Critical Issues in Child Welfare

Foundations of Social Work Knowledge
Frederic G. Reamer, Series Editor

Social work has a unique history, purpose, perspective, and method. The primary purpose of this series is to articulate these distinct qualities and to define and explore the ideas, concepts, and skills that together constitute social work's intellectual foundations and boundaries and its emerging issues and concerns.

To accomplish this goal, the series will publish a cohesive collection of books that address both the core knowledge of the profession and its newly emerging topics. The core is defined by the evolving consensus, as primarily reflected in the Council of Social Work Education's Curriculum Policy Statement, concerning what courses accredited social work education programs must include in their curricula. The series will be characterized by an emphasis on the widely embraced ecological perspective; attention to issues concerning direct and indirect practice; and emphasis on cultural diversity and multiculturalism, social justice, oppression, populations at risk, and social work values and ethics. The series will have a dual focus on practice traditions and emerging issues and concepts.

David G. Gil, *Confronting Injustice and Oppression: Concepts and Strategies for Social Workers*

George Alan Appleby and Jeane W. Anastas, *Not Just a Passing Phase: Social Work with Gay, Lesbian, and Bisexual People*

Frederic G. Reamer, *Social Work Research and Evaluation Skills*

Pallassana R. Balgopal, *Social Work Practice with Immigrants and Refugees*

Dennis Saleeby, *Human Behavior and Social Environments: A Biopsychosocial Approach*

Frederic G. Reamer, *Tangled Relationships: Managing Boundary Issues in the Human Services*

Roger A. Lohmann and Nancy L. Lohmann, *Social Administration*

Critical Issues In Child Welfare

Joan Shireman

COLUMBIA UNIVERSITY PRESS   NEW YORK

COLUMBIA UNIVERSITY PRESS
Publishers Since 1893
New York
Chichester, West Sussex

© 2003 Columbia University Press

Library of Congress Cataloging-in-Publication Data

Shireman, Joan F.
  Critical issues in child welfare / Joan Shireman.
    p. cm.—(Foundations of social work knowledge)
  Includes bibliographical references and index.
  ISBN 0-231-11670-5 (cloth : alk. paper)
  1. Child welfare. I. Title. II. Series.

HV713.S46 2003
362.7—dc21

                                        2003046067

∞
Columbia University Press books are printed
on permanent and durable acid-free paper.
Printed in the United States of America
c 10 9 8 7 6 5 4 3 2 1

*To my beloved grandchildren, David and Andrew,
Erika and Christopher, Amy and Sally, and to all the
children and young people who are our future.*

Contents

Acknowledgments   xv

About the Contributors   xvii

Introduction: Social Work and Child Welfare   1
    The Crisis in Child Welfare   2
    Child Welfare and Social Work: A Historical Connection   5
       Social Work   6
       Child Welfare   7
    Policy and Practice in Social Work and Child Welfare   9
    A Note About Case Examples   10

1   The Context of Child Welfare Services   13
    Changing Community Expectations   14
       Child Labor and Universal Education: A Legacy
         of Advocacy and Change   15
       Poverty   18
       The Changing Family   21
       Youth Violence, Delinquency, and Nonconformity   23
       Homelessness   25
       Substance Abuse   25
       Racism   26
       Women's Roles   27
    Child Maltreatment   28
       Child Fatalities   29
       Community Definitions of Maltreatment   32
       Neglect   35
       Physical Abuse   37

Sexual Abuse   38
Psychological Maltreatment   39
Critical Issue: Family Violence   41
Conclusion   46

2   A Framework for Child Welfare Services   52
    The Rights and Needs of Children   55
        The Needs of Children   56
        The Responsibility of the State for Its Children   60
    The Institutions That Have Served Children   65
        The White House Conferences   66
        The Children's Bureau   66
        The Child Welfare League of America   67
    The Judicial Framework   67
    The Legislative Framework   70
        Child Abuse Prevention and Treatment   71
        Interethnic Child Placement   72
        Income Maintenance   75
    Critical Issue: Permanency Planning   79
        The Theoretical Base   80
        The Empirical Base   82
        Legislative Responses   82
    Conclusion   85

3   The Child Welfare Services System   89
        with Katharine Cahn
    The Changing Role of the Public Child Welfare Agency   90
        The Federal Role in the Child Welfare System   92
        The Community Role in the Child Welfare System   97
        Public Child Welfare Under Stress   98
    The Interface of Public and Voluntary Agencies   102
        The Voluntary Agency   102
        Managed Care   103
    Interface of Child Welfare with Other Public Systems   106
        The Judicial System and the Child Welfare System   106
        Other Systems   110
    Responsibility to Those Served   114
        Formal Oversight   114
        Informal Oversight   115

The Interface of Systems   116
   Interdisciplinary Work   117
   Differing Perspectives   118
   Funding for Services   119
Critical Issue: Racism in the Child Welfare System   120
Conclusion   124

4 Community Services for Children and Families   128
   with Karen Tvedt
Families Needing Intensive Services   129
   Substance Abuse Treatment   130
   Mental Health Services   132
   Support for Incarcerated Mothers   133
   Family Violence   134
   Respite Care   135
Families Needing Some Extra Support   138
   Family Resource Centers   140
   Home-Visiting Programs   141
   Parent Training Programs   143
   Self-Help Groups   144
   Head Start   145
Meeting the Needs of All Families   146
   Income Maintenance   147
   Health Care   148
   Affordable and Safe Housing   149
Critical Issue: Child Care   150
   Historical Perspective: A Mother's Place Is in the Home?   150
   The Changing Economy and Workforce   152
   Parental Preferences in Child Care   153
   Child Care Costs   153
   Child Care Resources   154
   Quality of Care and Outcomes for Children   155
   Federal Child Care Policy   156
   Reexamining Child Care   156
   Possibilities for the Future   157
Conclusion   159

5 Crisis Intervention: Child Protection and Family Preservation 163
   The Nature and Extent of Child Maltreatment   164

Child Protective Services   165
    The Development of Child Protective Services   165
    The Public Agency Overwhelmed   168
    Intervention   172
Family Preservation   183
    The Concept   183
    Family Preservation Services   184
    The Three Original Intensive Service Models   185
    Community-Centered Practice   187
    Kinship Foster Care   188
Critical Issue: Appropriate Use of Family Preservation Services   189
    Evaluation   189
    Do Attempts to Preserve Families Put Children at Risk?   191
Conclusion   192

6   Investment in Foster Care   198
    Historical Perspective   199
        Congregate Care   200
        Foster Family Care   202
    Foster Care Today   207
        Number of Children in Care   207
        Characteristics of Children in Foster Care   210
        Characteristics of Foster Care   213
        Maltreatment in Foster Care   218
    The Foster Care Experience   219
        The Children's Original Families   220
        The Children   225
        The Foster Parents   229
    Outcomes   234
        Foster Children as Adults   234
        Facilitating Positive Outcomes   236
    Critical Issue: Establishing and Retaining Foster Homes
            to Meet the Needs of Children   237
        Recruitment of Foster Parents   237
        Assessment   238
        Training   240
        Retention of Foster Homes   241
    Conclusion   244

7   Expanding the Foster Care System: Other Types
        of Out-of-Home Care   250
    Shelter Foster Care and Assessment Centers   252
    Expanded Resources for Children Within Their Families   253
        Kinship Foster Care   253
        Whole-Family Care   259
    Care for Children with Special Difficulties in the Child
        Welfare System   261
        Specialized Foster Homes   261
        Group Care: Meeting a Range of Needs   267
        Group Homes   268
        Residential Treatment Centers   269
    Critical Issue: Institutional Care for Dependent Children
        as a Supplement to Foster Care   276
        Appropriate Uses   277
        Young Children   278
        Cost   279
        Maltreatment   280
        Outcomes   281
    Conclusion   282

8   Adoption   288
    The Framework of Adoption   289
        A Brief History of Adoption   289
        Major Adoption Legislation   294
        The Paths to Adoption   296
        Numbers of Children Involved in Adoption   300
    Protecting the Adoption Triad   301
        The Birth Parents   301
        The Adopting Parents   305
        The Children   307
    Adoption Outcomes   310
    Nontraditional Adoptive Homes   312
        Single-Parent Adoption   313
        Adoption by Gay and Lesbian Parents   315
        Transracial Adoption   317
        International Adoption   320
        Open Adoption   324

Critical Issue: Continuing Support for Postadoption Services   327
   The Need for Postadoption Services   327
   The Range of Postadoption Services   329
   Policy Implications   335
  Conclusion   336

9   At-Risk Youth   345
   with Charles Shireman
  Youth Without Homes   348
   Independent Living Programs   348
   Runaway and Homeless Youth   353
  Youth with Special Needs   357
   Sexual Minority Youth   357
   Youth of Color   358
  All Youth: At Risk   360
   Sexual Behavior   360
   Substance Abuse   362
   Solutions for Problem Behaviors   364
  Critical Issue: Juvenile Law Violations and Violators   365
   Extent of the Problem   367
   Societal Response   369
   The System's Clientele   370
   Prevention and Treatment   373
  Conclusion   378

10   Concluding Thoughts   383
  Major Policy Issues   385
   Comprehensive and Universally Available Services   386
   Shifting of Program Responsibility to the Local Level   388
   The Impact of Welfare Reform   388
  Outcomes   390
   Expanding Expectations   391
   The Impact of Outcome Measures on Service Provision   392
   Effective Intervention to Achieve Outcomes   394
  Toward More Effective Service: The Ideas of Major Scholars   396
   Freeing Workers from Investigations   397
   Increased Use of Adoption   397
   Community-Based Practice   398
   The Eradication of Poverty   400

Critical Issue: Recruitment, Education, and Retention
    of Child Welfare Workers   401
  Turnover Rates   401
  Social Work Education and Child Welfare   404
Social Work and Child Welfare: The Nature of the "Fit"   406
  Assumptions   406
  Values and Ethics   407
  Social Justice   408
  Advocacy   409
Conclusion   409

Appendix: Internet Resources   413

Index   415

Acknowledgments

This book is the sum of many years of reading, teaching, research, and conversation concerning child welfare and its many issues. It would not be possible to acknowledge all who have contributed to it. Students, with their keen questions and demands for social justice have been important in its formation. It was my good friend Frederic Reamer who suggested the possibility of the book. Katharine Cahn, Karen Tvedt, and Charles, my supportive husband, generously contributed their ideas as co-authors of three chapters. Kenneth Watson was kind enough to critique the chapters on out-of-home care, John Triseliotis the chapter on adoption; both offered excellent suggestions. Reviewers and editors have similarly improved the book as it progressed, and to them I owe many thanks. Conversations with Diane Yatchmenoff and the thoughtful staff of the five-year research project (described in the introduction) grounded the book in the practice world of child welfare. The voice of students found clear expression in Heidi Allen's thoughtful debate as the book took shape. Finally, I want to acknowledge my colleagues at Portland State University, without whose support it would not have been possible to complete the book.

About the Contributors

Joan Shireman is a professor at the Graduate School of Social Work at Portland State University, Portland, Oregon.

Katharine Cahn is the director of the Northwest Institute for Children and Families at the School of Social Work, University of Washington, Seattle, Washington.

Karen Tvedt is the director of policy for the Child Care Bureau, U.S. Department of Health and Human Services, Washington, D.C.

Charles Shireman is professor emeritus at the School of Social Service Administration, University of Chicago, Chicago, Illinois.

Social Work and Child Welfare

Child welfare is a specialized area of practice within which the values and skills of social work are implemented. Historically the fields of child welfare and social work have been intertwined, sometimes overlapping substantially—as in the time of the founding of juvenile courts or of child labor reform—and sometimes moving apart. Today child welfare seems to be moving apart from social work; a narrow definition of child welfare as a specialized field, focused on the protection of children, may exacerbate that separation.

One of the critical issues in the field of child welfare today is its definition. Some basic principles will make clear the point of view from which this book is written.

- There is no dichotomy between the welfare of the child and the welfare of the family. Every child grows best in his or her own family, if the family can provide proper care. Any policy that supports family life supports the welfare of children. Child welfare is, therefore, about the welfare of children and families.
- For a very small minority of children, there are concerns about safety within the family. Work with these children and their families requires a special set of skills that are unique to the practice of child welfare. Protective service requires the ability to assess family strengths and risks to the child. Out-of-home placement requires the ability to assess the needs of the child and the strengths of various placement options, and to match the two. It also requires knowledge of the meaning of separation to the child, and the ability to work with children to minimize this trauma.

- Skills needed to work with families and to work with out-of-home placement are of a high order and demand professional training. Though the need for professional skills is generally acknowledged when work with families is demanded, it is less accepted in the area of child protective services and out-of-home placement services. In part, this is due to the emphasis in the protective services arena on law enforcement rather than family-building. That emphasis may protect children but it does not enhance their overall well-being.

The definition of child welfare services used in this book encompasses the set of community-supported programs that enhance the welfare of children—a broad definition, but one which must be constantly in the minds of those who are advocates for children. It includes services available to all children as well as services targeted to specific groups of children. It includes services to prevent problems and services to remedy problems. It includes work with families who ask for help with the stresses of parenting and work with families who are involuntary clients. For practical reasons only, educational, recreational, and medical services receive little attention in this book, although they are all part of the comprehensive system of services to children and families. The focus of the book is on those programs that directly enhance the ability of families to care for their children by preventing, remedying, or ameliorating maltreatment, and that are within the realm of social work services.

The Crisis in Child Welfare

Child welfare services that enhance the growth and development of children in their own families tend to be valued by the community. These are services designed to support family life, such as day care, homemaker programs, family preservation programs, respite care, parenting classes, and family counseling programs. They are services into which most families enter voluntarily. Many are underfunded; the effectiveness of others has yet to be demonstrated. The array of available services continually changes as families, communities, and legislatures experiment with what can be funded, what can be sustained, and what is useful. These services face important challenges: how to expand small, successful model programs to serve larger populations; how to target services accurately so as to prevent the emergence of larger problems; how to secure and maintain funding.

Whereas such family-based and community-supported programs are challenged, the child welfare services whose goal is to protect children who may have been maltreated by their families are in genuine crisis. The crisis is most acute in the areas of protective services and foster care, though other parts of the child welfare system are also plagued by uncertainty and controversy. Crisis by its very nature cannot be sustained; it will be resolved by some change that restores a functional equilibrium to the system. It is our task to make sure that the new solutions for child welfare meet the needs of children.

The reasons for the crisis in child welfare are not complex. Higher community standards for the care of children, coupled with the deterioration of family stability and community cohesiveness have led to an overwhelming number of referrals of children thought to be in need of protection—almost 3 million in 1998 (U.S. Department of Health and Human Services 2000). A legacy of thirty years of unwillingness to fund children's services—or any social services—at a generous level has left public child welfare agencies with staffs that, in general, are not professionally trained and are managed by an intricate network of policy directives. The complex decisions that are involved in work with families and children under stress can overwhelm untrained workers, so that resignations and new hiring compound the problems of the child welfare agencies. Overwhelmed by the numbers of children and families needing help, the public child welfare system has narrowed its mission to focus on the protection of children, abandoning the range of services designed to meet the varied needs of children in many circumstances. Other community agencies have not had the resources to fully replace such services that once were publicly funded.

Despite considerable interest in the development of services to preserve families and to prevent the placement of children outside their homes, foster care has remained a staple of child welfare service. At the same time, demographic changes in family structure, especially the entry of women into employment outside the home, have produced an acute shortage of foster homes. Thus, foster care services have deteriorated: there are no longer enough foster homes to allow matching each home to the specific needs of the child; child welfare workers have neither the time nor the skills to provide supportive help to foster families as they care for children; and too often, when problems arise, children are removed from one foster home and placed in another. The problems of the children's families of origin are complex, and change is often slow and erratic, so it is difficult to move children out of foster care and back into their own homes. Long stays and multiple moves within the foster care system are damaging to children and intensify the shortage of foster homes.

Many suggestions have been advanced for resolving the crisis in child welfare services. One is to make the investigation of complaints of abuse and neglect a function of the police and criminal justice system, which has jurisdiction of criminal activity, and limit the child welfare system to the delivery of services. Another is to make investigation the sole function of public child protective services and to develop other child welfare services through the private sector. Another reform idea is to end mandatory reporting of maltreatment of children in the hope of greatly reducing the number of complaints that must be investigated (more than two-thirds of which cannot be substantiated). Ideas for reforming the foster care system have focused on making it much smaller through the use of family preservation programs, kinship foster care, and legislative limits on the time a child can remain in foster care. Other reform proposals have called for greater standardization and supervision of out-of-home care through the use of more institutional settings.

To each of these proposals a critical question must be addressed: Does this change meet the needs of children? The answers are usually unclear. Police, with their mission to protect, remove more children from their homes than do workers who see the long-range effects of foster care. Sometimes reports of suspected maltreatment made by neighbors or teachers lead investigators to situations where children are in real danger. Group care has been tried in other centuries and other countries, and it has drawbacks.

Another set of "reform" suggestions centers on increased resources for the welfare of all children. Lindsey (1994), for example, notes that

> more than 5 million children in the United States live in households with income less than "half of the poverty line"—a phrase that does not adequately reveal the depths of hopelessness these children daily experience. They are the poorest of the poor, subject not only to severe physical and sexual assault, but to hunger, disease, despair, and death. . . . The mission of the child welfare system is not to protect children from criminal abuse but to aid impoverished children. . . . The system should be judged by its success in reducing poverty among children, in providing them the means to break the cycle of poverty to become productive citizens.
>
> (PP. 177–78)

As a nation, we have not been generous with our children. Schools, child care, family support services—all need more resources. Income maintenance, to enable parents to care for their children, is a fundamental and unmet need. Child welfare services require greater resources, and those resources must be used effectively.

What do children from troubled families need? Primarily, they need safety and permanent, nurturing families. There are a thousand different ways to achieve these goals for children; indeed, each child's unique situation calls for a unique approach. Investing in professionally trained child welfare workers and then freeing them to use their skills while supporting them in their efforts is one route to addressing the many and varied needs of the children who come to the attention of the child welfare system. Though child welfare is an arena where many disciplines have important contributions to make, social work—with its focus on communities, family systems, and development through the life span and with its tradition of advocacy for the vulnerable—has particular value.

Child Welfare and Social Work: A Historical Connection

Child welfare has historically been a part of the social work profession. The early leaders in social work were deeply concerned about children and tireless in their advocacy for child labor laws, universal education, income maintenance, and other reforms that have benefited children. Imbued with a value system that emphasizes advocacy for the powerless in our society, social workers have long espoused the interests of children and their families. The advocacy of social workers, over time, is reflected in the following quotations.

> Nor, unfortunately, does there seem to be any reason for thinking that charities for caring for destitute, neglected, and delinquent children will soon become unnecessary. We learn to deal more and more wisely with those who are in distress, but the forces which produce poverty, neglect, and crime seem to be beyond our reach. The poor, the neglectful, and the vicious we shall have with us for a long time to come, and the hearts of the generous will continue to respond, both through individual and associate charity, and through governmental action.
>
> (FOLKS 1902:246)

We must also recognize that the co-morbidity of poverty, substance abuse, domestic violence, mental health issues, problems of maternal and child health, developmental disabilities, and child placement has been established beyond a reasonable doubt, and that service systems must address these multiple problems in a coordinated way if they are to meet the needs of clients.

(MEEZAN 1999:17)

Social Work

Social work has had a complex history. The early social welfare workers focused their efforts on reforming society to give the poor and vulnerable greater opportunity. Specht and Courtney, in their provocative book, outline the historical shift in social work from community concerns and advocacy for societal change to a fascination with psychotherapy and change within the individual.

It appears that throughout this century social work has been evolving toward a manifest destiny. Starting as the Cinderella of professions, left for years by psychiatry and psychoanalysis to do society's dirty work of tending to the poor and destitute, social work has finally been transformed into a princess. Sparklingly attired by her fairy godfather, Carl Rogers, she is off to dance at the psychotherapeutic ball with all of the other fifty-minute-hour professionals. Neither war, nor depressions, nor massive social upheavals have stayed her from her course.

(SPECHT AND COURTNEY 1997:163–64)

A profession is based on underlying constructs that "provide direction for the knowledge base, give a specific value orientation, and suggest research programs" (Kreuger 1997:22). Grounding in theory the dichotomy identified by Specht, Kreuger identifies the "grand narratives" of social work as the theories of Karl Marx, which identified the victimization of the economically disadvantaged, and the theories of Sigmund Freud, which laid the groundwork for interventions that might enhance an individual's ability to cope with the world. Kreuger suggests that although these "grand narratives" have been discredited, they still form the base of social work. It is immediately apparent that the two narratives point in different directions, one leading toward interventions to change society, the other toward interventions to help the individual get along in the existing society. In child welfare, both are at work in the simultaneous efforts to build a stronger community to support families and to enable individual families to cope with present circumstances.

The social work profession has its roots in the struggle to change the community so that individuals would have a better chance. The settlement houses that provided education for immigrants and were a center of endless reform efforts, the social survey movement that documented the plight of the economically disadvantaged, the early work of the first federal agency devoted to child welfare, the Children's Bureau, for the health and economic security of women and children—all were focused on changing conditions for the vulnerable. This advocacy and reform impetus laid a strong value base for the profession.

The second "grand narrative" has provided a different set of values that undergird direct practice. One is the belief that change is possible and that the individual is capable of lifelong growth. Another is respect for the uniqueness of the individual and for the individual's capacity to make judgments and guide his or her own life. The values of freedom and the right to privacy are buried in these constructs.

Clearly there are values that unite the two narratives, or the profession would have splintered. One is the idea that everyone should have access to opportunity and the ability to take advantage of that opportunity; one outcome of successful social work intervention is the maximizing of individual choices. Another is the idea that individuals are capable of making changes, both in themselves and in their communities. A third is the enhancing of individual responsibility to the community.

Specht suggests that the true mission of social work is that of building communities and working with individuals to accept responsibility as community members. Along with many in the profession, he advocates a return to this focus. Meezan, in his address on the future of children's services quoted earlier, makes the same point, noting also that community building is far easier to espouse than to accomplish. These ideas point toward a new direction in social work and child welfare—or perhaps it is a return to an older mission.

Child Welfare

The field of child welfare has also had a complex history. Its focus has shifted as communities identify new problems, but the struggle to find ways to enrich the lives of vulnerable children has remained paramount. Motivated by a desire to "save" children, early child welfare practitioners (whether town selectmen or the leaders of movements such as Charles Loring Brace's shipments of children to the farming families of the West) intended to educate children in the ways of religion and productive work, thus saving them from idleness and ruin. The late nineteenth and early twentieth centuries saw the rise of a child rescue movement as private child protective societies were formed to protect children from parental cruelty—an extension of the societies for the prevention of cruelty to animals. From these societies came the idea that children had rights and a fuller discussion of the rights of parents and the rights of children. In the early 1900s, the ideas of "scientific charity" and "social work" were introduced, bringing to the child rescue movement the idea that support within the child's own home might be a possibility and that, if a child were removed, reunification of the family should be a goal.

Through all of these child welfare "movements," the focus was on the individual child and family. At the same time, during the Progressive Era of the late nineteenth and early twentieth century, early social work introduced the idea in child welfare practice of changing the community conditions in which children grew. This era, in which social workers were prominent, brought an expansion of protections for children, such as child labor laws and the establishment of juvenile courts, and also an increased focus on programs that would benefit families, such as maternal and child health services and income maintenance. This dual emphasis on child protection and family enhancement endures today.

The Progressive Era was probably the time when the early social workers and the early child welfare workers were most closely aligned. Although part of the social work profession later wandered off into therapeutic halls, and child welfare was partly deprofessionalized, they have remained linked. The basic skills of work with individuals and families, as explicated in social casework texts, are grounded in the practical realities of everyday life. These fundamental skills have been very useful, helping individuals and families learn to solve problems, use strengths, and maximize the opportunities available to them in their communities. As social workers moved into positions in the child welfare system, they brought their skills to work with individual families, increasing the possibility of rebuilding families rather than removing children from them. However, neither social work nor child welfare has emphasized the important dimension of enabling individuals to contribute to their communities.

The strongest link between social work and child welfare is the work in both professions on developing communities to provide the opportunities people need while utilizing clinical skills to work with troubled families. Social workers struggle with the investigatory nature of protective work and with the concomitant intervention in family life. But when these functions are successfully brought together by a skilled social worker, using the basic principles of social work practice, the resulting opening of opportunities and choices for families and children can be impressive.

Policy and Practice in Social Work and Child Welfare

This is a book about the role that social work can and should play in child welfare services. It is a policy book, not a book about practice. But the two cannot really be separated, for policy shapes practice and practice shapes policy. Both, of course, should be informed by theory, empirical work, and the wisdom of long practice.

This book encompasses a vast array of information, and necessarily includes only superficial description of some important elements of the system. However, at the end of each chapter the reader will find a section in which a critical issue has been identified and explored in some depth. These critical issues were chosen because they are of central importance to child welfare services today, and their selection was limited to those for which a meaningful response is within the capacity of those working in the child welfare system. Some problems, such as poverty, are pervasive and shape all services to children and families. Some issues, such as physical and mental health or education, are critical to child welfare but fall within the purview of other systems with which child welfare must work cooperatively. The writer's choice of these critical issues will be controversial; the reader might well have selected others.

Child welfare services are firmly embedded in their communities. We will begin the exploration of policy in chapter 1 with a look at the community context of child welfare services, noting changes over time and the role of social work in the development of services to children and families. Chapter 2 examines the values and the conceptual and legal framework within which child welfare services operate. The complexity and the many components of the child welfare services system are the subject of chapter 3. The remaining chapters provide more specific consideration of the core services of child welfare: supportive services to families, child protection, foster care and other out-of home care, adoption, and services to at-risk youth. It is hoped that the reader will be captured by the journey.

A Note About Case Examples

Throughout the book, case examples are used to illustrate various facets of child welfare practice. Almost all of the examples are drawn from research completed at the Graduate School of Social Work at Portland State University in Portland, Oregon, under the auspices of the Child Welfare Partnership and the Regional Research Institute for Human Services. Child welfare practice with involuntary clients was examined in this research through interviews with families, caseworkers, foster parents, and community partners. Case examples often use the exact words of the participants to illustrate concepts developed in the text.

Briefly, the project monitored the implementation of a statewide practice reform in Oregon's State Office for Services to Children and Families. The practice model focuses on (1) the initial building of a relationship between caseworker and family through developing agreement about the needs of the child(ren); (2) a planning process that builds on family strengths and the family's perspective to identify needs and plan services, (3) services identified or crafted to meet specific needs; and (4) flexible funding to insure that services can be found or created as necessary to meet identified needs. The practice issues raised by the implementation of this model, particularly in protective services, are many and fascinating. For those who wish to explore the model and its implementation in greater depth, the research is described in a series of reports (Shireman, Yatchmenoff et al. 1998; Shireman, Yatchmenoff et al. 1999; Shireman, Eggman et al. 2000; Shireman, Rodgers et al. 2001) and is available at the project Web site: http://www.pdx.edu/SOC/pgSOCHome.shtml.

References

Folks, H. 1902. *The Care of Destitute, Neglected, and Delinquent Children.* New York: Macmillan.
Kreuger, L. W. 1997. "The End of Social Work." *Journal of Social Work Education* 33, no. 1 (Winter): 19–28.

Lindsey, D. 1994. *The Welfare of Children.* New York: Oxford University Press.

Meezan, W. 1999. *Translating Rhetoric to Reality: The Future of Family and Children's Services.* Ann Arbor: University of Michigan.

Shireman, J., S. Eggman, et al. 2000. "Strengths/Needs Based Services Evaluation: Interim Report, June 2000." Regional Research Institute for Human Services, Portland, Ore.

Shireman, J., A. Rodgers, et al. 2001. "Strengths/Needs Based Services Evaluation: Final Report, June 2001." Portland State University, Graduate School of Social Work, Portland, Ore.

Shireman, J., D. Yatchmenoff, et al. 1998. "Strengths/Needs Based Services Evaluation: Interim Report, June 1998." Regional Research Institute for Human Services, Portland, Ore.

———. 1999. "Strengths/Needs Based Services Evaluation: Biennial Report, June 1999." Regional Research Institute for Human Services, Portland, Ore.

Specht, H., and M. Courtney. 1997. *Unfaithful Angels: How Social Work Has Abandoned Its Mission.* New York: Free Press.

U.S. Department of Health and Human Services. 2000. *Child Maltreatment 1998: Reports from the States to the National Child Abuse and Neglect Data System.* Washington, D.C.: U.S. Government Printing Office.

CHAPTER 1

The Context of Child Welfare Services

Do Lawd, come down here and walk amongst yo people
And tak 'em by the hand and telt 'em
That yo ain't hex wid 'em
And do Lawd come yoself,
Don't send yo son,
Cause dis ain't no place for chillen.
—PRAYER COMPOSED BY SLAVES, 1866

As a new millennium begins, there is increasing recognition that the solutions to social problems lie within their broad societal context. Thus the task of promoting the welfare of the child demands a focus broader than the child, or even the child and family. The community provides the cultural and value framework within which families function, and it may or may not provide sufficient supports to enable the family to function adequately. Socioeconomic, cultural, and political forces combine to create a complex and ever-changing mix of demand, opportunity, barriers, and resources. Policy affecting the lives of children and families is formed as a result of this dynamic interaction.

The scope of the child welfare services available to children is dependent on the community's definition of the needs of children. The manner in which the community identifies those needs will depend to a very large degree on how the forces of the larger world shape the community, as well as upon the culture and resources of the particular community. Those family difficulties that are recognized as social problems change over time. This chapter traces those changes.

The community sets the standards of care it expects for its children, and the community sanctions and funds the child welfare workers who try to ensure that children have that care. But the social worker does not only carry out the wishes of the community. The social worker who, in the course of daily work, discovers conditions that harm children, has a responsibility to advocate for change. The worker must know the community intimately, for more and more, child welfare workers are called on to find and use community resources for the families they serve and to help develop community resources that those families need. Thus an important backdrop for a study of current child welfare policy is an overview of how community forces shape the lives of families and of how changing community definitions of social problems affect the commitment of resources.

The reader will discover the role of social work in alerting the public to the needs of children and mobilizing public opinion to support interventions that make life better for children. This introductory chapter discusses issues that continue to call for remedial attention if the world of the child is to be meaningfully enriched: poverty (and the related history of child labor), education that is often inadequate, the changing family, substance abuse, crime and delinquency, and the maltreatment of children. Racism underlies and compounds all of these issues. The role of women as caretakers of children demands constant examination. In later chapters we will examine the major ways in which social work and the allied professions have intervened in attempts to solve these social problems—never fully reaching goals, but succeeding in producing meaningful changes.

Changing Community Expectations

Community standards and customs change over time. Progress in bettering the lives of all children is evident if one begins a review of changing community standards with a look back to the condition of children in the eighteenth and nineteenth centuries. As the nineteenth century became the twentieth, child labor laws and compulsory education laws were passed. The first half of the twentieth century saw enormous strides in the guarantee of a basic income for families so that children could be cared for at home—and then the end of the century saw the erosion of this promise. The second half of that century saw increasing concern with child maltreatment as physical abuse, sexual abuse, and family violence were successively identified as major threats to children.

The programs and services integral to child welfare have shifted over time. The reformers of the Progressive Era (in the late nineteenth and early twentieth centuries) argued for a greater federal and state government role in the resolution of social problems. Those years saw an increasing development of government programs and movement toward federal standard-setting and provision of resources. Such programs continued to expand through the years of the New Deal (the 1930s) and the War on Poverty (the 1960s), then began to contract and grow ever more constricted in the last three decades of the century. Along with the contraction of these programs came progressive decentralizing of services as conservative political forces pushed for local control of social programs.

At the end of the twentieth century many social problems remain: too many children are poor; too many children do not have health care; too many children lack affordable, high-quality day care; too many children with special needs lack the services that would help. Families who are at risk need preventive services, and families in which children have been maltreated need a wider range of better-funded and more imaginative remedial services. But progress has been made, and social workers have often led the way.

The following sections review a few of the major social problems that affect our communities today, particularly those problems in which social workers, or their predecessor social welfare workers, have displayed a particular interest. We begin with the history of change regarding one social problem—child labor—to illustrate the impact that a determined group of child advocates, in this case social welfare workers, can have. It is an optimistic start to a look at a multitude of serious problems that face children today.

Child Labor and Universal Education: A Legacy of Advocacy and Change

From colonial times, it has been considered important that children learn the habits of work as preparation for adult life. Education was also valued as a necessity for governance in a democratic society. Closely linked to poverty, child labor was recognized in the late nineteenth century as a social problem, and the early social workers were instrumental in changing the conditions faced by children in the factories. This story serves as an example of the investment of social workers in the welfare of children.

Child labor regulated During the nineteenth century there was a growing recognition that factory employment kept children from becoming
educated and that a democracy would be ill served by a population that
could not read or write. Poor families depended on the wages of all family
members. Manufacturers were eager to employ children because they could
be hired for low wages and because their dexterity was an advantage. Thus
women and children formed a large proportion of the industrial workforce. Testimony before the Pennsylvania Senate in the 1830s described
the conditions of employment.

> The hours vary in different establishments; in some I have worked
> fourteen and a half hours. . . . It is most common to work as long
> as they can see; in the winter they work until eight o'clock, receiv-
> ing an hour and a half for meals. . . . The children are employed at
> spinning or carding. . . . I have known children of nine years of age
> to be employed at spinning—at carding, as young as ten years. Pun-
> ishment, by whipping, is frequent; they are sometimes sent home
> and docked for not attending punctually. . . . The children are tired
> when they leave the factory. I have known them to sleep in corners
> and other places, before leaving the factory, from fatigue. The
> younger children are generally very much fatigued. . . . The wages
> of children are not regulated by the number of hours they labor; I
> have known some to get no more than fifty cents per week; I have
> known some to get as much as $1.25.
>
> (ABBOTT 1938:280–81)

Compulsory public education It was around 1900 that the first laws
were passed by states forbidding the employment of children in factories.
Public schools and compulsory education and child labor laws were
linked; it was thought that children needed education, and feared that
children not in factories might be "idle" if not required to go to school.
The first compulsory education law in Illinois (1889)

> made unlawful for any person, firm, or corporation to employ or
> hire any child under thirteen years of age without a certificate, but
> the board of education was given authority to excuse any such
> child from school and to authorize his employment, provided his
> labor was needed for the support of any aged or infirm relative and
> provided the child had attended school at least eight weeks in the

current year. The system of allowing children to work if their relatives seemed to be in need meant, of course, that the children most
in need of the protection of child labor and compulsory education
laws would be entirely excluded from their benefits.

(ABBOTT AND BRECKINRIDGE 1917:69)

As further compulsory education laws were passed, the shortage of
schools and teachers became evident. A report to the Chicago school
board in 1896 complained that

until there are schools for the children, and a compulsory education
law that is enforced, the factory inspectors cannot keep all the children under fourteen years out of factories and workshops. . . . In
Chicago, the City Council has taken a distinctly retrograde step in
reducing the school appropriations by $2,000,000 for 1896–97,
thus checking the building of school houses, and depriving thousands of working-class children of the opportunity for school life
which primary schools are supposed to extend to all alike.

(ABBOTT AND BRECKINRIDGE 1917:81–82)

The development of a school system that could accommodate and educate
the many children now free to attend school was a massive undertaking,
one that is still in progress.

Social reformers—among them Jane Addams, Florence Kelley, Grace
and Edith Abbott, and Sophonisba Breckinridge—were active in support
of the child labor and compulsory education laws. Labor unions also
supported these laws because the employment of children at low wages
undercut their demands for better wages and working conditions. Of
course, there was strenuous opposition to these laws—from employers
and, sadly, from poor parents who "thought the sacrifice of their children necessary," and saw themselves as in great need of, and having a
right to, their children's earnings (Abbott 1938:263).

Early child labor laws protected only children in factories; laws protecting children in less regulated industries, such as street peddlers or
children working in home industries, followed more slowly. (The protection of children who work in the fields, particularly the children of
migrant workers, has still not been accomplished.) The first child labor
law in 1916 was followed by a series of attempts to enact federal legislation to protect children. All were declared unconstitutional, deemed to

overreach the regulatory powers granted to the federal government in the Constitution. An attempt to pass a constitutional amendment in the 1920s was unsuccessful. During this time many states passed laws regulating child labor, but not until 1938, with the passage of the Fair Labor Standards Act, did federal legislation succeed in restricting child labor (Costin, Bell, et al. 1991).

Universal education today By the end of the 1930s, then, there were laws protecting children from being exploited in difficult working conditions, and laws giving children the opportunity to be educated in public schools. Community support for these laws was widespread. The concept that the child needed to be trained to be a useful citizen had not been abandoned, but industrialization had given a different focus to that training: school became the route to productive citizenship. The community thus had taken major steps to change the status of children. It had also defined childhood as a special, protected time, lasting into the late teen years.

Although child labor and education laws greatly changed the condition of children, the problems they addressed are not completely in the past. There is continuing concern about children who work and whose schooling is disrupted; this is particularly of concern with migrant families who follow crops to work in the fields. There is also widespread concern about young people who do not complete the schooling necessary for productive adult lives. In 1995, 92.7 percent of white students, 86.8 percent of African American students, but only 57.2 percent of Hispanic students received a high school diploma or equivalency certificate (Children's Defense Fund 1998). This disparity is linked to poverty and to racism. Because schools are locally funded, those in poor communities have few resources; many African American and Hispanic children live in the poorest of our communities. The wealthiest schools spend 36 percent more per pupil than the poorest, and schools with large numbers of poor children have fewer books and supplies as well as teachers with less training (Children's Defense Fund 1998). Child advocates still have work to do to secure equal opportunity through universal education.

Poverty

Throughout the history of the United States, poverty has been—and has been recognized as—a problem for children. No community has been comfortable knowing that children are hungry, homeless, or without proper care. Social workers have often been instrumental in bringing recognition of this poverty to the community. Poverty lies behind other issues, such as child labor and child neglect. Just how little one has to have to be considered poor has varied over time, but there has always been concern about how to manage the care of and create opportunities for those at the bottom of the economic ladder.

Community explanations of poverty Attempts to solve the problem of poverty have been based at least in part on the explanation for poverty current in the community. In the United States there has always been a belief that careful planning, hard work, and industry would be rewarded with a comfortable standard of living. The early social welfare workers, such as Jane Addams, were influential in promoting an alternate view of poverty as a consequence of the forces of society, against which, too often, the individual could do little. The oppression of the poor by those better off became an important idea in some parts of the social work profession, and the battle against oppression that social work has always waged became also a battle against poverty.

Caring for the children of the poor has been a community concern in the United States since the first settlers arrived. Sometimes the solution has been to care for them in institutions so that the community could control their education and training; sometimes it has been to care for them in such a way that they could remain with their families. Private philanthropy and religious institutions have had an important role, at times greater, when there were few public programs, and at times of lesser importance. Accompanying the concern for children has been the worry that to provide sufficient help—particularly to give direct aid to families so they could care for their children at home—would encourage families to abandon their responsibility to support their own children and thus become dependent on the community.

Current patterns of income assistance for children began in the late 1800s, with the provision of income assistance to "worthy poor" families—that is, families who met the moral standards of the givers of assistance, such as those who were widowed or physically disabled. The Charity Organization Societies, private organizations devoted to a rational approach to the meeting of need, attempted to study the needs of families, searching for the causes of poverty, with the hope of eliminating poverty by eliminating its cause.[1] Recognizing the plight of women left with small children when their husbands died or deserted them, some states developed mothers' pensions. These also were allowances for the maintenance of "worthy" women and their children. However, the hardships of the great depression in the 1930s increased the numbers of the destitute and revealed the inadequacy of private and local relief efforts. The legislation that produced a guaranteed income "floor" for children, and its recent modification, are discussed in chapters 4 and 5. Though it contained the idea of an entitlement to a basic level of income, suggesting that poverty was not always the consequence of immorality, it was still restrictive and focused on help for mothers left alone to raise children. Though dated in its conception of family roles, Julia Lathrop's dictate of 1919 remains valid today:

> Children are not safe and happy if their parents are miserable, and parents must be miserable if they cannot protect a home against poverty. Let us not delude ourselves: The power to maintain a decent family living standard is a primary essential of child welfare. This means a living wage and wholesome working life for the man, a good and skillful mother at home to keep the house and comfort all within it. Society can afford no less and can afford no exceptions.
>
> (BRADBURY 1962:8)

The extent of child poverty Poverty and lack of opportunity make it difficult to nurture children adequately. Poverty in childhood is a persistent problem. Only in times of significant expenditure of public funds for social programs has the percentage of children living in poverty decreased substantially. For example, in 1976, at the end of the War on Poverty, 14.4 percent of children were living in families with income below the poverty line, defined as the amount needed to shelter, feed, and clothe a family at a minimal level. Reflecting the diminishing expenditures on social programs since that time, by 1996 the percentage had climbed to 20.5 percent, where it remained until the economic expansion of the late 1990s. Poverty among children then began to drop slightly, and stood at 18.9 percent in 1998 (U.S. Census Bureau 2000). Though it is encouraging to see the percentage living in poverty decrease, it is still astounding and shocking that in a country as rich as the United States almost a fifth of our children are very poor.

Poverty is not equally distributed among the races; in 1996, while only 10 percent of white children were poor, 40 percent of Hispanic children and 40 percent of African American children lived in families with income below the poverty line. Estimates for Asians and Pacific Islanders (a single census category) are similar to those for white children, about

12 percent living below the poverty line (U.S. Census Bureau 1999). The Census Bureau's sampling methodology results in too small a sample of Native American families to estimate the proportion living in poverty; other sources place it at 41 percent of the children (Meezan 1999). These figures are even more disturbing than the total poverty rates for all children. They indicate that almost half the African American, Native American, and Hispanic children in our country live at or below the poverty line; that is, they are very poor. Similar disproportion is found in the numbers of minority juveniles in institutions for delinquent youth and the numbers of African American and Native American children in foster care.

Young families (headed by a parent under age thirty) are particularly vulnerable; 41 percent of the children of these families were poor in 1994. Dependence on inadequate welfare benefits does not explain this poverty. Sixty-nine percent of the poor are working, and at the current minimum wage it is not possible for a single wage-earner working a standard forty-hour week to support a family (Children's Defense Fund 1998). This, of course, at least partly explains the great increase in households where both parents are working outside the home, and explains why single-parent, female-headed households are most likely to be poor. Recent welfare reforms, discussed in chapter 4, are expected to compound these problems.

The negative impact of poverty on family life and child development has been well documented. Poverty, and the compromises that are made in the attempt to cope with poverty, may well underlie subsequent negative experiences and poor outcomes.[2] If one accepts that poverty is most often the consequence of societal forces over which the individual has little control, it would appear that the eradication of poverty might be a major contributor toward attaining better outcomes for our children.

The Changing Family

The structure of the American family has been changing over the last hundred years; each significant change was probably viewed as a social problem by the contemporary community, and certain segments of it agitated to return to earlier ways. At the beginning of the nineteenth century, men held a dominant position in families as the sole provider of income, retaining almost all control of property and of decision making. If the parents separated, which happened rarely, the father retained custody of the children. Change has been gradual, aided by the increasing acquisition by

women of rights and economic power, and by judicial recognition of the
bond between mothers and children and of mothers' role as primary caretakers of children.

Women in the workforce The entry of women into the workforce has
created less change, either in the world of employment or in the home,
than might have been hoped. Although the proportion of women working
full time outside the home has increased greatly, women still carry the
major responsibility for the care of the home and the raising of children.
Though "family friendly" policies have been adopted in some work-
places, many jobs—particularly those that are low paying—are tied to
specific hours, have little or no flexibility, and carry few or no health
benefits. Child care has become vital, and working parents often search
desperately for high-quality and affordable child care. The critical issue
of child care will be explored further in chapter 4.

New forms of families The last half of the twentieth century has brought
a dramatic change in family composition. Divorce and remarriage have
created blended families. The divorce rate is high and stable—about half
of all marriages end in divorce. Men remarry, on average, three years after
a divorce; women after an average of six years. The acceptance of single
women bearing and raising children has created a single-parent family
structure so common that in November 1999 the Census Bureau reported
that more children were conceived or born out of wedlock than were conceived or born to two-parent families (U.S. Census Bureau 1999). Gay
men and lesbians raise children, sometimes as single parents, sometimes
with a partner. The result of all these factors is that about 60 percent of all
children can expect to spend some time in a single-parent home.

However, it is important to recognize that some of these changes do
not represent new situations, but rather a return to family patterns that
we have seen before. Though divorce rates have risen, death rates have
fallen; the average length of a marriage in eighteenth-century America was
twelve years, before death claimed a partner (Coontz 1992). Children
then also lived in blended families. When agriculture was a mainstay of
our economy, parents and children worked together to sustain the family.
With industrialization, the middle-class family emerged with the mother
at home and the children protected and educated, but this family structure
was supported by a working class in which both women and children
worked in the factories. Though it is often thought that geographic mobility
and a tendency, beginning in the 1950s, to establish homes containing
only parents and children have separated the generations, Coontz (1992)

points out that these are changes in community ties, not family ties, and that contact with extended family has not diminished in recent years. The recent explosion in kinship foster care, in which aunts and uncles, grandparents, and other relatives take in children and care for them, adds credence to this idea and suggests that intergenerational support, as well as contact over distances, remains an important dimension of family life.

There is now greater acceptance of the single person—usually the mother—raising a child than there has been in the past. Generally, research concerning relationships between single parents and their children has indicated that these are strong families with the capacity to nurture on a daily basis and to cope with crisis (Hanson, Heims, et al. 1995). The greatest problem for single mothers has been poverty, for there is only one wage, and a woman's wage is generally less than a man's. The fact that children living with only one parent are almost five times as likely to be poor as children living with both parents cannot be ignored.

Poverty, of course, complicates other aspects of the single parent's life—finding affordable day care, finding time to take children to doctors and dentists and to go to school appointments, finding a way to have some respite from the constancy of parenting. All of these factors contribute to difficulties in parenting and to stress, which in turn may contribute to child abuse and neglect.

Concern about large numbers of single women raising children alone has led to discussion of the role of fathers. Child support has always been the responsibility of absent fathers; recent legislation makes it more difficult to evade payment. Services designed to help fathers become a part of the lives of their families are beginning to develop, and federal funds are for the first time being directed at helping young men gain skills for productive employment in the hope that they can then support their families. The contrast with the patriarchal family of the previous century is striking.

Youth Violence, Delinquency, and Nonconformity

Youth violence has been seen as a social problem for a long time, and continues to be a concern of the community. In 1997, one out of every five people arrested was a juvenile. Some 123,400 of these arrests were for violent crimes (including 2,500 for murder), and 701,500 were for property crimes (Snyder and Sickmund 1999). Between 1990 and 1999 the number of juveniles arrested for drug violations had increased 132 percent (U.S. Department of Justice 2000). Guns are a problem; the Annie E. Casey Foundation reports that every two hours a child dies of a gunshot wound, and that 70 percent of murders by juveniles under age fifteen are by firearms (Annie E. Casey Foundation 2000). A disproportionate number of arrests involve African American youth.

Young people who do not conform to community standards but are not necessarily delinquent, are also of concern to communities. Runaway youth, homeless youth, and youth who are truant from school and engage in risk-taking behavior are often seen by the community as in need of services, guidance, and perhaps control. For many years such youngsters were treated as delinquents; federal law now forbids their classification as delinquents, but alternative services have been slow to develop. The needs of these young people are explored in chapter 9.

The early social welfare workers played an important role in establishing the principle that youth in trouble were children to be taught and "rehabilitated" rather than criminals to be prosecuted. Early attempts at control focused on deterrence; in the 1800s, children over the age of seven who were delinquent were treated as adult criminals, facing the same criminal procedures and penalties as did adults. The last hundred years have seen changes in the type of institutions to which juveniles were committed and in the court procedures preceding such commitment. The first changes, initiated by social reformers around the end of the nineteenth century, moved toward the ideal of rehabilitating the juvenile offender. Instead of prison with adult offenders, "training schools" for delinquent and nonconforming youth were established.[3] Probation was another important innovation. Also important was the establishment of juvenile courts, with their informal procedures and their goal of rehabilitation. Julia Lathrop, a resident of Hull House,[4] was instrumental in organizing the movement that resulted in this first juvenile court, which was seen as a monumental change and quickly copied in other states. By 1945 all states had enacted legislation to establish juvenile courts (Downs, Moore, et al. 2000).

In the 1990s punishment as the means of deterring crime became more popular. The extent of juvenile crime, and its violence, makes this "get tough" reaction understandable. Emphasis is on the safety of the community rather than the welfare of the youth. In chapter 9 these changes, and their impact on the protection of the community and the rehabilitation of youth, are explored.

Homelessness

Related to poverty, homelessness is a problem for many families with young children. Although hard economic times have always led to some displacement and migration of children and families, the proliferation of working families who are simply unable to afford housing seems to be a fairly recent urban phenomenon. It is estimated that about a third of the homeless are families with children; a 1997 survey by the U.S. Conference of Mayors found that families with children made up 36 percent of those in homeless shelters (Children's Defense Fund 1998). The proportion might be higher if not for the fact that children are sometimes removed from families and placed in foster care for reasons related to homelessness. Young families with young children are particularly at risk for losing their homes; these families tend to have lower wages and high child care expenses. In 1997 the Children's Defense Fund reported that 38 percent of these 5.8 million families paid more than 30 percent of their incomes for housing, with 900,000 paying more than 50 percent (Children's Defense Fund 1998). Unfortunately, the supply of affordable housing for those with very low incomes is diminishing. At the same time current federal policy initiatives granting greater discretionary power to local housing authorities regarding the use of federal housing subsidies may worsen the situation if local authorities decide to lower subsidies or raise qualifying income levels.

Lack of adequate shelter is particularly hard on children. Poor housing with inadequate heating or deteriorated plumbing poses risks to health; old housing presents the risk of lead poisoning from older lead-based paint; structural deterioration may put young children at risk of accidental injury. Poor families often move from place to place in an attempt to secure better housing; these moves are disruptive to the older child's school experience. And, of course, the ultimate crisis of losing a home and living in a car, in a shelter, or even with relatives, creates a situation that is transient by definition, entailing enormous disruption and stress.

Substance Abuse

Substance abuse is a relatively recent addition to the list of social problems recognized by the community. For years alcohol has created tremendous difficulties for families and children, but alcoholism has been considered a personal or family problem, not a target for community intervention. The use of illegal drugs and the quest to obtain them have destroyed families and created even greater chaos. The extent of drug use and its linkage with violence and illegal activity have clearly made it a community problem.

Parents abuse substances at a lower rate than the general population; still, 11 percent of children in the United States live with at least one parent who is in need of treatment for substance abuse. Of these, 3.8 million live with a parent who is alcoholic, 2.1 million live with a parent who uses illicit drugs, and 2.4 million with a parent who abuses both alcohol and illicit drugs (U.S. Department of Health and Human Services [hereafter, U.S. HHS] 1999). Only a small percentage of these children will ever come in contact with the child welfare system; of those who do, the primary complaint will be neglect. Children of substance-abusing parents are more likely to be placed in foster care, and remain there longer, than children whose parents have other problems (U.S. HHS 1999). The growth in the numbers of young children in foster care is associated with the appearance of crack cocaine in the major cities, though causality cannot be demonstrated. It is estimated that for about two-thirds of the children in foster care, parental substance abuse is a problem (U.S. HHS 1999).

Racism

It might be said that racism is the hidden social problem of our time—not hidden from those who experience it, but hidden from the mainstream community that must provide the resources to combat it. It affects children in many ways. And, as a not-yet-recognized social problem, it becomes the special responsibility of social workers.

The extent of racism, and its impact on children and on the child welfare system, is discussed as a critical issue for the system in chapter 3. The statistics that show the extent to which children of color live in poverty document deteriorated communities, inadequate schools, and the despair of parents. These are children who are being denied opportunity in an affluent society. Throughout this book the reader will find the impact of racism documented over and over again in the various child welfare services. Of related concern are the more subtle and still less recognized biases that arise from the largely white and middle-class culture of child welfare agencies.

Women's Roles

The feminist perspective has in recent years helped us see clearly that society still defines the "proper" roles for women as marrying, having children, and caring for husband, children, and household. This framework is important in child welfare, for built into the child welfare system is the expectation that mothers will care for and protect their children. When this does not happen, mothers are blamed and expected to be the catalyst for family change. Child welfare workers often focus on work with mothers toward accomplishing changes in family functioning that will result in adequate care of children.

A different lens, however, may refocus work. Maluccio, Pine, et al. (2002) suggest that feminism is a lens through which to view the experiences of vulnerable women and their children and critically examine their needs and societal responses to them. For example, the concept of the feminization of poverty refocuses attention on the fact that currently most poor people in the United States are women and children. A feminist approach would focus on the causes of poverty—what pushes women into poverty or inhibits escape from it—such as workplace discrimination, lack of child support, premature and single parenting, undereducation and insufficient training, and racism (p. 20).

These same authors point out that the traditional view of women as responsible for caregiving does not extend to poor women, who are virtually forced to seek employment rather than rely for any extended period of time on public income assistance. They suggest that "as a result, these women may be viewed as doing neither wage-earning or parenting well enough" (p. 21). Swift (1995) carries these ideas further, suggesting that the structures of society make it extremely difficult for poor women to fulfill their expected roles, and suggesting that with its unrealistic expectations society has "manufactured" bad mothers.

Because child welfare work focuses so intensely on mothers, it is imperative that we deliberately and frequently step back and view our work through a feminist lens. Though the needs of children may impel action, and though family change may be the children's greatest need, we must always be conscious of the responsibility to advocate for change in the societal conditions that contribute to impoverished or aversive family life for children. We must be aware of the burden that poor mothers carry as they raise their children.

Child Maltreatment

Central to the concerns of child welfare, and certainly defined by the community as a problem, is the maltreatment of children by their caretakers, usually family members. Abuse and neglect are the issues that engender the most community concern, the most community debate about appropriate policy, and the most criticism of existing child welfare services. Services in place to protect children also consume most of the resources of child welfare agencies.

Pecora, Whittaker, et al. (2000) remind us that child maltreatment, though usually thought of in the context of family, occurs also at the community, societal, and institutional levels. At the community level, it occurs when the problems outlined earlier in this chapter result in inadequate support for families as they care for children—safe housing, adequate educational and employment opportunities, equal opportunities, and a violence-free environment. At the societal level it is reflected in unrealistic expectations for women and the cultural condoning of violence toward children and women. At the institutional level, maltreatment occurs when schools, legal authorities, or institutions designed to care for children and families fail to provide adequately for all children. Most child welfare intervention is focused at the family level, though in recent years community intervention has received increasing attention in the social work literature (for example, Adams and Nelson 1995; Meezan 1999). Certainly we as policy makers and practitioners need to keep all four levels in mind as we focus on child maltreatment.

The number of reports of child maltreatment is continuously rising. The Third National Incidence Study of Child Abuse and Neglect, a survey of professionals that attempts to discover the actual incidence of abuse and neglect both reported and known about but not reported to authorities, found a 67 percent increase between 1986 and 1993 (U.S. HHS, National Center on Child Abuse and Neglect 1996). State and national statistics show that the number of reports rose from 416,000 in 1976 to almost 2 million in 1985 (Kadushin and Martin 1988), to 2,974,000 in 1999 (U.S. HHS 2001).[5] After investigation, workers substantiate about a third of these reports, concluding that abuse or neglect severe enough to meet statutory definitions has taken place. The reasons for the increasing numbers are unclear. It is possible that there is indeed more maltreatment. We have noted the growing fragmentation of families and the many stresses facing young families. Traditional community supports—a

network of relatives and neighbors, the church, the well-staffed school—
may no longer be in place, particularly in transient and impoverished communities. It is possible that community standards for the care of children
have again risen, as they certainly have since the turn of the century. Whatever the reason, child welfare agencies are dealing with increased numbers
of reports and increased numbers of substantiated cases of maltreatment.

It is important to understand how community definitions of child
abuse and neglect have changed over time. Neglect and physical abuse
were recognized first, followed by sexual abuse. More recently, communities have become concerned about the exposure of children to family
violence. As each of these types of abuse was recognized as a social problem, a pattern of service delivery was repeated. At first children were
"rescued" and removed from their homes. Gradually knowledge was
gained about ways to keep children safe in their own homes in each of
these situations, and more sophisticated work with families began.

Most families whose children are abused, neglected, or at risk of maltreatment are poor, young, and subject to other stresses. These families
and their children can often benefit from a host of supportive services,
which can enhance family life, prevent maltreatment, or enable a family
to use its strengths to continue to care for its children even if maltreatment has occurred. There have been a number of interesting demonstra-
tions of these methods of family preservation. The work of delineating
the characteristics of parents who neglect, physically abuse, or sexually
abuse children is in its early stages; as this work progresses more effective
intervention programs may become possible. Such services are the subject
of chapter 4.

In some instances the maltreatment has been so severe—or the risk of
further maltreatment is so great—that the children need substitute care;
substitute care is explored in chapters 6 and 7. Substitute care may also
be needed by older children who have entered into a struggle with their
families, so that because of their own behavior and attitudes parental
guidance is no longer available to them. Among these are the children at
risk who are the subject of chapter 9.

Child Fatalities

The death of a child due to caretakers' abuse or neglect is a shocking and
tragic event. Such deaths are relatively rare, although intense media
attention tends to magnify the impact of each death. In 1999, the last

year for which federally collected data are available, 1,100 children are estimated to have died in the United States as a result of maltreatment (U.S. HHS 2001). This rate has remained fairly stable over the past five years, and the number seems consistent with the estimates of other reporting sources.[6]

Most fatalities involve very young children. In 1999, according to federal statistics, 42.6 percent were under one year of age, 86.1 percent under six—an age span during which children are relatively helpless and are easily injured. Most maltreatment (87.3%) occurs at the hands of one or both parents; this is also true of fatalities (89.1%). Many child deaths were associated with more than one type of maltreatment. Physical abuse, alone or combined with neglect, was the cause of almost half (48.8%) of the child fatalities in 1999; neglect alone caused 38.2 percent of child fatalities (U.S. HHS 2001).

Available statistics undoubtedly underestimate the number of fatalities, both because of child deaths that are attributed mistakenly to natural causes, and because of lack of coordination among the many systems tracking child deaths. Coordination of reporting systems so that police, health departments, and the child welfare department are all working together, where it has occurred, has led to the identification of more fatalities due to maltreatment. Increased use of interdisciplinary child fatality review teams perhaps offers the best hope for understanding the scope and nature of child fatalities and for implementing appropriate prevention efforts. These are teams, usually with representatives from police, health, and child welfare offices, the court system, and other related disciplines, that review all child deaths not clearly attributable to natural causes. Review teams seek to establish what happened and to identify patterns and risk factors that present special danger to children. The interdisciplinary nature of the teams permits many points of view to be explored. Increasing study of fatalities has led to the discovery of certain common occurrences and to corresponding public education campaigns. Perhaps the most notable example is the recognition of the number of fatalities that occurred when a baby or small child was shaken, and the "Never Shake a Baby" campaign that resulted. The campaign provided new information to the public and has apparently had considerable impact.

When fatalities due to maltreatment occur, they mobilize a community and often lead to criticism of child welfare workers. It is assumed that the child welfare system should have been able to protect the child. However, it is clear that at least half of the families in which a child died after maltreatment were never known to the child welfare system. Of those who were known to the system, only about 15 percent apparently had received intensive family preservation services or foster care; in 1999, federal data show that only 12.7 percent of the families of children who died had been provided family preservation services in the five years preceding the deaths, and only 2.7 percent of the children had been returned to their homes from foster care (U.S. HHS 2000). It is not known how many families in which a child died had been known to the child welfare agency and receiving community-based preventive services. Nor do we know how many of these families were reported to the child welfare system, perhaps had brief contact during an investigation, but were not linked to services. Partial information is contained in a fifty-state survey by Darro and Mitchell in 1990, cited by Lindsey (1994), which found that half of child abuse fatalities had been active child welfare cases at the time of the death.

If we could predict which families were most likely to severely injure or kill their children, preventive services might be put in place. However, the risk factors that lead to child fatalities are imperfectly understood. Numerous instruments exist to assess the risk of abuse; all demonstrate "imprecision and low reliability in predicting abuse" (Lindsey 1994:117).[7] It might be expected that risk factors in a family in which a child dies due to maltreatment would be greater in number or intensity than those that lead to severe, nonfatal abuse. It is not clear that this is so. There is little research. It has been suggested that "homicide is not simply an extreme form of interpersonal violence. Rather, homicide is a distinct form of behavior that requires a distinct explanation" (Gelles 1996:85–86). Supporting this idea is a statewide analysis in Oregon of family factors associated with severity of abuse or neglect, reported by DeHaan (1997). That analysis, based on case reading, found families in which a child died to be more similar to families where abuse or neglect was classified as "mild" than to those where it was classified as "moderate" or "severe." The best predictor of future behavior seems to be past behavior, and thus prior severe injury or death of a child is definitely considered a risk factor. Beyond that, there is a great need for more data to inform assessments of the potential for fatal maltreatment.

Perhaps typical is the story of a recent fatality in Portland, Oregon. The story begins with an intensive and highly publicized search for a missing three-year-old, who had disappeared, apparently while his mother was sleeping, from the tent in which he and his young mother were living. There had been two reports of child neglect, both investigated, neither thought to be serious. No services had been provided to the family. The search ended when the child was found fourteen days later, battered to death. The mother's boyfriend has been accused of the murder. As the shocked community laid flowers and teddy bears at the door of the abandoned house where he died, one person left a note that read, "Little Mr. P., Sorry we let you down as a society; we can now only have you as a memory."

Community Definitions of Maltreatment

Community definitions of maltreatment have changed over time, as the standards of the community have changed. Generally, these definitions have reflected the increasing recognition of childhood as a life stage during which there are particular developmental needs, and of children as persons with rights. This view has gradually replaced earlier perspectives in which children were seen as property under the absolute control of their parents.

Neglect Neglect has always been present. It can be defined as child maltreatment by failure to meet a child's basic needs, though the definition of basic needs may vary over time and across cultures. Neglect can be physical, emotional, medical, or educational. In its most severe form it is life-threatening. In all instances, the developmental consequences of neglect are serious.

Reviewing the definitions of neglect offered by child welfare scholars, Swift (1995) notes that descriptions of physical neglect predominate: inadequate food, clothing, and shelter; inadequate supervision; abandonment. Emotional neglect has, she notes, received increasing attention in recent years, though it remains difficult to define. Failure to thrive, a condition in which infants or small children fail to gain weight and develop as expected, is often thought to result from a combination of physical and emotional neglect. Often discussed is the issue of whether there is a universal definition of neglect, or whether it varies according to cultural tradition and community setting. Definitions of neglect generally focus on the acts or omissions of parents, though Giovannoni and Becerra (1979) reported that more community consensus is achieved when the definition focuses on harm to the child. The repetitive or chronic nature of neglect is another common aspect of its definition.

Physical neglect occurs when parents do not provide for the basic needs of a child. Most common are inadequate food, clothing inappropriate for the weather, lack of a home, or a home in which conditions are unsafe—either because of physical hazards or because extremely poor housekeeping has resulted in health hazards. Failure to provide adequate supervision, including leaving children alone when they are young, is a common neglect complaint. Another form of neglect consists of leaving children for long periods with a substitute caretaker without planning with the caretaker about the time of return. Abandonment is an extreme form of neglect.

Medical neglect occurs when parents fail to obtain needed medical care for a child. This can involve very complex ethical issues if there is a religious reason that medical assistance is not sought. Some churches teach that reliance on prayer is the proper course of action in illness; some forbid blood transfusions or other medical procedures. In these instances the neglect is defined by the community and the remedy enforced by the court. The following example was reported in the *Oregonian* newspaper in October of 1999:

In Oregon in 1998 a child died at home after a fairly protracted illness that was diagnosed, after his death, as diabetes. The parents had been greatly concerned about the child's physical decline and his discomfort and had called in the pastor of their church to pray with them for the child's recovery. They had not sought medical help. Oregon law protected them from charges of neglect because of their adherence to an organized religion that prohibited medical intervention.

In the examination of this law and the pressure for its repeal that followed the boy's death, the *Oregonian* examined the recent history of members of this church. It discovered an inordinate number of women who had died in childbirth, and of children who had died of diseases fairly easily handled with standard medical care. In this patriarchal sect, it was women and children who paid the price of the set of beliefs.

Educational neglect occurs when parents fail to comply with laws concerning school attendance. This is, of course, a fairly simplistic definition. Parents sometimes do not send their children to school because they do not approve of what is being taught; courts have upheld the right of parents to "home school" children if their religious beliefs are in conflict with material taught in the schools. Sometimes children are kept out of school to watch smaller children, to act as an interpreter for a non-English-speaking parent, to accomplish errands, or otherwise to help in the household. Some children do not go to school because parents simply cannot organize family life to get up and get started in the morning. And some children truant because school is in some way intolerable for them. All of these, with the exception of home schooling, constitute educational neglect and each, clearly, has a very different remedy.

Physical abuse Physical abuse is defined as deliberate physical injury to a child, regardless of the reasoning or intent of the abuser. It had always been of concern, and instances of extreme physical cruelty (combined with neglect) led to the founding of Societies for the Prevention of Cruelty to Children, the child rescue movement mentioned in the introduction. Physical abuse includes severe physical punishment (such as beating, scalding, poisoning, or close and aversive confinement of a child), or any nonaccidental action that creates the possibility of harm to the child. Though they vary among the states, statutes that define abuse emphasize that a child must have received serious injury, or be at substantial risk of injury, in order for the state to intervene in the family against the parents' wishes. The line between appropriate physical punishment and physical abuse is drawn differently in different communities and among different cultural groups, which, of course, makes a precise definition difficult.

Sexual abuse Sexual abuse is subject to many definitions, and the prevalence rates vary with the definition. A common denominator of the definitions is the use of power to involve a child or immature adolescent in sexual activities for the gratification of the abuser. An important element is that, because children cannot comprehend the nature of sexual activities, they are unable to give informed consent. Sexual abuse "includes incest, sexual assault by a relative or stranger, fondling of the genital areas, exposure to indecent acts, sexual rituals, or involvement in child pornography" (Panel on Research on Child Abuse and Neglect 1993:59).

Psychological maltreatment Psychological maltreatment has increasingly been recognized as important, though it has been difficult to identify. Emotional neglect occurs when a parent is unavailable to meet the psychological needs of a child; it is difficult to define, sensitive to cultural differences, and specific to the developmental stage of the child (Garbarino, Guttmann, et al. 1986). Components of psychological abuse include unpredictable verbal belittling and constant depreciation of the child. Parental indifference also constitutes psychological abuse. Intervention in situations of psychological abuse is usually impossible unless parental actions have been severe enough to cause recognizable behavior disturbance in the children.

Psychological abuse (which often accompanies other maltreatment) prevents children from developing to their full potential. Unpredictable parental responses create a state of constant watchfulness and anxiety, which interferes with other learning. Belittling and depreciation rob a child of self-esteem. Indifference may be even more devastating, conveying the message that the child is not even worth attention. These are serious consequences that can be as crippling as the consequences of other forms of maltreatment.

Neglect

Neglect is the most common of all forms of maltreatment. In 1999, there were approximately 482,000 substantiated instances of neglect—neglect serious enough for protective services to become involved (U.S. HHS 2001). The Third National Incidence Study estimates that 879,000 children were neglected in 1993; that is twice as many as in 1986 (U.S. HHS, National Center on Child Abuse and Neglect 1996). Reports of neglect are increasing faster than reports of other forms of maltreatment (Garbarino and Collins 1999). Probably only the most severe neglect is reflected in statistics such as those cited. Much neglect is chronic, and it is very difficult to differentiate between minimally adequate care and neglect. Over the years it can be observed that whenever there is an increase in staff in a protective service agency, the proportion of neglect cases rises as workers have the capacity to reach out and serve more families.

Parents who chronically neglect their children appear to lack the capacity or the energy or the resources to recognize and respond to their needs. Family and environmental stress, and lack of family and community supports, are often evident. Large families have been associated with neglect (Giovannoni 1985; Polansky, Chalmers, et al. 1981; Nelson, Saunders, et al. 1993). Some studies have found single parents more likely to neglect (U.S. HHS, National Center on Child Abuse and Neglect 1996). Most families who neglect their children are poor; the Third National Incidence Study reports that children who live in the poorest families (with incomes under $15,000 per year) were 45 times more likely to be neglected than those from upper-income families ($30,000 or more per year). Substance abuse also appears to play a role in neglect (Gelles 1999).

Most research on neglect focuses on the mother's role, for women are usually the primary caretakers of young children. The focus can be through the feminist lens, explored earlier, which emphasizes society's conflicting expectations that women will both be self-supporting and be good parents. Most empirical study of neglect has, however, been through a more traditional lens, which emphasizes the needs of the child.

The classic pattern of neglect involves the isolated, disorganized, and apathetic mother who does not perceive her children's needs, does not believe that anything she could do would meet their needs, and further has little support and few resources. Polansky named this the "apathy-futility syndrome" (Polansky, Chalmers, et al. 1981). Crittenden (1999) suggests that it is the failure to form productive human relationships that distinguishes those who neglect their children. Young (1964), in a classic portrayal of neglect, identifies the emotional deficits in the childhood of the neglecting parent. Poverty, isolation, and a mother who is disorganized, apathetic or depressed, and perhaps involved in substance abuse, mark a "typical" neglectful family. It is a difficult situation in which to intervene.

Failure to thrive in infants or small children can be due to neglect, difficulties in feeding, or both; it is a condition diagnosed when a child fails to gain weight as growth charts predict, instead falling into the very lowest weight percentiles. It can be an organic condition, and it is vital that a proper diagnosis be made. Young children who have the serious nutritional deficiencies evidenced by the failure to gain weight and height may suffer cognitive and emotional difficulties. Particularly if the cause is neglect, early intervention to establish attachment to a nurturing caretaker is important.

Neglect has serious consequences. At its most severe, malnutrition in an infant or very young child can lead to developmental delay or even death. Profound neglect, as seen recently in the "orphanages" of some Eastern European countries, where children may be afforded minimal physical care but have no opportunity to interact with caregivers, can lead to an apparent inability to form social attachments, with consequent language and behavioral difficulties. Cognitive difficulty, poor impulse control, and insecure attachment to adults have been identified as outcomes of family neglect (Gelles 1999). School-age children who are neglected and unkempt are often shunned by their peers, creating social isolation that further distorts normal development. Gelles states that "when researchers do disentangle the effects of other forms of abuse and the impact of poverty and structural influences, it appears that neglected children suffer the worst outcomes" (1999:285).

Physical Abuse

Pediatric radiologists working with X rays in the 1960s were the first to recognize a pattern of multiple fractures at different stages of healing in the long bones of small children. The extent of these injuries to children was first documented in a national survey in which 302 children were discovered hospitalized due to physical abuse (Kempe, Silverman, et al. 1962).

States responded in the next decade by passing laws aimed at protecting children from physical abuse; most of these laws mandated reporting of suspected abuse and granted the reporter immunity from prosecution for slander. The passage of the Federal Child Abuse Prevention and Treatment Act in 1974 provided assistance to states for the development of child protection programs. Administering the provisions of this act became a central concern of the Children's Bureau, the federal agency formed in 1912 to promote child welfare.

Because the focus of concern was relatively narrow and dramatic, the new laws enjoyed widespread support. Publicity resulted in increasing numbers of reports of suspected abuse. For example, in 1971 in Dade County, Florida, after a campaign to educate the public about child abuse and their responsibility to report it, the number of reports of suspected abuse increased, in the course of one year, from 17 to 19,120 (Lindsey 1994). Protective service workers were overwhelmed, there and in other states, and have remained overwhelmed ever since.

In 1999, states recorded approximately 176,000 substantiated reports of physical abuse, which constituted 21.3 percent of the substantiated maltreatment reported (U.S. HHS 2001). Physical abuse is generally easier to verify than other types of abuse, because a child's injuries are visible and can often be identified as having been intentionally inflicted.

While agreeing that physical abuse is unacceptable, communities are less clear about determining where on the continuum between physical punishment and abuse intervention is warranted. Definitions of abuse rely on judgments and are culturally bound. Different cultural groups may have different ways of providing guidance and discipline. Abuse can be said to have occurred when parents have behaved in a way unacceptable to their community and when the child has been injured or is at serious risk of injury because of parental actions.

In a very early study of child abuse, Young (1964) distinguished two types of persons who abuse children. She noted that most abuse began as a parental reaction to some action of the infant or child, a reaction that was inappropriate or too severe, or grew out of control. Kadushin and Martin (1981) examined this kind of abuse in detail, documenting the manner in which it became an "interactive event" between parents and older children. However, Young suggested, a much smaller number of abusing parents seem to derive pleasure from their power over the victim and appear to lose sight of the original incident in their absorption in the child's suffering. Large epidemiological studies have identified circumstances associated with abuse: poverty, unemployment, a new baby, a child with disabilities, social isolation (Gil 1970; Straus, Gelles, et al. 1980). Characteristics of abusive parents, such as involvement in the criminal justice system, substance abuse, and family violence have been identified (Straus, Gelles, et al. 1980). However, Young's two categories still seem to make sense. Clearly the risk assessment and planning for the child's safety will be very different in the two situations.

Physical abuse can have serious physical consequences. Elmer (1977) followed a group of severely physically abused children for several years after the abuse, and found that a high proportion of them had serious physical disabilities or had limited cognitive function due to head injuries that occurred during the abusive episode. Even more evident is the emotional disturbance, often expressed as aggression, that follows physical abuse, even if the child is removed from the abusive home. This has become particularly evident as the adoptive parents of children who were removed from their own homes after abuse have sought postadoption mental health services for their children.

Sexual Abuse

Sexual abuse was not recognized as a community problem until the late 1970s; its recognition was in part due to the voice of the feminist movement. The feminist movement saw child sexual abuse and rape as related examples of inordinate male power in a patriarchal society, and worked to bring both to public awareness.

Substantiated sexual abuse accounts for about 11.3 percent of all substantiated maltreatment (U.S. HHS 2001). As with other types of maltreatment, the number of reports doubtless represents only a small proportion of actual incidence. Prevalence studies yield a variety of estimates; the discrepancies reflect the different definitions and methods used to gather data. Using the broadest definitions, as many as one in four women have been identified as sexually abused (Finkelhor 1984). There is increasing recognition that boys are also sexually abused. Boys seem less willing to come forward and report sexual abuse; possibly because of the implications for their male self-image.

The characteristics of those who sexually abuse children have not been well defined. Most are heterosexual men. Family systems have often been part of the explanation, with the mother often identified as the family member who is distant from the daughter and unable to protect her. Feminists point out that this model blames the woman when the man is the actual perpetrator. Finkelhor (1984) proposes a model that describes the dynamics of sexual abuse but does not attempt to explain why the initial impetus to sexually abuse a child would arise.

In addition to the physical harm that can come to a child through sexual abuse, the emotional harm can be extensive. Sexual abuse distorts a child's developmental process, and this can lead to a devalued self-image, difficulties in relationships, and precocious sexuality. The most extreme manifestation of long-term harm seems to be the post-traumatic stress syndrome, in which severe symptoms can be disabling.

Psychological Maltreatment

Though psychological maltreatment accompanies almost all abuse and neglect, by itself it is less frequently reported and less frequently established than other forms of abuse. In part this is because of the linkage of child protective services with the legal system; unless psychological abuse or neglect has been severe enough to cause demonstrable harm to the child, with either physical or behavioral manifestations, it is difficult to prove in court. Psychological maltreatment thus has the lowest reported incidence rate, 0.09 victims per 1000 children in 1999 (U.S. HHS 2001). This rate has been relatively constant over the last five years.

Psychological maltreatment takes different forms at different stages in child development. As outlined by Garbarino, Guttmann, et al. (1986), it involves a "pattern of psychologically destructive behavior" that constitutes "a concerted attack by an adult on a child's development of self and social competence" (p. 8). The attack can take five forms: rejecting, isolating, terrorizing, ignoring, and/or corrupting, and will be manifested in differing behavior at different child developmental levels. For example, rejecting behavior in the parent of an infant takes the form of rejecting the child's overtures so that the formation of a primary attachment relationship is thwarted. In early childhood, the child is excluded from family activities. As the child reaches school age, the parent "consistently communicates a negative definition of self to the child" by belittling accomplishment, scapegoating, and using labels such as "dummy" or "monster." In adolescence the parent refuses to acknowledge the changing roles within the family, either infantilizing the adolescent, continuing to criticize and humiliate the adolescent, or, ultimately, expelling the adolescent from the family (p. 25).[8] The psychic destruction wrought by consistent parental behaviors such as these is evident.[9]

Descriptions of parents who psychologically maltreat their children read much like descriptions of parents who abuse or neglect their children. Poverty, isolation, and substance abuse create strain in family life. The parents have not been adequately nurtured themselves as children, have had poor role models, and have little to give. Parents have unrealistic expectations, which their children fail to meet. The interventions prescribed are similar to interventions for any abuse or neglect; Garbarino, Guttmann, et al. (1986) outline interventions to reduce stress on the family, interventions to resolve problems among family members, and interventions to mobilize community resources. They emphasize the importance of individualizing interventions to address family needs.

Psychological abuse and neglect have serious consequences. Abuse, with its belittling, scapegoating, and isolating behavior by parents leads inevitably to struggles with self-esteem, to anger and possibly violence, and to estrangement from family life. Many of the "at-risk youth" described in chapter 9 have been victims of psychological abuse. Psychological neglect has equally devastating consequences, particularly in infancy and early childhood. If a child's attempts at attachment are consistently rejected, the basis for distorted developmental patterns and lifelong difficulty has been laid. This is most dramatically seen in the children in the orphanages of Eastern Europe who have become known to the Western world in the last ten years. These children's emotional needs were profoundly neglected. From experience with those who were adopted and brought to the United States or Western Europe, we know that they have manifested multiple developmental difficulties. However, the attention and nurture of adoptive homes has been remedial for many. The world should watch and learn from the experiences of those who remained institutionalized in Eastern Europe.

Critical Issue: Family Violence

At the end of the twentieth century, social workers in child welfare became aware of the potential impact of family violence on children. Prior to the feminist movement of the 1980s, family violence was largely unrecognized or, if recognized, thought of as a problem that should be handled within the privacy of the family. Feminists raised the consciousness of the community about the extent of family violence and the damage—both physical and emotional—that it could do to women. Violence is more likely now to bring police intervention and to involve the criminal justice system. A network of services has developed for battered women, prominent among them battered women's shelters, in which women can find safety. Domestic violence services attempt to form a protective network around a battered woman, to enable her to discover her options, and to assist her in leaving the violent situation. Still, in the long run women often have few protections against a determined and violent partner.[10]

It was gradually recognized that a parent who was violent toward a spouse might also be violent toward a child. Physical and sexual abuse were the first types of abuse to be linked to family violence. Children also often "get in the way" of family violence, being hurt simply because they are present or because they try to protect the victim. Most recently, question has been raised of whether children in violent homes experience considerable distress or psychological abuse; recent research has found that children in violent homes manifest emotional and behavioral problems even if they have not been directly abused. The constant anxiety and watchfulness demanded in a violent home will, at a minimum, have serious consequences for child development, whether or not the child actually becomes part of the violence.

Domestic violence is a pattern of assaultive and coercive behaviors used against an intimate partner. Although there are instances of women as the aggressors in domestic violence, far more often women are the victims. Domestic violence occurs across all social strata and cultural groups, though its interpretation may differ from culture to culture. Once it emerged as a social issue, and counting began, many were amazed at the extent of family violence. It is estimated that between 2 million and 4 million women are severely battered each year (Straus and Gelles 1986). FBI statistics estimate that between 1,400 and 1,500 women are murdered every year by current or former husbands or boyfriends (Dykstra and Alsop 1996).

Domestic violence and child maltreatment are linked. Data concerning the overlap between spousal violence and child maltreatment has for the most part been gathered from families who have been identified as needing services. It comes from two sources: studies of family records of children known to protective services, and analysis of information from women who have sought services related to abuse. Investigation of family factors from protective service caseloads and studies that begin by identifying women who have sought help yield an estimate that in 30 to 60 percent of the instances in which either spousal violence or child maltreatment is identified, it is likely that both exist (Edleson 1999).

In an attempt to ascertain actual incidence rather than relying only on events severe enough to have been reported, *Woman's Day* magazine recruited 775 women who saw themselves as victims of spousal violence and asked about their children. The mothers reported that in 70 percent of the families the children were also being maltreated, and more severe woman abuse was linked to more severe child maltreatment (Bowker et al. 1988, reported in Edleson 1999).

There is no question that children in violent homes are aware of the violence. A recent four-city telephone survey asked mothers about their children's involvement in abusive episodes, and most mothers reported that the children were aware of the abuse. Children were reported to be drawn to the room as a violent episode began, but then to leave. About a quarter of the children called someone for help, and another quarter attempted to intervene physically. The more pervasive and violent the abuse, the higher the proportion of children involved. Family stability and the relationship of the abuser to the mother and child were factors that influenced the involvement of the children (Edleson, Mbilinyi, et al. 2001).

The extent of the developmental hazard to a child who witnesses abuse without being a direct victim is well documented. Studies measuring children's behavior through standardized mental health instruments have found that children who have been in violent homes display more externalizing problem behavior, more internalizing problem behavior, and less social competence. Not surprisingly, they display more anxiety and lower cognitive and verbal abilities. And, perhaps most worrisome, they display lowered self-esteem and less empathy (Peled, Jaffe, et al. 1995). This lowered self-esteem and lessened empathy may be the personality traits that set the stage for another generation of violence.[11]

Concerned about the risk of harm, and the actual harm, that children experience in violent homes, child protective service systems have in recent years begun to intervene in situations of family violence. The intervention demands complicated decisions and demands new ways of conceptualizing child safety and family preservation. Historically, child welfare workers have tended to expect that mothers could protect their children, to blame them when they could not, and to remove children from them if children's safety was compromised. Child welfare workers often find it difficult to intervene in such a way that the child will be protected and the mother neither endangered nor revictimized by the intervention.

For the child protection worker, the safety of the child is the most important consideration. Child protective services also work within the framework of preserving the family for the child if at all possible, and child welfare workers are not used to thinking of preserving only a part of the family for the child. In order for the child to be safe, the abusive family member must leave the home, or the mother must be helped to move to a situation in which she can protect the child. However, unless the family violence has been judged serious enough for court intervention, fathers are not likely to leave the home, and if they do leave they are likely to return promptly. The child protection worker must then decide whether the extent and severity of the violence is such that the risk of harm to the child warrants intervention.[12] At the same time the worker must decide whether an intervention that separates a child from his or her family is likely to do more harm than good.

This is a complex decision, for the growing body of research makes clear that many family factors interact to mitigate or exacerbate the risk of harm; some mothers are able to protect their children from abuse, from neglect, and from emotional harm. Morton (2002) notes that safety assessments must consider safety in the context of individual caretakers and individual children. Complicating matters is the fact that the time of a move from home has been demonstrated to be the most dangerous time for mother and children (Mills, Friend, et al. 2000).

Intake interviews triggered by child maltreatment allegations may be an excellent way to discover domestic violence and to open possible avenues of help for desperate women. However, the intervention of a protective service agency into a family may itself make the family situation more dangerous. A first reaction to protective service contact is often defensiveness and anger. The very fact that a protective service agency knows of the situation and is attempting to intervene may provoke further violence against the mother or children, who are now blamed for "telling" and may be suspected of exaggerating the situation. As is often the case when working with a new type of maltreatment, workers must make difficult decisions in uncharted territory; the removal of children may occur more often than would be ideal.

Child welfare interventions, focusing on safety of the child, create tension between child welfare and domestic violence organizations. The ultimate aim of both services is to empower women and enable them to protect themselves and their children. Domestic violence services view women who have been assaulted as victims who are relatively powerless to control the abuse. The goal is to shelter them and to help them with the economic and psychological barriers they face in establishing an independent home. The removal of children is often viewed as a further victimization of the mother.

As in other forms of abuse, it is the abuser who ought to leave the home. Intervention should ensure the child's safety, help the mother protect herself and her children, and hold the perpetrator of the violence accountable (Schechter and Edleson 1999). However, neither the child welfare worker nor the domestic violence organization worker has the power alone to make this happen. Community systems must be mobilized. The police and the court system can be helpful. If any reason can be found in records of even minor past offenses, the abuser can sometimes be picked up and jailed for a day or two, giving the abused woman time to leave with her children and move to a safe place. Substantiation of child abuse or domestic violence complaints may enable a court to order the perpetrator out of the home.

A woman's ability to move away from her partner is dependent on her resources—both financial and emotional—and the resources of her community. As has been noted, the time of leaving an abusive relationship is very dangerous, both for the woman and for her children. Shelters offer respite and focus on supporting and empowering. When leaving a shelter, a woman often faces poverty, homelessness, harassment from the former partner, and the behavioral problems of children whose lives have been disrupted (Schechter and Edleson 1999). The same kinds of family support resources that are useful in any family preservation situation can be helpful at this time.

The child welfare establishment has historically been optimistic that remedial programs, such as anger management training, would be effective in helping a child abuser learn other ways of interaction with children. This optimism is not shared by the domestic violence organizations, which tend to view the rehabilitation of an abuser as an extensive and dubious project. And they may be right. When there is serious domestic violence in the home and a mother has been unable to protect her children, she is unlikely to be able to do so in the future unless the abuser's behavior changes. The effectiveness of intervention and education programs for batterers is debated by researchers and practitioners; certainly it varies greatly between programs (Schechter and Edleson 1999). Many of the tragedies of children returned home only to be abused again may be due to the system's underestimating the extent to which the abuser controlled the family through violence.

Child welfare is entering new territory as it moves toward intervention in families known to be violent. Child welfare agencies must learn from the wisdom and caution of the network of services that have developed protocols for keeping women and children safe while decisions are made. Immediate decisions have to be differentiated from long-term planning; though a child may need to be separated from the mother for reasons of safety, the long-term attachment of child and the mother should be considered when long-term plans are made. Lyon (1999) discusses the difficulties an abused woman faces in leaving an abusive partner and in convincing the court that she can protect her child, and urges that termination of a mother's parental rights occur only if it is evident that the mother cannot protect the child and if there is a prospective adoptive home ready for the child.

Domestic violence organizations and child welfare agencies are increasingly making attempts to work together. Conflicting goals create a major obstacle to collaboration: child welfare workers focus on child safety and tend to blame mothers for not protecting children, while domestic violence organizations tend to trust the mother's judgment and work to empower the mother. Successful collaboration seems to depend first on articulation of common goals (Beeman, Hagemeister, et al. 1999). Cross-training of workers, the hiring of battered women's advocates as part of the child welfare system, and the development of domestic violence protocols for investigators have also proved effective in promoting cooperation (Aron and Olson 1997; Whitney and Davis 1999). However, it must be recognized that there are complex policy and practice issues to be resolved as child protection workers learn how to assess risk and work to benefit children and families in these situations.

It is not only domestic violence organizations and the child welfare system that need to learn more effective ways of working together. Knitzer (2001) writes of a population dependent on public welfare and affected by depression, substance abuse, and domestic violence. She suggests that welfare reform and a national goal of seeing that every child enters first grade ready to learn may provide a framework for positive intervention in the lives of these families. Early childhood services (Head Start, child care, preschool, home-visiting programs, family resource programs) can provide a point of entry, as can welfare reform, substance abuse programs, family violence services, or mental health services. So can child welfare protective services. Coordination of these services will not be easy—it will demand examination and reconciliation of the differing value bases, as well as integration of diverse federal programs with different sources of funding and, at the local level, the blending of funds for different services.

These are challenges that child welfare must take up, if we are to learn to intervene effectively in situations of domestic violence where children may be in danger. As we learn, we must be careful. A pro forma intervention to inform a woman of services—and to make a child welfare worker feel that he or she has not ignored a bad situation—may do more harm than good. Removing a child to ensure safety, when it is possible that the child could have remained with the mother, may do more harm than good. Skills developed through long experience with these families must be learned, disseminated, and utilized.

Conclusion

These, then, are some of the major social problems that affect children, and with which the community has grappled over the past three hundred years. This rather long and involved chapter has established the connection between the social conditions the community defines as problematic and the services the community wants to see provided to promote the welfare of children; it has also shown how social workers (or, before the profession was established, social welfare workers) discover and document problems through direct work with those who are suffering. It is evident that, repeatedly, community problems have been discovered by those working directly with affected families, and have been brought to the attention of the community so that some action could be taken.

Attention seems to move from one issue to another, and although an earlier issue is not fully resolved, interest is keen to resolve the newly discovered problem. In addition to their responsibilities in bringing new issues to the consciousness of the larger community, social workers must also try to keep attention focused on older, unresolved problems.

This mission of social work is complicated. Today communities have become so heterogeneous that the voice of the community is often split. Perceptions of need vary. There is little consensus about whether the responsibility for building family supports rests with the community, or whether the individual family unit should be self-sufficient. There is a gap between what society says it wants to do and what it will fund. These are critical issues for children. In order to work effectively with the community, and within the community, the social worker and child welfare practitioner need to understand these forces and learn how to work with them to create change.

Notes

1. Sidney Zimbalist, in his *History of Social Work Research* (New York: Columbia University Press, 1969) gives a good account of this work and of its impact in the development of the social work profession.

2. Lisbeth Schorr, in *Within Our Reach: Breaking the Cycle of Disadvantage* (New York: Anchor Press, 1988) details many of these compromises and their impact on children. She also examines programs that have had a positive impact in these circumstances.

3. Nina Bernstein, in *The Lost Children of Wilder* (New York: Pantheon, 2001) documents the use of prison-like institutions for the care of dependent children (children who are dependent on the state for care but have broken no laws) in very recent times.

4. Hull House, founded by Jane Addams, was a renowned settlement house in Chicago. Located in a poor section of the city with a largely immigrant population, it became both a community center and a center from which a rich array of research and scholarly discourse arose. Many of the early advocates for social reform were associated with Hull House; this work became a foundation of the social work profession.

5. The sources of the data cited here are explained in greater detail in chapter 3.

6. See Lindsey (1994) or L. B. Costin, H. J. Karger, et al., *The Politics of Child Abuse in America* (New York: Oxford University Press, 1996), for thorough discussions of these numbers.

7. A. Turnell and S. Edwards, in *Signs of Safety: A Solution and Safety Oriented Approach to Child Protection Casework* (New York: Norton, 1999), turn

around the concept of risk and examine the safety factors present in a household; this work is innovative and theoretically appealing but has not been empirically validated with large populations.

8. Garbarino, Guttmann, et al. (1986:23–43) provide descriptions of the five dimensions, illustrating each with case examples that make it clear how to recognize emotional abuse and/or neglect.

9. An excellent description of the experiences of a psychologically abused child, and the adult she became, is contained in Jane Hamilton's novel *The Book of Ruth* (New York: Anchor, 1988).

10. It is difficult to imagine a violent home. Anna Quindlen's novel *Black and Blue* (New York: Random House, 1998) conveys the anxiety and despair of such a home.

11. Excellent reviews of this research can be found in L. C. Carter, L. A. Welthorn, and R. E. Behrman, "Domestic Violence and Children: Analysis and Recommendations" (*The Future of Children* 9, no. 3 (1999): 4–20), and in A. Fleck-Henderson, "Domestic Violence in the Child Protection System: Seeing Double" (*Children and Youth Services Review* 22, no. 5 (2000): 333–54).

12. Risk of harm is a problematic reason for state intervention in family life. Of course, we want to protect children from injury before it happens. However, when no damage to the child can be demonstrated, there can be serious questions about violation of the rights of the parents.

References

Abbott, E., and S. P. Breckinridge. 1917. *Truancy and Non-attendance in the Chicago Schools.* Chicago: University of Chicago Press.

Abbott, G. 1938. *The Child and the State: Apprenticeship and Child Labor.* Chicago: University of Chicago Press.

Adams, P., and K. Nelson. 1995. *Reinventing Human Services: Community and Family-Centered Practice.* Hawthorne, N.Y.: Aldine de Gruyter.

Annie E. Casey Foundation. 2000. *Kids Count Data Book: 2000.* Washington, D.C.: Annie E. Casey Foundation.

Aron, L., and K. Olson. 1997. *Efforts by Child Welfare Agencies to Address Domestic Violence: The Experience of Five Communities.* New York: Urban Institute Press.

Beeman, S. K., A. K. Hagemeister, et al. 1999. "Child Protection and Battered Women's Services: From Conflict to Collaboration." *Child Maltreatment* 42: 116–26.

Bradbury, D. E. 1962. *Five Decades of Action for Children.* Washington, D.C.: U.S. Department of Health, Education, and Welfare.

Children's Defense Fund. 1998. *The State of America's Children.* Washington, D.C.: Children's Defense Fund.

Coontz, S. 1992. *The Way We Never Were*. New York: Basic Books.

Costin, L. B., C. J. Bell, et al. 1991. *Child Welfare: Policies and Practice*. New York: Longman.

Crittenden, P. M. 1999. "Child Neglect: Causes and Contributors." In *Neglected Children: Research, Practice, and Policy*, edited by H. Dubowitz. Thousand Oaks, Calif.: Sage.

DeHaan, B. 1997. "Critical and Fatal Child Maltreatment in Oregon: Escalating Violence or Distinct Behavior?" Ph.D. diss., Graduate School of Social Work, Portland State University.

Downs, S. W., E. Moore, et al. 2000. *Child Welfare and Family Services: Policies and Practice*. Boston: Allyn and Bacon.

Dykstra, C. H., and R. J. Alsop. 1996. *Domestic Violence and Child Abuse*. Englewood, Colo.: National Resource Center on Child Abuse and Neglect.

Edleson, J. L. 1999. "The Overlap Between Child Maltreatment and Woman Abuse." St. Paul, Minn. Available at http://www.vaw.umn.edu/Vawnet/overlap.htm.

Edleson, J. L., L. F. Mbilinyi, et al. 2001. "How Children Are Involved in Domestic Violence: Results from a Four-City Telephone Survey." Available at http://www.mincava.umn.edu/link.

Elmer, E. 1977. *Fragile Families, Troubled Children: The Aftermath of Infant Trauma*. Pittsburgh: University of Pittsburgh Press.

Finkelhor, D. 1984. *Child Sexual Abuse: New Theory and Research*. New York: Free Press.

Garbarino, J., and C. C. Collins. 1999. "Child Neglect: The Family with a Hole in the Middle." In *Neglected Children: Research, Practice, and Policy*, edited by H. Dubowitz. Thousand Oaks, Calif.: Sage.

Garbarino, J., E. Guttmann, et al. 1986. *The Psychologically Battered Child*. San Francisco: Jossey-Bass.

Gelles, R. J. 1996. *The Book of David*. New York: Basic Books.

———. 1999. "Policy Issues in Child Neglect." In *Neglected Children: Research, Practice, and Policy*, edited by H. Dubowitz. Thousand Oaks, Calif.: Sage.

Gil, D. 1970. *Violence Against Children: Physical Abuse in the United States*. Cambridge, Mass.: Harvard University Press.

Giovannoni, J. M. 1985. "Child Abuse and Neglect: An Overview." In *A Handbook of Child Welfare: Context, Knowledge, and Practice*, edited by J. Laird and A. Hartman. New York: Free Press.

Giovannoni, J. M., and R. Becerra. 1979. *Defining Child Abuse*. New York: Free Press.

Hanson, S. M. H., M. L. Heims, et al., eds. 1995. *Single Parent Families: Diversity, Myths and Realities*. Binghamton, N.Y.: Haworth Press.

Kadushin, A., and J. Martin. 1981. *Child Abuse: An Interactional Event*. New York: Columbia University Press.

———. 1988. *Child Welfare Services*. New York: Macmillan.

Kempe, C. H., F. N. Silverman, et al. 1962. "The Battered Child Syndrome." *Journal of the American Medical Association* 18(1): 17–24.

Knitzer, J. 2001. *Promoting Resilience: Helping Young Children and Parents Affected by Substance Abuse, Domestic Violence, and Depression in the Context of Welfare Reform*. New York: National Center for Children in Poverty.

Lindsey, D. 1994. *The Welfare of Children*. New York: Oxford University Press.

Lyon, T. D. 1999. "Are Battered Women Bad Mothers? Rethinking the Termination of Parental Rights for Failure to Protect." In *Neglected Children: Research, Practice, and Policy,* edited by H. Dubowitz. Thousand Oaks, Calif.: Sage.

Maluccio, A. N., B. Pine, et al. 2002. *Social Work Practice with Families and Children*. New York: Columbia University Press.

Meezan, W. 1999. *Translating Rhetoric to Reality: The Future of Family and Children's Services*. Ann Arbor: University of Michigan.

Mills, L. G., C. Friend, et al. 2000. "Child Protection and Domestic Violence: Training, Practice, and Policy Issues." *Children and Youth Services Review* 225:315–32.

Morton, T. 2002. Failure to Protect? In *Child Welfare Institute: Commentary*. Duluth, Ga: Child Welfare Institute.

Nelson, K. E., E. J. Saunders, et al. 1993. "Chronic Child Neglect in Perspective." *Social Work* 386:661–71.

Panel on Research on Child Abuse and Neglect, Commission on Behavioral and Social Sciences and Education, National Research Council. 1993. *Understanding Child Abuse and Neglect*. Washington, D.C.: National Academy Press.

Pecora, P. J., J. K. Whittaker, et al. 2000. *The Child Welfare Challenge: Policy, Practice, and Research*. New York: Aldine de Gruyter.

Peled, E., P. G. Jaffe, et al. 1995. "Introduction." In *Ending the Cycle of Violence,* edited by E. Peled, P. Jaffe, and J. L. Edleson. Thousand Oaks, Calif.: Sage.

Polansky, N., M. A. Chalmers, et al. 1981. *Damaged Parents: An Anatomy of Child Neglect*. Chicago: University of Chicago Press.

Schechter, S., and J. L. Edleson. 1999. *Effective Intervention in Domestic Violence and Child Maltreatment Cases: Guidelines for Policy and Practice*. Reno, Nev.: National Council of Juvenile and Family Court Judges.

Snyder, H., and M. Sickmund. 1999. *Juvenile Offenders and Victims: 1999, National Report*. Washington, D.C.: Office of Juvenile Justice and Delinquency Prevention.

Straus, M. A., and R. J. Gelles. 1986. *Physical Violence in American Families*. New Brunswick, N.J.: Transaction Books.

Straus, M. A., R. J. Gelles, et al. 1980. *Behind Closed Doors: Violence in the American Family*. New York: Anchor.

Swift, K. J. 1995. *Manufacturing Bad Mothers: A Critical Perspective on Child Neglect*. Toronto: University of Toronto Press.

U.S. Census Bureau. 1999. "Estimates of the Population of State by Age, Sex, Race and Hispanic Origin: 1990–1998." Washington, D.C. Available at http://www.childstats.gov/ac1999/econ1a.htm.

———. 2000. "Poverty, 1998." Washington, D.C. Available at http://www.census.gov/hhes/poverty/poverty98/table 5.html.

U.S. Department of Health and Human Services. 1999. *Blending Perspectives and Building Common Ground: A Report to Congress on Substance Abuse and Child Protection.* Washington, D.C.: U.S. Government Printing Office.

———. 2000. *Child Maltreatment 1998: Reports from the States to the National Child Abuse and Neglect Data System.* Washington, D.C.: U.S. Government Printing Office.

———. 2001. *Child Maltreatment 1999: Reports from the States to the National Child Abuse and Neglect Data System.* Washington, D.C.: U.S. Government Printing Office.

U.S. Department of Health and Human Services, National Center on Child Abuse and Neglect. 1996. *Third National Incidence Study of Child Abuse and Neglect.* Washington, D.C.: U.S. Government Printing Office.

U.S. Department of Justice. 2000. *Crime in the United States 1999: Uniform Crime Reports.* Washington, D.C.: U.S. Government Printing Office.

Whitney, P., and L. Davis. 1999. "Child Abuse and Domestic Violence in Massachusetts: Can Practice Be Integrated in a Public Child Welfare Setting?" *Child Maltreatment* 42:158–66.

Young, L. 1964. *Wednesday's Child.* New York: McGraw Hill.

CHAPTER 2

———— ✦ ————

A Framework for Child Welfare Services

The task of each family is also the task of all humanity—this is to cherish
the living, remember those who have gone before, and prepare for those
who are not yet born.

MARGARET MEAD

The first chapter explored the changing nature of the problems that
the community recognizes as affecting the welfare of children. This
chapter is about attempts to intervene to alleviate some of those
problems.

The framework within which child welfare services are delivered has
three components. One is the value system of both the community and
the professionals delivering services. Another is the legal framework:
laws, court decisions, and policy developed to implement this legal framework. The third might be called the conceptual framework—the ideas
that flow from logical analysis of policy, from the wisdom of practice,
and from the study of community conditions. A basic value of child welfare is that all children have a right to safe, permanent, nurturing homes.
Note that the value is expressed in terms of children, not adult clients.
This value is operationalized in the child welfare goals developed by the
a broadly representative consultation group working with the Children's
Bureau:

Safety: the protection of children from abuse or neglect in their own
homes or in foster care.

Permanency: children having stable and consistent living situations (such as living with their families, living with adoptive families, or living with legal guardians), continuity of family relationships, and community connections.

Well-being: families having the capacity to provide for their children's needs, children having educational opportunities and achievements appropriate to their abilities, and children receiving physical and mental health services adequate to meet their needs.

(U.S. DEPARTMENT OF HEALTH AND HUMAN
SERVICES [HHS], CHILDREN'S BUREAU 2000:2-1)

These are the outcomes that are expected as child welfare services are delivered. The preference that the child remain within his or her original family is a reflection on society's valuing of family and reluctance to have the state interfere with family life. The specific mention of educational needs and physical and mental health needs points to the multiple systems involved in the welfare of children and families.

The legal framework, which is reviewed in this chapter, reflects attempts to shape intervention toward these outcomes; some laws emphasize family connections, others emphasize permanency.

Part of the conceptual dimension is examination of the nature of child welfare services. A fundamental issue is whether child welfare services can be short-term, crisis-oriented services linking families to community services, or whether in order to fulfill their mission of keeping children in safe nurturing homes they must be long-term services to sustain families. Linked to this is the issue of the best roles for law enforcement, courts, and child welfare services. Also linked is the issue of the entitlement of all families to have basic needs met (as in education for children), versus the provision of community services only when need can be demonstrated (as in current income maintenance laws). These major questions underlie much of the discussion of this book.

Child welfare shares the value system of social work, but differs from other areas of social work in that it places primary emphasis on the child. The "best interests of the child" guide interventions in child welfare—though how these best interests are to be determined is often open to debate. Because children grow best in families, interventions usually are directed toward parents and other adults. But the well-being of adults, including parents, is subservient to the well-being of children in child welfare policy and practice, and this distinguishes it from other social work enterprises.

Always basic to child welfare services has been supporting children's families in providing safe, permanent, and nurturing care. This goal has been expressed through the development of supportive services in the community and, more recently, through the development of specific techniques of intervention to preserve families that are at risk of dissolution. In recent years the pressures of heavy intake, budgets, and workloads have caused public child welfare agencies to retreat from this family support role. A patchwork of community agencies has grown up to provide these services; their work will be explored in chapter 4. It is questionable, however, whether this pattern of services is sufficient to support family functioning and to protect children.

The major function of public child welfare agencies has become child protection. When children cannot safely remain with their own families, the state intervenes, either to provide services to make the family safe for the children or to provide alternative safe care. Always open to question is the degree of risk that can be tolerated by the community. The right of the state to intervene when children are reasonably safe but when the family does not provide adequate nurture, reasonable discipline, acceptable medical care, or educational opportunities, is also often debated.

The outcomes of child welfare services provide a framework by which to judge their effectiveness. Basically, the community wants children's needs to be met. Because there is evidence that children's needs, particularly those of young children, are best met in families, the community wants children to be in families. If a child cannot remain at home, foster family care, rather than institutional care, is the preferred option for most children. Substitute out-of-home care is intended to be temporary. Returning to the original family under improved conditions, and with supports in place to insure that the improvement is sustained, is outcome that best meets the needs of most children. If this cannot be achieved, we want children to be in permanent alternative homes. And we want children, if possible, to maintain their connection to their original family.

Family is being increasingly broadly defined in child welfare. We no longer mean the nuclear family of parents and children; rather, family has come to mean the extended family. Homes of extended family members maintain a family connection and are a much-used resource, though workers must often bring their best creative skills to bear to make sure these homes enjoy the legal protections that will provide permanency. Long-term foster care or institutional care can sometimes provide continuity of care while family ties are maintained. Adoption provides another route to permanency, but one that may make it more difficult to retain a child's connection to the original family. These options are explored in chapters 6 and 7.

Some children have special needs. Special types of family care may be called for temporarily to meet those needs, or treatment in a residential setting may be necessary. The services available to meet such specific needs are explored in chapter 8.

Beginning with the assumption that children have a right to have their basic needs met, this chapter first identifies those needs, then discusses the state's right to interfere in family life to make sure they are met. The public policy base of these intervention decisions is outlined. The chapter also explores the way in which the conceptualization of successful child welfare services has changed over time, as communities have recognized first children's need for families, then for permanency, and, most recently, for continuing connection to their original families. The chapter then focuses on the achievement of permanent homes for children, the dominant theme of recent legislation.

The Rights and Needs of Children

Child welfare philosophy and thinking rests on the premise that children are individuals, and so have rights, most basically the right to have their needs met in at least a minimal fashion.

> There is a growing acceptance of children as separate entities entitled not only to having their needs met but also to having their rights respected. In recognizing children's rights, society has moved from a perception of children as belonging to their parents to one that sees children as belonging to themselves in the trust of their parents.
>
> (KADUSHIN AND MARTIN 1988:219)

The state will intervene to protect the rights of children, and to see that their needs are met, if parents fail in this responsibility.

The Needs of Children

The needs with which child welfare policy is primarily concerned are safety, nurture, and guidance sufficient to provide the opportunity to become a productive member of society. These needs are, in our society, met by adults with whom a bond can be formed that will provide safety and the emotional basis for optimal development. These adults are usually the biological parents, but children's needs can be met, if the commitment is there, by extended family or by unrelated families through long-term foster care or adoption. The community has, to a large extent, delegated the responsibility for protecting children's rights to child welfare agencies and juvenile (or family) courts.

Food and shelter Children need a place to stay and someone to care for them. This very basic need is so obvious that it seems to scarcely require comment. However, it has absorbed a good deal of the attention of the child welfare community through the years. The detailed story of the development of ways to care for children whose original homes could not care for them is told in the chapter on foster care. This brief introductory section describes the early and continuing recognition of this need and touches on the difficulties with its satisfactory resolution.

In the early days after this country was colonized, children who were dependent on the state for care were housed in almshouses—orphans as well as children whose parents were unable to support them financially. This practice was combined with indenture, the apprenticing of children to learn a productive trade. The goal of these services was to see that basic needs were met and that children were raised to follow the their community's moral precepts and contribute to its economic well-being.

It was recognized by the social reformers of the nineteenth century that the mixed-age environment of the almshouse was not a good one for the moral education of children. This led to the development of orphanages, institutions solely for children. The early orphanages were indeed for orphans; many were founded following epidemics or historical passages during which many adults died leaving children without care. But orphanages soon began also to care for children of impoverished families, particularly families in which one parent had died and the other parent needed child care in order to work. Orphanages also indentured children old enough to work.

The placing of children in foster homes began as a movement to give family homes to the street children of New York City; children were sent by train to the "wholesome" farms of the newly settled West—Pennsylvania, Indiana, Illinois, and Michigan—again with the hope that a family would provide the moral upbringing and the training in a productive trade that would produce good citizens. The merits of family homes versus institutional care were sharply debated through the early years of the twentieth century; adequate supervision of foster homes was one of the main points of contention. Finally, about midcentury, family foster care, local and thus more easily supervised, became the preferred mode of care for children who could not remain in their own homes.

As noted earlier, in recent years many more women have entered the workforce. At the same time other community forces have resulted in an increasing number of children needing placement outside their own homes for their safety, leading to long stays in foster care as their families struggled with intractable difficulties. This combination of events has severely strained the foster care system in the last twenty years. There have been many attempts to bring fewer children into foster care and to shorten children's stays in foster care. Extensive use of relatives has developed as an extension of the foster care system. There is discussion of the use of institutional care, particularly for older children, to relieve the demand for places in the foster care system. And, finally, recent federal legislation has accelerated the movement of children out of foster care and into adoption. However, the foster care system is currently in crisis, and some type of change will occur in the next few years—a part of the continuing struggle to provide food and shelter for children.

Safety There is no argument about the necessity for children to be safe. In a situation where a child has been severely injured, or where neglect is so extreme that children are exposed to serious health hazards, or where no one is consistently supervising a child, it is often necessary to remove the child from the current home to a place where appropriate care will be provided. The capacity of a competent parent, or of extended family, to protect a child is part of the decision about whether the child can remain in the home.

In more ambiguous situations, many questions arise about the placement of a child in out-of-home care. There may be a risk of injury to the child, but the child has not been visibly harmed. Or there may be a question about whether parental actions are so extreme as to constitute abuse, or whether parental incapacity or absence is sufficient to be considered neglect. There may be difficulty in disentangling the reports of various family members. The parents' rights to practice their own religion may be in conflict with community standards for health care or education of children. The cultural practices of the family may differ from those of the mainstream community. Neither the child welfare worker nor the community itself may be sure what the proper answers are in these situations. Questions also arise about what kinds of changes need to be made, and how it can be assured that they have been made, before the child is returned to the original home.

These are the debates that have given rise in the public press to stories suggesting that attempts to preserve families expose children to great risk. The most dedicated professional judgment may prove fallible. When headlines tell of a child left in a home and later maltreated there, or of a child returned to a home that proved unsafe, an indignant public demands to know why the child welfare workers are not doing their work properly. On the other hand, the community also values the privacy of the home and the right of parents to make decisions about the care of their own children, so a removal that seems unnecessary can generate just as much controversy. If safety were the only concern, decisions would be easier. But concerns about safety must be considered along with parental rights and the needs of families.

Nurture and guidance The right to the nurture and guidance needed for optimal child development is also easier to state as a value than to operationalize. As a nation, we have done little thinking about how we want our children to "turn out." What qualities do we want them to have? What do they need to have as children in order to develop these qualities?

Community consensus around certain negatives emerges from terrible events; we do not, for example, want our adolescents to be dangerously violent. But debate rages about what contributes to violence. Answers range from the relatively simple issue of access to guns, through more complex questions about role modeling and the consequences of violence in the media, to even more complex suggestions about the effects of indifferent parenting or of biological changes induced by very early experiences.[1]

The identification of positive adult traits and their childhood origins is vitally important. Theorists have identified the course of positive child development, describing the physical, emotional, and cognitive competencies that can be expected at different ages and developing a theoretical foundation to explain a positive course of development (see, for example, Erikson 1950).[2] Vera Fahlberg, a noted pediatrician and psychiatrist who has written extensively on child development, explains:

> Parents are responsible for creating the environment that helps children achieve their maximum potential in terms of physical, intellectual, and psychological development. The child's job is to make use of the environment. Neither can accomplish the other's work; it is only in the context of the parent-child relationship that the child is able to successfully move through the stages of child development.
>
> (FAHLBERG 1991:21)

Thoughtful guidance and discipline, opportunities for learning, nurturing of self-esteem, and appropriate medical care are all conditions that parents, or parent substitutes, have a responsibility to provide. The presence of the necessary conditions for good development can be evaluated and used as measures of the effectiveness of services.

As chapter 1 pointed out, changing community standards affect the our assessment of whether children are receiving the nurture and guidance that is their right. Currently we demand a higher standard of care for children than in the past. Extreme physical abuse is no longer condoned as punishment. The harm sexual abuse does to children has been acknowledged. Emotional abuse is beginning to be recognized. Universal education is seen as necessary, and it is no longer thought right to hold children out of school to work in factories or on farms. It is expected that children will be sheltered in clean, warm homes and have adequate food, though the economic programs to make this possible are only marginally in place. Children are expected to receive adequate health care; this standard has given rise to extensive debate about the economics of making health care affordable and accessible to all children.

Nothing is as clear-cut as the foregoing paragraph implies, however. The point at which poor care becomes chronic neglect is never clear, nor is the point at which physical punishment becomes abusive. Emotional maltreatment is even harder to define and to identify. Ethical issues abound.

Attachment Perhaps the most complex of children's rights is based on the need to form an attachment to caretakers—usually parents—who will provide the secure base from which development can proceed. In the 1950s child development experts first articulated the drastic consequences to the infant bereft of stimulation and maternal care (Bowlby 1951) and the destruction of the sense of trust, on which future emotional development rests, when these attachments are disrupted (Littner 1950; Robertson 1958). These theoretical developments had major consequences for child welfare policy. They have led to the closing of large institutions that cared for young children and to the strong preference for care in the "least restrictive setting"—the setting that most closely resembles family in community. They also led to the realization that removal from home to foster care was a traumatic event for a child, and that multiple moves from home to home could be devastating. Permanency planning, with the goal of insuring that every child had a home in which he or she could remain until adulthood, became an overriding policy imperative in child welfare.

Permanency has been a difficult concept to operationalize. It begins with the attempt not to remove the child from his original home, and continues with the attempt to rehabilitate that home if the child has been removed, or to find a new, permanent home (usually adoptive) for the child. This quest for permanence will be explored in detail later in this chapter.

Another facet of attachment has recently become increasingly important in child welfare. There has been increasing recognition that for some children separation from the family of origin gives rise to serious issues concerning their own identity. Foster children need to know why they are in foster care, and they do better if they have visits from their own families (Weinstein 1960). Foster children tend to perceive themselves as having diminished status, a perception often reinforced by interactions with other children and their families.[3] In adolescence, both foster and adopted youth may internalize this stigma, further eroding their identity development (Kools 1997). Some adopted adults search very intently for their birth parents, demonstrating a need to know their heritage.

Recognition of these issues has made efforts to maintain connection with the original family a key part of planning for children who are separated from their families. Difficult decisions inevitably arise. A foster home with extended family may not offer permanency. An adoptive home may not permit continued contact with the original family. An institution may offer permanence and contact with the family, but may be a more restrictive setting than a family home would be. Guided by a policy framework that emphasizes family care, permanent homes, and continued connection with the child's own family, the child welfare worker will seek the best combination of services to meet the individual needs of each child.

The Responsibility of the State for Its Children

Child welfare professionals do intervene in family life when it is determined that children's needs are not being met: when it appears that children are being abused or neglected and need help. But what should the limits of this intervention be? The state has assumed a responsibility for protecting all its citizens, including children and others who are powerless. Under what conditions does this responsibility justify intervention in family life?

Legal tradition affirms that the state is, ultimately, the parent to all children, and has a right and responsibility to see that children are not in danger. Under this concept, known as *parens patriae*, the state has an obligation to protect the rights of children. "With the concept of *parens patriae*, a third party is introduced into the parent-child relationship, providing the child with some assurance of outside protection and support" (Kadushin and Martin 1988:219).

Our society also has a strong tradition of protecting the autonomy and privacy of family life. A basic principle of the American community, and of law, is the integrity of the family and the right of the family to make its own decisions and govern itself in its own way, as long as those actions do not interfere with the rights of others. When parents are thought not to be meeting the needs of their children, the responsibility of the state as a protector of its children is delegated to the child protective agency, which may call upon the authority of the court to assert its right to intervene. The child protective agency also has the responsibility to continue to work with the family until the children are no longer in danger. Families, therefore, often are involuntary clients.

The juvenile court Under English common law, which became the basis for our legal system, children over the age of seven were considered capable of distinguishing between right and wrong and could be charged as criminal offenders. It was an era of severe punishments, which were thought to deter further criminal behavior. The courts were expected to deal justly with offenders; the concept of justice was that of balancing the crime and the punishment, and meting out punishments based solely on the nature of the crime. Thus young people could be, and were, put to death, deported, whipped, and imprisoned (Abbott 1938).

The concept that children were not criminals but delinquent, and that the punishment should be based on the needs of the individual child with the goal of rehabilitation, was revolutionary. Jane Addams, Julia C. Lathrop, and Lucy L. Flower, all social workers resident at Hull House, developed the idea of a new type of court for children. The Chicago Bar Association worked to provide a legal base for the new idea. Courts of equity, which exercised the power of the state to protect children whose welfare or property rights were in jeopardy on the basis of the merits of the individual case, became the legal basis for the new juvenile courts. The judge was to deal with the problems of "erring children" as a "wise and kind father," according to the statute creating the court (Abbott 1938).

The first juvenile court was established in Cook County, Illinois, in 1900. This was the first statutorily created juvenile court in the United States and possibly in the world. The Chicago Bar Association sponsored the bill that established the court. It was an era of social reform, and the idea captured the imagination of many who were working to advance the cause of children. By 1925 all but two states had juvenile courts and, usually, probation services.

Based on the concept of *parens patriae*, the juvenile court established informal procedures designed to individualize the judicial response in the hope of rehabilitating the young offender or helping erring parents to learn new ways. Jane Addams wrote that "there was almost a change in mores when the Juvenile Court was established. The child was brought before the judge with no one to prosecute him and no one to defend him— the judge and all concerned were merely trying to find out what could be done on his behalf" (Downs, Moore, et al. 2000:190).

The informal proceedings of the court relied on background reports from probation officers rather than on the presentation of evidence. As the court assumed responsibility for the welfare of the child, delinquency was broadly defined. A complaint was usually termed a "petition in behalf of the child." Because the goal of the court was rehabilitative, it was presumed that the court would uphold the juvenile's rights even though the constitutional due process guarantees afforded to adults were not enforced.

In a 1967 Supreme Court case known as *In re Gault,* this presumption was challenged, and the Court extended many of the established due process safeguards to minors in juvenile court proceedings. In a particularly egregious case, a fifteen-year-old boy had been sentenced to the state industrial school for up to six years. The offense had been minor, the parents had not been properly informed of what was happening, the complainant had not appeared at the hearings, and the sentence was long. Such denial of liberty, the Supreme Court said, required the protection of basic rights including timely notice of charges and hearings, notice of the right to counsel, and the right to confront witnesses.

In the ensuing years, the procedures of the juvenile courts have become more adversarial as the protections of due process have been applied. Downs, Moore, et al. (2000) outline these due process rights for parties in juvenile court matters. Note that they apply to persons charged with abuse and neglect as well as to juvenile offenders.

> Right to notice and opportunity to be heard. This means they have a right to know in advance what the charges are; who is making them; what evidence they have to support the charges; the date and time for the court hearing; and the right to bring evidence in support of their side of the story.
>
> Right to representation. This means that parents charged with abuse or neglect and youth charged with delinquent offenses have a right to an attorney. If they cannot afford one, then they have a right to have one appointed at public expense. Children in neglect and abuse matters may or may not have a right to attorney representation, depending on the state statute. They do have a right to have someone speak on their behalf—often a guardian ad litem.
>
> Right to remain silent or privilege against self-incrimination. This means that parents and youth charged with delinquent offenses can choose to not speak on their own behalf and the court cannot interpret that as an admission of or presumption of guilt.
>
> Right to confront and cross-examine witnesses. This means that parents charged with abuse or neglect and youth charged with delinquent offenses have a right to challenge verbally and with documents the testimony and statements of any witnesses.
>
> (P. 192)

Thus the courts have recognized the rights of children and have shaped juvenile court procedures to protect those rights. In this process, the juvenile court has become adversarial in nature. The protections are important, but the flexibility and rehabilitative potential of the earlier juvenile court have to a great extent been lost, both for the delinquent child and for the family charged with maltreatment of children.

Rights of parents The court also, of course, protects the rights of parents. Reflecting a long history of law and custom giving parents control and decision-making authority over their children, court decisions tend to support parents' rights. The state is wary about intervening to protect children unless the need can be clearly presented.

Though laws are generally written to give child welfare workers broad latitude in investigating a child maltreatment complaint, family privacy retains some protections. Only if a child is believed to be in danger may entry be made to the home without consent. Without a search warrant issued by the court, there are limits on the extent to which a worker can investigate the home or examine children (Stein 1991). When a child is removed, parents have the right to notice of a hearing, to be present at a hearing, to be represented by an attorney, and to confront and cross-examine witnesses (Stein 1991). Usually state law sets a definite period of time (often two or three working days) within which this hearing must occur. During the course of a placement, the court periodically reviews the status of the case, and the parents have the opportunity to present their evidence that a child should be returned.

Federal law requires that social workers make "reasonable efforts" to maintain children in their own families and to reunite separated children and parents. This concept of reasonable effort is a mediating ground between the rights of parents and the need of children for protection. The Adoption and Safe Families Act (discussed later in the chapter) has placed reasonable efforts within the context of children's safety, exempted certain situations from the requirement of reasonable efforts, and limited the time for which these efforts must be employed. Still, caseworkers are required in almost all situations to document to the court that they have tried to keep child and parents together, and this guarantee of services is an important protection for both children and parents.

Implications for child protection One of the basic ethical questions faced by all helping professions concerns the obligation to intervene. There is a duty to aid those who ask for help. But what about those who do not ask? In some areas of child welfare work, particularly protective service work, the family is not asking for help. Social work has always had difficulty in adapting its philosophy and intervention techniques to work with involuntary clients. There is concern that the values of the more powerful are being imposed on the vulnerable; this is a real concern and must be remembered as issues of cultural values and racism in child welfare services are explored in later chapters. Though social workers, with their focus on protection of the vulnerable, may tend to think intervention should occur whenever children's rights are compromised, and may define children's rights very broadly, they should be warned by prior experience. It has been a hallmark of totalitarian societies in the twentieth century to maintain control of their populations through invasion of family life and absorption of children into communal programs.

This is, obviously, a major point of tension in child welfare services. Many of the criticisms of the child welfare system come from those who believe that social workers invade family life, impose their own values, and place children out of the home unnecessarily. The privacy and integrity of the family unit allows for the variability that makes a society vibrant, and it nurtures the individual freedom that is so prized. Remembering a history of the imposition of values and of moralistic judgments about who deserved help, social workers in child welfare, as in other services, must remain careful.

The Institutions That Have Served Children

Until the beginning of the nineteenth century, parents—particularly fathers—had almost complete control over the lives and activities of their children. The idea that children had rights to care that could be established against parental wishes gained acceptance in the late nineteenth and early twentieth centuries along with the rights of women. Perhaps first was the idea that children should be protected from extreme neglect and cruelty, established in New York in 1875 when, in response to a dramatic instance of abuse and neglect, the state intervened under laws pertaining to the protection of animals. As a result, the first Society for the Prevention of Cruelty to Children was organized. The first juvenile court was established in 1899. Restriction of child labor, coupled with the push for universal education, put additional limits on the absolute discretion of parents. At the same time, public income support provided a growing federal role in helping disadvantaged families. Any review of the federal role in the development of child welfare services must begin with the assumption by government, early in the twentieth century, of certain responsibilities to improve the lives of children. The leaders in this movement are names familiar in the history of social work.

> It was a tempestuous, challenging period in the development of social welfare. Today's child welfare workers owe much to the early national leaders—Jane Addams, Julia Lathrop, Lillian Wald, Florence Kelley, Grace and Edith Abbott, and others—who labored with such dedication for the protection and enhancement of child life. These were among the influential persons who brought about the establishment of the juvenile court, the passage of mothers' pension laws among the states, child labor legislation, and the inauguration of the White House Conferences.
>
> (COSTIN, BELL, ET AL. 1991:20)

The White House Conferences

In 1909, Theodore Roosevelt for the first time called on leaders to confer about the care of dependent children.[4] One of the recommendations of this conference was that there be a department at the federal level concerned with the issues of children. The Children's Bureau was established in 1912. Subsequent White House Conferences have addressed topics of particular importance at the moment; the topics provide a picture of changing community concerns. These high-profile conferences have focused attention on the issues being debated and have helped to shape child welfare services.

The Children's Bureau

Fact-finding, investigation, and reporting were the original functions of the Children's Bureau. It has also had the important function of advocating for legislation and programs beneficial to children. In 1935, the additional responsibility of administering grant programs was given to the Children's Bureau, and with it the responsibility of providing consultation and stimulating better services for children in the states. A list of the programs administered by the Children's Bureau, all of which are the result of federal legislation, illustrates the broad range of child welfare issues to which the federal government has turned its attention. The state grant programs require various amounts of matching money from the states and are administered by the state child welfare agencies. Some of the major programs are identified here:

- Title IV-E Foster Care funds states to assist with the costs of foster care and with the support services that surround foster care.
- Title IV-E Adoption Assistance provides funds to states to assist in the maintenance of, or to allay the costs of meeting special needs of, older and handicapped children who have been adopted, and for administering the adoption subsidy program.
- The Independent Living program provides services to foster children who are sixteen and older to help them make the transition to independent living.
- Title IV-B, subpart 2, the Promoting Safe and Stable Families program, provides funds to assist in the preservation of families for children or, if this is not possible, in the placement of children in adoptive families.

- The Medical Neglect/Disabled Infants State Grants help states respond to reports of medical neglect.
- Community-Based Family Resource Program Grants are provided to states to help in the development and implementation of community-based family resource services.
- The Children's Justice Act helps states develop and implement programs designed to improve the investigation and prosecution of child maltreatment, with a particular emphasis on sexual abuse.

Full descriptions of these programs, and others, can be found on the Children's Bureau Web site, at http://www.acf.dhhs.gov/programs/cb.

The Child Welfare League of America

Founded in 1920, the Child Welfare League of America is the nation's oldest and largest membership-based organization. Its membership exceeds one thousand private and public agencies. One of its important contributions is the publication of standards of practice for most areas of child welfare work, which are periodically revised to incorporate new ideas. The league also publishes a major journal, *Child Welfare*. Annual regional conferences and many national conferences are important vehicles for the discussion and dissemination of knowledge. Advocacy for public policy initiatives that benefit children has been another important aspect of the Child Welfare League's work. A description of the organization's work can be found at its Web site, http://www.cwla.org.

There are many other organizations important to the conceptualization and delivery of children's services and to the development of public policy. Some of the major ones, along with information about their useful Web sites, are listed in the appendix, Internet Resources.

The Judicial Framework

A series of Supreme Court decisions have established the balance between the rights and responsibilities of parents, the rights of children, and the interest of the state in protecting its future by protecting children from harm. There is a long tradition of parental control over decisions affecting their children, and many Supreme Court decisions have reinforced these parental rights. However, the Court has also established that children have rights—though these rights may be limited by children's vulnerability and need for protection, and by immature cognitive processes that impair decision making. Children's rights to protection from parental abuse, neglect, and exploitation were established in the nineteenth century, but it was not until the 1967 *Gault* decision (reviewed earlier in this chapter) that the Supreme Court established the right of juveniles to due process protection when their freedom was threatened by the power of the state.

> The evolution of children's rights in America is divided into four periods: pre-nineteenth century, 1800–1900, 1900–1967, and 1967 forward. Prior to the nineteenth century children were considered their parents' property to do with as they saw fit. In the nineteenth century with industrialization and urbanization leading to neglect, abandonment, and exploitation of children, benevolent laws and institutions were established to offer protection to children. In the early years of the twentieth century, juvenile courts and the attitude of benevolent oversight of orphaned, abandoned, neglected, abused, and delinquent children predominated. *In re Gault* and *Kent v. United States,* decided by the U.S. Supreme Court in 1966, marked the beginning of the children's legal rights era.
>
> (DOWNS, MOORE, ET AL. 2000:47)

In very general terms, Supreme Court interpretations of law have established that parents have the right to the care and custody of children, and the responsibility to provide financial support, physical and emotional care, and guidance.[5] They must also see that the child has medical care and education. The courts have valued the diversity of family lives, and have moved very cautiously to intervene. Education and medical care are two areas in which court decisions have affirmed the rights of parents to make decisions that are in keeping with religious tenets, even when a larger society might think these decisions harmful.

The definition of family has been before the court in various cases for many years. Fathers never married to the children's mothers have gained some legal rights in recent decades, if they have had a consistent relationship with the children and have provided some financial support. The awarding of custody to same-sex couples is still uncertain, subject to individualized circumstances. "Judicial prejudice against homosexual parents in child custody cases remains despite the fact that the child's best interests standard is the overriding one for all states" (Downs, Moore, et al. 2000, p.55). The question of what constitutes a family has often come before the courts in recent years.[6] Does a family include grandparents, and do they have rights? In a disputed adoption, who is the child's family? In a series of decisions, the Court has generally determined, or has supported state courts in determining, that biological parents have the right to raise their children, without interference from the state, until they are judged to be unfit.

In all of the decisions concerning the rights of parents and the rights of children, the courts are defining the extent to which the state may use its police powers to intervene in family life. The responsibility of the state to provide for children once it has taken custody of them has not been the subject of Supreme Court decisions. It has, however, been the basis of class action lawsuits in several states. These lawsuits represent attempts to reform the child welfare system through court judgments and through the court-ordered funding of whatever reforms or obligations are decided upon. Decisions favorable to plaintiffs in these cases have laid the judicial groundwork for the assumption that the state has a responsibility to provide services to children.

An emerging issue, under the Adoption Assistance and Child Welfare Act of 1980 and the Adoption and Safe Families Act of 1997 (reviewed later in this chapter), is to what lengths the state must go, having assumed custody of a child, in making "reasonable efforts" to reunite a child with family. Early decisions suggest that procedural requirements, such as completion and periodic review of case plans, may be enforced by the court, whereas requirements to provide specific services may not (Downs, Moore, et al. 2000:53).

In summary, parents are viewed as having the right to care for their children, to have their custody, and to make major decisions about their care. The courts have been hesitant in infringing on the rights of parents. Most decisions favor biological parents. There is an interesting series of cases under way now that will begin to determine the rights of extended family. The concept that children have rights independent of their parents has been affirmed by the courts and is expressed in the due-process provisions of the juvenile courts. The right of the state to use its police powers to intervene in family life when parents abuse, neglect, or exploit their children has been affirmed; the responsibility of the state once it has intervened is less well defined.

The Legislative Framework

The legislative framework of child welfare consists of the laws that have been enacted in the attempt to resolve the social problems described in chapter 1 and to guarantee stable, nurturing homes to children. In the United States, federal legislation tends to set standards and broad outlines of service delivery, offering funding incentives to follow those guidelines. The laws of particular states contain the various means of implementing federal initiatives. If, as is often the case, a federal initiative is underfunded, its impact will be compromised. Court decisions also modify legislation, as the courts act to void laws or to modify their interpretation. In this brief overview, only those federal laws most directly tied to child welfare policy will be reviewed.

As these laws make evident, social policy in the United States generally focuses on providing remedies for particular groups experiencing difficulties, rather than providing for all families. The assumption is that adequate families do not need the support of governmental programs. A good example is the current income maintenance program, examined in more detail in chapter 4, which provides governmental support only to families that can demonstrate that they do not have adequate income to support their children. The European children's allowances, which grant a sum to every child to enhance their well-being, by contrast, operate under the assumption that most or all families need additional support and that it should be easily available without stigma. Policies that address defined population groups with specific problems are called residual policies.

The history of federal legislation, from the New Deal in the 1930s through the 1980s, was one of increasing movement toward federal standard-setting in child welfare services, with the stricture that if public funds were to be spent, the programs they financed should be overseen by public authority. This movement was reversed in the 1990s, with increasing emphasis on state development and control of child welfare programs. The main vehicle for this change has been the federal "block grant" system, in which states are given blocks of money for specific needs, and challenged to develop programs that will meet the unique needs of their own citizens. This shift in focus is evident in income maintenance, in attempts to develop programs to prevent child abuse and neglect, and in the development of programs to provide foster care and permanency planning for children.

Child Abuse Prevention and Treatment

The Child Abuse Prevention and Treatment Act of 1974   As discussed in chapter 1, in the 1960s physical child abuse was brought to community attention by the publicizing of the "battered child syndrome" (Kempe, Silverman, et al. 1962). One response was the passage of the Child Abuse Prevention and Treatment Act of 1974, which provided federal funding to help states develop programs to intervene and protect children who were abused or neglected. Two provisions have had particular impact: the requirement of mandated reporting and the establishment of the Center on Child Abuse and Neglect.

The Child Abuse Prevention and Treatment Act established mechanisms for the reporting of suspected child abuse and neglect, mandating that the states establish means for this reporting. In most states, certain professionals are mandated reporters, meaning that they must report any knowledge of child maltreatment. All reporters are given immunity from prosecution for libel. Immediate difficulty arose when these reporting programs were developed, as the public became educated about the indicators of abuse and neglect and the means to report it. Child welfare agencies were unprepared for the vast numbers of reports made by a concerned public. The necessity of investigating large numbers of reports of child maltreatment changed the nature of public child welfare services, as the resources of child welfare agencies were increasingly devoted to protective services.

The act also established the National Center on Child Abuse and Neglect, which became a center for the collection of data and a leader in shaping prevention services through the provision of grants, consultation, and national conferences. The full scope of the center's activities is described at its Web site, at http://www.calib.com/nccanch.

Issues in child protection   Attempts to protect children also conflicted at times with the civil liberties of parents. A protective service investigation is invasive of family privacy. If the allegation proves to be unfounded, as is true of the majority of reports, there is justified parental resentment. Attempts to improve the identification of abuse led to registries of children injured, so that a child with multiple injuries over time could be identified even if taken to different hospitals and doctors. However, these registries contained the names of adults suspected of abuse in the absence of any proof that it had occurred, a violation of the basic legal presumption of innocence until guilt is demonstrated. The age of computers has made the checking of data systems and the sharing of information so easy that the issue assumes even greater importance. Purging computerized records of unfounded abuse or neglect complaints solves one problem, but destroys the capacity of the protective service agency to track multiple complaints, over time, about the same family. Agencies continue to face difficult issues concerning confidentiality and information sharing.

A continuing problem with reporting, and with centralized data collection, has been the definition of maltreatment. The laws of the fifty states differ, sometimes markedly. Thus it is difficult to compile meaningful national statistics. The imprecision of definitions of maltreatment has also led to difficulties in public interpretation of the laws, to criticism of child protective agencies for not acting in cases of perceived maltreatment, and probably to underreporting due to uncertainty about what should be reported.

Prevention The reporting laws of the Child Abuse Prevention and Treatment Act have received so much attention that the development and funding of programs aimed at prevention has not been emphasized. By necessitating the commitment of resources to the investigation of complaints, mandated reporting diverted the resources of child welfare agencies from prevention programs. Prevention programs, which will be further discussed in chapter 5, remain poorly conceptualized and underfunded. Their effectiveness has been difficult to demonstrate; the prevention of a low-incidence behavior is difficult to document.

The Title XX amendments to the Social Security Act authorized payment to the states for services that would prevent maltreatment, prevent placement in foster care, and provide appropriate placements when needed. These funds were limited to children already receiving AFDC or Social Security Disability payments. In 1981, this funding was converted to a block grant to the specific states, allowing states to spend with fewer restrictions. This initiative too has been underfunded, and its prevention services have received the least attention.

Interethnic Child Placement

The Indian Child Welfare Act The United States is an increasingly multicultural society, and issues related to the bias of child welfare services toward white, middle-class values and customs arise continually. We have already noted the disproportionate numbers of nonwhite children who are poor. Questions arise, and will be explored in later chapters, about the disproportionate numbers of children of color in foster care and in the juvenile corrections system, about the lack of family preservation services for families of color, and about the lack of same-race adoptive homes for children of color. However, only for Native American children and families have these questions been responded to with federal legislation.

The Indian Child Welfare Act (ICWA), adopted by Congress in 1978, was the end point of a history of attempts to forcibly assimilate Native American children into mainstream society and to remove them from their cultural roots. From the 1800s on, federal policy was to remove Indian children to boarding schools, where they were taught the language and ways of their European conquerors, and where the attempt was made to "eradicate the 'Indianness'" in young people (Mannes 1995). In 1958 the Bureau of Indian Affairs and the Child Welfare League of America established an Indian Adoption Project. The goal of this project was the removal of children from the poverty and perceived neglect of the reservations, and the adoptive placement of these children. Adoptive placements were usually with white families. These transracial placements fit the earlier Bureau of Indian Affairs policies of educating Native American children in the mainstream, white culture; the placements were also congruent with the ideal of racial integration, which was a goal of the civil rights movement of the time. Ten years later this project had placed 395 Native American children (Mannes 1995). A follow-up study showed that the children seemed to be developing well in their adoptive homes and that the adoptive parents were satisfied (Fanshel 1972).

However, a study conducted by the American Association on Indian Affairs in 1969 showed that in states with large Native American populations, between 25 and 30 percent of the children had been placed for adoption with white families, and that Native American children were much more likely to experience out-of-home placement than other children (Mannes 1995). This loss of their children was devastating for the tribes. At the same time, as a result of the War on Poverty, tribal governments were increasingly administering human service programs. The addition of child welfare responsibilities seemed reasonable.

ICWA gives the tribal court exclusive jurisdiction over Native American children who live on reservations, and, when a child living off the reservation is removed from his or her home, mandates notification of the tribe and gives the tribal court the right to take jurisdiction. These provisions apply in child custody proceedings, such as foster care placements, attempts to terminate parental rights, and preadoption and adoption placements (Jones 1995). The law applies to all children who are members of a federally recognized tribe, and the determination of membership is made according to the rules of the tribe (Jones 1995).

ICWA has aroused considerable controversy as it has been applied. With its primary focus on the preservation of family and tribal ties, at times its application has seemed to conflict with the best interest of the child, as that interest is understood by the mainstream culture. It can disrupt existing families, for example when a tribe refuses to approve an adoption by non-Indian foster parents of a Native American child placed with them by a birth parent. The power given tribes to make decisions about their children means that sometimes parents are not able to make their own plans for a child, which is hard for the mainstream culture to understand. Tribal decisions also appear sometimes to deprive children of opportunities for family life that a non-Indian placement could offer.[7]

Child welfare workers have, in general, been slow to recognize the importance of the kinship network and the tribe in the organization of Native American culture. If in no other way, the act has been useful in bringing attention to the unique needs of Native American children and, by association, the unique needs of all children who are not part of the dominant culture. It has become one of the means through which issues of cultural sensitivity and social justice surface in child welfare agencies.

The Multiethnic Placement Act of 1994 and the Interethnic Adoption Provisions Amendment of 1996   The Multiethnic Placement Act (MEPA) may be viewed as a legislative attempt to increase the numbers of adoptive homes for children of color, many of whom in 1994 were remaining in foster care for very long times. It may also be viewed as an attempt to increase the numbers of very young children available to white couples who wish to adopt. It is certainly an expression of the legislative desire that children be moved to permanent adoptive homes.

The Multiethnic Placement Act represents the most recent episode in a long debate about transracial adoption, which, in the United States, usually means the placement of a child of color in a white adoptive home. In 1975 the National Association of Black Social Workers issued a strong statement condemning transracial adoption, using much the same logic as that of the Indian Child Welfare Act. Transracial adoption ceased almost immediately, its prohibition generally becoming unwritten policy within child-placing agencies. Continued lobbying by organizations of adoptive parents and by persons who wished to adopt, and a stream of research demonstrating that the outcomes of transracial adoptions were much like those of other adoptions, led to the passage of MEPA.

The intent of MEPA is to decrease the amount of time that children of color wait to be adopted. It accomplishes this by preventing discrimination on the basis of race, color, or national origin, and by encouraging the recruitment of foster and adoptive homes that can meet the needs of waiting children. This law was strengthened by an amendment passed in 1996, the Interethnic Adoption Provisions Amendment (IEPA), which explicitly prohibits denying a person the opportunity to become a foster or adoptive parent on the basis of the race of the applicants or the race of the child. Native American children are exempt from the provisions of MEPA and IEPA, which are superseded by the Indian Child Welfare Act.

Evaluation of the wisdom of this legislation, of course, depends on the perspective of the reader.

Income Maintenance

It was a major advance for children when, in the late nineteenth century, the idea arose that poor children should be cared for in their own homes rather than in institutions. The Charity Organization Societies pioneered this approach, searching for the causes of poverty and ways to eradicate it, but at the same time giving funds for maintenance of the home to those deemed worthy—mainly widows who had young children at home and who were determined "respectable."

Aid to Dependent Children Aid to Dependent Children (ADC) was established by Congress in 1935, as part of the Social Security Act, to provide income assistance to women and children without a male wage-earner in the household. It was a response to the Great Depression, when private charities no longer could meet the need of families. Its intent was to enable women to stay home and care for their children, both because this was an accepted model of family organization, and because in a time of great unemployment the government did not want women taking scarce jobs from men. ADC was a means-tested program; that is, assistance was available only to those who could prove they did not have adequate income, and as family income rose, the amount of aid would decline. The program contained both state and federal funding, and the amount of assistance varied among the states. Historically, from the time of the Elizabethan Poor Laws, policy makers have worried that even very marginal levels of support might take away the incentive to be self-supporting; this is one reason welfare payments have always been low. In the 1950s, when it was thought that the availability of assistance to single women with children but not to intact families was causing fathers to desert, the law was changed to provide assistance to families without adequate income regardless of family composition, and in 1962 the name was changed to Aid to Families with Dependent Children (AFDC).

Twenty years later a majority of women were no longer staying at home caring for their children while their husbands supported the family. Working women, struggling to organize their households, care for children, and meet the demands of full-time jobs, increasingly contrasted their position with that of women receiving income from the government and staying home with their children. Swelling welfare rolls raised public concern about women who had children while very young and unmarried, with no plan for support other than public welfare. It was feared that welfare payments were supporting unwise decisions, or even encouraging immoral sexual activity.

The first major response to these changing times occurred at the federal level in 1988 with the passage of the Family Support Act, which introduced the idea that the recipient of AFDC had a responsibility to seek paid employment. Job training programs, child care, and help in finding work were introduced. However, changes in the numbers of welfare recipients were modest, and the low-paid jobs to which recipients moved too often did little to alleviate their poverty.

Welfare reform By 1995, determination to end expenditures for AFDC had hardened. Little attention was paid to statistics about the short time most recipients used AFDC benefits, about births to single women across income categories, or about the difficulty women with limited education and no job skills had in earning a living wage. The time for welfare reform had come. The stated goals of this reform were to promote work and to strengthen the two-parent family structure.

Thus, in 1996, Congress passed the Personal Responsibility and Work Opportunity Reconciliation Act (PRWORA). The idea that poverty was the result of economic forces shifted; public policy once again focused on individual improvidence as the cause. The reforms essentially changed a program of entitlement to income assistance into one that set strict limits on the number of years a family could receive assistance, while offering training programs and child care to make employment possible.

Temporary Assistance for Needy Families States were given considerable flexibility in establishing Temporary Assistance for Needy Families (TANF) programs that provided limited income assistance with varied time limits, combined with job training. The focus shifted from determination of income eligibility to counseling to promote employment. Families would be allowed two years of assistance before employment was expected. The legislation set a limit of five years of total lifetime assistance. States were allowed to provide exemptions to these rules for no more than 20 percent of their welfare rolls, and incentives were offered to states for success in moving families off welfare rolls. The federal government block-granted the money for TANF assistance, so that states were free to implement the program in any way consistent with the goals of the legislation. In many instances states set timelines more stringent than that of the federal government.

In the first years of the program's implementation, the economy was strong and the states were successful in moving many families from welfare to employment; in 1992, 5.4 percent of the population received income maintenance payments; by December 1999 that number had dropped to 2.3 percent. Though many of these jobs were at low wages, paying an average of $6.60 to $6.80 per hour, earnings had increased since the beginning of welfare reform (U.S. HHS 2000). It is, however, difficult to support a family with a single low-paying income from forty hours per week of work. The percentage of children living in poverty has declined slightly, but still hovers just below a fifth of the child population.

Despite the strong economy, many states supplemented private-sector job programs with public employment, seeing it as a temporary expedient to teach job skills and serve as a bridge to full employment. These programs were expensive, providing wages as well as child care, and were not intended to be permanent. Of course, the first families to move from welfare were probably those with the most education and job skills, and it is not known what will happen when those with little education and no job experience reach the limits of the time they can receive assistance.

The Social Security Act Another source of income for children has been the Social Security Act. The Survivor's Insurance program, established in 1939, provides benefits to dependents of a deceased worker who has paid social security taxes. Benefits are indexed to inflation. In 1989, 1.3 million children received survivor's insurance. When the program was enacted in 1939, death was the usual reason for the absence of a father; thus it was expected that survivor's insurance would eventually replace the needs-based Aid to Dependent Children, providing an income floor to which all children would be entitled.

Also administered by the Social Security Administration is Supplemental Security Income (SSI), established in 1972. This program provides monthly payments to needy blind and disabled persons. Many states supplement these payments. In recent years children with emotional disabilities have been considered eligible to receive SSI. Relatively few children receive SSI, but these are the children with many needs who will often require extensive services.

Earned Income Tax Credit The Earned Income Tax Credit also serves as a source of help to many low-income families with children. Families with low earnings receive credit against their income tax for each dollar they earn. With increasing income, the credit becomes smaller. If a family with low income does not have to pay taxes, the credit is refundable. In 1997, the Earned Income Tax Credit provided assistance to 18.5 million poor and near-poor families; $26.8 billion in claims were expected, of which 81 percent would be refunded in direct payments. (U.S. Congress 1998). This approach to the provision of income assistance is favored by many because it assists poor families through the relatively straightforward means of the tax system, and avoids stigmatization.

Child support A major federal and state effort also developed in the 1980s to help mothers obtain child support from absent fathers. In part, this arose from the same civic outrage that fueled the welfare reform of 1995. In 1984 and 1988, amendments to the federal child support law made it more likely that child support would actually be collected. Requirements that employers deduct court-ordered child support from paychecks have been particularly useful. However, such requirements do little if the father is unemployed, or employed as casual labor, and seeks to evade payment.

Nutrition Federal programs have also attempted to supplement children's nutrition. The major program is food stamps, available to families who can prove low income. These vouchers can be used at the store to buy food items. As part of the welfare reform in 1995, qualifications for obtaining food stamps became more stringent. Other federal programs target children of low-income families directly. The Supplemental Food Program for Women, Infants and Children (WIC) targets pregnant women and their children under age five; it has been very successful in reducing malnutrition during a crucial period of child development. Subsidized school breakfast and lunch programs can also have a major impact on children's ability to learn. Because they target children directly, these programs have been less affected by recent cutbacks than have cash assistance programs.

Critical Issue: Permanency Planning

A cornerstone of the framework within which child welfare services are delivered is permanency planning. Permanency planning has become an organizing principle of child welfare, and the achievement of permanency for children is a commonly used outcome measurement.[8] It means, simply, consistent planning so that each child achieves a home that will provide safety, nurture, and guidance throughout childhood, adolescence, and the young adult years. It is *home*—a place to come back to.

Permanency planning begins with the decision about whether a child should enter state care, and with the attempt to support the child's current home so that a move can be avoided. If a child must enter foster care, the goal is as few moves as possible. If the next move can be back to the child's original home, that is the preferred option. If this is not possible, the second preferred option is termination of parental rights and formal adoption, by a member of extended family if that is appropriate or, if not, by the current foster family or a home newly recruited. All of these plans secure for the child a home where the intent is permanency, and where that intent is backed by the sanctions of a legally established parent-child relationship.

Sometimes, such plans are not options for a particular child. An older child, even though unable to return home, may not want to be adopted because the original parent-child bond is so strong. Relatives may not wish to upset delicate balances within the extended family by participating in the often adversarial court processes involved in the termination of parental rights. For some children, particularly older children, foster parents may not want to adopt, and a new adoptive home might not be found. Courts are often protective of parental rights, and sometimes refuse to terminate them even when children cannot return home. But these are not reasons to abandon permanency planning for children; indeed, children in such situations are even more in need of creative planning to secure for them a home where the intent is permanency even in the absence of legal support.

Court-ordered guardianship, which transfers most responsibility and authority to make decisions concerning a child's life (such consent for medical procedures), is increasingly being used to secure some legal support for placements in which adoption is not a good option. Guardianship transfers some decision-making responsibility from the state to the caretakers of the child. Foster care placements with relatives are often long-term and stable, but relatives may continue to want the support of the child welfare agency; guardianship can provide some legal support for these placements and some protection from erratic interference by the biological parents. Nonrelated foster parents also may be reluctant to adopt—usually, it has been found, because the needs of the child are so extensive that foster parents continue to want the financial resources and professional guidance of the child welfare agency behind them as the child grows (Meezan and Shireman 1985).

Sometimes even more creative solutions are needed for a particular child, and the goal may become stability in a living situation rather than a declaration of permanency. If a troubled adolescent is able to make a reasonable adjustment in a group home, with periodic temporary returns to an acute care unit or a residential treatment center, and this plan works over a period of time, should it not be considered a successful plan for that particular child? If a foster family has successfully cared for a seriously developmentally delayed and physically challenged child over a period of years, and wishes to continue but does not wish to assume the responsibility of lifetime care without the assistance of the child welfare agency, has this child not achieved a stable home? If a deeply committed grandmother cares for a child and plans to continue to care for the child—who is actually within his family and, it might be said, not in temporary care at all—is another plan necessary? In all of these instances, stability has been achieved for children, and the intent is permanency. These are second-best solutions, in that they lack the legal supports of guardianship or adoption and continue to demand agency involvement, but they do represent stability for children.

The Theoretical Base

The emphasis on permanency began with the recognition that without a continuing interaction with a consistent caretaker, children did not develop well. In 1951 Bowlby drew together the findings of other observers in a monograph that, by demonstrating the devastating physical and developmental consequences for children raised in institutional settings without the interaction of maternal care, changed the then current thinking about care of infants and very young children (Bowlby 1951). Foster care, where the child was able to form an attachment to a consistent caretaker and had the stimulation of family living, became the preferred mode of caring for young children.In fairly rapid succession, other observers documented and reported the depression of young children separated from parents, foster parents, or other long-term caretakers, noting a sequence of anger, depression, and finally apathy, in which normal development ceased (Robertson 1958). Though it soon became evident that the effects of separation were being confounded with the effects of the sensory deprivation of an institutional setting, this work had the important effect of bringing out the damage to young children that separation from family could cause.

This body of literature, expanded and reinforced through the years, has formed the theoretical base for the emphasis on permanency for children. Fahlberg writes of problems in attachment being manifested in psychological or behavioral problems, cognitive problems, and developmental delays (Fahlberg 1991). It is useful to distinguish three types of attachment problems: (1) those that stem from a traumatic relationship, (2) those that stem from interrupted relationships, and (3) those that stem from profound neglect (Bourguignon and Watson 1987). A traumatic relationship, such as the relationship in a severely abusive family, may make the child afraid to risk another attachment. Interrupted relationships, which make the child reluctant to trust, create another type of attachment problem; Ner Littner, in a theoretical monograph based on his clinical observations, documented the destruction of a child's ability to trust and to form new attachments if old attachments were repeatedly disrupted (Littner 1950). This is the type of attachment problem that grows from repeated moves in foster care. Finally, attachment problems can come from profound neglect that deprives the infant of the opportunity to make a primary attachment; these are the difficulties found in infants cared for in orphanages.

A key to this theoretical base is the determination of who is the child's "real" family. When a child spends a long time with any family, including one that is not the original biological family, attachment bonds form. The concept of the "time clock of the child" is important here; two or three years is a long time in the life of a young child—a large proportion of his or her life (Goldstein, Freud, et al. 1973). The bonds that form may be so strong that this family becomes the child's psychological family, so that the child's developing attachment and sense of security would be best served by remaining there.

The Empirical Base

For more than forty years there has been evidence that too many children placed in foster care tended to "drift," without planning for more permanent homes, in foster care. "Foster care drift" has become a major concern of the critics of the child welfare system, and of the system itself.

In 1959, Maas and Engler produced a careful, national study, revealing that more than half of the children placed in foster care would not return to their own homes; indeed, children who had been in foster care for eighteen months were likely to remain more or less permanently in out-of-home care with all the possible uncertainties that implies (Maas and Engler 1959). Almost twenty years later, a series of studies demonstrated that children were, indeed, still drifting without planning for long periods of time in foster care (Fanshel and Shinn 1978; Gruber 1978; Knitzer, Allen et al. 1978). Again the alarm was raised. At the same time, it had been demonstrated that adoptive homes could be found for older children growing up in foster care (Emlen, Lahti, et al. 1976). The quest for permanent homes for all children became, and has remained, the essential goal of child welfare services.

Legislative Responses

The Adoption Assistance and Child Welfare Act of 1980 In the early 1980s, it seemed that the concern about finding permanent homes for children had mobilized the child welfare community and that large numbers of children were moving out of foster care, either back home or into adoptive homes. The movement was aided by the passage of the Adoption Assistance and Child Welfare Act of 1980 (Public Law 96-272). This legislation provided a policy framework and fiscal incentives consistent with what was considered best practice at the time. It required states to make "reasonable efforts" to preserve families for children, both before removing a child to foster care and in attempting to return a child from foster care. It also required that a permanency plan be established for each child in foster care and that progress toward implementation of the plan be reviewed periodically by the court. Federal matching for adoption subsidies was also provided for in this law. The law was important because it directed federal funding streams toward family preservation work and because it recognized the importance to children of a permanent home.

The number of children estimated to be in foster care in the United States fell from 400,000 in 1977 to approximately 276,000 in 1984 (Kadushin and Martin 1988:355). A series of studies demonstrated that even parents who had lost touch with a child in a foster home often were interested in having the child return home, and that adoptive homes could be found for other children (Hargrave, Shireman, et al. 1975; Emlen, Lahti, et al. 1976; Jones, Neuman, et al. 1976). The idea of adoption changed; children of preschool and school age who needed homes were now classified as adoptable.[9] Children with disabilities, older children, children with behavior problems—adoptive families could be found for most. Age proved to be the greatest obstacle: the adoption of adolescents was particularly difficult to secure. It was predicted that by the 1990s the foster care population would consist of young children who needed very short-term care during a family crisis, and of adolescents who would grow up in stable foster homes where, often, they had lived for many years.

Unfortunately, however, the predicted reduction in the use of foster care yielded to a tide of family difficulties. Concurrently with the rise in the use of crack cocaine in the inner cities, concurrently with rising concern about the number of children who had no father active in parenting, concurrently with the divergence of income distribution in the United States, with the poor growing ever poorer, the number of very young children entering foster care began to grow.

The daunting problems of affected families have been difficult to resolve. Neither poverty nor substance abuse, can be overcome without protracted effort. Children began to spend longer in foster care, until in 1999 (as in 1959) if a child was in foster care for a year, she was likely to still be there after three years.

At the same time, foster homes became more difficult to recruit, as more women entered the workforce. Foster homes also became more difficult to retain, as the resources of child welfare agencies were stretched by increasing intake and less support was available to sustain foster care. The stability of foster home placements diminished, so that the young children who remained in care for three or more years were all too likely to experience multiple placements. Of course, budgets were also strained by the need to provide more and more foster care placements. These forces combined to introduce a renewed urgency to permanency planning.

The Adoption and Safe Families Act The goal of the federal Adoption and Safe Families Act of 1997 is to expedite permanency planning. It sets a time limit for the child's stay in foster care. The law says that when a child has been in placement for fifteen of twenty-two months, the state shall file an action to terminate parental rights, except when the child is placed with relatives, or when there is compelling reason not to file such an action, or when services have not been provided to the family. It thus sets a time limit on the "reasonable efforts" required to rehabilitate a family for a child.

An important intended effect of this legislation is to energize both the child welfare system and the parents of placed children, so that agencies provide services promptly and parents quickly become involved in those services. The child welfare agency must demonstrate in court that it has made "reasonable efforts" to provide services and to engage parents in their use. The intent of the legislation is to end the long periods of time during which children remain in foster care while parents either receive few services or engage only marginally in the use of services.

The act provides that in aggravated circumstances the court may decide that efforts to rehabilitate the home for the child are not necessary. Such circumstances include a parent having caused the death of another child through abuse or neglect, a parent having seriously injured any child through maltreatment, a parent having starved or tortured the child, or the child being abandoned. Again, the intent is to identify families to whom the court will not return children, and to move those children quickly toward adoption.

Reflecting a changing climate, this legislation views relatives as extended family. Though exceptions to the time limits must be granted by the court, it is expected that children will be allowed to remain indefinitely in the care of relatives. As placements with relatives begin to be viewed as permanent homes rather than temporary foster homes, it will be interesting to see whether child welfare agencies begin routinely to help these families seek guardianship, and whether they begin to withdraw the services that support foster home placements. Will these homes of relatives actually become permanent homes?

Legislation seldom solves a problem as neatly as it intends. Whether child welfare workers will actually be able to find adoptive homes for these children, or to create adoptive homes from relative or nonrelative foster homes, remains to be seen. Whether courts will actually be willing to terminate the rights of parents who appear to be trying, but have not succeeded in rehabilitating the home for the child, also remains to be seen. Most important, this is an opportunity for the emergence of new forms of adoption, new forms of permanency, and new ways for parents to remain in the lives of their children. The Adoption and Safe Families Act will challenge the creativity of the line worker in the child welfare agency.

Conclusion

The framework of the child welfare system, outlined in this chapter, guides policy development and service in the field. Examination of the values of social work and of child welfare show an underlying congruence, with the most notable tension surrounding the identification of the child as the primary client in child welfare. The underlying values of social work and of child welfare change gradually, remaining a reasonably constant touchstone for those working in child welfare. The legislative and judicial framework may change much more rapidly in response to changing community concerns, though it too remains consistent in its attempt to find a balance between protecting the integrity of families and promoting the safety and well-being of children.

Outcomes of interventions are expected to dictate service delivery. Determination of outcomes has always been difficult for child welfare. At a high level of abstraction, outcomes of safety, permanence, and well-being for children are agreed upon. The outcomes that the system can hope to measure, and thus strives toward, are factors which we think promote those abstract goals. They are (1) reasonable efforts, as legislatively defined, to preserve or rehabilitate the child's own home; (2) achievement of a permanent family home for each child; (3) preservation of children's ties to their original extended family; and (4) services that enable those caring for children to meet the unique needs of each child. At issue is whether an outcome that relies on continued, long-term services to support a family and its children will be acceptable to the community, which dictates the legislative framework and funds the services. In some instances, not all of the desired outcomes can be reached. The duty of the caseworker is to achieve the best balance possible among these factors.

The social worker in the child welfare agency, actually interacting with families and children, is in an important position to evaluate the impact of any policy. Through their advocacy for their clients, backed up by data gathered during the course of their work with children and families, social workers can provide the impetus for needed policy change. It is this advocacy, added to the voices of the community, that results in legislative change, and it is an important professional responsibility of the social worker and the child welfare worker.

Notes

1. In a fascinating book, *Ghosts from the Nursery: Tracing the Roots of Violence* (New York: Atlantic Monthly Press, 1997), Robin Karr-Morse and Meredith Wiley describe the research that documents the impact of violence on the developing brain of a young child, and describe the monumental consequences of these developmental changes. The book is easily understood by those of us who are not scientists, and it provides a glimpse into a new stream of research that in the coming years will have enormous impact on social work.

2. The relative importance of innate developmental processes and the environment has been seriously debated among experts in child development. A consensus seems to have arisen that an environment must be present that allows the unfolding of genetically programmed development while also stimulating and encouraging that development.

3. For a vivid account of this dynamic from the perspective of the foster child, the reader might want to read *The Lost Boy: A Foster Child's Search for the Love of a Family,* by David Pelzer (Deerfield Beach, Fla.: Health Communications, 1997.

4. *Dependent children* is a term commonly used in the child welfare field to mean children in state custody—children dependent on the state to have their basic needs met. Courts that deal with the legal status of these children and arbitrate decisions about their care are called *dependency courts*. Dependent children are distinguished from delinquent youth—youth who are in state custody because they have violated a law. To add to the confusion, *dependent* is often used to describe children dependent on their parents, as in tax law or in income maintenance statutes.

5. Downs, Moore, et al. (2000, chapter 2) provide an excellent summary of Supreme Court cases that have established the principles reviewed here. Much of the material of this section is drawn from that source.

6. Michael Shapiro, in *Solomon's Sword* (New York: Random House, 1999), explores this question thoroughly and thoughtfully.

7. In her novel *Pigs in Heaven* (New York: Harper Perennial, 1993), Barbara Kingsolver has sensitively and warmly described the impact of the Indian Child Welfare Act on an adoption.

8. Long used by many agencies and state systems as an indicator of success, the achievement of permanency for children in foster care was identified as the third of seven outcome measurements by the Department of Health and Human Services, Administration for Children and Families, August, 1999.

9. The 1970s were wonderfully exciting years in adoption. Prior to that time it was thought that families would adopt only healthy infants. The demonstration project in Oregon (Emlen, Lahti, et al. 1976) was convincing in its ability to find adoptive homes for a third of the children in its sample who were in foster care (another third returned home). Other agencies were publicizing their work in placing severely handicapped infants and young children, as well as older children. For example, Christopher Unger and his coauthors, in *Chaos, Madness, and Unpredictability: Placing the Child with Ears Like Uncle Harry's* (Chelsea, Mich.: Spaulding for Children, 1977), documented the work of Spaulding for Children, a Michigan placement agency that pioneered in the adoptive placement of older children. New recruitment techniques and new placement and post-placement support techniques developed. Adoptive homes were even sought, and found, for adolescents during this time. "No child is unadoptable" became the slogan of the era.

References

Abbott, G. 1938. *The Child and the State: The Dependent and the Delinquent Child.* Chicago, Ill.: University of Chicago.

Bourguignon, J. P., and K. W. Watson. 1987. *After Adoption: A Manual for Professionals Working with Adoptive Families.* Springfield: Illinois Department of Children and Family Services.

Bowlby, J. 1951. *Maternal Care and Mental Health.* Geneva: World Health Organization.

Costin, L. B., C. J. Bell, et al. 1991. *Child Welfare: Policies and Practice.* New York: Longman.

Downs, S. W., E. Moore, et al. 2000. *Child Welfare and Family Services: Policies and Practice.* Boston: Allyn and Bacon.

Emlen, A., J. Lahti, et al. 1976. *Overcoming Barriers to Planning for Children in Foster Care.* Portland, Ore.: Regional Research Institute for Human Services.

Erikson, E. 1950. *Childhood and Society.* New York: W. W. Norton.

Fahlberg, V. I. 1991. *A Child's Journey Through Placement.* Indianapolis: Perspectives Press.

Fanshel, D. 1972. *Far From the Reservation.* Metuchen, N.J.: Scarecrow Press.

Fanshel, D., and E. B. Shinn. 1978. *Children in Foster Care: A Longitudinal Investigation.* New York: Columbia University Press.

Goldstein, J., A. Freud, et al. 1973. *Beyond the Best Interests of the Child.* New York: Free Press.

Gruber, A. A. 1978. *Children in Foster Care: Destitute, Neglected, Betrayed.* New York: Human Sciences Press.

Hargrave, V., J. Shireman, et al. 1975. *Where Love and Need Are One.* Chicago: Illinois Department of Children and Family Services.

Jones, B. J. 1995. "The Indian Child Welfare Act." *The Compleat Lawyer* (Fall): 18–23.

Jones, M. A., R. Neuman, et al. 1976. *A Second Chance for Families: Evaluation of a Program to Reduce Foster Care.* New York: Child Welfare League of America.

Kadushin, A., and J. Martin. 1988. *Child Welfare Services.* New York: Macmillan.

Kempe, C. H., F. N. Silverman, et al. 1962. "The Battered Child Syndrome." *Journal of the American Medical Association* 18(1): 17–24.

Knitzer, J., M. L. Allen, et al. 1978. *Children Without Homes.* Washington, D.C.: Children's Defense Fund.

Kools, S. 1997. "Adolescent Identity Development in Foster Care." *Family Relations* 46:263–71.

Littner, N. 1950. *Some Traumatic Effects of Separation and Placement.* New York: Child Welfare League of America.

Maas, H., and R. Engler. 1959. *Children in Need of Parents.* New York: Columbia University Press.

Mannes, M. 1995. "Factors and Events Leading to the Passage of the Indian Child Welfare Act." *Child Welfare* 74(1): 264–82.

Meezan, W., and J. Shireman. 1985. *Care and Commitment.* Albany: State University of New York Press.

Robertson, J. 1958. *Young Children in Hospitals.* New York: Basic Books.

Stein, T. J. 1991. *Child Welfare and the Law.* New York: Longman.

U.S. Congress. 1998. "Green Book." House of Representatives, Washington, D.C. Available at http://aspe.os.dhhs.gov/98gb/intro.htm.

U.S. Department of Health and Human Services. 2000. *Temporary Assistance for Needy Families (TANF) Program: Third Annual Report to Congress.* Washington, D.C.: U.S. Department of Health and Human Services, Administration for Children and Families, Office of Planning, Research, and Evaluation.

U.S. Department of Health and Human Services, Children's Bureau. 2000. *Child Welfare Outcomes 1998: Annual Report.* Washington, D.C.: U.S. Government Printing Office.

Weinstein, E. 1960. *The Self Image of the Foster Child.* New York: Russell Sage Foundation.

CHAPTER 3

The Child Welfare Services System

with Katharine Cahn

Ah, Love! could you and I with Fate conspire
To grasp this sorry Scheme of Things entire,
Would not we shatter it to bits—and then
Re-mould it nearer to the Heart's Desire!

RUBAIYAT OF OMAR KHAYYAM

A primary function of child welfare services is the protection of children. Agencies plan for safety and provide services that establish children in safe, nurturing, and permanent homes—if possible, as part of their original families. The principal provider of these services is the public child welfare agency. The public agency does not operate alone, however. To accomplish its task, the agency sometimes contracts with other agencies for family preservation, foster, and/or adoptive services, refers families to other organizations for services, and works closely with law enforcement and the courts. Additionally, those working in the child welfare system must work cooperatively with other systems. Interaction with the legal system and the court is constant; because most clients have multiple problems, workers must also be able to cooperate with income maintenance delivery systems, schools, disability services, substance abuse programs, women's domestic violence services, the mental health system, the public health system—the list continues. Such interface of systems is difficult, but necessary if we are to be effective in serving clients with multiple needs.

The system for the protection of children begins at the level of community, with the community's responsibility to identify those children who are in need of help and report those situations to the child protection agency. Laws concerning mandated reporters are in place in every state, but many calls come from neighbors and family. The child protection agency is expected to investigate those reports, sometimes with the participation of law enforcement; to act in instances where the child has been harmed or there is threat of harm; to plan services with the family; and to put those services into effect. If the investigating social worker feels that the child's safety cannot be assured in the family home, the authority of the court may be invoked to protect the child by removal.

Ideally, the network of cooperating agencies, public and private, nonprofit and for-profit, would be such that every family referred to a child protection agency received appropriate service. For example, when a referral alleging maltreatment is made, if investigation does not show that there is sufficient risk to the child to warrant the state's intervention in the family, there would still be a "safety net" of community agencies to which the family can turn for support. The work of these family support agencies will be explored in chapter 4. If the report is more serious, and the public agency accepts the case, contracting agencies may provide family preservation services; these services are described in chapter 5. If the child needs placement, the subject of chapter 6, the public agency may have its own foster homes and may also contract for specialized foster home care, described in chapter 7. Residential care, also discussed in chapter 7, is almost always provided by contracted organizations. If a child cannot return to his or her own home, an alternate permanent arrangement, such as adoption, becomes the plan of choice. Adoption services, the subject of chapter 8, are provided by both public and private agencies; public child welfare agencies usually concentrate their adoption services on those children in their foster homes. The system thus begins with community responsibility for the identification of maltreatment, and depends on an interlocking set of cooperating agencies throughout the case to bring about desired outcomes, all under the watchful eye of the courts. The child welfare system is just that—a system—not the province of one agency alone. This chapter explores that system.

The Changing Role of the Public Child Welfare Agency

Few would disagree that the goal of the whole child welfare system, with its many interlocking agencies, is to protect children. Child safety is the primary concern. Attachment and child well-being are also important, so that protection is to be accomplished, if possible, while children remain in their own homes; if they must move, the system seeks to achieve safe, permanent homes quickly, preferably with their original families.

In the past, the public child welfare agency itself was the source of a broad array of services to promote the welfare of children. In recent decades, rising community expectations for the care of children have combined with the disintegration of family structure—and of the community structure that has traditionally supported families—to produce a continuing rise in reports of child maltreatment without corresponding increases in funding or services. The capacity of child protection agencies has been stretched to the point where many are unable to deliver on community expectations within the limits of current staff and budgetary resources. "Child abuse is not just a social phenomenon in and of itself," wrote Lindsey in 1994, "but an issue that has affected child welfare practice as nothing else has ever done, transforming child welfare policy in a way that obscures the traditional focus of what child welfare is all about" (p. 158).

Most public child welfare agencies have adapted to these increased demands by narrowing their range of services, using more stringent definitions of maltreatment, and/or declining to serve some categories of children (such as behaviorally disturbed adolescents or children with developmental disabilities who require out-of-home care for reasons unrelated to abuse or neglect). This adaptation has not been totally successful, however, at least in part because other community resources have not increased their capacity to work with the families and children no longer served by public child welfare agencies. The community has not fully understood this new, narrow definition of the public child welfare agency's mission—or, having understood it, does not accept it. It may take a whole system to meet the needs of children and families, but the responsibility for seeing that those needs are met is still placed on the public child welfare agency alone.

In a major text on child welfare, written in 1992, the authors lamented the open intake policies then current among public child welfare agencies, noting that no agency could hope to do everything well. The writers lauded the new move toward narrowing intake and focusing on protection (Pecora, Whittaker, et al. 1992). Now, a decade later, the wisdom of that move seems less certain, and child welfare agencies are having difficulty articulating their mission. A goal of protecting children, even when that mission is articulated to include the assurance that the children will enjoy permanent, nurturing homes, is too narrow. Too many children who are old enough to protect themselves from serious physical injury are turned away and left unserved. Too many young children have important needs unmet.

> It is no longer possible for child welfare to remain a relatively small service system addressing the needs of a limited number of children who require out-of-home care or protective services. The problems of families and children demand that the child welfare system broaden its scope and diversify its practice approaches into a wider arena of family and child services. The child welfare system must forge new relationships with families, with neighborhoods and communities, and with other organizations in the service delivery system.
>
> (DOWNS, MOORE, ET AL. 2000, P. 25)

The Federal Role in the Child Welfare System

The federal role in the development of child welfare services has been, generally, one of attempting to see that all of the children in the United States had access to the services necessary for their welfare. Since the eighteenth century, when the first orphanages were founded, there have been local, private charities offering services for children. In the public realm, the pattern in the United States has been for each state to develop its own set of services. Thus the approach of the federal government has been to set standards and then to offer funding to state programs that meet those standards. The federal government also has special projects at the national level; a current important project is the building of a national data system.

The shaping of services The federal government's presence in child welfare services began with the inception of the Children's Bureau in 1912. The founding of the bureau, the first federal agency with a social policy agenda, was a great achievement of the Progressive movement. Under strong leadership, the Children's Bureau encouraged "public responsibility" for social problems. Its research and advocacy supported mothers' pensions, public health clinics, juvenile courts, and, beginning in the 1920s, the establishment of public child welfare agencies (Costin, Karger, et al. 1996; Rosenthal 2000).

The passage of the Social Security Act, and its authorization of public funds for staffing and administration of public child welfare agencies, created the opportunity for the founding of such agencies. Many in the private sector were, however, worried by this increased public role, fearing both the regulation and the competition that might come from the public sector. In order to pass the child welfare amendments to the Social Security Act a compromise was necessary; funds for the establishment of public child welfare agencies were to be restricted to largely rural states, where the presence of private agencies was limited (Rosenthal 2000). To the present time, the public presence in child welfare is stronger in the western than in the eastern states.

The federal role in the shaping of child welfare services is apparent in the legislation reviewed in chapter 2. That legislation and the history of the Children's Bureau embody the federal government's efforts to stimulate states toward programs and practices believed to be beneficial. One can trace the evolution of community concerns through the first Children's Bureau initiative on maternal and child health, the activity to secure income maintenance for families with children, legislation to encourage mandated reporting of child maltreatment, and services to assist those children. In more recent times, federal legislation pushed states toward family preservation services. This emphasis shifted again with passage in 1997 of the Adoption and Safe Families Act. ASFA is an expression of the renewed emphasis on safety as a central concern and of the assertive commitment to move children promptly toward permanence, even if it means adoption rather than family reunification.

Federal money comes to the states through specific programs established by law, as well as through grants for specific purposes. Usually the spending of federal money is strictly controlled, and extensive reporting is necessary to demonstrate that it has been used exactly as intended—part of the paperwork burden of child welfare work. Federal legislation and initiatives have considerable influence upon state policy. The rewards attached to joining the federal initiative produce this influence, particularly if, as with foster care, federal funds for a category of service are not capped.[1] State agencies make every attempt to draw federal dollars, and their program initiatives tend to follow the most available funds. In recent years, as part of the devolution of federal authority to the states, federal regulations have increasingly been waived so that states could more flexibly spend money as local needs dictated.

The sharp increase in the number of children in foster care in recent years is often cited as an example of federal funding shaping services. Title XX of the Social Security Act is a capped entitlement, meaning that states are entitled to a specific amount each year for social services. It is a block grant, so that states are free to spend their share for any social services; most states use this as a major source of funds for child protection. Title XX was established by Congress in 1977 and was not indexed for inflation; between 1977 and 1993 the value of Title XX funds was diminished 56.6 percent by inflation (Costin, Karger, et al. 1996, p. 152). In contrast, federal funds for foster care and adoption assistance have been more readily available through Title IV-E, an uncapped entitlement, or open-ended funding source, in which state expenditures are matched by federal funds according to a specific formula. Though there is an investment of state funds, there is no limit on the amount that can be matched. The availability of these federal funds does shape practice, though the extent of the influence is unclear. According to Costin, Karger, and colleagues, "by the early 1990's incentives accompanying federal matching funds were clearly influencing state child welfare practices. . . . In order to capture federal revenues, cash-starved state child welfare agencies began removing children from their families" (1996:154). However, it could be argued that it was not the availability of federal funding but the breakdown and increasing distress in families, in part due to widespread substance abuse—making it difficult to protect children within their own families—that led to the rising numbers of children in foster care.

Level of funding The public has never been generous with dollars for child welfare. Abuse and neglect, crisis intervention services, and the need for foster care are seen as problems of the poor. Because poverty is often conceptualized as the product of individual improvidence, communities have historically shown little interest in providing funds for poor families. This is reflected in numerous public programs, most notably income maintenance programs (which will be discussed in the next chapter), but also in child welfare. Later sections of this chapter will describe the increased demands made on child welfare in recent years, and the manner in which the system's response has been limited and shaped by both the level of funding and its source.

Data systems Another aspect of the federal role has been the attempt to develop national data systems. Data is essential to the management of any system, necessary for the tracking of funds and for policy making. Accurate data about the characteristics and service needs of children is particularly important in a time when decision making and service delivery are being transferred from the public to the private sector. Good data is needed to determine whether public money is being used to purchase the intended service and whether this service is delivering on the investment by producing beneficial outcomes. However, the United States has never maintained a national data system to track protective services, children in out-of-home care, or adoptions. What exists is a mix of systems, from which fairly good approximations can be drawn, but no solid database to inform the establishment or amendment of policies.

There are several sources of national data. In 1993 the federal government published rules for the State Automated Child Welfare Information Systems (SACWIS). One part of this system is the National Child Abuse and Neglect Data System (NCANDS), which reports data required from the states by the Child Abuse Prevention and Treatment Act, as amended in 1996, as well as other data reported by the states. Another part is the Adoption and Foster Care Analysis and Reporting System (AFCARS). The state systems are to contain data about child protection, family preservation and support services, foster care and adoption, and independent living. They are also to interface with income maintenance data systems, and they are to "provide for intrastate electronic data exchange and data collection systems" (House Committee on Ways and Means 1998:811). Although federal matching funds were included as an incentive for the development of the systems, as well as financial penalties for failure to participate, not all states have completed development of SACWIS. The data system is currently at least partially operational for thirty-three states, and fourteen more are working toward this goal (U.S. HHS, Children's Bureau 2002). Although the SACWIS data system has been slow to develop, data are available from almost all of the states through the NCANDS and AFCARS data systems. The slow progress of the more comprehensive system reflects the difficulties of building a data system and the need to invest time in training personnel to use it. Statistics and outcome reports are being issued from both NCANDS and AFCARS.

National organizations have been important in supplying missing data and supplying data in differing formats. The Child Welfare League of America is developing national data and has established an ambitious Web site at which data from the states are available. The site contains predetermined tables, and it is also possible to download data and create custom tables. Although each state has a data system that provides the information necessary to manage that state's system, there are obstacles to the aggregation of state data to create a national picture. One major difficulty with combining data is that different states use different definitions for the same terms. A sample of the explanatory notes on one of the Child Welfare League's statistical tables, concerning children in out-of-home care, illustrates this problem:

Arkansas: Out-of-home care data includes children in foster care, rela-
tive/kinship care, residential, therapeutic foster care and emergency
shelter care.

Georgia: The number of children in out-of-home care includes children
who are in the legal custody of the State but are in the physical custody of their parents.

Kansas and Vermont: Out-of-home care data includes juvenile offenders
in addition to children in need of care.

Maryland: Out-of-home care includes foster care, kinship care, and
some pre-finalized adoptive placements. Also includes a number of
children in foster care or kinship care aftercare.

Oregon: The number of children in out-of-home care in paid placements only.

Rhode Island: Out-of-home care data includes juvenile probation youth
who are in placement.

These statements, of course, raise a series of questions about which children
might be included, or not included, in the data of other states.

The American Public Human Services Association maintains the Voluntary Cooperative Information System (VCIS), which gathers national data
from the forty-one states that participate. Not all states provide information on every question, and this data is subject to the same definitional
variation as that of the national data systems and the Child Welfare
League of America. The VCIS has been invaluable in providing detailed
data not available from other sources, particularly data that goes back in
time to show trends.

National data on the incidence of child abuse and neglect is also available from the National Incidence Studies of Child Abuse and Neglect
(NIS). Three of these studies have been conducted, reporting incidence in
1980, 1986, and 1993; another one is expected to be available soon. The
reports are based on a nationally representative sample population, and
inquiries are made not only of protective service workers but also of
other investigatory agency personnel and of professionals in schools, hospitals, and other major agencies. Respondents are asked about child maltreatment that they have observed and reported, and about maltreatment
observed and not reported. The studies attempt to ascertain the incidence
of actual maltreatment, not just reported maltreatment.[2]

The Children's Defense Fund also provides yearly reports on indicators
of child well-being, and the National "Kids Count" initiative, funded by

the Annie E. Casey Foundation, offers state-level data. Reports from both organizations are available in written form and on the Internet. Some individual states also provide reports on certain aspects of their protective service and foster care systems as well as data generated by individual research projects that may be representative of national trends. Waldfogel (1998) describes these many data sources, and their uses, in a recent and invaluable article.

It is possible to work with this mix of data, focusing on information that comes from reliable sources and is in agreement with data from other sources. However, the lack of a national data system has, for decades, proved an impediment to policy makers and the providers of child welfare services.

The Community Role in the Child Welfare System

During the 1970s, states developed laws that mandated the reporting of child abuse and broadened the definition of reportable abuse. Television and newspaper publicity informed the public of the existence of abuse and how to recognize it, emphasizing the responsibility of every citizen to report child abuse and neglect. These campaigns also stressed that reporters could remain anonymous and would be immune from prosecution for libel. The response was overwhelming. By 1976 there were 416,000 reports; by 1985 almost 2 million (Kadushin and Martin 1988). In 1999 almost 3 million reports of maltreatment were made to protective service agencies (U.S. Department of Health and Human Services [hereafter, U.S. HHS], Children's Bureau 2001b).

This vast increase in the number of reports to be investigated, and in the numbers of families and children identified as needing services—in the absence of corresponding increases in funds—challenged the capacity of child protection agencies. As chapter 5 discusses more extensively, reports were so numerous that it was not possible to investigate them all or to investigate quickly. The failure of child protective agencies to respond to the reports of other professionals created strains within the system of cooperating agencies. Failure to respond to citizen reports created serious public relations difficulties. Failure to respond when a child died created public outcry.

Social workers are mandated reporters. This means that if, in the course of work with an individual or a family, a social worker learns of child maltreatment, that maltreatment must be reported to child protective services. This requirement creates a dilemma in some instances. If the social worker thinks that the services offered by the local protective service agency are intrusive and authoritarian and will do more harm than good, the worker may be reluctant to report. If the social worker has a good relationship with the family, he or she may fear that the report will be seen as a betrayal, disrupt the relationship, and result in the family's not receiving the help they need. However great the temptation not to report, the social worker must keep in mind the legal obligation to report. There is also an ethical obligation, for most social workers do not have the specific training and skills needed to deal with child maltreatment. Such situations highlight the social worker's obligation to advocate for changes in the local protective agency' response, so that it is more certain that a family and child will be helped by the report.

Public Child Welfare Under Stress

Responding to calls from doctors, police, teachers, and grandparents who believe a child has been mistreated, caseworkers knock on doors, ask personal questions, look inside refrigerators, and check children's bodies for bruises and burn marks. They have the power to take children temporarily from their homes and parents, if the risk of harm appears severe. They also have the discretion to determine that nothing serious happened, or that it is safe for the child to remain home while the parents are urged to change. The stakes are high. Overestimating the degree of danger could needlessly shatter a family and rupture the child's closest relationships. Underestimating the danger could mean suffering or even death. The decisions caseworkers make every day would challenge King Solomon, yet most of them lack Solomon's wisdom, few enjoy his credibility with the public, and none command his resources.

(LARNER, STEVENSON, ET AL. 1998:4)

Public child welfare agencies are struggling with the pressures of increased workload, limited funding, and a watchful community critical of their performance. Community standards for caregiving are rising at the same time that family structure is changing and communities seem to be offering less support to families. The great increase in referrals for protective service investigation is one factor in this increased workload.

Another factor is the increasing complexity of the family problems presented to child welfare agencies, such as substance abuse or addiction, necessitating longer and more intensive work with families and often resulting in foster care placements and the need for intensive work with children and foster parents. Foster care is also in crisis, with the number of available homes declining at the same time that the number of children needing placement is rising. Child welfare workers need training, supervision, and an organization that will support them in difficult decision making and service delivery. Funding has not increased sufficiently to provide the needed resources. And the public is increasingly aware, and critical, of the system's deficiencies in meeting the needs of children.

Increases in numbers of children needing help The increase in reports of maltreatment has had a major role in placing public child welfare agencies under stress. Each report demands investigation and either protective services or, if the situation is less serious, the mobilization of community support services to aid a stressed family.

Public agencies can control their intake only through definition of the populations they will serve; they cannot, as a private agency can, say they have "no room" for new cases. The pressure of large workloads is placed on public agencies by the broad definition of maltreatment that brings cases to them, and by their mandate to serve all children who need protection. Some have suggested narrowing these definitions (Hegar and Sullivan 1994, for example)—and most states have done so—so that intervention in family life is warranted only when there has been demonstrated harm to the child or when a family can be identified as "high risk." However, we do not know at what point mild abuse escalates into more serious abuse. Child neglect poses another problem: each individual incident seems low risk, but the cumulative effects of chronic neglect can be terribly damaging to a child's development. More fatalities among children in public child welfare caseloads are associated with neglect than with abuse (U.S. HHS, Children's Bureau 2001b:40).

If the public agency attempts to bring caseloads down to a manageable size by narrowing the definition of maltreatment in order to limit intake, a second resource issue arises for the system as a whole. In many jurisdictions, there is no existing network of private agencies with sufficient capacity to serve "low-risk" families who need help. Working with "low-risk" families early on to prevent more serious problems is widely acknowledged as best practice. However, very little federal funding is available for such family support and family preservation programs, and already strapped state budgets can rarely accommodate bringing this part of the system up to full capacity.

Foster care Though most children who come to the attention of child protective agencies can remain in their own homes, approximately 10 percent need placement in foster care (U.S. HHS, Children's Bureau 2000:5–3). The main point of entry of children into foster care is through the protective service system. For children who need placement, the ideal approach is for the worker to select a home that is prepared to handle the issues of the particular child, is geographically close so that parents can visit, is comfortable in terms of language or culture (ideally, is a family member who has been assessed for safety), and has few enough children that it can attend to the needs of the newcomer. Unfortunately, the child welfare worker rarely has the opportunity to choose with such care. Changing demographics—particularly an increase in the number of single-parent homes and the entry of women into the workforce—coupled with low reimbursement rates and limited recognition, have resulted in a steadily declining number of available foster homes. Often, foster children are adopted by their foster parents, further contributing to the attrition of foster homes, and at the same time underscoring the importance of choosing the original placement with care, even though it may at first seem temporary. Thus, despite the high stakes, the worker usually has very limited resources from which to choose when making a foster placement.

The systemic response to this issue has been to attempt to decrease dependence on foster care. At best, this is done by keeping children in their own homes through intensive services to the family or, when there has been a placement, moving children back home or into adoptive homes as quickly as possible. Policy initiatives leading to more frequent placement of children with relatives have decreased agency reliance on nonrelative foster homes. These are the tenets of family preservation and permanency planning, and they are good policy. However, the need for foster homes remains. The shortage of homes means that children are often placed wherever there is an available bed. Inappropriate placements lead to moves, and each move damages the child. VCIS data for 1990 indicate that, while 43 percent of the children in foster care had only one placement during the last three years, 27.5 percent had two placements, and 6 percent had six or more placements (House Committee on Ways and Means 1998). The foster care system is subject to almost as much criticism as the child protection system.

The provision of foster care, described in more detail in chapter 6, requires collaboration between the agency caseworker and the foster parent, and sometimes between the public agency and a private contractor. In many states, virtually all aspects of the foster care program are operated by private agencies, while in other states this responsibility is shared, with some children in the direct care of state agency foster homes and others in the care of private contracted agencies. Under a contracted system, the private agencies are responsible for recruitment, training, licensing, and management of their own foster homes, under the oversight and monitoring of the public agency.

This system of the state contracting with private agencies to provide foster care is beleaguered by funding and oversight challenges. Often, the public agency's payment rate does not cover the full cost of providing good foster care. A responsible private agency will, to the extent possible, supplement the funds received from the state. Other contractors will attempt to find savings in the foster care program, often through providing less supervision and support to foster homes. Of greatest concern are the for-profit providers of foster care, who organize services in such a way that both expenses and a profit can be met.

Continuity of services is also difficult to maintain with a system of contracted foster care. Often, different agencies are working with parents and with foster parents, making planning and service delivery more complicated. When a child has been in foster care and returns home, support services to the family are often necessary; these are seldom provided by an agency contracting to provide foster care.

Recruitment, training, and retention of qualified personnel Across the child welfare system, staff recruitment, training, and retention are issues of concern, but the problem is nowhere so pressing as in the public child welfare agency. The investigation of each child maltreatment complaint, the assessment of the risks to the child, and the assessment of the family's capacities demand a high level of clinical skill. The complexity of the problems faced by the families and the children necessitate similar levels of skill in the provision of direct service or the arrangement and supervision of services from a variety of other agencies. Each case requires difficult decisions that may have grave impact on the life of a child.

There is a surprising lack of empirical research documenting the characteristics, educational background, and training needed to do this work. Social work has long been allied with child welfare, and many think that the philosophy and skills taught to social workers are effective in child welfare work. Most child welfare agencies provide in-service training to build on the educational background of their employees, though in times of budgetary difficulties training is too often sacrificed to maintain direct services. However, it does little good to recruit staff members with the proper background, train them to do the work of the specific agency, and then have them leave.

The problem of staff turnover in child welfare is the critical issue explored in the final chapter of the book. Here it is sufficient to note that, according to a 2001 survey by the Child Welfare League of America, annual turnover for protective service workers and other caseworkers in public agencies approaches 20 percent; in private agencies it is 40 percent (Drais, Cyphers, et al. 2001). Staff turnover leaves vacancies, starting the cycle of recruitment and training again. The repetition of recruitment and training consumes needed resources, and it wastes the experience and practice wisdom of the workers who have left. Vacancies cause caseloads to rise for remaining personnel, increasing the risk to children. It is vital, therefore, to discover the reasons for turnover and to put the support structure in place that will maximize workers' satisfaction and desire to remain in the agency.

The Interface of Public and Voluntary Agencies

The past decade was a time of devolution of responsibility for social services toward smaller and local units. Just as the burden of services is tending to shift from the federal to the state levels of government, so it is shifting from public to private social welfare organizations. Indeed, in public policy discussions the term "privatization" has replaced "public-private partnership." This is a reversal of the trend begun at the start of the century.

The Voluntary Agency

A private or voluntary agency is established by a group of citizens interested in a particular cause or program. The orphanages established in the eighteenth and nineteenth centuries were voluntary agencies, and many of them still exist, often with changed names and evolved functions. Others have been formed much more recently for specific tasks, ranging from the youth development activities of the Boy Scouts and Girl Scouts to the crisis-response work of Homebuilders, or to serve particular ethnic or racial groups in the community, such as One Church, One Child. The citizens who form a private agency usually form a corporate body and obtain a legal charter outlining the services they plan to implement. Private agencies are subject to state licensing if they provide out-of-home care. Although private agencies become part of the child welfare system through contracts with the public agency, it is rare for a private agency to rely for its funding on public contracts alone. As one source of funding, private agencies often become members of a local fund-raising organization such as a United Way; they must demonstrate to the organization before each fund-raising campaign that they are providing the intended services.

A private agency can be strictly local or can be part of a national organization. Some private agencies have a religious affiliation that provides support as well as an obligation to observe the religious tenets of the affiliated organization. The management of a private agency is usually responsible to a board of directors composed of prominent citizens, responsible for major policy decisions and for fund-raising. Thus the services of the private agency retain a community base, and the agency can often exert policy and programmatic pressure on the legislature through influential board of directors members.

There has always been argument about whether public or private agencies were more likely to develop innovative services. At the time of the founding of public agencies, private agencies were thought to be caught by their traditions and investment in buildings, and unwilling to move toward innovations such as foster care. Later, the innovations of the private sector, disseminated through the Child Welfare League of America, became the source of many new practices. Certainly it is in the private sector that one finds the greatest variety in policy, philosophy, and services, and this variety allows for experimentation. However, bringing these innovations "up to scale" for all children served by the public agency has proved to be no easy task. A private agency often has the opportunity to narrow its intake, focusing an innovative intervention very precisely on the population of children and families most likely to benefit from it.

This multiplicity of private agencies with different focuses has meant that children's services delivered through the private sector were of uneven quality. Standard-setting, so that children throughout the United States receive roughly equivalent opportunities, has been an ambition of all federal child welfare programs. The capacity to set standards has come with the delivery of federal funds. Private child welfare agencies have used public funds since the time when townships purchased places in orphanages for destitute children. However, the major influx of federal funds into private agencies occurred in the 1960s, during the War on

Poverty. Before that time, federal funds had been available only for administration and staffing of public child welfare agencies. In 1962, provision was made for federal payments for foster care. The 1967 Social Security amendments authorized the use of federal funds for the purchase of professional services. Federal expenditures increased dramatically, from $194 million in 1964 to $3 billion in 1982 (Rosenthal 2000).

Although concerned about the standardization and regulation that might follow this influx of public funds into the private sector, private agencies reached for the new source of income. The Child Welfare League of America issued position papers warning that private agencies must retain their own missions and standards and that, in order to keep their independence, they should accept only a portion of their budgets from public funds. By 1986, private child welfare agencies received 59 percent of their income from governmental sources (Rosenthal 2000).

The movement of public dollars into private child welfare has accelerated since 1980. In an era when it was thought that private enterprise was more efficient than public, the buying of services from private agencies increased. Cost containment has been part of the motivation, leading to an expansion of purchase of services under managed care standards. Governments are also beginning to buy child welfare services from for-profit agencies. In many public child welfare agencies, most services other than protective services are contracted to private agencies. As this privatization increases, concerns arise about the enforcement of standards for quality care.

Managed Care

Managed care is essentially a strategy of organizing care to control costs, with a goal of efficiently providing the entire range of services needed. Having originated in the medical world, it depends on the ability to diagnose precisely, specify a known average length and type of care to match the diagnosis, and measure outcome. For a long time it seemed that the managed care approach would not come to the world of child welfare, where such a level of specificity is not possible.

However, managed care has indeed emerged in child welfare. In 1998, a Child Welfare League of America survey reported that twenty-nine states had policy initiatives in place that called for privatization of services with elements of managed care included in the shaping of contracts. Though this represents many plans in many states, the authors estimate that only about 10 percent of the child welfare population is affected.

The models vary widely in size, focus, methods of organizing services, and risk-sharing. The most commonly contracted services involve out-of-home care of a more specialized nature than regular foster care, though some states have initiatives focusing on family preservation and support services. No state has privatized its child abuse and neglect investigations; in every state the public agency remains the gatekeeper (McCullough and Schmitt 1999).

States have developed these managed care initiatives to fit the particular needs of their systems, with the goal of providing a full array of services for all children. Some are contracts with a single provider, almost always a not-for-profit provider. Some use a lead provider model. Lead provider contracts stimulate the development of service delivery networks, as a lead agency takes on case management and subcontracts with an array of providers to obtain the needed services. Risk-sharing is common. "Due to uncertainty about accurately pricing child welfare services, . . . many initiatives that include risk-sharing have built in risk adjustment mechanisms to protect against losses that would jeopardize the survival of contractors or the quality of services delivered" (McCullough and Schmitt 1999:39).

Given the current popular distrust of government, and the perception that the private sector delivers more cost-effective services than do government agencies, the movement toward increased sharing of case management and service delivery between the private and public sectors will doubtless continue. The public agency is entering into an environment of shared responsibility. However, the public agency continues to retain legal authority for most child welfare cases and is held liable, both in the courts and in the court of public opinion, if anything goes wrong with a case.

Whether this privatization and managed care initiative is good for children is open to question. Troubling stories are reported of providers spending relatively little on direct services to children and diverting funds into administrative costs or profits,[3] but troubling stories are also reported of poor services to children delivered directly by the public child welfare system. Any change from one model of service provision to another will hurt children in the short run because changes of caseworkers, and perhaps of foster homes, are likely to delay decision making about their cases.

There is probably no perfect mix of public and private services. As appealing as it may be, any change in the current structure, such as privatization, should be entered into carefully and with a great deal of attention to avoiding the interruption of services to children and families. Effective systems for monitoring the process of service delivery are needed in both the private and public sectors, for children are very vulnerable. The monitoring of process should not be lost amid the current interest in outcomes.

Managed care is usually controlled by monitoring of outcomes as well as process. However, outcome measures for child welfare have always been problematic. The appropriate indicators of ultimate good outcomes are open to debate. For example, McCullough and Schmitt (1999) describe a Cook County, Illinois, managed care initiative in which time in relative foster care was reduced substantially. Costs were obviously reduced. Whether this was a good outcome for the children, however, depends on whether more time with relatives was really needed, and whether the children had moved to a better situation. The outcomes that are possible to measure are not necessarily the outcomes that are most telling in the highly individualized world of child welfare services.

The Interface of Child Welfare with Other Public Systems

The Judicial System and the Child Welfare System

The courts are a major player in the child welfare system because families are often involuntary clients, under court order to change their mode of living if they wish to keep their children. Every step of the child welfare process is guided by the courts. Only with juvenile court involvement can a child be removed from his or her parents for more than a brief emergency period. As the child's case moves through the system, juvenile courts provide oversight, determining whether reasonable efforts are being made to maintain family ties. Sometimes family or criminal courts are also involved in aspects of the case.

The interface of the criminal justice system and the protective service system is not always easy. In decision making about the handling of abusive and neglectful families, courts and social service agencies do not always agree. Even when they may agree as to outcomes, agency and court procedures can be at odds, delaying the progress of a case and preventing timely resolution.

Juvenile court involvement A key aspect of the Adoption Assistance and Child Welfare Act of 1980 (Public Law 96-272) was the institution of increased supervision of the work of public agencies through periodic court reviews, as well as by court-appointed citizen review boards or internal administrative review mechanisms. Citizen review boards are made up of community volunteers, appointed by the court. Their overall mission is to assure accountability for children in foster care. A citizen review board's charge is to ensure that all family members have been involved in developing a permanent plan for a child, and that children are moved as rapidly as possible into permanent homes or are well prepared for independent living. In periodic reviews of children in foster care, all interested parties are invited to appear. The board asks questions, listens to points of view, and makes findings and recommendations to the court and to the child welfare agency.

Courts have also developed voluntary agents, often called court-appointed special advocates (CASA), to assist the guardian ad litem (usually an attorney from the public defender's office) in representing the child's interests in court. Judicial oversight, as well as administration of advocacy programs such as citizen review boards and CASA programs, is typically provided by the state's dependency court system.[4] The intent of court involvement is to promote timely decision making, helping children move more quickly to a safe and permanent home. However, the addition of multiple players and systems is a mixed blessing. It introduces a level of complexity that can create its own delays, unless all players understand one another's roles and learn how to collaborate well in the best interests of the child.

Since the passage of the Adoption Assistance and Child Welfare Act of 1980, the child welfare agency and the courts have been inextricably intertwined in the service of children. The professional cultures and practices of the two make for an uneasy partnership. Clashes between the adversarial nature of legal decision making and the more holistic, systemic nature of social work practice can cause misunderstandings and delays. In the legal system, members of families (parents and children) become "parties" who are "adversaries" in a legal proceeding. This has the result of putting the two sets of players most likely to hold the keys to resolving the issue (the parent/family on the one hand, and the agency on the other) at odds with one another in a situation where collaboration and full sharing of information might produce a better outcome.

Increased oversight can cause tension. Agency social workers, accustomed to being considered "experts," equate court oversight with questioning of their judgment; indeed, many are ill prepared (by education or temperament) for the evidence-based, adversarial, argumentative procedure of the courtroom.

To further complicate matters, a third player was added. Many began to feel that the child welfare agency, forced to balance child protection against parental rights and constrained by agency budgets, could not be trusted to champion only the best interests of the child. Traditionally the guardian ad litem represented the child in court, but this office was often so overwhelmed that its representatives could not really get to know the children and their situations. To ensure that there was one person looking only from the point of view of the child in a court proceeding, many state court systems established CASA (court-appointed special advocate) programs, which assign trained volunteers to many children in the dependency system.

Courts, citizen review panels (in some states), and CASA programs are now an integral part of the child welfare system. They have established their own data systems, compete with other parts of the system for funding, and have their own challenges with staff recruitment, education, and training. The establishment of these systems added to the complexity of the system, while at the same time offering more layers of protection and advocacy for children and parents.

The role of the agency social worker now includes the responsibility to negotiate relationships with each of these systems effectively. More time is spent in citizen review board and court hearings, as well as meeting with the many players involved in the service delivery sector, and the child welfare social worker needs well-developed collaborative skills such as the ability to present a case in court and to a team, the ability to understand a wide array of other systems, and the ability to negotiate. Sharing decision making is challenging for the most highly trained professional, and it is a major part of a child welfare social worker's job today.

The Children's Bureau, recognizing that refinement of these interagency processes would benefit children, passed the Court Improvement Program as part of the 1993 Omnibus Budget and Reconciliation Act. This program provided funding for multi-year initiatives designed to assess and strengthen the dependency court processes called for in the Adoption Assistance and Child Welfare Act of 1980. Some courts are investing in more training for judicial officers, others are streamlining court processes like the docketing of cases, and still others are developing community resources to help families.

To mitigate the worst impacts of the adversarial process on the delicate tissue of a family system, jurisdictions across the country are experimenting with alternative methods of dispute resolution for dependency cases. These include the use of mediation, pretrial conferences, family group conferencing, and other forms of family decision making. Some courts and agencies are also implementing methods to empower families to participate more effectively in the process, such as providing special classes on how the dependency court works or assigning mentors or advocates to explain the system.

Involvement of other court systems The criminal courts and family courts, as well as the delinquency side of juvenile court, also impact the public child welfare system. For example, many families are involved in the criminal justice system. Parents are incarcerated; children need care and parents need, somehow, to maintain bonds with their children. Perpetrators of child abuse are, inconsistently, subject to criminal prosecution. Family violence involves both the criminal justice and the child welfare systems. Custody issues can be settled in family court. And, of course, adolescents with serious behavior problems often move from the child welfare system to the juvenile justice system. The need for interdisciplinary understanding among the legal and the social service professions has been neglected and, as court involvement increases, needs to be addressed. Adding to the challenge, coordination of the services of several court systems will be needed to assure the best outcomes for children.

Criminal courts are involved if a crime such as child endangerment or child sexual abuse is alleged. In these cases, a defense attorney may advise the parent not to admit guilt and not to participate in services such as substance abuse treatment or sex abuse counseling that might imply guilt prior to resolution of the criminal case. This delays permanence for children (while quite properly protecting a parent's legal rights). Some states are addressing these delays by improving coordination between the criminal and dependency courts in matters of scheduling or by prioritizing child welfare cases on the docket in criminal court.

Parents may be involved in family court in matters connected or unconnected to the dependency. Domestic violence, while posing dangers to children, will be addressed by law enforcement and family court, and may or may not come to the attention of the dependency court. Parents incarcerated for crimes not related to their parental capacity present a particular challenge to the timely resolution of child welfare cases. How long should a child wait for the chance to be raised by a parent now in prison? Can attachments be maintained? For how long? Can good parenting skills be acquired or demonstrated by a parent behind bars? Dependent youth may also become involved in the delinquency system.

Some jurisdictions are addressing this problem of multiple court systems by introducing unified family courts where all matters may be reviewed by the same judge, and where a family may have access to a case management system that can coordinate hearings on the same day.

Other Systems

Many social service systems affect the families who become involved with the child welfare system. Many children are involved in Head Start or other early childhood education programs; almost all children are involved in the public school system.[5] The medical system, of course, is important for all families. These systems are, at least in their broad outlines, known to most of us. The mental health and developmental disability services systems are less familiar. Child welfare workers will work with many children with varying degrees of developmental disability and with children who have serious emotional disturbance. Because these children have particular needs, and because early recognition of their problems and early intervention are important, child welfare workers need to be familiar with the systems that serve these children.

Developmental disabilities Developmental disabilities have been defined in federal legislation concerning SSI assistance in terms of the limits to functioning they present. Although earlier assistance was limited to children with certain categories of disability, principally mental retardation, a 1990 Supreme Court decision mandated the use of a more functional definition of disability. Developmental disability was then defined as a severe, chronic condition that is caused by mental or physical impairment and makes self-care, language, learning, mobility, and/or self-direction difficult (Hughes and Rycus 1998:21). The welfare reform of 1996, however, removed the functional limitation assessment and created other restrictions; as a result many fewer children will be eligible for SSI income (Pecora, Whittaker, et al. 2000:114).

Children with serious developmental disabilities were once routinely institutionalized, in the belief that they would be more content among others of similar capacity. The evidence is clear, however, that children cared for in their own families achieve better developmental outcomes, and the focus of services has shifted to the provision of support services to enable families to care for their children at home.

Developmental disabilities can be both a cause and an effect of child abuse and neglect. Children perceived as different, or who are demanding, are at higher risk for maltreatment. In addition, the extraordinary demands for special care that some of these children present can result in neglect when parents simply cannot manage to meet those demands. Physical abuse, particularly if it involves head injury, can be a cause of serious developmental disability. Recent research demonstrates that both neglect and abuse of young children distort normal brain development, leading to severe behavioral disorders. Drug or alcohol use by pregnant women can result in damage to the fetus, and some child welfare systems automatically treat babies born with drugs in their systems as abused children.[6]

Serious emotional disorders, such as autism, can clearly be considered developmental disabilities. There can be debate about whether other emotional disorders reach the threshold of pervasive interference with a child's development that the definition demands.

Children's mental health Child welfare workers will meet many children with serious emotional disturbance. There is little doubt that among the consequences of severe abuse and neglect are emotional and behavioral disturbance. In a thoughtful review of the empirical evidence linking these events, Dore (1999:7) notes that various studies of children entering the child welfare system have found between 30 and 60 percent to be exhibiting clinical levels of emotional or behavioral disorders. The evidence is fairly clear that the severity and the frequency of maltreatment and the developmental stage of the child are associated with later emotional or behavioral disturbance (English 1998). Probably it is not the maltreatment alone, but also the poverty, substance abuse, depression, and family violence associated with the maltreatment that lead to later problems. Thus it can be expected that a high proportion of children entering the child welfare system through its protective services will exhibit serious emotional or behavioral problems.

Additionally, some children come into out-of-home care in the child welfare system specifically because of serious emotional disturbance. Some of these children are unable to function in a family setting and need the structure and intensive therapeutic intervention of a residential setting. Others may do well in therapeutic foster homes. For the families of these children, the cost of such treatment programs presents a serious obstacle. In many states, although the families have voluntarily approached the system for help, the state takes custody of these children, often labeling them "neglected," before helping to meet the costs of care. This procedure creates unnecessary hardship for the family and presents an unnecessary obstacle to the eventual reunification of the youngster with the family. It is a good example of the failure of two service systems to coordinate their procedures.

Coordination of systems The effective interface of these multiple systems is seldom achieved. Such coordination depends on shared values, shared language, shared philosophies of individual planning for children, and, at best, shared funding streams.

The mental health, developmental disability, and child welfare systems are not well coordinated at the federal or state levels, where policy is outlined and funding streams developed; coordination is often somewhat better at the local level where practitioners interact to coordinate services. On the philosophy of maintaining children in their own homes whenever possible and using the least restrictive setting possible, the child welfare, mental health, and developmental disabilities systems are all in agreement.

Child welfare services and services designed for children with developmental disabilities are usually separated at both federal and state levels.

> The services are funded from different sources, administered by separate bodies, and delivered by separate local agencies. Service delivery objectives often appear to be quite different, each focusing on the remediation of different conditions and defined by the perception of quite different presenting problems. And, while services are available, they remain inaccessible due in large part to barriers erected out of philosophical and legislative differences among agencies and programs.
>
> (HUGHES AND RYCUS 1998:12)

Comprehensive plans, of course, begin with cooperation among systems to "wrap around" services (borrowing a term that originated in the mental health field) to enable families to care for children in their own homes. These services may begin to involve the child welfare system if the child is abused or neglected, or if the demands the child makes on the family necessitate respite care or foster care. The term "wrap-around services" is now commonly used in child welfare to mean comprehensive services.

At the federal level, leadership in the development of mental health services for children has come through the Child and Adolescent Services System Program (CASSP). This initiative, begun in 1985, has provided states with funds to hire specialists to improve child mental health services and to create linkages with other child-serving systems, thus developing local systems of care. It has also supported several research and training centers that have been important in developing and disseminating information.

The State Comprehensive Mental Health Services Plan Act, Title V of Public Law 99-660, passed in 1986, applies to children as well as adults. Under it, states are required to develop comprehensive plans for children with serious emotional disturbance. These plans are funded through mental health block grants to states. However, it is quite possible that the more visible mental health needs of adults, as in the past, will crowd out those of children as states implement these block grants.

For children who are either developmentally disabled or seriously emotionally disturbed, school can be both a source of difficulty and an important avenue toward optimum development. The Individuals with Disabilities Education Act (IDEA) of 1990 mandates "free, appropriate, public education" in "the least restrictive setting" for all children with disabilities, starting with identification and intervention for infants and toddlers, and including early intervention programs for children aged three to five as well as appropriate school planning for school-aged children. Individual Family Service Plans are developed for the infants and toddlers; Individual Education Plans (IEP) for the older children. Parents are to participate with the schools in the development of these plans, and may request a due process hearing if they disagree with a school's assessment or planning for their child. The plans are reviewed yearly (Hughes and Rycus 1998:117–18). The child welfare worker may well have a role in helping parents advocate for their children in the school system.

If these children enter the child welfare system, careful assessment and individualized planning are vital for them. As for all children, the first efforts should be to insure safety and well-being in the child's own home. Respite care can be an important resource in this endeavor, as can various home-visiting and parent education programs. Early childhood intervention programs can be critical in maximizing a child's developmental capacity and helping a child manage behavior so that he or she will be ready for school. Sometimes children's own families are unable to manage care if the child is particularly difficult, and family resources stretched too thin.

Income assistance is available for the families of many of these children through the disability provisions of SSI. Expenses for specialized care can, however, be extraordinary. For example, as discussed in the previous section, in order to be able to pay for residential care for their children with serious emotional disturbance, families in many states are required to surrender custody and have the children declared dependent so that the state will pay for care, a practice distressing to parents and incongruent with a philosophy of strengthening the family.

For the child who is developmentally disabled or has mental health problems and cannot remain with the original family, foster care and adoptive care are appropriate. Placements must be carefully made and supported with intensive services. Some children will need medical foster homes, therapeutic foster homes, or even residential care, at least temporarily. The recruitment and support of foster and adoptive families for these "hard to place" children is discussed in chapter 8.

Responsibility to Those Served

All social service systems are, of course, ultimately responsible to those they serve. It is easier to lose this sense of responsibility in child welfare than in some other systems, for those served are poor, young, and have relatively little power. Public oversight is a "watchdog" that helps to keep the system responsive; nevertheless, social justice issues constantly arise.

Agencies that have the authority to intervene in family life, insist on lifestyle changes, and if necessary remove children, inspire fear. These same agencies have the responsibility to provide services, or to organize the network of community service providers, so that families are enabled to take better care of their children. Partly because of the immense power and responsibility entrusted to these agencies, the public is constantly overseeing their work. The formal channels for public oversight are in the federal funding system and in the court system. The media act as the informal system of review of agency functioning.

Formal Oversight

When the federal government spends its funds on child welfare services in the states, it wants to know how those funds have been spent, and wants assurance that federal standards for services have been met. The reporting requirements thus constitute a system of oversight. An unintended consequence of this system, of course, is the enormous burden of paperwork it entails, which increases the workload pressure on the service-providing agencies.

The oversight role of the court, including court-sponsored programs such as CASA and citizen review boards, was described earlier in this chapter. In addition to the court, other bodies provide oversight and add checks and balances to the system. Interdisciplinary child protection teams that review child protection decisions are in place in many states. Some states have set up placement oversight panels for Indian children, providing cultural expertise and a connection to the tribes for Native American children who come into care. Although their forms vary, these case-level oversight and planning mechanisms are now an integral part of the child welfare system in every state.

Case-level oversight is not always welcome; busy caseworkers often see the demand for review as an indication that their decision making and casework are not trusted. To get the best results for children, a social worker must be skilled at presenting a case to a team, distilling the case facts to clear points, and identifying the key practice issues for discussion. In this way the social worker can engage the team or review board as a partner in planning for children.

Informal Oversight

The news media represent an influential, though informal, review system for public child welfare agencies. Everyone has read the newspaper stories, and seen the television newscasts, about cases in which a complaint of maltreatment has been made and investigated, and a child has been left with a family only to be seriously harmed. Everyone has also read stories of the removal of children from their homes over the protests of the parents, and wondered whether the removal was necessary. Such publicity can have a demoralizing effect on workers inside the agency, who worry that one of their cases could be the next headline. However, such media coverage can work to the advantage of the system as well. In the hands of a skilled administrator, these stories can secure the political momentum for desired policy or practice changes, or can leverage increased public funds. The media does not only monitor child protection through highlighting difficult decision making. There are also frequent pieces on the system as a whole—the workload pressures of the protective service worker, the difficulties of the child in foster care, the problems families have in accessing services. Thus the community is kept informed about the health of its child protective system. An agency that can manage to maintain a regular flow of such "good news" stories can build a reservoir of goodwill to draw on when the "bad news" hits.

Because the state has the authority to remove children and to decide where to place them, it at times creates situations in which parents or relatives feel they have been unjustly treated. VOCAL, which stands for Victims of Child Abuse Legislation, is a parent organization that has been an active voice for reform. Grandparents' organizations have also grown up in several states to lobby for the rights of relatives to have children placed with them, and to visit when that is not possible. These organizations also keep the public informed about child protection, usually through publicity and lawsuits in response to perceived mistakes of the child protection system. Some states have also established child advocacy or ombudsman's offices, usually reporting directly to the governor, to provide checks and balances in case of over- or underzealous child welfare work.

Though this public scrutiny is healthy, it increases the stress on the child welfare worker. It is always more difficult to work when someone is watching. The stakes are very high—a child's safety. Decision making in child welfare is not fail-safe. A worker must often act before information is complete, and not every decision turns out well. Every worker must deal with the risk that a decision may end up being discussed on the front page of tomorrow's paper. Public criticism can erode morale. Supports provided by in-service training, supervision, team participation, and interdisciplinary work can help, but will not solve the problem entirely. The pressure has an impact on workers' attitudes toward families and on the energy and creativeness they bring to their interactions with families.

The Interface of Systems

It is clear from the discussion in this chapter that the child welfare system is not one agency or profession; it is a complex, interlocking network of agencies and professionals that includes other systems such as mental health and education. This means that the fate of children and families is shaped by the policies, program constraints, and professional cultures of very different worlds. Effective advocacy for children requires that a social worker be informed about, and alert to, the opportunities and constraints presented by colleagues from other disciplines. It requires coordinated interdisciplinary work, both at the level of work with the individual and at the level of understanding and accessing the many systems that impact families.

Interdisciplinary Work

The historically separate development of the many systems serving children and families has created differing value systems, different language, and different sets of laws and regulations, all of which tend to separate the systems. These are obstacles that must be overcome for effective interdisciplinary work.

For example, legal professionals and social workers often seem at odds, because differing professional cultures and ethics are inculcated from the very first day of their professional training. A law student is taught to argue, to defend a point of view, to operate only from facts and not from subjective information. The student learns an ethical obligation to zealously defend the client's stated position, regardless of personal opinion on that position. By contrast, the social work student is taught to look at a situation holistically, and to seek solutions that will best meet the needs of all players. Emotional and subjective information are considered valid, though social workers are taught to examine their assumptions closely for class, race, or other biases.

Confidentiality standards can challenge interdisciplinary work. For example, drug treatment professionals and therapists have a very high threshold of confidentiality, a condition of receiving federal funds in the case of drug treatment professionals. Those standards can be frustrating to child welfare agency workers who think that the information collected by clinics is necessary for decision making regarding children's well-being. Clear contracting and requests for information in accordance with federal confidentiality standards, releases of information designed to meet the needs of multiple agencies, and involvement of the client in decision making are all approaches to managing these dilemmas with integrity.

The connection between law enforcement and child welfare agencies is vital to child (and worker) safety and to good outcomes. Law enforcement officers often (and in some states are legally required to) accompany child welfare workers on a home visit that is likely to end up in a removal. The training law enforcement officers receive in maintaining safety and in gathering criminal evidence are invaluable in the child welfare arena. The legal authority of a police officer is vital to many child welfare interventions. Clear interagency protocols and established channels for communication and problem solving can result in powerful partnerships between law enforcement and child welfare social workers for the benefit of children. Around the country, strong working agreements between child welfare workers and law enforcement officers have proven to be the best way to address the problems of domestic violence and of substance abuse in violent settings.

Many referrals to child protective services come from schools. Although they are mandated reporters, many educators are not familiar with the boundaries and mission of the child welfare agency. Without this context, educators may consider the narrowly defined intake criteria a sign of lack of responsiveness or lack of caring on the part of the child welfare agency. Cross-training sessions to explain child welfare agency constraints, intake criteria, and how to refer a case can help this situation. Conversely, child welfare social workers need to work closely with schools to help children succeed. A child who has been abused or neglected can present behaviors that make it hard to manage a classroom. Communication about the special health and behavioral supports a child will need to succeed, and mechanisms to negotiate funding for those supports, are characteristic parts of a system that works well.

Differing Perspectives

Throughout this chapter, child welfare has been discussed as a system of interlocking players as if child safety and well-being were the primary focus for all participants. This is not always true. Some partners whose services are essential for the safety of the child do not necessarily hold the child's safety as their central concern. For example, an organization that shelters and supports battered women may perceive the removal of their children as a further victimization of its clients. Similarly, a drug treatment provider will be concerned primarily with the recovery of the parent and may advocate for a long period during which the parent is relieved of the stress of parenting; the parent is their client, not the child. It is not that other organizations are careless or heedless of child safety issues; in fact, they often raise critical concerns about child safety and have important information to offer, for example, about a client's relapse. But frustrations and problems will arise unless each participating agency clearly understands the role played the others and respects their commitment to their primary client.

With such understanding, communication and coordinating mechanisms and interagency protocols can be developed that take the agencies' differing perspectives into account. But a key concept may be agency flexibility. As any service matures, it develops a flexibility of response attuned to the situation presented. Thus it may be time for child welfare services to begin to modify their traditional investigative approach to all families; in family violence situations, an approach that emphasizes partnering with the parent to assure safety may be more appropriate than an investigation. Similarly, the new focus on permanency within a short time frame as a preferred outcome for all families may not always lead to the best practice; when neglect is related to substance abuse, for some families the ultimate goal of family reunification may be more important than the timeline to the reunification. The examples could be continued. The implementation of such ideas will, of course, demand imaginative caseworkers who are determined to fight for the best for their clients, support of the idea from agency management, and willingness to enter the policy arena. Innovation and flexibility in one system—such as that engendered by the new focus on early permanency as a preferred outcome for all families—often sparks a similar response in another system.

Funding for Services

Categorical funding streams—different agencies having different sources of funds—are one of the biggest challenges to the smooth functioning of the vast interagency system this chapter has described. It can take years to develop an understanding of the various funding streams of each of the interagency players. Developing this "systems savvy" will make a child welfare social worker or advocate more effective.

From the mental health field comes the concept of "wrap-around services," an array of services that can be "wrapped around" the client, driven by the needs of a child, adult, or family rather than by the shape of the service delivery system. This useful conceptualization has been taken up by child welfare, and its implementation demands coordination at the systems level. Most public child welfare agencies do not, however, have funds that will enable the purchase of services from other agencies on a case-by-case basis (Waldfogel 1998:109). Flexible funds that can be accessed by the worker to meet particular needs are a new idea in public child welfare, one that has great promise.

Another fundamental service delivery problem is posed by the basic casework provided by CPS, which in many cases is the primary service families receive from CPS. Because they are large public bureaucracies engaged in a high-stakes enterprise, CPS agencies tend to adopt a uniform approach to all cases, prescribing specific procedures that must be followed in each case rather than encouraging a customized approach that takes into account the fact that families coming to the attention of CPS are a varied group whose needs change over time. Although standardized procedures exist to ensure that the delivery of services is fair, responsible, and equitable, they often mean that families do not get a response that is sufficiently tailored to their needs.

(WALDFOGEL 1998:109)

Developing flexible "pots" of funding, and using funds from one player as match to leverage increased funding from another, are strategies that have brought greater integration and the experience of a more seamless system of services for children and families.

Critical Issue: Racism in the Child Welfare System

Statistics demonstrate that a disproportionate number of African American and Native American children are involved in the child welfare system. In 2001, it was estimated that 64 percent of the children in out-of-home care were children of color, and half of those were African American (Morton 2001). A disproportionate number are reported to the protective service system, and they are more likely to be placed in foster care. Children of color spend a longer time in foster care and are less likely to be reunited with their families or to be adopted. The interpretation of these statistics is complex, but it is important in determining whether racism is part of the child welfare system and in what parts of the system it operates.

If more children of color are actually mistreated, then the high proportion in the system is explained. The Third National Incidence Study found that family income was related to the incidence of maltreatment and that children of single parents were more likely to be maltreated (U.S. HHS, National Center on Child Abuse and Neglect 1996). Of course, as we noted in chapter 1, single parenthood and poverty are closely related. Race is associated with poverty; families of color have historically been economically disadvantaged. Certainly the stresses of poverty make child rearing more difficult. Poverty limits opportunity and generates frustration. Poor communities often lack resources to support struggling families.

Many of the most poverty-stricken communities have fallen prey to a culture of drugs and violence. The environment creates obstacles to the healthy development of children and families. Thus it might be expected that children of color would experience a higher incidence of abuse and neglect.

However, the Third National Incidence Study reports finding no race differences in the actual incidence of maltreatment (U.S. HHS, National Center on Child Abuse and Neglect 1996:8–7). Yet the numbers of children for whom reports of maltreatment were substantiated in 1998 varied markedly by race: 20.7 African American victims per 1,000 children of the same race in the population, 19.8 Native Americans or Alaska Natives, 10.6 Hispanic victims, 8.5 whites, and 3.8 Asians or Pacific Islanders (U.S. HHS, Children's Bureau 2000:2). This suggests that African American and Native American children receive differential attention somewhere in the process of referral and investigation.

A higher proportion of the African American and Native American children who enter the system because of maltreatment end up in foster care. About 28 percent of white children are placed in foster homes, while 72 percent receive services in their own homes. In contrast, only 44 percent of African American children receive services in their own homes, and 56 percent enter foster care (U.S. HHS, Children's Bureau 1997; Morton 2001). As a result, although African American children make up roughly 15 percent of the population, 51 percent of the children in foster care are African American. Native American children are 1 percent of the population and almost 2 percent of the foster care population nationally. White children, Hispanic children, and Asian children are underrepresented in foster care. Table 6.4 (page 212) displays this data.

Recent studies have been able to pinpoint some of the ways in which children of color and their families receive differential treatment. A series of studies have indicated that families of color receive fewer services, have fewer visits with their children in foster care, and have less contact with their caseworkers (Courtney, Barth, et al. 1996:107–13). Kinship foster care has expanded in recent years and may be considered a mark of cultural awareness, exemplifying the appropriate use of the care system of another culture. It is more frequently used for African American children than for white children. However, kinship foster homes generally receive fewer support services than do regular foster homes, and among kinship foster homes, African American homes received fewer services than white homes (Berrick, Barth, et al. 1994).

Courtney, Barth, et al. (1996), reviewing studies from several states, concluded that African American children were likely to remain in out-of-home care longer than white children. The average stay of all children in foster care in 1990 was seventeen months; African American children had an average stay of twenty-four months (Select Committee on Children 1990:39). Placement stability is another measure of the quality of the out-of-home care experience. Data on placement stability for children of different races is scarce, and results are mixed (Fanshel and Shinn 1978; Goerge, Wulczyn, et al. 1994). Children in kinship care tend to remain in foster care longer than children in regular foster care, but the placements tend to be more stable (Scannapieco, Hegar, et al. 1997:483).

The large number of children of color in out-of-home care raises questions about the effectiveness of family preservation services for these families. Morton (2001) suggests that there is no indication that African American families in the child welfare system have more problems than white families, and he suggests that it is tempting but unwise to think that the problems are substantively different. Race has not been a variable extensively examined in the studies of family preservation. Schuerman, Rzepnicki, et al. (1994), in a large study of family preservation in Illinois, found differences between families in the urban areas, where approximately 90 percent of the sample were African American, and more rural areas, which were predominantly white. Urban families tended to have problems related to child neglect, often due to substance abuse, while more rural families were more likely to be referred due to emotional problems, difficulties with relationships, and child behavior problems. The family preservation program was more successful in reducing the risk of placement for families with marital and emotional problems, and less successful in avoiding placement for families with cocaine problems. Thus the family preservation program was more successful with white families, but the difference could be related to the nature of the presenting issue and only indirectly to the race or ethnicity of the family or to the worker's skill or investment. This interpretation is congruent with that of Rodenborg (2001), who reports that her secondary analysis of the National Study of Protective and Preventive Services data indicates that even if white and African American families receive similar services, those services may be a better match to the needs of the white family than to the needs of the African American family. She notes that less than a quarter of the children in her sample had poverty-related needs met by the child welfare system, while 80 percent of the caretakers needing mental health or behavioral health services received them. The data are provocative, inconclusive, and worthy of serious attention.

In the area of adoption, race is hotly debated. Historically, children of color have left the foster care system for adoption at a much slower pace than white children. In 1998, of the 110,000 children waiting for adoption, 56 percent were African American; 28 percent were white (U.S. HHS, Children's Bureau 1999). The pressures of large numbers of children lingering in foster care led to the passage of the Adoption and Safe Families Act (ASFA); the problem of African American children spending long periods in foster care, and of large numbers of them waiting for adoptive homes, led to passage of the Multiethnic Placement Act of 1994 (MEPA) and the Interethnic Adoption Provisions Amendment (IEPA) in 1996.[7] These laws encouraged adoption and attempted to remove barriers; they imposed severe penalties on any agency that delayed an adoptive placement to await a race-matched home. (It should be noted that the act explicitly exempts Native American children who are protected by the Indian Child Welfare Act.) MEPA mandated, but did not fund, increased efforts at recruitment of adoptive homes among families of color.

The extent to which these new policies will enable larger numbers of African American children to move to adoptive homes remains to be seen. Early data suggest that more children are being freed for adoption; by September 1999, it was estimated that 127,000 were waiting for adoption. The data also suggest that a higher proportion of the African American children are finding adoptive homes; of the waiting children, 42 percent were African American and 32 percent white. Forty-three percent of adoptions from foster care in 1999 were adoptions of African American children (U.S. HHS, Children's Bureau 2001a).

Although these many indicators raise questions about inequities in the child welfare system, they do not provide guidance about how to improve child welfare services to erase the differences. It is evident that a bias against African American families appears early in the decision-making process. This is reinforced with every decision. Child welfare workers are predominantly white and middle class; services may be tailored to a similar community rather than matched to the needs of the African American community. Common sense suggests that the hiring of more minority child welfare workers would improve service delivery to populations of color, but there has been little conclusive research on the effectiveness of that strategy (Courtney, Barth, et al. 1996).

Given the level of poverty in the African American community, it may be that longer times in foster care and difficulty in finding adoptive homes are rooted in a system larger than the child welfare system. However, it is notable that Hispanic children, equally poor, are underrepresented in child welfare services. If this is in part because of differences in family and community structure, it provides a hint that services to support family functioning may be critical.

Conclusion

The need for interdisciplinary and intersystem collaboration is evident even from this brief exploration of the many systems that interact to provide for the protection of children and for services to enhance their well-being. Such cooperation will require increased understanding by all players of the various systems' distinct goals, their definitions of the primary client, their value systems, and their modes of working. The potential of interdisciplinary work and intersystem collaboration has been demonstrated in a variety of special projects around the country, but maintaining and expanding it will demand constant, thoughtful attention and work. Additionally, those working in the child welfare system should be aware of the indicators of racism, be constantly alert to its influence, and advocate strongly for policies that will mitigate its presence.

Notes

1. Capped funding is that in which the federal government allocates a certain amount to the states for a specific program; when that is spent there is no more. Funds for foster care are matched by the states, but there is no upper limit on the funds.

2. We will meet these National Incidence studies later in the chapter—they provide valuable insights into child protection, as well as providing data that suggest racism and other possible inequities in child welfare services.

3. For example, a series in the *Denver Post* reported on Colorado's largely privatized foster care system, in which 57 percent of foster children are placed in homes supervised by private businesses. The lead story not only reported serious maltreatment occurring in inadequately supervised foster homes, but also described the flow of public funds to support these foster care businesses, which were considerably more expensive but seemed to be providing essentially the same level of

care as public foster homes (P. Callahan and K. Mitchell, "Foster Care Too Often Fails to Keep Kids Safe," *Denver Post,* May 21, 2000).

4. Though some states have separated the dependency courts and the courts that handle delinquent youth, in many states these are combined in a court labeled "juvenile court"—meaning a court that handles matters pertaining to youth under the age of eighteen. Some states are developing "family courts," which commonly handle all matters relating to those under eighteen and to family matters such as divorce and child custody.

5. For an excellent discussion of the importance of schools in child welfare work, see A. N. Maluccio, B. Pine, et al., *Social Work Practice with Families and Children* (New York: Columbia University Press, 2002).

6. R. Karr-Morse and M. S. Wiley, in *Ghosts from the Nursery: Tracing the Roots of Violence* (New York: Atlantic Monthly Press, 1997), present a thorough and very readable discussion of the emerging knowledge of the effects of maltreatment on the development of the brain.

7. The provisions of ASFA, MEPA, and IEPA are outlined in chapter 2. Their implementation, their impact on services, and the issues surrounding transracial adoption are more extensively explored in chapter 8.

References

Berrick, J. C., R. Barth, et al. 1994. "A Comparison of Kinship Foster Homes and Foster Family Homes: Implications for Kinship Foster Care as Family Preservation." *Children and Youth Services Review* 16:34–50.

Costin, L. B., H. J. Karger, et al. 1996. *The Politics of Child Abuse in America.* New York: Oxford University Press.

Courtney, M. E., R. P. Barth, et al. 1996. "Race and Child Welfare Services: Past Research and Future Directions." *Child Welfare* 75(2): 99–137.

Dore, M. M. 1999. "Emotionally and Behaviorally Disturbed Children in the Child Welfare System: Points of Preventive Intervention." *Children and Youth Services Review* 21(1): 7–30.

Downs, S. W., E. Moore, et al. 2000. *Child Welfare and Family Services: Policies and Practice.* Boston: Allyn and Bacon.

Drais, A., G. Cyphers, et al. 2001. *The Child Welfare Workforce Challenge: Results from a Preliminary Survey.* Washington, D.C.: American Public Human Services Association.

English, D. 1998. "The Extent and Consequences of Child Maltreatment." *The Future of Children* 8(1): 39–53.

Fanshel, D., and E. B. Shinn. 1978. *Children in Foster Care: A Longitudinal Investigation.* New York: Columbia University Press.

Goerge, R. M., F. H. Wulczyn, et al. 1994. *Foster Care Dynamics: California, Illinois, Michigan, New York and Texas—A First-Year Report from the Multistate Foster Care Data Archive.* Chicago: Chapin Hall Center for Children.

Hegar, R. L., and R. Sullivan. 1994. "Are Legal Definitions of Child Abuse Too Broad?" In *Controversial Issues in Child Welfare,* edited by E. Gambrill and T. J. Stein. Boston: Allyn and Bacon.

House Committee on Ways and Means. 1998. *1998 Green Book: Section 11, Child Protection, Foster Care, and Adoption Assistance.* Washington, D.C.: U.S. Government Printing Office.

Hughes, R. C., and J. S. Rycus. 1998. *Developmental Disabilities and Child Welfare.* Washington, D.C.: Child Welfare League of America.

Kadushin, A., and J. Martin. 1988. *Child Welfare Services.* New York: Macmillan.

Larner, M. B., C. S. Stevenson, et al. 1998. "Protecting Children from Abuse and Neglect: Analysis and Recommendations." *The Future of Children* 8(1): 4–22.

Lindsey, D. 1994. *The Welfare of Children.* New York: Oxford University Press.

McCullough, C., and B. Schmitt. 1999. *CWLA Managed Care and Privatization Child Welfare Tracking Project: 1998 State and County Survey Results.* Washington, D.C.: Child Welfare League of America.

Morton, T. 2001. "Where Does It Begin?" In *Breaking the Silence: A Candid Discussion on the Disproportionality of African American Children in Out-of-Home Placement,* edited by G. D. Rooney. St. Paul: University of Minnesota School of Social Work.

Pecora, P. J., J. L. Whittaker, et al. 1992. *The Child Welfare Challenge: Policy, Practice, and Research.* New York: Aldine de Gruyter.

———. 2000. *The Child Welfare Challenge: Policy, Practice, and Research.* Second edition. New York: Aldine de Gruyter.

Rodenborg, N. 2001. "Response from the Field." In *Breaking the Silence: A Candid Discussion of the Disproportionality of African American Children in Out-of-Home Placement,* edited by G. D. Rooney. St. Paul: University of Minnesota School of Social Work.

Rosenthal, M. G. 2000. "Public or Private Children's Services? Privatization in Retrospect." *Social Service Review* 74(2): 281–306.

Scannapieco, M., R. L. Hegar, et al. 1997. "Kinship Care and Foster Care: A Comparison of Characteristics and Outcomes." *Families in Society* 78(5): 480–88.

Schuerman, J. R., T. L. Rzepnicki, et al. 1994. *Putting Families First: An Experiment in Family Preservation.* New York: Aldine de Gruyter.

Select Committee on Children, Youth, and Families. 1990. *No Place to Call Home: Discarded Children in America.* Washington, D.C.: U.S. House of Representatives.

U.S. Department of Health and Human Services, Children's Bureau. 1997. *National Study of Protective, Preventive and Reunification Services Delivered to Children and Their Families.* Washington, D.C.: U.S. Government Printing Office.

————. 1999. AFCARS Report No. 1. Available at http://www.acf.hhs.gov/programs/cb/publications/afcars/report1.htm.

————. 2000. *Child Maltreatment 1998: Reports from the States to the National Child Abuse and Neglect Data System. Highlights.* Washington, D.C.: U.S. Government Printing Office.

————. 2001a. AFCARS Report No. 6. Available at http://www.acf.hhs.gov/programs/cb/publications/afcars/report6.htm.

————. 2001b. *Child Maltreatment 1999: Reports from the States to the National Child Abuse and Neglect Data System.* Washington, D.C.: U.S. Government Printing Office.

————. 2002. "Child Welfare State Projects." U.S. Department of Health and Human Services, Administration for Children and Families, Office of State Systems, Washington, D.C. Available at http://www.acf.hhs.gov/programs/oss/sacwis/cwsstat.htm.

U.S. Department of Health and Human Services, National Center on Child Abuse and Neglect. 1996. *Third National Incidence Study of Child Abuse and Neglect.* Washington, D.C.: U.S. Government Printing Office.

Waldfogel, J. 1998. "Rethinking the Paradigm for Child Protection." *The Future of Children* 8(1): 104–20.

CHAPTER 4

◆

Community Services for Children and Families

with Karen Tvedt

To the extent a society protects and invests in its children, so will it ensure its future. To the extent that it does not, it imperils its existence.

LINDSEY 1994

The community services that support the functioning of children and families are interfacing systems. Many public systems, such as education and health systems, are used by virtually all families with children, and many private institutions, such as religious and recreational programs, have points of contact with them. A large number of families in contact with the child welfare system are involved in the justice system, and a great many are in need of income maintenance or income supplements, as well as child care. Navigating a path among these systems, each with its own policies and procedures, can be daunting. There is always the possibility that a family who requires help but is not fully eligible for services in any system may "fall between the cracks." Families access services at the community level, and it is there that whatever coordination of services exists most often takes place.

Family support services can be conceptualized as a pyramid-shaped continuum (figure 4.1). The services must rest on the secure base of the adequate resources needed by all families. As one ascends the pyramid, the number of families needing the services decreases and the intensity of the service increases. The middle tiers represent both broader services that assist in building parenting capacity and services targeted to specific problems. The top depicts the realm where the courts may mandate compliance with the service for the protection of children. This chapter discusses

FIGURE 4.1   Continuum of Services

Out-of-home care
Justice system institutions
Residential treatment centers
Therapeutic homes
Foster family homes

Families in crisis
Intensive family preservation services
Child protective services

Families needing intensive services
Substance abuse treatment
Mental health services
Domestic violence services
Services for children with incarcerated parents
Respite child care

Families needing some extra support
Home-visiting programs
Family support centers
Parent and child education programs

All families
Adequate income, housing, health care, child care, education, and recreational services

selected community-based services found toward the pyramid's base. Child protective services and intensive family preservation services are described in chapter 5, and out-of-home care is the subject of chapters 6 and 7.

Families Needing Intensive Services

A high proportion of the families who enter the child welfare system because their children need protective services are involved in the criminal justice system or have problems of substance abuse. Some have mental or physical health needs, many are overwhelmed by the demands of children with physical or behavioral difficulties, and family violence is common among them. These families are in need of specialized assistance if they are to successfully raise their children.

Substance Abuse Treatment

Substance abuse, as was noted in chapter 1, is a pervasive problem. It occurs in between one-third and two-thirds of families in contact with the child welfare system (U.S. Department of Health and Human Services [hereafter, U.S. HHS] 1999:1–2). Most children in substance-abusing families live with their parents throughout their childhood; 11 percent of children in the United States live with at least one parent who is either an alcoholic or in need of treatment for abusing illegal drugs (U.S. HHS 1999:1–2). Although the child welfare system commonly uses the "solution" of placing children in foster care until the parent is "clean and sober," it is probably more realistic to focus on careful assessment of the type of support available to parents that might enable them to care for their children, even if the parents are not completely successful in ending their use of alcohol or drugs.

Although the impact of prenatal exposure to alcohol or, to a lesser extent, drugs, can be very serious, evidence is accumulating that the quality of the postnatal environment is critical in helping the child overcome these handicaps. Parent-child interaction needs encouragement and support, as well as monitoring. If the child is placed in foster care and the mother referred for substance abuse treatment, it may be a long time before they are allowed to be together again.

Of course, children seldom enter the child welfare system because of parental substance abuse alone. Most families in the child welfare system have multiple problems. This complex set of difficulties prevents effective parenting. An early task of the child welfare worker is to distinguish whether substance abuse is the reason for the maltreatment or whether the relief of other familial stresses will be effective. Substance abuse treatment programs are moving toward new models that use case managers to help families address their multiple problems, as well as toward increased use of residential treatment approaches in which mothers can have young children with them.

Further complicating intervention, the timelines of planning are relatively short once a child is in foster care, both because children's development proceeds at a rapid pace and because the Adoption and Safe Families Act (ASFA) mandates permanency in little more than a year. Waiting lists for many treatment programs are long, particularly for those designed to meet the needs of women with children. Substance abuse is a chronic problem. Most of those who succeed in conquering an addiction do so over a period of years, during which they are counseled to live lives as free from stress as possible, and usually after one or more relapses. Less than one-third of substance abuse treatment clients achieve sustained abstinence after their first attempt at recovery. Another third eventually achieve long-term recovery but only after repeated episodes of relapse (U.S. HHS 1999). Increasingly, practitioners and policy makers recognize the importance of accommodating these recovery patterns:

> Families often come with serious problems to service systems which are fragmented, and as such are limited in their ability to facilitate safety, permanency, and sobriety. The Adoption and Safe Families Act recognizes the importance of time to children and establishes an expectation of urgency in decision making regarding their welfare. The imperative for timely decisions for children and the time frames necessary for recovery should also create a sense of urgency for policy makers and providers of service. Those of us who work in the areas of substance abuse and child welfare services must recognize the immediate need to eliminate barriers to effective treatment.
>
> (U.S. HHS 1999:8–8)

Horn (1994) writes that the current model of child welfare, in which a family is supposed to be "fixed" during a child's brief stay in foster care, will not work when substance abuse is the underlying problem causing child maltreatment; rather, a new model is needed. Adoption will be appropriate for some children. However, when a child does go home, increased use of home visitation and protective service monitoring will also be needed, and cases that are open for a long time should not be considered to have poor outcomes. Horn (1994) also notes the need for increased tolerance of repeated episodes of foster care as parents relapse. The use of relatives for foster care is, he suggests, the best way to insure that children will return to the same foster home each time foster care is needed. Foley (1994) adds that for some of these children long-term foster care will provide the greatest stability and should be an acceptable plan.

Mental Health Services

Mental health services can be even more difficult to access, because they are scarce and often not well covered by insurance plans. However, substance abuse and mental illness present similar issues in that individuals often become stabilized, only to destabilize a few months later. Both problems require specialized treatment and long-term planning. Perhaps the most difficult and fundamental aspect of the interaction between mental health and child welfare is the assessment of the degree of threat to the child's well-being posed by the illness and, if the threat is great, of the probability that the parent will have periods of reasonable stability that are sufficient in length for raising a child.

Among the families we know is a Vietnamese single parent. Ms. V. is quite alone; she left Vietnam among the boat people and after time in a refugee camp came to the United States as an unaccompanied minor. She has four young children, the oldest eight. Each has a different father, and none of the fathers remains in contact with her. She came to the attention of protective services when she responded to neighbor complaints about her children's behavior by threatening to kill herself and her children. She was also observed chasing her children with a knife, threatening to kill them for misbehavior. This situation raised many questions for the protective service worker.

Is her mental health status such that she is likely to carry out her threats? Or is she expressing a lesser degree of despair in a way more congruent with her culture than with mainstream American culture? Can she be referred to appropriate diagnostic and treatment services and receive them quickly so that decisions can be made about the necessity of placing her children? Can she access community mental health services to sustain her functioning, so that if the children must be placed to assure their safety, the placement will be brief? Or if the mental illness is serious and pervasive, will it prevent her caring for her children for a long period of time to the extent that an alternative family, perhaps an adoptive family, should be considered?

These are the types of questions that weigh on child welfare workers. It may not be easy to find answers.

Community mental health services have been chronically underfunded. With the deinstitutionalization of the mentally ill in the 1960s came the promise to provide mental health services in the community. Adequate funding for these services never materialized. The presence of homeless mentally ill persons on the streets of many major cities is a testament to our failure to provide care. With services in short supply, both parents and children who need mental health assessments or treatment may be forced to endure long waiting periods or be unable to access services at all. Again, delayed access to services for parents can conflict with the short timelines for planning for children.

Support for Incarcerated Mothers

Parents in the criminal justice system face great difficulties in developing or retaining bonds with their children; because mothers are usually the primary caretakers of children, this is of particular concern when they go to prison. Furthermore, the number of female prisoners has increased in recent years, from about 6,000 in 1972 (Beckerman 1994) to 63,000 in 1998 (Young and Smith 2000:130). More than two-thirds of these women have children. While their mothers are incarcerated, the children live with their fathers (about 20%), with grandparents (about 50%), with other relatives (about 20%), in foster care (about 8%), or with friends or in other arrangements (Young and Smith 2000:131). The relatives who care for these children are subject to all of the stresses of kinship foster care, reviewed in chapter 7. Income may be supplemented through Temporary Assistance for Needy Families (TANF) grants. Higher subsidies, without time limits, are available if these homes become kinship foster homes. However, some families are reluctant to go that route because it means they must share decision-making responsibility for the child with the state child welfare agency.

When children are in formal foster care, the public child welfare agency assumes responsibility for overseeing their care and planning for their future. Most mothers plan to reunite with their children after incarceration. However, if sentences are long and the children young, child welfare agencies may consider the benefits to the child of placement in an alternative permanent home. To participate in this planning, incarcerated mothers must be in contact with the caseworker, take part in the discussion of case plans, and be notified of and able to attend each case review (Beckerman 1994). Given the strictures of prison life, ensuring that mothers have this access requires child welfare workers to be energetic and organized.

Another, more subtle concern for incarcerated mothers is how they can develop and maintain a strong attachment to their children and work on their parenting skills so that when they are discharged they will be good parents. That prisons are often located in remote sites, and visitation strictly monitored and often uncomfortable for the visitors, can hinder this process.[1] However, scattered programs throughout the prison system attempt to bring children into the lives of incarcerated parents in ways that are as natural as possible and promote parent-child interaction. A small number of progressive prison systems are beginning to develop residential wings in which infants and very young children can remain with, and be cared for by, their mothers. It is a wonderful opportunity for observing mother-child interaction, teaching parenting skills, and supporting the growth of a new family.

> *Unfortunately, the experience of a young woman we learned of recently is more typical. She was in prison when her child was born. She had the baby with her for the twenty-four hours that both remained in the hospital. Then the child was placed in foster care—in this case not with relatives but in a home the mother was unfamiliar with. There was a family planning meeting about the future of the child. The mother was informed of the date and time of the meeting, but the caseworker did not explain its purpose. The court did not request her presence. No one requested transportation. Nobody thought of modern technology such as a speakerphone. Thus she did not attend.*
>
> *This mother will be released from prison within a year or two—most mothers emerge from prison within a relatively short period of time. Will she have lost her parental rights because she has had no opportunity to demonstrate her ability to parent? If she retains the right to raise the child, how will she and her child bond, when there has been no opportunity for interaction? These are the difficult questions that highlight the need for closer cooperation between the child welfare system and the corrections system.*

Family Violence

As noted in chapter 1, it is estimated that between 30 and 60 percent of the time, violence toward women is accompanied by violence toward children (Edleson 1999). Increasingly, family violence results in involvement with the criminal justice system, and sometimes in the incarceration of the offender. Systems must work together to protect children in violent families, while affirming the capacity of the victims of violence to control their lives. The women's shelter movement, the criminal justice system, and the child welfare system may all be involved. Because most victims of family violence are women, intervention methods that encourage women to protect themselves have been developed within a feminist framework. The goal is to empower the victim so that she can either leave the abuser or create a system to protect herself and her children. Child welfare services, when they intervene to protect children, can revictimize the woman, who is implicitly accused of not protecting her children. If space is not available in a shelter (there are often waiting lists), the children may be removed from the mother while she waits for placement. This philosophical conflict, explored more extensively in chapter 1, has only begun to be recognized. Battered women's shelters and services and child welfare services have started to develop protocols so that they can together serve these troubled families.

Respite Care

The discussion of respite care could appear in any of several chapters in this book, for respite care is important to any family whose coping capacities are stretched by caring for children, whether they are birth families, foster families, or adoptive families. It can take place in a family or a group setting. Considering that probably its most common use is to prevent the placement of children in foster care, this chapter seems the most appropriate.

Not too long ago, children with severe developmental delays and physical disabilities were cared for in institutions. As it came to be recognized that these youngsters had better opportunities to develop to their full capacity within the community, more and more families kept them at home. Institutions that had given lifetime care to these youngsters were gradually closed, as were the institutions that had served the mentally ill. In all spheres of care for people with disabilities, there was a movement to get people out of the isolation of institutions and to expose them to the opportunities of community life.

The development of respite services accompanied the deinstitutionalization movement. As parents began to care for children with disabilities in their homes, the need emerged for occasional relief from the extensive demands of their care. Respite care can be critical in enabling a birth family to continue to care for a child. It can be critical too in avoiding the need to remove child from one foster home to another. Families who have adopted children with complex needs and severe behavioral problems find respite care invaluable. Whether it takes the form of day care, family care, or institutional care, the goal is to provide relief to the primary family so that continuity of care can be maintained for the child.

Early sources of funding were Medicaid waivers, in individual cases of families caring for a physically disabled child, and through the Child and Adolescent Service System Project, which provided money to states for the development of services to children with emotional handicaps. In the early stages funding was, however, uncertain. In 1988 the financial base became more stable when federal funding was provided under the Temporary Care for Children with Disabilities and Crisis Nurseries Act of 1986 (as amended). Under the provisions of this act, grants are awarded for the development of programs to support families of children who are at risk for abuse or neglect or who have disabilities. Various renamings and consolidations of the act have occurred since, each increasing the collaboration among community programs to support families. The latest consolidations emphasize collaboration among family preservation efforts, family resource centers, and respite care providers.

As broadly defined, respite care is used by almost all parents in the form of school or child care, after-school programs, summer camps, or just a grandmother or baby-sitter coming in for an afternoon. Children with special medical or behavioral needs can be very challenging to care for, however, and parents have difficulty finding neighborhood services with the appropriate expertise.

Respite care can take the form of group care of children, usually coupled with interventions that teach and support positive parent-child interactions. Crisis nurseries emerged early in the respite care movement to provide day care relief for families of children with disabilities. Their larger role has been in the prevention of abuse and neglect: the observed interaction of parents and children in the nursery setting offers opportunity for assistance in the development of parenting skills.

Ms. W. was a single mother with three young children. The oldest, a four-year-old, was a particularly trying little boy. He was very active and did not seem responsive to Ms. W.'s disciplinary attempts. More and more she found herself yelling at him and hitting him in frustration. A visiting nurse, there to help with the youngest (very new) member of the family, suggested a relief nursery.

A plan was formed. The four-year-old went to the relief nursery five afternoons a week. Twice a week Ms. W. stayed with him for an hour, and staff members watched her interact with him and made suggestions to enhance parenting skills. But, most important, Ms. W had time without him, to get

> *her house in order, to tend to her younger children, and even sometimes to nap while they napped. The relief from the constant and challenging care of this boy made a great difference in Ms. W.'s patience and parenting capacity when he was at home. The possibility of abuse, and possibly even of an out-of-home placement, disappeared.*

Family respite care is usually planned on an individual basis; that is, a single family becomes the respite care provider for a particular child. The discontinuity occasioned by respite care is not ideal for children and is minimized if the same family is used each time a respite is needed. Often a respite family receives general training in meeting the child's special needs, but the provider is also encouraged to follow the instructions of the parents and to attempt to maintain continuity for the child between home and respite. Communication between the two families is vital, and often the caseworker assumes the role of facilitating that communication.

> *The M. family had taken in Mr. M.'s sister's new baby as a foster child eight years ago. They had comforted her incessant crying and held her and talked to her as she grew, and had grown very attached to her. Sadly they recognized that she was very slow in mastering developmental tasks. Even more sadly, they recognized that her abilities to reason and to manage her emotions had been affected by her mother's drinking before she was born. Nevertheless, when it became apparent that her mother was not going to be able to make a home for her, the M.s decided to adopt the child. By the time she was eight years old they were exhausted, their marriage was strained, and their older children were clamoring for some time to do things together without the constant distraction of a constantly-in-trouble sister. Mr. and Mrs. M. began to consider the possibility of another family for the girl.*
>
> *A respite foster home proved a better answer. The M.s sought help from the agency that had handled their foster parenting and adoption and learned about the possibility of respite care. Interviews and observations enabled the worker to get to know their daughter and the methods they used to manage her behavior. The foster home that was selected had received training as a respite home, emphasizing communication with the child's own family and commitment to managing behavior as the family did. The daughter went to the respite home for one weekend a month.*
>
> *Once she got to know the family, the child rather enjoyed the change of pace and different activities provided. She seemed content to go and content*

> *to return home—though of course she tried to tell each family what the other one let her do. That was when communication between families became important. And the M.s greatly enjoyed a weekend a month when they could focus on themselves and their older children and do the things that cannot be done with an active eight-year-old . . . though sometimes they missed her.*

Respite care is beginning to assume its place in the continuum of services for children with special needs, whether they are in their own homes or in foster or adoptive families. The most important point about respite care is that it is always viewed as temporary and focused on enhancing and stabilizing the parent-child relationship.

Families Needing Some Extra Support

Family support services can, to some extent, be conceptualized as services that have developed to provide help to families, as the mobility of the twentieth century began to remove parents and children from their extended families and from closely knit communities. Many of these services perform functions that resemble roles played by extended families or community organizations, such as religious institutions and neighborhood clubs.

By establishing settlement houses in the late nineteenth century, Jane Addams and others pioneered family support programs and access to services for community residents. The work of the settlement houses embodied many of the concepts of modern community support programs. They used what is now termed an ecological model, recognizing that the lives of families were in many ways impacted by the communities in which they lived. Through a combination of political advocacy, classes, political discussion groups, and recreational programs, they worked to improve life for community residents. They empowered participants to create change in their families and communities. They also opened their doors to all members of the community, not just families who had specific problems.

The social reform movement of the 1960s gave impetus to the development of family support programs. Volunteers in Service to America (VISTA) worked in many communities, empowering residents to change their communities to better meet their own needs. Head Start, a comprehensive preschool program for disadvantaged children, was probably the most directly influential family support program begun in that era. "Head Start's developers were the first to design a national education program acknowledging the interrelatedness of health, nutrition, parent involvement, and children's learning" (Allen, Brown, et al. 1992:14). Parent-child centers were funded under Head Start to provide low-income parents of infants and toddlers guidance in stimulating early development and to assist families with nutrition, health information, personal and economic problems, and obtaining social services. More recently, concern about the number of teen parents, and their difficulties, has led to many programs focused on providing information, support services, and usually child care so that parents can finish high school.

Family support programs—with their key principles, identified by Allen, Brown, and colleagues (1992), of empowering and strengthening families, making participation voluntary, developing parenting skills, and nurturing community connections—fit the political agendas of almost everyone. With their goal of strengthening families, they appeal to the most conservative members of society; with their promise of assistance in obtaining educational, emotional, or more specific resources, they fit liberal philosophies.

Despite this almost universal appeal, family support services are usually small programs offered by private agencies. Funding has traditionally come from local sources, supplemented by grants from foundations and government programs and charitable giving by the community. Funding has been scarce, and most programs report much greater need than they can meet. Many of the family support programs have focused on the prevention of child abuse and neglect. Because resources are limited, some have targeted their services to high-risk families, whereas others have made services available to all families within a limited geographic area.

There have been a few publicly funded programs. Head Start, though it began as an educational program for young children, evolved into a program in which involvement of families and concern about the overall well-being of children were important. Healthy Start, a program that targets at-risk families and provides extensive home-visiting services, began in 1975 in Hawaii with funding from the National Center on Child Abuse and Neglect. In 1984 the Hawaii legislature authorized its expansion in collaboration with the Hawaii Department of Public Health.

The Family Preservation and Support Services Act of 1993, an amendment to Title IV-B of the Social Security Act, continued funding for family preservation, and it authorized funding for family support services offered through state child welfare agencies. This funding gave a more solid base to family support programs: in 1997 the U.S. General Accounting Office reported that states were expanding their family services, using 44 percent of the federal dollars for family support services and 56 percent for family preservation (Downs, Moore, et al. 2000:81). Given that in the last ten years public child welfare has narrowed its focus to work with only those families where relatively serious maltreatment has occurred, this expenditure doubtless reflects the recognition that these family support services have to exist somewhere in the community. It indicates an attempt to build a community service structure that will meet the needs of families who are no longer eligible for service in the public system but who can benefit from help.

Family Resource Centers

Family resource centers are as varied as the communities they serve. Usually located in a neighborhood house, they offer a variety of educational programs, services, and support. Many have "drop-in" programs, children's play groups, and self-help groups focused on a variety of difficulties. Some have home-visiting programs. Most have close links to other community services and can help families access the services that the family resource center does not provide. Some, in the tradition of the settlement house, are active in advocacy and in facilitating community change. Allen and colleagues begin a description of five varied family resource centers:

> Imagine a place . . .
>   . . . where a young mother can go for support and encouragement when she feels overwhelmed by her responsibilities at home.
>   . . . where she and her children can drop in for a hot lunch, visit with other mothers while the children play, and get some professional advice about a child's special health needs.
>   . . . where someone has time to sit and talk with her about her own education goals and help her plan the next step toward reaching them.
>   . . . where a group of parents can sit and talk with a professional about how to help their children cope with violence in their neighborhood.

> . . . where a parent who has just completed a drug treatment
> program or had her children returned from foster care can find out
> about available community resources.
>
> (ALLEN, BROWN, ET AL. 1992:5)

Such programs are indeed in the tradition of the settlement house and
also at the forefront of the integrated services, "one-stop-shopping"
models of current social work. Note the community outreach in the program description—such resource centers help with everyday difficulties
and are a starting place for work on more complex issues.

Home-Visiting Programs

Home-visiting programs reach out to families with young children. They
focus on the important early years in a child's life and aim to influence
parental behavior in order to optimize children's development. Research
that shows the importance of very early years to child development and
early program evaluations that show positive changes in parenting have
made these programs popular; there are now thousands across the country.
Unlike the home-visiting programs of the Charity Organization Societies,
which sought to identify the "worthy poor," current home-visiting programs seek to be inclusive. They also reach out to families that may be
too isolated or mired in troubles to access community programs.

The programs vary in explicit goals and in home visitor qualifications.
Some programs target high-risk families; others attempt to serve all families in a geographic area. Engaging families in the use of these programs
is a major difficulty: only about half of the families originally targeted
receive extensive help. With few exceptions, evaluations using control group
designs have failed to find statistically significant changes in behavior as a
result of the home visiting. What changes there are usually manifest themselves in parent attitudes (Gomboy, Culross, et al. 1999).

The most extensive home-visiting program is Healthy Families America
(HFA), a nationwide support program modeled on Hawaii's Healthy
Start. Begun in 1992 by Prevent Child Abuse America (then known as the
National Committee to Prevent Child Abuse), it has now been implemented
in more than three hundred culturally and geographically diverse communi-
ties and has a presence in forty-four states (Daro and Harding 1999).

Healthy Families America has a dual commitment: system reform and
development of community capacity to support families, on the one hand,

and the provision of direct services to families, on the other. Most effort has gone into the development of the individual home-visiting programs. Although they vary in their outreach strategies and specific goals, all the programs deliver services of sufficient intensity and duration to assist families during the child's early years—services can continue until a child is five years old (Daro and Harding 1999).

One question raised about home-visiting programs is whether it is possible to use paraprofessionals or whether specific skills are needed. A survey in the late 1990s of the HFA sites showed that 9 percent of the visitors had some college or an associate's degree, 35 percent were college graduates, and 9 percent had postgraduate training. The most common areas of specialization were child development (25%), social work (20%), education (11%), and nursing (10%) (Daro and Harding 1999:157). Given the small percentage of workers in the field with education beyond college, one would guess that these programs use visitors with a bachelor's of social work degree. Because of the generalist nature of the home visitor's work, this seems appropriate.

The evaluation of these programs takes place through a research network established by Prevent Child Abuse America, which attempts to bring together the evaluations of its own individual programs and the evaluations of other home-visiting programs. The intent is to build a knowledge base for the development of home-visiting programs. Although there have been few rigorous evaluations, initial data indicate that the programs seem to be meeting the goal of preventing maltreatment and promoting positive parent-child interaction. However, it has been noted that

> although several communities have implemented strong, intensive home visitation programs, none of the efforts covered by these early evaluations has been taken to scale (that is, none has provided access to support services for more than 20 percent of the communities' newborns and their parents). Nor have they fully incorporated the type of community change recommended in HFA's overall theory of change. HFA efforts are not well integrated into existing child welfare response systems, nor have they become an integral component of public health care systems.
>
> (DARO AND HARDING 1999:168)

The building of this family support programs network is itself an attempt to convert "to scale" the home-visiting programs of individual communities. It remains to be seen whether, as they become more universal, these programs can retain the intensity and extent of services that seem to have a positive impact on some families.

Parent Training Programs

Parent training programs are similar in their goals to home-visiting programs. However, parent training is primarily a cognitive approach: the teaching of parenting skills. Usually this takes place in a group setting, though some parent training programs have options such as one-to-one instruction in the parents' homes. Community-based parent training programs are usually found in school and public health settings, where there are groups of young parents-to-be or of parents naturally assembled. Because all parents have some doubts and difficulties while raising children, parenting workshops are offered throughout the community to parents of all socioeconomic backgrounds.

There is probably no service more frequently purchased by child welfare agencies than parent training. One of the causes of maltreatment is lack of knowledge about child development and about what children can do at various ages. Parent training programs are an excellent vehicle for conveying this knowledge. They are also useful in teaching techniques of behavior management. It is also expected that participation in a parent training group will increase awareness of others' needs and thus increase family support and cohesion. Enhancement of self-esteem and general improvement of child-rearing skills are hoped-for outcomes. In addition, parents find support in meeting with other parents and discussing mutual difficulties and solutions.

There are many parent training curriculums and approaches to curriculum delivery. Among the parent training programs, the Incredible Years Training Series has received some attention recently; a description of it provides a good example of a parent training program. As reported by Webster-Stratton (2000), the Incredible Years Parents, Teachers, and Children Training Series uses group discussion, videotape modeling, and rehearsal of intervention techniques to assist parents of children aged two to ten who have conduct problems. Based on cognitive social-learning theory, it teaches reinforcement skills and nonviolent discipline techniques. The primary goal is to reduce these conduct problems while increasing children's social, emotional, and academic competence; improving parental competence and strengthening families are also goals. The program can also be used to help teachers learn techniques for managing classrooms.

Evaluation of the Incredible Years program has been unusually rigorous. A series of studies, using randomly assigned control group designs, have consistently shown positive gains for participating parents across different socioeconomic groups. One study with a one-year follow-up demonstrated that gains are maintained. Another, randomized study was conducted to determine which component of the program was most effective. All proved effective; a self-administered video component alone was the least costly and produced changes comparable to group therapy, but was not as well liked by participants (Webster-Stratton 2000).

Self-Help Groups

Self-help groups have become popular in American culture, perhaps another manifestation of American independence and individualism. They are common in substance abuse treatment; Alcoholics Anonymous is perhaps the best known. Those for parenting often address issues related to children with particular characteristics: transracially adopted children, children adopted when older, foster children, children with particular medical problems, and children with behavioral disturbances.

Parents Anonymous is one of the best-known self-help organizations. Its philosophy embodies the values of family empowerment and professional guidance based on recognition of family strengths that are the hallmark of the best current child welfare services. Founded by a parent in 1970, it is the oldest of the child abuse prevention organizations. Each year, approximately 100,000 parents come together in Parents Anonymous groups "to learn new skills, transform their attitudes and behaviors, and create long-term positive changes in their lives" (Rafael and Pion-Berlin 1999:1). With a program philosophy of shared leadership, each group has a parent leader and a professionally trained facilitator. Children's groups run simultaneously in some settings; in others, child care is provided. Many state and local organizations also run twenty-four-hour telephone help lines for parents seeking immediate help with their responses to their children. There is a strong public awareness component to the program, including outreach to potential participants.

Parents join Parents Anonymous because they want to change their behavior toward their children and because they seek help, information, and support in managing specific issues facing their families. Sometimes attendance is mandated by a court order or child protective services agreement. The groups reach across gender and racial lines. About a third of the participants are male. Fifty-one percent of the participants are white; 22 percent are Hispanic, 21 percent African American, 5 percent American Indian, and 1 percent Asian or Pacific Islander (Rafael and Pion-Berlin 1999:4).

To join a Parents Anonymous group takes some courage; it involves the recognition that one's own behavior needs to be changed. Parents at risk of involvement in the child welfare system are often stigmatized and often socially isolated. The organization's ability to reach out successfully across racial groups speaks to its capacity for developing culturally appropriate services when parents themselves are in leadership positions. Cameron and Birnie-Lefcovitch (2000), describing a parent mutual aid program in child welfare, report that "members expressed a pride, a sense of ownership and protectiveness towards the program, and an enthusiasm about their involvement that is hard to match in programs designed and delivered solely by professionals" (p. 435).

Each group has a parent leader and a professional leader. The professionals come from many different disciplines. Maintaining true joint leadership can be difficult for professionals, particularly those who have been working in child welfare. The shared decision making differs from their usual mode of working. Some find it difficult to accept that parents are as competent as professionals to assess the needs of children and to plan meetings that will help other parents meet those needs. Specific training and supervision in the shared leadership role may be necessary.

There have not been rigorous outcome evaluations of Parents Anonymous. The literature on self-help groups suggests that the support of other parents faced with similar situations can lead to a positive changes in self-esteem and attitudes toward parenting, as well as positive changes in perceived social support (Cameron and Birnie-Lefcovitch 2000).

Head Start

Head Start is the largest of the early intervention programs specifically targeted at children at risk—those whose environment is impoverished to the extent that they are likely to experience delays in mental development and start school at a disadvantage. Begun in 1965 as part of the expansion of social programs at that time, it is a national program that has served more than 15 million children (Karoly, Greenwood, et al. 1998).

Head Start was designed as a comprehensive intervention, with a home-visiting as well as a child care center component. Concern about school readiness dominated the early years of the program, however, and the classroom component and its effect on children's IQ scores have received most of the attention.

There is a vast body of research literature concerning Head Start. Early studies showed few cognitive gains, and those that did exist seemed to disappear early in the following school years. In a 1974 review, Broffenbrenner emphasized the importance of family in fostering development and advocated emphasis on the parent participation component of the program as a remedy for the fading of early gains (Broffenbrenner 1974, reported in Karoly, Greenwood, et al. 1998). Parent involvement has become a more important component of Head Start, and more recent studies have found more favorable and lasting effects on test scores and school attainment (Karoly, Greenwood, et al. 1998:44).

The High/Scope Perry Preschool Project of Ypsilanti, Michigan, deserves particular note. Created in 1962 as an attempt to remedy the poor school achievement of disadvantaged children, it used highly trained teachers and very small classes. The home-visiting component was also important, and fairly intensive work was done with some families. The number of children served was small—123 children in all. There was also a randomly assigned control group, and the two groups of children and families have been followed for more than twenty-two years. Outcomes have been positive. Children enrolled in the program had short-term IQ gains that tended to disappear later. However, academic achievement was maintained: program participants had more successful school careers and were more likely to graduate from high school. Crime and delinquency rates were lower and incomes higher (Schweinhart, Barnes, et al. 1993). Reading the report, one senses a domino effect at work—a better start led to earlier academic success, which led to greater commitment to school, and subsequently to better outcomes. One is tempted to wonder whether the national Head Start programs might have similar results had they been funded to provide a similar intensity of service.

Meeting the Needs of All Families

All families need adequate income, housing, health care, child care, education, and recreational and spiritual programs in order to successfully raise children. In the United States, we have decided to assume public responsibility for the education of children. Although many difficulties remain in securing education of equal quality for all children, some of which were noted in chapter 1, education is at least recognized as a family support service that the state should provide to all children. Other fundamental needs, the state has decided, should be met through the individual efforts of families. Only if a family demonstrates its inability to provide for itself will the state step in with "residual" programs. This section briefly reviews some of these basic programs. The next section looks in greater depth at child care, a pressing need in our changing society.

Income Maintenance

As discussed in chapter 2, the United States has opted for a policy of residual help to families and children in poverty, stepping in when there is a crisis or in certain desperate circumstances, rather than developing a program that would ensure all children, as an entitlement, a basic standard of living. In this policy one sees the United States' commitment to individualism and self-sufficiency. In all other advanced, industrialized countries, programs such as children's allowances create a basic income level for all children, regardless of their family's income level, as an entitlement. The following case excerpt shows the predicament some parents face trying to maintain a sufficient level of income while caring for children.

One of the families we knew was a single mother with five children; the oldest was nine, the youngest a toddler. She came to the attention of protective services when a neighbor called the police to complain that the children had been left alone. The police arrived to indeed find the children alone. By the time their mother returned from the grocery store with supplies for Thanksgiving dinner, the children had been taken to foster care. They were returned to her care after the holiday weekend, on condition that the children be properly supervised.

Thus began a saga that continued for several months and was not resolved when we last interviewed the mother. Ms. G. had some clerical skills and experience, and she could find low-wage employment without too much difficulty. When she was not working, she took good care of her children. When she had work, she had difficulty arranging child care. Sometimes she left them alone for short periods of time when the alternative was to miss work; then neighbors would report to protective services that the children

> *were again unsupervised. Sometimes she was late to work in order to wait for caregiver or missed a day's work when things really went wrong. She would miss enough work, or be late often enough, that she would lose her job. She would stay home and care for her children, and the protective service worker would feel that all was going well. Then the TANF worker would be insistent that she look for new employment, and the cycle would begin again.*

The philosophy of income maintenance legislation is to provide little enough help that families are encouraged to be self-supporting, while providing employment counseling and child care sufficient to allow mothers with small children to obtain full-time employment. Time limits on the duration of income assistance are an added incentive to join the workforce. Ignored are the difficulties of supporting a family on a minimum-wage job, even if parents work full time, and of attaining full-time child care for young children. In the strong economy of the 1990s, with rapid job growth rates, welfare reform had success in moving recipients to employment. Experiences during economic downturns are likely to be different.

It is unlikely that any prosperous and peaceful community will allow children, in large numbers and over time, to be homeless or hungry. Just how these children will be provided for, when there is no longer income assistance for their parents, is uncertain. It is possible that there may be additional stress on the foster care system or that congregate care may again become an option for children. It is almost certain that more families will struggle with extreme poverty and with unmet needs for housing, medical care, and child care. Sad effects on children's lives can be expected.

Health Care

Every other industrialized nation in the world has universal health coverage, whereas in the United States only those over sixty-five years of age have guaranteed coverage. Almost 20 percent of our families whose members are under sixty-five have no medical insurance. Eighty-five percent of them have at least one family member working, usually at a low-wage job that does not provide medical insurance benefits. They do not earn enough to afford insurance. *Consumer Reports* (September 2000) states that for these families, medical care often consists of treating the presenting symptom but does not provide the diagnostic work and follow-up necessary to manage serious or chronic illness. Although in many communities free or low-cost medical care and prescription drugs can be obtained in neighborhood clinics, which are funded by a mix of federal, state, and local dollars, capacity falls far short of the number of patients seeking help. The number of people seeking care from these clinics has increased by 45 percent in the last decade.

Health care is available to very poor children and families through Medicaid (and to those over sixty-five through Medicare). The program has made a difference: before Medicaid was enacted in 1966, poor families were dependent on charity, and many went without needed medical care. The advent of Medicaid coincides with a dramatic drop in infant mortality rates and with decreases in death rates from childbirth (72% decrease), from influenza and pneumonia (53%), from tuberculosis (52%), and from diabetes (31%). In addition, children covered by Medicaid are more likely to receive immunizations and preventive health care than are uninsured children (Schorr 1988:125). Medicaid has been separated from welfare under TANF, and there are concerns about the dropping Medicaid rolls that seem to have resulted as families have been diverted from welfare and moved into the workforce.

Growing recognition that the purchase of health care is not within the means of many families has led to at least the beginnings of a movement to insure that children have access to health care. The Oregon Health Plan, which has used a Medicaid waiver and state funds to extend coverage to low-income children—the plan is able to afford this by refusing to pay for certain extremely expensive procedures—is an example of a program that developed out of these concerns. Certainly, good health care is an important component of the well-being of children.

Affordable and Safe Housing

The lack of affordable housing was discussed in chapter 1. Unfortunately, there is little to add about social programming to address this problem. The absence of programs in this sphere demonstrates the "philosophical redirection of public policy to eliminate the role of the federal government in housing" (Mulroy and Ewalt 1996:125). About a third of the homeless are families with children (Children's Defense Fund 1998). Although the vast majority of poor families live in private rental housing, in 1996 there were 4 million people in public housing, and the median household income of those families was $6,420. Sixty-four percent were people of color; about half had children (Mulroy and Ewalt 1996).

Current initiatives focus on the use of subsidies and vouchers to help the poor afford private rental housing. The success of this program, of course, depends on the availability of low-rent housing and the willingness of landlords to rent to poor families with children. However, the supply of affordable housing for those with very low incomes is diminishing. There are no federal policy initiatives to increase levels of housing subsidy or to assure that subsidized housing is reserved for the very poor. Innovative programs in public housing and subsidized housing have begun to show success in providing stable, safe, and affordable housing (Mulroy and Ewalt 1996). However, there is no vocal constituency to publicize and promote these projects. The resultant transient living and sometimes homelessness is a major problem for families with children, and safe and affordable housing can make the difference between a family that stays together or is reunified, on the one hand, and long-term foster care for children, on the other.

Critical Issue: Child Care

With the changing labor market, increased numbers of working parents, and the shift in welfare policy from economic maintenance to work for low-income families, child care has emerged as a critical support to most families with young children. Increasingly, quality child care supports a broad range of public policy goals including family economic self-sufficiency, child health and well-being, school readiness, economic productivity, and our collective future. For low-income and at-risk families especially, child care has a lot of potential, largely untapped, to support parents, child development, and early intervention.

Unlike in most other modern industrialized countries, attitudes about the appropriate role of mothers and individual family responsibility in the United States have limited our collective involvement in child care. To the extent that a child care system exists, it has evolved as a privately purchased service, dependent on market forces and what parents can afford. Government involvement at federal, state, and local levels has typically been limited to minimum health and safety requirements for child care providers and subsidies to promote low-income working families' access to the child care market.

Historical Perspective: A Mother's Place Is in the Home?

Child care was always essential when economic hardship forced both parents to work or when a single parent was forced to support the family.

Records of the orphanages of the 1800s document the admittance of children because a single parent needed child care so that employment would be possible (McCausland 1976). In the factory conditions of the nineteenth century, both women and children worked long hours under dangerous conditions. Older neighborhood women sometimes provided care for children too young to work. And because so many young girls were the caretakers of younger siblings, settlement houses formed "little mother groups" to teach these girls how to care for their siblings (Nasaw 1985). Infant schools and day nurseries first emerged in Europe and then in the United States with the dual purpose of instilling societal norms and values in young children and freeing parents to work (Fein and Clarke-Stewart 1973; Schorr 1974; Steinfels 1973).

Within the middle and upper classes, the cults of motherhood and domesticity evolved during the 1800s and early 1900s. Gordon argues that early social workers viewed women's involvement with home and family as critical to women, children, and the social order (Gordon 1973). This view of the role of women emerged along with the notion that male workers should earn "family wages," an ideal that did not become a reality for many of them, especially those who were ethnic minorities.

In arguing for widows' pensions, the women's and early social work movements unified behind widows' pensions and argued that mothers should not work but rather care for their children at home. Jane Addams is quoted as saying that the working immigrant mother is "bent under the double burden of earning the money which supports her children and giving the tender care which alone keeps them alive" (Fein and Clarke-Stewart 1973:16). This belief that mothers should not work outside the home influenced the creation of Aid to Dependent Children, discussed earlier in this chapter and in chapter 2.

During World War II, when large numbers of mothers were needed in the labor force, Congress passed the Community Facilities Act, also known as the Lanham Act. Funding for the Lanham Act nurseries was provided through Department of Education budgets (Steinfels 1973; Tuttle 1992). Believing that the care of mothers was vital to young children, many social welfare workers remained opposed to any service that seemed to encourage mothers to work outside the home. Prior to the act's passage, articles and speeches warned against women working. Frances Perkins, the only woman in Roosevelt's Cabinet, is quoted as saying to the Children's Bureau staff, "What are you doing to prevent the spread of the day nursery system which I regard as a most unfortunate reaction of the hysterical propaganda about recruiting women workers?" (Goodwin 1994:416).

By the end of the war, almost $50 million had been spent on child care; in July 1945, more than 1.5 million children were being served. Despite 5,914 letters, wires, cards, and petitions in favor of keeping the Lanham Act nurseries open, the effort resulted in a mere four-month extension in funding (Tuttle 1992). There is evidence that many social workers did not support continuation of the nurseries, and at least one governor accused advocates of retaining the nurseries of being communist sympathizers.

After World War II, the social work profession continued to view children whose mothers worked as deprived. Although day nurseries were encouraged to "incorporate much of the educational methods of the nursery school into their programs," they were also urged to provide casework services for parents (Department of Social Security 1949:1). At the national level, Beer wrote, "the day nursery is a social agency because of its connection with a social problem, the employment of the mother," and, he noted, "the plight of children left without a mother all day" (Beer 1957:10).

The Changing Economy and Workforce

In the last quarter of the twentieth century, wages for working-class men and women in the United States stagnated and fell. This was accompanied by growing disparities in income and wealth between rich and working-class Americans. The changes in the economy, combined with expanded opportunity for females and a greater number of single-parent households, contributed to dramatic increases in the labor-force participation of mothers. Hernandez (1996) argues, "If children had available only the income from fathers living in the home, then the relative poverty rate would have fallen sharply during the 1940s, much more slowly or not at all during the 1950s and 1960s, and it would have increased substantially during the 1970s and 1980s."

In 1996, 59 percent of mothers with an infant or toddler under three years of age were in the workforce. Of mothers whose youngest child was between three and five, 67 percent were working. This compares with 39.2 percent with infants or toddlers and 46.8 percent with children under six in 1980 (U.S. Congress 1998). In 1995, during a typical week, more than 11 million children under five were in child care while their parents worked (Smith 2000). The care arrangements used by families included relatives (50%), day care centers or preschools (30%), care by a nonrelative in the child's home (9%), and care by a nonrelative in a provider's home (21%). Five percent of parents arranged for care for their children at the parents' workplace. Among relatives, 30 percent of caregivers were grandparents. Multiple care arrangements were common: 44 percent of preschool and 75 percent of school-age children regularly spent time in more than one child care setting per week.

Parental Preferences in Child Care

Research indicates that parents look for provider warmth and attentiveness and for someone they can trust. In addition, safety, health, price, convenience, and flexibility are considered important. Using a parent survey instrument, "Quality of Care from a Parent's Point of View," Emlen (1999) found that parents balance work, family, and child care demands by developing their own "flexibility solution." If they lack flexibility in their job or family, they look for it in child care, for example, choosing informal care as opposed to center care, which tends to be less flexible in terms of scheduling.

Child Care Costs

In an analysis of data from the fall 1995 Survey of Income and Program Participation, the U.S. Bureau of the Census found that child care costs had increased in real terms between 1986 and 1995 (Smith 2000). The amount paid varied by type of care used, child age, race, size of family, family income, and region of the country. Although a lower percentage of low-income families (those earning less than $1,500 per month) paid for child care, when they did pay for care, it consumed a large part of their budget (35 percent of their income as compared to 7 percent for higher-income families).

A PARENT: I work full time at a prominent business in my community. When I first moved here, I had to look for child care for my six-month-old son. I tried every possible program available that provides help to low-income families for child care. I found that a single mother who makes $8.50 an hour is not considered low income. I did not qualify for welfare. I was told that there are over 350 people in my area on a waiting list for non-welfare-related child care. They told me to apply anyway, but not to count on any help. Child care can average from between $350 to

$600 per month, per child. That is almost two weeks worth of pay for me. After paying rent there is no money left over for monthly bills, not to even mention my son's food, diapers, and clothes. At this point, I feel I have only two options: (1) I can quit my job and go on welfare so that I can then qualify for child care assistance, or (2) I can keep my job, along with my pride, impose on my family members to provide day care at a great expense to them, and struggle severely with monthly finances, all the while continuing to live in poverty.

Child Care Resources

Child care is provided, as was noted earlier, by relatives, in child care centers, and in private homes. Centers vary in size depending on available space and personnel, community child care demand (centers tend to be larger in urban and suburban areas), and regulations. Family child care homes typically operate in the dwelling of the provider; the numbers of children depend on the ages of the children, the size of the home, the experience of the provider, and the availability of an assistant. Although states vary in whether they regulate small family child care homes, most states do regulate homes for larger groups of children (from seven to twelve children). All states license child care centers, but certain categories of centers, such as those operated by churches or schools, may be exempt from licensing requirements.

Although most home child care providers operate as small businesses, centers operate as both for-profit and nonprofit organizations. Despite increased federal and state funding for child care subsidies in recent years, parent fees continue to be the primary source of revenue in child care. Because child care is a staff-intensive business, personnel costs average 50 to 70 percent of center budgets, with variations relating to profit versus nonprofit sponsorship (Willer, Hofferth, et al. 1991; Helburn and Culkin 1995).

Even though staffing costs dominate child care budgets, child care workers receive very low wages. One study found that most child care workers earn just over $12,000 per year and that the average child care teacher subsidizes the cost of care by $5,238 per year in foregone wages as compared to what they could earn in other female-dominated industries (Helburn and Culkin 1995). Centers report widespread difficulties in recruiting and retaining qualified personnel. Given research that indicates the interrelationships among staffing, staff education and training, and quality of care, this staff shortage and staff turnover has serious implications for the field.

Without resources to augment what parents are able to pay (such as in-kind assistance with facility costs, charitable funding, or government grants), child care providers are forced to make difficult trade-offs among parent fees, staff wages, and the quality of care provided to children.

Quality of Care and Outcomes for Children

In reviews that summarize research dealing with child care quality and the effects it has on child development, Scarr and Eisenberg (1993) and Zaslow (1991) identify three stages or waves of child care research. Consistent with historical views of child care, the early wave of research was concerned with attachment and whether or not children were harmed by child care and by separation from their mothers. The second wave of research caused concerns to surface about the quality of child care in the United States and demonstrated that quality of care does make a difference in results for children, especially low-income children. In recent years, however, some researchers have called for a more ecological approach to child care research. Third-wave child care research seeks to examine child care and child outcomes in the context of the family and community. A new group of researchers are using complex modeling techniques and large data sets to examine the interrelationships among variables judged to relate to supply, choice, cost, quality, and children's developmental outcomes. These studies find complex relationships between regulation and such market responses as cost, ratios, quality, and demand for care.

Other researchers are developing research designs to examine child care issues in the context of the family. Most notably, the National Institute of Child Health and Human Development is conducting a longitudinal study that has followed children since infancy in 1991 (NICHD Early Childhood Research Network 1996). This study examines the relationship between child care experiences and characteristics and developmental outcomes for children. It uses multiple methods and takes into account family characteristics. So far, the study seems to have found that although child care quality is associated with cognitive and language development in children, family characteristics such as maternal sensitivity, family income, and home environment have greater implications for children's development than does child care quality. However, it has also found that when child care fails to meet a child's needs, that factor combines with family risk factors to result in less than optimal development for some children.

Federal Child Care Policy

Despite President Nixon's veto of the Comprehensive Child Development Act in 1971, progress was made in the 1970s toward increasing resources for child care through the provisions of Title XX of the Social Security Act, under which the federal government provided the states with funds to initiate "comprehensive social services programs directed toward achieving economic self-support and preventing dependence" (National Association of Social Workers 1987:787). During the early 1980s this support was eroded, as Title XX funding was cut and as business involvement in child care was encouraged. By the mid-1980s, the changing economy, changing family structures, and early welfare reform efforts, along with cuts in federal support to child care, began to reveal the gaps in the nation's child care system. A number of state governors formed task forces to develop recommendations for improving child care services and systems. National and state coalitions formed a powerful advocacy voice. The Child Care and Development Block Grant Act was signed into law in 1990 as a discretionary program subject to annual appropriation; it was the culmination of a lengthy debate about the role that federal government should play in child care. Funds were granted to states, territories, and tribes with the requirement that the money be spent primarily on child care subsidies to facilitate low-income families' access to the child care market. States were required to provide subsidized families with choices from among the same types of care available to privately paying families. The focus on subsidies for low-income working families and parent choice continues in the Child Care and Development Fund, the child care block grant established under the Personal Responsibility and Work Opportunity Reconciliation Act of 1996 (the welfare reform legislation).

Reexamining Child Care

Child care continues to be enmeshed in conflicting attitudes about the role of mothers, even though a majority of mothers are now in the labor market within a few months of giving birth. Twenty-first-century families are dealing with a child care system shaped by the values and realities of the late nineteenth century and by the failure to proactively establish a continuum of family supports during the transition from an agricultural to an industrialized economy.

Efforts in recent years to increase federal involvement in child care demonstrate how embedded child care is in history and ideology. Although the Child Care Development Fund is but one of several major efforts to respond to the child care needs of working families, it involves the largest appropriation of funds and represents the broadest expression of federal policy. Oriented largely toward the child care needs of the poor and of at-risk families, the service is intended primarily to enable low-income parents to work rather than to further the development of children. The fund's connection with welfare reform and with TANF perpetuates the association of poverty with those receiving child care assistance, a stigma that creates obstacles for both low-income and middle-income people as they pursue child care solutions.

In the congressional debates over the Child Care and Development Block Grant and, later, the Child Care Development Fund, market interests won out over those who advocated for strategies more analogous to public education, Head Start, or even the military child care system. Underlying the Child Care Development Fund is the assumption that if parents are given necessary resources, including vouchers and information, market forces will produce the supply and quality of care needed by low-income families. This assumption does not fully take account of the failures inherent in the child care market, including (1) the extraordinary challenges faced by low-income parents, who struggle to manage work, family responsibilities, and child care and who often work in jobs that lack benefits and require nonstandard work hours; (2) disregard of society's human and collective interest in the long-range development of all children; (3) implicit subsidies made by child care workers in the form of foregone earnings; and (4) the failure of the market to produce the high-quality services that have been shown to benefit low-income children.

Possibilities for the Future

With the influx of mothers into the labor force and the observance of TANF work requirements, even individuals who embrace traditional values have difficulty arguing against the need for child care, especially for low-income working families. In contrast to earlier efforts, the Child Care Development Fund builds on the existing market approach to child care and devolves responsibility for decisions about eligibility, copayments, regulations, and quality initiatives to states. By sidestepping these decisions and administrative issues, the fund's directors have avoided potentially contentious issues, and a strong coalition of organizations and individuals has remained united around advocacy for child care issues.

Although successful, this approach has its costs. The early care and education system is fragmented, with significant variability from state to state. In the absence of a coherent long-range vision for the system, efforts appear to emerge from a few loosely formulated principles related to access to care for low-income children, improved training and compensation for child care workers, and incentives for quality. Quality efforts are initiative driven: little evaluation and research are conducted to demonstrate the effectiveness of programs and determine whether they better the living conditions of families and children; thus many questions remain. To improve the quality of care for children, should we eliminate access to unregulated providers through the Child Care Development Fund? Do we truly want to regulate grandmothers? If we limit informal care, what are the implications for families who work nonstandard hours, live in rural communities, or have a child with special needs? If low-income families can't find care that meets state requirements, will they be forced to use unpaid care or to pay for care out of their own limited budgets? Is the impulse to limit choice under the Child Care Development Fund class biased because we don't seem to discuss taking similar steps for middle-income families who use the child care tax credit? Do policy makers know whether full-day, full-year, early childhood programs in conformance with Head Start Performance Standards produce better results for children compared to some combination of part-day preschool and informal care? How should incentives for quality be prioritized with respect to adequate reimbursement for all providers? Can we demonstrate how child, family, and program outcomes correlate with current public investment? In that regard, how do we avoid overpromising gains or subjecting young children to inappropriate assessments?

There are no easy answers to these and other questions that impact child care policy. Thoughtful policy makers, practitioners, and advocates struggle daily to understand the possible effects of policy choices, taking into account what research—however inadequate—indicates, and balancing goals and needs that often seem competing. Clearly, a greater amount of quality research is needed.

Despite the intensity of efforts at national, state, and local levels to improve child care services and systems, there is very little explicit discussion of long-range goals. Where are our efforts taking us? How will we know when we get there? Most individual policy makers, advocates, researchers, and practitioners undoubtedly have a vision for a rational system of early care and education. It may be that the system would eventually become part of public education or that full-day, full-year Head Start would subsume early care and education for young, low-income children. Others may envision a plan whereby block grants for early care and education are allocated to the states and the states become responsible for implementing a coherent system. Some may want to see mothers returning from the workforce to the home. But each of these visions involves potential winners and losers. Incremental efforts and consensus politics avoid the potential for conflict among those working on child care issues and make it possible to respond to the needs of varied interests.

That said, it is essential to reflect critically on what we are working toward. Is our vision limited by traditional views about the role of mothers and the belief in individual responsibility, or can we recognize the roles that class, race, and sex play in creating an uneven playing field? To what extent does our own peculiar investment in the current system shape our views about the types of changes that are possible and desirable? Federal child care policy as expressed through the Child Care Development Fund is oriented toward providing the working poor with access to the child care market. In what ways does that keep us rooted in the past and limit our vision of what is possible?

A revamped child care system might have a stable infrastructure and a funding base less vulnerable to political winds than our current mix of vouchers and tax policies. While allowing for parental choice, that infrastructure, including standards and funding, could be institutionalized through a system analogous to the public education system. Parents would contribute to the cost of care, but quality would not be dependent on what parents could afford. Paid parental leave would be available to the primary caretakers of infants. And, with a more stable funding base, child care workers could receive wages commensurate with their education, experience, and responsibilities.

Conclusion

All of the community support services reviewed in this chapter are critical to child welfare services. Until the last few years, many were incorporated into the structure of the public child welfare system. Others have developed as innovative programs to meet the needs of families as new needs appeared or existing ones were recognized. Many are now linked to public child welfare agencies through contractual arrangements. These are the services that provide the specialized interventions, and the ongoing support, that enhance the functioning of families in our complex society.

In this chapter discussions of basic family support have been somewhat more extended then the discussions of more specialized services. This emphasis reflects the opinion of the writers. Child care is a vastly important issue as family structures change and parents move into the workforce. Furthermore, the stresses of poverty are associated with a host of social problems, among them child maltreatment. The literature on the prevention of child maltreatment suggests that more generous provision at this basic level of support to all families might have enormous impact. Finally, if this base is not sound, the core child welfare services reviewed in the next chapters will have little to build on and will falter.

Notes

1. This dilemma is described in Janet Fitch's moving and beautifully written book *White Oleander* (Little Brown and Co., 1999). The book follows the experiences of a mentally ill mother, incarcerated because of a murder, and her young daughter in foster care.

References

Allen, M., P. Brown, et al. 1992. *Helping Children By Strengthening Families: A Look at Family Support Programs.* Washington, D.C.: Children's Defense Fund.

Beckerman, A. 1994. "Mothers in Prison: Meeting the Prerequisite Conditions for Permanency Planning." *Social Work* 39, no. 1 (January): 9–14.

Beer, E. S. 1957. *Working Mothers and the Day Nursery.* New York: Whiteside, Inc., and William Morrow and Company.

Broffenbrenner, U. 1974. *A Report on Longitudinal Programs. Vol. 2, Is Early Intervention Effective?* Washington, D.C.: Department of Health, Education, and Welfare.

Burchinal, M. R. 1999. "Child Care Experiences and Developmental Outcomes." In *The Silent Crisis in Child Care,* edited by S. W. Helburn. Thousand Oaks, Calif.: Sage. 563

Cameron, G., and S. Birnie-Lefcovitch. 2000. "Parent Mutual Aid Organizations in Child Welfare Demonstration Project: A Report of Outcomes." *Children and Youth Services Review* 22(6): 421–40.

Children's Defense Fund. 1998. *The State of America's Children*. Washington, D.C.: Children's Defense Fund.

Daro, D. A., and K. A. Harding. 1999. "Healthy Families America: Using Research to Enhance Practice." *The Future of Children* 9 (Spring/Summer): 152–78.

Department of Social Security. 1949. *Standards for Day Nurseries in Washington*. Olympia: State of Washington.

Downs, S. W., E. Moore, et al. 2000. *Child Welfare and Family Services: Policies and Practice*. Boston: Allyn and Bacon.

Edleson, J. L. 1999. "The Overlap Between Child Maltreatment and Woman Abuse." St. Paul, Minn. Available at http://www.vaw.umn.edu/Vawnet/overlap.htm.

Emlen, A. 1999. *From a Parent's Point of View: Measuring the Quality of Child Care*. Portland, Ore.: Portland State University and the Oregon Child Care Research Partnership.

Fein, G. G., and A. Clarke-Stewart. 1973. *Day Care in Context*. New York: John Wiley and Sons.

Foley, R. 1994. "The Insufficiency of Statutory Protections." In *When Drug Addicts Have Children: Reorienting Child Welfare's Response,* edited by D. J. Besharov. Washington, D.C.: Child Welfare League of America.

Gomboy, D., P. L. Culross, et al. 1999. "Home Visiting: Recent Program Evaluations. Analysis and Recommendations." *The Future of Children* 9 (Spring/Summer): 4–26.

Goodwin, D. K. 1994. *No Ordinary Time*. New York: Simon and Schuster.

Gordon, M., ed. 1973. *The American Family in Social-Historical Perspective*. New York: St. Martin's Press.

Helburn, S., and M. L. Culkin. 1995. "Cost, Quality, and Child Outcomes in Child Care Centers." University of Colorado, Denver.

Hernandez, D. J. 1996. "Trends in the Well Being of America's Children and Youth." U.S. Department of Health and Human Services, Washington, D.C.

Horn, W. F. 1994. "Implications for Policy Making." In *When Drug Addicts Have Children: Reorienting Child Welfare's Response,* edited by D. J. Besharov. Washington, D.C.: Child Welfare League of America.

Karoly, L. A., P. W. Greenwood, et al. 1998. *Investing in Our Children: What We Know and Don't Know About the Costs and Benefits of Early Childhood Interventions*. Santa Monica, Calif.: Rand.

Lindsey, D. 1994. *The Welfare of Children*. New York: Oxford University Press.

McCausland, C. L. 1976. *Children of Circumstance*. Chicago: Chicago Child Care Society.

Mulroy, E. A., and P. L. Ewalt. 1996. "Is Shelter a Private Problem?" *Social Work* 41, no. 2 (March): 125–28.

Nasaw, D. 1985. *Children of the City at Work and at Play*. New York: Oxford University Press.

National Association of Social Workers. 1987. *Encyclopedia of Social Work*. Silver Spring, Md.: National Association of Social Workers.

NICHD Early Childhood Research Network. 1996. "Characteristics of Infant Child Care: Factors Contributing to Positive Caregiving." *Early Childhood Research Quarterly* 11:269–306.

Rafael, T., and L. Pion-Berlin. 1999. "Parents Anonymous Strengthening Families." *Juvenile Justice Bulletin* (April): 1–11.

Scarr, S., and M. Eisenberg. 1993. "Child Care Research: Issues, Perspectives, and Results." *Annual Review of Psychology* 44:613–44.

Schorr, A. L. 1974. *Children and Decent People*. New York: Basic Books.

Schorr, L. B. 1988. *Within Our Reach: Breaking the Cycle of Disadvantage*. New York: Anchor, Doubleday.

Schweinhart, L. J., H. V. Barnes, et al. 1993. *Significant Benefits: The High/Scope Perry Preschool Study Through Age 17*. Ypsilanti, Mich.: High/Scope Educational Research Foundation.

Smith, K. 2000. *Who's Minding the Kids? Child Care Arrangements*. Washington, D.C.: U.S. Bureau of the Census, Household Economic Studies, Current Population Reports.

Steinfels, M. O. B. 1973. *Who's Minding the Children? The History and Politics of Day Care in America*. New York: Simon and Schuster.

Tuttle, W. M. 1992. "Rosie the Riveter and Her Latchkey Children: What Americans Can Learn About Child Day Care from the Second World War." *Child Welfare* 74(1): 92–114.

U.S. Congress. 1998. "Green Book." U.S. House of Representatives, Washington, D.C. Available at http://aspe.os.dhhs.gov/98gb/9ccare.htm.

U.S. Department of Health and Human Services. 1999. *Blending Perspectives and Building Common Ground: A Report to Congress on Substance Abuse and Child Protection*. Washington, D.C.: U.S. Government Printing Office.

Webster-Stratton, C. 2000. "The Incredible Years Training Series." *Juvenile Justice Bulletin* (June): 1–23.

Willer, B., S. L. Hofferth, et al. 1991. *The Demand and Supply of Child Care in 1990: Joint Findings from the National Child Care Survey 1990 and a Profile of Child Care Settings*. Washington, D.C.: National Association for the Education of Young Children.

Young, D. S., and C. J. Smith. 2000. "When Moms Are Incarcerated: The Needs of Children, Mothers, and Caregivers." *Families in Society: The Journal of Contemporary Human Services* 81(2): 130–41.

Zaslow, M. J. 1991. "Variation in Child Care Quality and Its Implications for Children." *Journal of Social Issues* 47(2): 125–38.

CHAPTER 5

Crisis Intervention: Child Protection and Family Preservation

> I felt my standpoint shaken
> In the universal crisis.
> But with one step backward taken
> I saved myself from going.
> A world torn loose went by me.
> Then the rain stopped, and the blowing,
> And the sun came out to dry me.
>
> ROBERT FROST

This chapter is about families in which the children are at risk. Either children have been harmed through their caretakers' abuse or neglect, or children are at risk of harm. These are children who need immediate action for their protection. In this chapter we are nearing the top of the pyramid described in chapter 4 and considering very intensive services needed by a relatively small proportion of families. We are also considering the very center of child welfare services.

Downs, Moore, et al. (2000:218–19) note that child protection services are distinct from other child welfare services in several important ways: (1) Services are authoritative; the agency initiates the service and the family is an involuntary client, (2) services carry increased social agency responsibility; decisions must be accurately made, and the agency cannot withdraw until the child is safe, (3) the community expects the protective service agency to carry out its work effectively, and (4) protective services must maintain a delicate balance in the use of authority, including the authority of the legal system, in relation to the child, the parents, and the community. These attributes make protective services extremely complex; they do not negate the principles of good social work practice.

Community interest in protective services is intense. The current debate about whether children too often remain with families when they are at risk of harm is taking place in the larger community as well as within the profession. It is often framed as a question of "family interest" versus "the best interest of the child." There are not really two sides here, for the best interest of the child usually lies in the preservation of the child's own family. Public discussion focuses on a vast middle ground of cases, in which the threats to a child's safety and the strengths of a family are not easy to determine. Unfortunately, errors can have devastating consequences for the child. Publicity about child fatalities—actually very rare—fuels the debate. Corresponding data about the emotional damage to children in foster care has focused on inadequacies in the foster care system rather than on whether their own families might have been strengthened so the children could stay in them.

The Nature and Extent of Child Maltreatment

The numbers presented chapter 1, in the discussion of child maltreatment as a societal issue, gave some idea of the scope of the problem. There are more than three reports of maltreatment for every substantiated case: in 1999, for example, 2,974,000 reports and 826,000 victims were reported by the states (U.S. Department of Health and Human Services [hereafter, U.S. HHS], Children's Bureau 2001). These numbers have been likened to the tip of an iceberg, and it is a good analogy. We know from the data of the National Incidence Studies, explained and used in chapter 3, that there are half to two-thirds as many unreported incidents of maltreatment as there are those reported. And the numbers of incidents of maltreatment that are never known outside the family, and thus known neither to professionals nor to the child protection system, are probably many. These constitute the hidden, or submerged, portion of the iceberg.

Statistics mean little if the severity of the maltreatment is not examined. Statutory definitions of abuse and neglect are generally quite restrictive and are intended to prohibit intervention in family affairs unless serious harm has been done to a child or the child is clearly at risk of such serious harm. Those in the field report that families coming into the protective service system are more distressed, and the harm done to children more severe, than in the past (Bartholet 1999). The families present multiple problems—poverty, substance abuse, family violence, involvement in the criminal justice system. And, because of a culture that respects family privacy, the overloaded child welfare system, and the continued lack of funding for family support services, the families are deeper into their troubled patterns by the time protective services intervene.

Child Protective Services

The Development of Child Protective Services

Although the independence and privacy of the family has always been valued and protected in the United States, the society has nonetheless strived to provide for the care of children who were being brought up in a way that did not meet community standards.

Saving children For the first two centuries of this country's history, the mode of providing for such children was to "save" them from their families. These were primarily the poorest of families, and the removal of the children was often justified as a means of preventing the children from developing "slothful ways of life that led to idleness and moral degradation" (Costin 1985:35). The legal basis for intervention was established gradually, following the English common law principle of *parens patriae,* the concept of the state as responsible for the well-being of its youth. The children were usually placed in institutions, from which they were often indentured in order to learn a trade. Placement of children in foster homes began in the mid-nineteenth century. (Chapter 6 begins with a summary of the history of placement alternatives in the United States).

Rescuing children Child rescue was a distinct social reform movement that sought to establish the rights of children and to establish the responsibility of the state to discover and rescue children who were being abused or neglected. The responsibility of government to protect children began to be recognized about 1825. In 1872 a "deeply concerned lady" wrote to the *New York Times,* "Do not forget the creatures whom God made in his own image, and to whom he has given a soul that may be saved by saving the body. These dumb creatures [animals] will not meet you in the life to come, but if you rescue but one human being, angels will envy your reward" (Costin, Karger, et al. 1996:61). Societies with the specific mission of protecting children first emerged amid the publicity following the exposure of the condition of a badly abused and neglected little girl, Mary Ellen, in New York City in 1873. Laws on the books that punished those cruel to animals were invoked, with the idea that surely children deserved the same protection that animals enjoyed. Elbridge T. Gerry, the attorney in the case of Mary Ellen, became the first executive of the New York Society for the Prevention of Cruelty to Children when it was formed in 1875 (Downs, Moore, et al. 2000). By the early twentieth century there were three hundred such private societies dedicated to protecting children, "under the umbrella of the American Humane Association," in the Northeast and the Midwest (Schene 1998:26).

Sharing the philosophy of the animal protection movement, which was the original focus of the American Humane Association, the Society for the Prevention of Cruelty to Children sought to rescue children from bad families and to punish the parents who maltreated them. Gerry, in 1872, stated the purpose: "Our object is . . . to rescue the child who is being ill-treated, and to deter the brutal from similar acts by bringing to punishment all those who injure children" (Costin 1985:43).

Competing philosophies Competing ideas about helping families and children developed during the Progressive Era. The Charity Organization Societies wanted to understand and eliminate poverty. Poverty was thought to be both fault and responsibility of the individual, and the friendly visitors of the Charity Organization Societies were to "provide a role model, advice, and instruction" so that the poor could "rid themselves of poverty." Though it soon became apparent that the poverty of many families was due to circumstances beyond their control, the idea of working directly with intact families to resolve problems would have a major impact on social work (McGowan 1983:56). A second philosophy was that of community action to improve conditions for families, and thus to improve conditions for children. The settlement house movement, the formation of labor unions to bargain for living wages, the advocacy for public education and the end of child labor, the mothers' pension movement—all were part of this thrust.

Although the child rescue movement also engaged in community advocacy, that advocacy was focused on building a system of legal rights for children, and the child rescue movement emphasized its distinction from other social movements (Costin 1985). The ideas of the Charity Organization Society, and of the settlement house movement, began to influence some societies, though Gerry stoutly resisted them. The Massachusetts Society, under C. C. Carstens, was noted for its emphasis on work to strengthen families; when, in 1921, Carstens became director of the new Child Welfare League of America, these ideas became dominant. The new philosophy of child protection included work with families, temporary out-of-home care and an attempt to preserve the child's own family whenever possible, and some emphasis on prevention of abuse and neglect (Costin 1985; Schene 1998).

Increasing recognition and government responsibility These developments "set the stage for what were to become the hallmarks of the child welfare field during the twentieth century: bureaucratization, professionalization, and expanded state intervention in the lives of children" (McGowan 1983:59). The Children's Bureau was founded in 1912, the first recognition that the federal government had responsibility for the welfare of children (McGowan 1983). The Social Security Act of 1935 was another step in the entry of the federal government into child welfare, with Aid to Dependent Children, which provided an entitlement to a basic income, and Title IV-B, Child Welfare Services, which provided limited funding to states for protective services. Publicly funded agencies began to take over the protective functions formerly carried out by private Societies for the Protection of Cruelty to Children (Schene 1998). Still, until the middle of the twentieth century, child protection was a minor part of child welfare work; the major thrust of the field was toward improving conditions for all children.

The focus shifted toward child protection in the 1960s after the discovery of what came to be called the "battered child syndrome" (Kempe, Silverman, et al. 1962). Pediatric radiologists began to recognize a pattern of multiple fractures of the long bones of very small children. Such fractures, in different stages of healing, could only be the result of severe physical abuse over time. It was hard to imagine that parents or other caretakers could deliberately and repetitively hurt children. At first it was thought that this must be a rare occurrence. The extent of physical abuse of children was first documented in a national survey of hospitals, which found 302 children in hospitals because of physical abuse. The discoveries of the pediatricians astounded and horrified the public.

Over the next decade, many new state laws aimed to protect children from physical abuse. In 1974 the federal Child Abuse Prevention and Treatment Act (CAPTA) was passed. It provided funds to assist states in developing systems that encompassed mandated reporting of suspected child abuse or neglect, public social service departments to investigate reports, and systems to keep track of substantiated cases of maltreatment.

CAPTA also established the National Center on Child Abuse and Neglect, which developed standards, became a clearinghouse for information, and eventually began a program of grants for research to promote better understanding of abuse and neglect and ultimately the development of effective interventions. CAPTA also offered funds to states that met its standards to develop child protection services, but the funding was always limited. In 1975 Congress passed Title XX of the Social Security Act, which gave states funds they could use for child protection. By 1980, three-fourths of those funds were being used for foster care rather than to support families (Schene 1998:29).

The Public Agency Overwhelmed

Mandated reporting One of the provisions of CAPTA was the requirement that states, if they wanted to receive any funds distributed under the act, enact statutes requiring professionals who had contact with, or learned of, child maltreatment to report that maltreatment to law enforcement or child protection agencies. All reporters of maltreatment, whether mandated or not, were assured of immunity from prosecution for libel as part of this reporting statute. To receive CAPTA funding, states were also required to disseminate information to the public about the prevention and treatment of child abuse and neglect. These provisions accomplished their intent of bringing children in need of protection to the attention of authorities that could protect them; they also had unforeseen effects.

During the 1970s, states developed their own laws that mandated reporting of child abuse, and broadened the definition of reportable abuse. "The idea that all suspicions could be investigated seemed feasible in the 1960s, when physicians naively estimated that perhaps 300 families nationwide battered their children" (Schene 1998:10). But the number of reports has grown steadily, as noted in chapter 1, reaching 416,000 by 1976, nearing 2 million by 1985, and approaching 3 million in 1999.

Child protection in question The vast increase in the number of reports to be investigated, without corresponding increases in funds, has precipitated the current crisis in child protective services. Each report should be investigated, for a child may be in danger. However, the volume is such that not all reports are actually investigated. A 1988 study found that the laws of forty-four states allowed agency discretion in deciding which reports to investigate. The same study documented the extent of both written and unwritten policies that allowed some reports to be "screened out" and to receive no follow-up (Wells, Stein, et al. 1989), a situation that apparently persists. Data from the National Child Abuse and Neglect Data System (NCANDS) indicate that almost 40 percent of reports to children's protective service agencies were "screened out" and not referred for investigation (U.S. HHS, Children's Bureau 2000a:vii).

Data from the Third National Incidence Study[1] indicates that the extent of suspected maltreatment is considerably greater than the number of reports. Investigation occurs for only 28 percent of the children thought by a professional to be maltreated under the definitions of the study, either because the maltreatment is not reported or because the case is screened out without investigation by the protective service agency (U.S. HHS, National Center on Child Abuse and Neglect 1996:7–16). Situations that are not reported or not investigated are, of course, generally those considered to be low risk, but the fact is that in each instance someone thought a child was in trouble and needed help.

Only about one-third of the referrals that are investigated are substantiated (U.S. HHS, Children's Bureau 2000a, 2001). In other words, in about two-thirds of the situations it is determined that maltreatment serious enough to warrant state intervention cannot be demonstrated. It is not known how many of those families investigated are linked to community services that might help with whatever conditions prompted the report. The protective service agency's staff time is thus spent largely on investigation, with only a small proportion devoted to work with the families of those children who really need protection.

Targeting the reasons for abuse   One difficulty in providing effective protective services is that we do not have much idea what causes child abuse. We do know that many things are associated with it. Until the causes are better understood, however, the design and targeting of services will remain problematic. The pursuit of that understanding takes place within a variety of theoretical frameworks, such as those emphasizing psychological profiles of the parent(s), socioeconomic explanations, and ecological frameworks that emphasize the interaction of parents, child, and environment (Giovannoni 1985; Pecora, Whittaker, et al. 1992).

Most of the empirical evidence about maltreatment comes from sociological theory. We know that poverty is associated with child maltreatment. The vast majority of poor families, of course, neither abuse nor neglect their children. However, the great majority of families to whom child abuse and neglect have been attributed live in poverty or near-poverty circumstances. This finding has been obtained across a range of methodologies and definitions. Moreover, poverty is the single most prevalent characteristic of these families, who tend to be the poorest of the poor.

(PELTON 1989:38)

Unemployment, crowded housing, family size, and social isolation have also been identified as factors contributing to child maltreatment—and all of these, of course, are often associated with poverty.

Some contend that the closer living conditions of the poor, and the exposure of these families to public programs, expose abuse and neglect that might remain hidden in more affluent families; but such arguments are not sufficient to account for the overrepresentation of poor children among those maltreated. More convincing are explanations that focus on how the stress of poverty creates the context for maltreatment. Crowded, unsafe housing and lack of resources can also be direct causes of accidents—which often are categorized as abuse or neglect.

African American families are disproportionately represented in statistics of abuse and neglect. These children are also overrepresented in the foster care system (U.S. Congress 1998) and in studies of child fatalities due to maltreatment (Costin, Karger, et al. 1996:146). This is doubtless in part because high concentrations of African American families live in the poverty-stricken centers of our large cities, and are very poor. The interpretation of this data is complicated, however. In a national study of service delivery, it was found that when families had the same characteristics and problems, African American and Hispanic children were more likely to be placed in foster care than white children (U.S. HHS, Children's Bureau 1997). The National Incidence Studies indicate that the actual incidence of maltreatment does not differ among races; the differences are apparently in reporting and response (U.S. HHS, National Center on Child Abuse and Neglect 1996).

Single mothers head many of the families with whom public child protection workers have contact. Certainly it might be supposed that the difficulties of parenting would be increased when there was no partner to share the burden. However, studies of single mothers show them to be, in general, competent women who cope well with their situation (Hanson, Heims, et al. 1995). Poverty has a serious impact on the single mother. If their children were born when they were young, single mothers often have limited education and limited opportunity for earning a living wage. Women earn less than men in every arena. Child care is expensive. These factors together made public assistance a good solution for many women; welfare reforms are ending this option. Whether it is single parenthood or poverty that contributes more to child maltreatment is not clear.

Psychological factors must be an element in child abuse, for most poor families manage to raise their children without maltreatment. Young (1964), in her early research, generated perhaps as complete a portrait of the abusive parent and the neglecting parent as has been developed. Polansky, Chalmers, et al. (1981) expanded upon that research and coined the term "apathy futility syndrome" to describe neglecting parents. Kadushin and Martin (1981) conceptualized physical abuse as an interactive event in which the behaviors of the child provided context and triggered the abuse by the parent; these ideas are borne out in studies of families in which a single child who is different, or particularly demanding, is singled out for abuse or neglect. Intergenerational theories of abuse and neglect have received some support, though it is clear that many adults who were abused as children do not abuse their children. Most of our empirically based knowledge is about the context of abuse and neglect, not the actors.

Interactive or ecological frameworks are familiar to social workers, and seem to make sense in the context of child abuse.

Factors resident in the child, the parent, the family interaction, the neighborhood, and even the broader community have all been noted as associated with the occurrence of child mistreatment. One formulation of how this myriad of factors may interact to precipitate child mistreatment emphasizes the relationship between family stresses and family supports. . . . For example, the stresses of poverty—material deprivation and social and personal frustration—unless mediated by intrapersonal resources in conjunction with environmental supports and supplementation can result in situations of child maltreatment.

(GIOVANNONI 1985:210)

This interaction of factors is well illustrated in the case of substance abuse. Substance abuse is a central issue for many of the families involved with the child welfare system (U.S. HHS 1999). Historically it has been associated with child abuse and neglect (Brace 1872). The rise in the numbers of children in foster care in the late 1980s and 1990s coincided with the introduction of crack cocaine to the inner cities. Substance abuse crosses class and race lines, but is most often encountered by child protection agencies when it coexists with poverty. Perhaps the two-parent family, with the support of extended family and with the resources to pay for child care and after-school programs, can manage with a substance-abusing parent—the damage done to children in such families remains unknown to the child welfare system. When those resources are not available, children are left alone, not fed, neglected as their parents pursue their quest for drugs; or, worse, they are assaulted by a parent in a drug-induced state. These are the children that come to the child welfare system.

A more encouraging finding concerns a population in which poverty and powerlessness have not predetermined child maltreatment. Hispanic families, among our poorest families, are not overrepresented in child maltreatment statistics, in foster care, or in fatality statistics. This may mean that protective services are not reaching effectively into the Hispanic community and that these children are not receiving the services they need. Or it may mean that there is something protective in the Hispanic family structure. A California study by Hayes-Bautista, Hurtado, and colleagues has suggested the latter, finding traditional family structure more intact, with Hispanics exhibiting higher rates of labor force participation and higher rates of family formation than do African Americans or whites (Hayes-Bautista, Hurtado, et al. 1992, reported in Costin, Karger, et al. 1996). Hispanic people are, of course, of many different origins. The group studied probably were primarily of Mexican origin, a people in the process of moving from abject poverty to something better. Hope may be an important factor. This is an aspect of our national life that needs further study, for we know very little about the factors that hold family life together in the midst of poverty.

Intervention

Risk assessment Child protective work entails heavier responsibility than most other social work. When a child protective worker makes an assessment of the safety of a home for a child, he or she must make a decision that could alter the course of a family's life. A decision to do nothing is as important as one to intervene, and the nature of the intervention entails another set of decisions. The worker's skill in engaging the family in assessment and planning, while making firm use of the authority to protect children, will also have a profound impact on future work with the family.

> *When a neighbor saw the three-year-old toddler on the roof of a two-story house, he called the police, who responded immediately. When they knocked on the door, it took a long time to get any response. The father had been asleep, and had locked the children, a five-year-old and three-year-old twins, in a bedroom while he slept. When police gained entry, they found the house in "deplorable" condition.*
>
> *The police, ready to take the children to foster care, called Child Protective Services. When the mother came home from work, she found police and protective service workers still there assessing the situation.*

The protective service worker may conceptualize the task in a number of different ways. If he is part of a "substantiation-based" system, intervention will occur only when there is evidence, which the court is likely to accept, that an incidence of maltreatment has occurred and is serious enough that punishment of the perpetrators (if only through removal of the child from their care) is justified. If the focus is risk assessment, the role of the protective service worker is not to determine whether a crime has occurred or who did what, but to determine more holistically the nature and extent of the future risk to a child, based on an array of factors. Finally, the worker may focus on safety, attempting to determine the capacity of the family to ensure the child's safety.

Both a risk assessment and a substantiation model start with investigation of the maltreatment—what has occurred, any prior history of maltreatment, how family members perceive the incident. A risk assessment looks, in addition, at strengths and risks in such domains as parental capacity (including whether it is compromised by substance abuse, mental illness, developmental delays, etc.), level of family support, the child's age and developmental status, and any history of abuse in the parents' lives. In theory, the risk assessment approach allows for a more systemic and strengths-based view of the child in the context of the family. For example, a risk assessment model should be more capable of raising the alarm about the cumulative harm of a neglecting family. However, in practice, even when the public agency works on a risk assessment model, the court system still demands proof that abuse has occurred before it will sanction the removal of a child. After more than ten years of experimentation in many states, the risk assessment approach has failed to produce the hoped-for reform.

The model that focuses on safety rather than risk is relatively new. Turnell and Edwards (1999) describe it as a process in which the focus is not on the incident, but on the family's capacity to maintain safety for the child. Such models are complex to put into practice, for they demand a different approach than the more traditional risk assessment. Numerous practice techniques are part of this model. The promise is that, if a partnership for decision making and planning can be developed with a family, that partnership can create real change in the family's child-rearing practices.[2] How useful this model will be in practice probably depends on the willingness of protective service workers to allow families a role in decision making, and on whether the model has sufficient strength to enable many cases to be handled without court involvement and thus avoid drifting into a substantiation model.

Using a focus on safety, the worker and the parents began to assess the extent to which the family was able to keep their children safe from harm.

THE MOTHER: I was impressed, very impressed. Very happy that she was willing to work with us. She wasn't out to get the kids. She wasn't out to get us. She took a real impartial look at the situation. She wanted to see what the situation really was, and not what it just appeared to be at the time.

The father explained that he was ill, and medication had made him sleepy. Once before when he had gone to sleep the children had gone outside, and neighbors had complained about the lack of supervision. He thought the children would be safe locked in the bedroom. The parents were aware of the danger the child had been in, and were ready to take action. With the worker, they made a plan.

THE FATHER: She talked to you like you were a person instead of someone who had done something wrong.

Parents and worker together decided that the children needed a clean, safe, and sanitary home, with safety locks on the windows. They needed to have parents who understood the children's need for safety and supervision, and a father awake, aware, and engaging with the children when they were his responsibility.

The decision about placement The major decision made by the protective service worker is whether it is safe to leave the children in the home, or whether for their immediate safety they must be moved to out-of-home care. A decision to leave a child in a home is as fraught with consequences as a decision to remove a child. The task demands a specialized knowledge of the impact of separation on children, and of the techniques that can help a child deal with the trauma. All the clinical skills of assessment and intervention used in social work are needed.

The decision to place a child in foster care has profound consequences for both child and family, and one would hope such a decision would be made only after careful analysis of all factors. Lindsey's (1994) review of the literature on this decision making reveals the lack of scientific or theoretical basis for the decisions, so that a lack of consistency between workers, and between judges, is not surprising. More disturbing is his analysis of the reasons that children are placed in foster care. Using a large sample of children referred to a public child welfare agency, he used a discriminate function analysis in an attempt to discover the factors that predicted placement and those that predicted services to children in their own homes. The single most important predictor of placement in foster care was adequacy of income source. Families with no steady income, either from self-support or government support, were more likely to have children removed. "Clearly government income support (i.e., welfare) prevents placement" (Lindsey 1994:141). Another large study modifies this finding, noting that children from families with adequate income from wages are least likely to be placed in foster care (U.S. HHS, Children's Bureau 1997).

Even if parents do not agree with the worker that the children need placement, the worker has the authority to remove the children. The judgment of the worker will be reviewed in court within a specified time period, usually twenty-four hours or one working day. At that hearing, parent, child, and agency may each be represented by an attorney. The task of each attorney is to present the facts that will support the wishes of his or her client; with all the facts and arguments presumably before him, the judge makes a decision. The child may be returned to his family, returned with some protective supervision, or ordered into temporary foster care, with a review date set. The court review protects all parties.

If there is agreement on the appropriate plan for the child, the placement may be made voluntarily, without court involvement.

> *The plan they made was for a temporary placement of the children, return home when the physical condition of the home had improved, and later some follow-up services to prevent future difficulties. The worker was firm that the children were not safe in the home, given the current condition of the home. They were placed with grandparents, whom they knew, for the weekend. Over the weekend the parents were to clean up the house. Locks needed to be installed on the windows.*

Services provided Beyond the immediate protection of children, the goal of protective service work is to strengthen family functioning so that the children can remain safely in the home or, if placed, return soon. The services provided to effect this goal are those of the protective service agency as well as other specialized community services to meet specific needs. It is important that services be tailored to fit the needs of the individual family. And it is important, if the family is to engage in the use of services, that the family see the need for such help. Otherwise, services will be viewed as a series of "hoops" through which a family must jump in order to reclaim their children.

Family group decision meetings Family meetings are an important part of many protective service systems that do not function in an authoritarian mode. They give a family a voice in decision making, and they can be effectively used to help a family make an appropriate plan. The practice of family group meetings originated in New Zealand and is based on the same philosophy as the safety-focused risk assessment described earlier in the chapter. In family group meetings the family, after reviewing the situation with professionals and learning about available resources, is left alone to decide what should happen in the case. Family group meetings have been shown to reduce foster care placement as families come up with innovative plans to care for their children. Parnell and Burford (2000) suggest that these meetings can become a way for the protective service worker to pull together a team of "allies" to work together to strengthen the family and build a "sustaining community" for the family.

Family unity meetings were introduced in Oregon in the late 1980s. These were somewhat different in character from the family group meetings. They brought together all of those in the natural helping network who were involved in the problem—parents, grandparents, other relatives, church members, neighbors, as well as the protective service worker. In these meetings the problem was examined, and those present came up with suggestions for resolving it, often offering to help in the resolution. The protective service worker was present throughout the meeting and had the ultimate decision-making authority.

Another variant is the family decision meeting. This format emphasizes the inclusion of community partners in case planning; it is part of the effort to build a community system of care. A family decision meeting is a planning meeting of the immediate family, close relatives, and those professionals that may be involved in service delivery to the family; there may be several meetings as a case progresses. These meetings are well liked by community partners (such as mental health professionals, school personnel, and probation officers), and families also see them as a vehicle for having their ideas included in decision making (Shireman, Eggman, et al. 2000). However, families need extensive preparation for these meetings so that they know whom they may invite, can anticipate the number of professionals that will be there, and feel comfortable in expressing their ideas during the meetings (Rodgers 2000).

In an interesting twist, in each of these models the meeting is managed by a facilitator who is outside the protective services system, and not a family member. The assumption is that the child protection worker and the family are adversaries, and the facilitator is needed to mediate between them. But the assumption of an adversarial relationship may not be valid when initial work of a protective service worker with a family has gone well.

The family we are following in this chapter's case example did not have a formal family decision meeting. Instead, planning was done in a series of meetings between the parents and the worker. A meeting might have increased the involvement of the grandparents and of community agencies. And, certainly, had it not been relatively easy to develop a plan, a family meeting would have been helpful.

The family participated in parenting classes, and received some help in organizational and budgeting skills to improve home management. . . . The grandparents provided money for the locks for windows; had this not been possible, a fund was available within the agency to be used flexibly to make such purchases. In addition, the child who had been on the roof was tested for possible ADHD.

THE FATHER: She left about all of it up to us.

THE MOTHER: Kind of guided it. At least she made it feel like it was up to us. I mean, if we had resisted, she might have said you have to do it. But she really went about it in a way, she left a lot of it up to us. . . . She was listening. She was opening up to listen to us about what we thought. . . . She pointed out, "Well, maybe this is a need. Maybe parenting classes would help with supervision skills."

The extent and appropriateness of services The extent of services received by those children who are found to be in need of protection is largely unknown. It is estimated that services are provided to between 40 and 60 percent of those who have substantiated cases of abuse or neglect. Many child protective agencies target services to the highest-risk cases, which unfortunately means that many families who have neglected their children, the most often reported category of maltreatment, receive no services (English 1998:49). Bartholet (1999) reports that a review of New York cases revealed that half of the substantiated cases were closed on the same day they were substantiated. A California study found that 67 percent of the cases in which maltreatment had been documented were discharged from intake; it is not clear what brief services may have been offered during the intake process (Inkelas and Halfon 1997:151). Placement in out-of-home care occurs for about 21 percent of the children whose maltreatment is substantiated (U.S. HHS, Children's Bureau 2001).

More services are given to families and children prior to a child's placement in out-of-home care than after a placement has occurred (Lindsey 1994: 145). A California study of 676 case records found that "Few referrals to social or health services of any kind (during the current investigation in 1993) were recorded for the majority of cases, despite high levels of documented problems. Referrals for AFDC or Medicaid were provided in two cases. Treatment for drugs or alcohol was provided to fewer than 1 percent of families, while drug or alcohol problems were noted in more than 50 percent of families" (Inkelas and Halfon 1997:148). Lindsey reports a personal communication from Richard Barth, a distinguished researcher, whose California data indicates that only 9 percent of the children who are reported to protective services receive any services (Lindsey 1994:120). Thus an extremely small proportion of families actually receive substantial services.

In their review of research and analysis of services offered as part of child protection, Faver, Crawford, and colleagues (1999) document the lack of service delivery for many families and the inappropriateness of the services offered. With limited services available, families are offered what there is. Short-term services tend to be more available, and are often used with families who need long-term help. Many services are targeted toward a single problem, whereas families have multiple problems. Foster care may be provided more often than necessary because matching federal dollars are available for state expenditures for foster care, regardless of the amount spent, whereas funds for treatment and prevention are capped at a fixed amount. And finally, if families have not been involved in the planning of their services, they may believe them to be inappropriate and engage in them only to satisfy the child welfare agency, which has the power to take or return their children.

These findings are echoed in the 1994 national study of service delivery, in which it was documented that brief service is common; 78 percent of the children in the child welfare system remained at home, and 64 percent of those cases were closed within three months. (If there was foster care the median length of service was twenty-six months.) Parental substance abuse, mental health problems of either child or parent, and lack of housing are associated with long service periods (which usually include foster care); duration of services was thus related to the needs of the children and families. The most commonly provided services were parent training, provided to 37 percent of the families, and mental health outpatient treatment, provided to 24 percent of the families. However, for only a quarter of families homeless or experiencing housing problems were housing services provided; educational services were provided for only 6 percent of parents lacking a high school diploma. Substance abuse services were provided to 17 percent of the families, half of those that workers thought needed such services (U.S. HHS, Children's Bureau 1997).

These are appalling data, outlining a serious failure to protect children and to enable their families to care for them. It should not be thought that those who actually deliver services are unaware of this, or that they are unconcerned. The uninvestigated cases, the unsubstantiated cases, and the substantiated but unserved cases represent families for whom intervention might be helpful, but is not offered because resources are limited. Decisions to screen out reports are influenced by workload pressures (Wells, Stein, et al. 1989; U.S. HHS, Children's Bureau 2000a). Decisions abut whether to substantiate cases and offer services may be influenced by these same pressures, more often than one might wish.

Thus the volume of the workload seems to have led to a situation in which caseworkers, without the training and support services they need, are spending most of their time investigating reported abuse and neglect but are offering very few services, and often inappropriate ones, as a result of those investigations. Certainly such a situation wastes the resources that the agency does possess.

Outcome and case closing Risk assessment is an ongoing process, occurring throughout the period of a worker's interaction with the family. A case that has been opened in protective services because there is risk of maltreatment cannot be closed until that risk is low. Whatever factors created risk when the case was opened must have been modified, or the factors that created safety must have been strengthened. This assessment clearly demands a holistic review, with the family, of the child's situation. Outcome is a broader concept, asking not only if the child remains safe over time, but if the child is better off because of the protective service intervention. Is the child safe? Have ties to the family been preserved? Has the family been strengthened in its ability to care for the child? Have extended family or community resources been activated to provide continuing support to the family? In sum, is this family better off because of protective service intervention? The family in our example would clearly answer "yes" to that question.

THE MOTHER: I was kind of leery about it [parenting classes] at first, but once we started going it was like yes, this is really helpful.

And concrete services, offered by another agency in the community, were even more helpful.

THE MOTHER: She brought out information on ADHD and different ways for treating that . . . she brought out information on budgeting and kind of went over it. . . . She brought out activities to do with the kids; she brought out zoo passes. . . . A recipe for homemade play dough. Just different things.

The result of the services? In the words of the parents, the protective service intervention

brought back focus on being a healthy family again. . . . The house is organized and it is easier to deal with the [ADHD] child without all the clutter. . . . We put locks on windows and cupboards; it made me think more about what I am leaving down and putting it up. . . . We take more time with the children, and the children have noticed a difference in how we interact.

Reabuse rates If children go home from foster care, if cases are closed in protective services, do children remain safe? The most frequently used measure in answer to this question is the rate of reabuse, usually measured by substantiated reports of abuse or neglect. National data show that of the children who entered foster care in 1998, 10 percent were entering within twelve months of a prior episode in foster care, and 7 percent a longer time after a prior stay (U.S. HHS, Children's Bureau 2000b). Botsko and Festinger (1994) found that children in more problematic and difficult cases were more likely to reenter foster care. Unmet service needs, when there was no planning to meet those needs, were also associated with reentry.

Reabuse of children that does not rise to the level of seriousness necessitating foster care is doubtless more prevalent. The National Study of Service Delivery found that 40 percent of the families in its sample, about half of whom were receiving in-home services, had had one or more case openings prior to the current service period (U.S. HHS, Children's Bureau 1997). A California study of 646 cases opened in protective services (a systematic sample from county caseloads) found that 48.8 percent had had a previous protective service case opening. Substance abuse, family instability, and economic stress were found in higher proportions among those cases that had experienced prior openings. Few children had received substantive services. Eighty-one percent of the children with prior case openings had never progressed beyond an investigation; the authors speculate that this "recycling" may be a characteristic of cases that "hover" just below a threshold that would warrant intensive services or foster home placement (Inkelas and Halfon 1997). Nevertheless, such families clearly have serious problems.

Cultural issues Child protection services must, obviously, be responsive to the customs and needs of the diverse families encountered by the system. However, studies demonstrate striking racial disparities in the child protection system. Children of color are more likely to come into the child welfare system than white children (Close 1983). Although the incidence of abuse and neglect is apparently identical, families of color are more likely to be reported to the child protective services system (U.S. HHS, National Center on Child Abuse and Neglect 1996). Assessment results for children of color are harsher and more pessimistic than for white children (Stenho 1982). And African American and Native American children are more likely to be placed in foster care (U.S. HHS, Children's Bureau 1997).

It is obviously important to consider the cultural background and traditions of a family when making decisions about protective services. The dominant community's standards, likely to be internalized by the child welfare agency, can be at odds with the standards of subcultures within the community. And the accusation is often made that the child welfare worker, generally from a middle-class, white background, imposes the standards of that culture as families are assessed.

It can help to have clear definitions of abuse and neglect that are specific in describing serious deficiencies in child care. But they do not provide completely satisfactory answers. For example, definitions of neglect state that lack of supervision constitutes neglect. Care delivered under a different set of cultural rules can look abusive—for example, Russian emigrant parents using severe physical discipline may appear to be abusing their children.

Ideas about appropriate punishment also vary from culture to culture. Defining physical abuse in operational terms—for example, as physical discipline that leaves marks on the child—is also helpful, but still leaves room for differing interpretations. For some cultures, particularly people who have been oppressed, teaching instant obedience has been a way to keep their children safe, and physical discipline teaches instant obedience.

Culture includes social class, a variable that can introduce many differences in standards and expectations. Costin, Karger, and colleagues (1996) point out that we commonly ignore class differences and that there is a "politically correct" tendency to note that child maltreatment occurs in all classes. In fact, child maltreatment is concentrated in poor communities and poor families. Assessment and intervention must be carried out with understanding of the constant struggle faced by those in poverty, and with attention to the larger circumstances of the family as well as to family dynamics.

Social workers believe in diversity; the profession's value system suggests that it is not right to impose "middle-class Anglo-Saxon" ways on other cultures. They also believe in the right of the child to appropriate nurture and guidance. In order to make case-by-case decisions, the child welfare worker must translate policy into workable practice guidelines. An important consideration is the examination of the internal cultural dissonance of any set of parental behaviors; if the behaviors are outside the usual practices of the culture, they are much more likely to be abusive or neglectful in the eyes of both the larger community and the subculture (Korbin 1981). However, this evaluation demands a solid understanding of the culture within which the family lives. In the process of developing these practice guidelines, workers may have to advocate for modification of agency policy in order that it become culturally responsive.

> *Cultural issues with the family were minor, for the worker and family were of similar backgrounds. The worker did, however, discuss briefly her increased tolerance for poor housekeeping, developed in working with lower-class families whose housekeeping standards were different, but who successfully raised children.*
>
> *They [the police] don't see homes like we see all the time. . . . They wanted us to come and remove the kids right away. Just get them out of there. . . . They see that narrow vision sometimes.*
>
> *The family did not mention cultural differences in their interview.*

Family Preservation

It is evident that child protection is probably the most child-focused of the child welfare services. If a child is not safe, if care does not meet community standards, the child will live elsewhere. Yet this very child-focused approach has led to poor outcomes for children, as they have been removed from their original homes and left in the limbo of foster care too long. The last two decades of the twentieth century have seen two major initiatives which it was hoped would create better outcomes for children. Intensive family preservation services, discussed in this section, have attempted to improve conditions so that children could remain at home. Kinship foster care, discussed in chapter 7, has expanded the concept of family to include the extended family of grandparents, aunts and uncles, and cousins, and it attempts to keep the child within that extended family.

The Concept

One aspect of protecting children from emotional harm is the maintenance of their primary attachments, best accomplished through preserving children's own families. It is one of the means toward the end goal of protecting children.

Family preservation is both a concept and a set of services. As a concept, it has guided child welfare in an on-again, off-again way over time, retreating as the child rescue movement took shape, advancing with the idea of mothers' pensions and income maintenance, retreating with the "discovery" of child maltreatment in the 1960s and '70s, advancing as an alternative to foster care toward the end of the century, and most recently, retreating with ASFA and a new emphasis on adoption. The goal of preserving families has always been in the background of child welfare services; it is the impetus behind the family support services explored in chapter 4 and the array of services targeted to the prevention of abuse and neglect.

An interesting aspect of family preservation in the past fifteen years has been the expansion of the concept of family. We noted in chapter 1 that a smaller proportion of families now consist of the traditional mother-father-child constellation. Blended families, single-parent families, families with same-sex parents, intergenerational families—all have become more prevalent. Family has come to mean the large extended family of grandparents and aunts and uncles and cousins, as well as all of the traditional and nontraditional forms a family can take today. These are the families that the child welfare system attempts to preserve for children.

Bartholet notes that family preservation is "a mindset that dominates the thinking of people who make and implement child welfare policy from top to bottom, in the public agencies and the private foundations, in the courts and the legislatures" (1999:114). The idea of keeping families together is appealing, both to a public that values family life and to child welfare personnel who have witnessed how poor a parent the state can be. There is serious disagreement, however, about how the concept should be implemented.

Although critics of family preservation may point to particular cases in which the policy has influenced worker or court decisions that compromised the safety of children (Gelles 1996; Bartholet 1999), there is no real disagreement about these tragic instances in which mistakes in judgment have clearly been made. The controversy focuses on family situations in which the risk is less dire and the questions concern the potential of parents to acquire the attitudes and skills necessary for success. The problems lie in the implementation of the concept. How much help should parents be given, and for how long? Which do children need more urgently, stable homes or homes with their biological families?

Family Preservation Services

"Family preservation" has come to signify any set of services with the goal of maintaining the child in the family, or even, sometimes, simply the decision to allow a child to remain at home without providing services to the family. It is impossible to evaluate the outcomes of such a broad range of interventions and noninterventions, whose only common thread is that the family remains intact. To evaluate the outcome of family preservation and assess it as a policy, it is necessary to narrow the discussion to a specific set of services, based on shared assumptions about the family and delivered with the intent of enabling the family to provide an adequate home for its children.

> What is revolutionary about the family-based services movement is its rejection of a world view which blames families for their failures in child rearing and sees foster care or institutional placement as the best way to save children. In place of this old world view, the family preservation movement holds forth a new vision: one which sees that families are worth saving, as well as children. . . . The new model of child welfare differs from the old paradigm in valuing families' strengths and respecting their needs and views, even in the face of serious child maltreatment. Family-based workers recognize that an essential part of their job is to instill hope and engage families in a process of change which is both goal-oriented and time limited. And while preventing placement is most frequently seen as the primary goal of family-based services, families, workers, and agencies all know that this can only be achieved through improvement in family functioning, social, material, or psychological, which allows children to remain *safely* in their own homes.
>
> (NELSON AND LANDSMAN 1992:3)

This kind of family preservation services—a particular model of intensive, crisis-oriented service delivery—is the subject of the remainder of this chapter. The reader should bear in mind that long before this particular model of intensive services was developed, family preservation services were part of the child welfare system.

The Three Original Intensive Service Models

Nelson and Landsman (1992) distinguish three models of intensive family services: crisis intervention, home-based treatment, and family treatment. These models share the philosophical base outlined in the preceding quotation, but they use different theoretical models and they vary in the intensity, duration, and place of service.

Homebuilders The first of the intensive family preservation models was Homebuilders, developed in the state of Washington in the 1970s. Homebuilders is a short-term, intensive intervention program. It is based in crisis theory, which postulates that because a crisis state cannot be maintained, its presence opens an opportunity for change. Families are referred to Homebuilders from protective services when there is a high probability that children will need placement in foster care. Each Homebuilders worker carries only two cases at a time; the workers are available to the families as needed, at any time. They work mainly in the home, but also anywhere else they are needed. Their work ranges from counseling interventions to help in cleaning an apartment. This intensive service is brief, lasting between four and eight weeks, and is based on social learning theory. The goal is the limited one of stabilizing the family so that placement of children outside the home is not necessary (Kinney, Haapala, et al. 1990).

Evaluation was built into Homebuilders from the start. Early evaluations showed that the families served experienced very low rates of placement. These findings, and the attractiveness of the philosophical base, generated great enthusiasm for the model.[3] Later evaluations have not shown the model to be superior to other forms of service in preventing placement, but it meets the needs of some families and continues to be a much-used model.

The home-based model The home-based model has many of the characteristics of Homebuilders, but it arises from family systems theory. The family as a whole is the target of intervention.[4]

Families receiving services according to a home-based model participate in the assessment of their situation and in setting treatment goals. Interventions take place over more extended periods, and workers carry ten to twelve cases at a time. Family therapists provide a wide range of services, in addition to the coordination of services provided by other agencies.

Family treatment model The third model is the family treatment model. Also based on family systems theory, this model is a much more traditional therapeutic model. Sessions can take place in the therapist's office as well as in the home, and interventions often consist only of family therapy. Services are less intensive than those provided in the preceding two models, and can extend over an indefinite length of time. Workers carry more cases. There has been little formal research on the effectiveness of the family treatment model. Over time, its originators have come to think that it is most effective in work with families in which there are difficulties with adolescents.

When family preservation services are discussed in general terms, usually it is either the Homebuilders or the home-based model, or a blend of the two, that is being discussed.

Community-Centered Practice

So new that it does not yet have an agreed-upon name, community-centered practice is based on the idea that successful family life can take place only in concerned and supportive communities that have the resources to offer opportunity and hope to residents. With its roots in the settlement house movement and the beginnings of social work, community-centered practice is the newest idea in the family preservation literature.

> Community social work views professional services as marginal compared to the amount of help and care that is provided in informal social networks and avoids usurping natural helpers and creating disempowering reliance on formal services. Rather than "objects of concern," clients are seen as equal citizens with the same capacities and rights as professionals. In this new light, the professional's task is to promote partnership and collaboration by identifying strengths and mobilizing resources in the community, reframing situations, and modifying destructive patterns.
>
> (ADAMS AND NELSON 1995:17)

Many of the ideals of community social work are applied to child welfare in the community partner concept, since the late 1990s being promoted by the Edna McConnell Clark Foundation. The reforms envisioned in this approach would narrow the scope of child protective services so that they dealt only with high-risk families, while building a network of community agencies to work with families who need support and help but do not require authoritative intervention. Waldfogel (1998, 2000) reports the experiences of Florida, Missouri, and Iowa in implementing a community partner approach to protective services, noting that it is modeled on British experience.

The Patch Project in Iowa is an example of a community-centered practice model. A team of workers delivers child protective services and other family support services to a specific neighborhood, or "patch." The

Patch teams "offer accessible, flexible, and holistic services based on their knowledge of the local cultural and physical environment and on the formal and informal partnerships they develop in their neighborhood, or patch" (Adams and Krauth 1995:87). Workers report spending more time with clients; drawing on both formal and informal neighborhood resources; and defining family problems more holistically, giving more attention to the impact of poverty, housing, mental illness, and substance abuse on the safety and well-being of children (Waldfogel 1998).

The promise of this approach lies in its emphasis on the community conditions that make it difficult to raise children. It offers hope for prevention of abuse and neglect. With its basis on listening to community residents as they define their needs, and its reliance on the voluntary use of services by stressed families, the model offers great promise for real changes in communities and families. It rests on the premise that parents, even those who are abusive or neglectful, want to do well by their children and will engage in services to improve their parenting.

Bartholet (1999) points out some of the dangers of the community partner approach. She questions the assumption that child protection is overinclusive, serving families in which there is relatively little risk to children, and thus that funds could be diverted from child protection to develop community-based services. If low-risk families were to be served in the community, voluntarily and without court supervision, Bartholet questions whether children would really obtain the protection they need. The approach would direct funds to high-poverty neighborhoods, where they are sorely needed, but she cautions that those funds might be diverted from core child protection services, leaving children at even greater risk. These are interesting questions about a dynamic new way of conceptualizing child welfare services. Both the community-based approach and the concerns it raises deserve serious consideration.

Kinship Foster Care

The placement of children who cannot remain in their own homes into the care of relatives has grown tremendously in the past fifteen years. An important reason for this growth has been the acute shortage of foster homes; the use of relative homes has taken some pressure off the foster care system. But kinship foster care is also a part of the family preservation movement: a major impetus for its growth has been the expanded concept of family and the increasing investment in keeping children within their extended families. A full discussion of kinship foster care, though it would not be out of place here, appears in chapter 7 because so many of the complex issues involved in foster care pertain to relative foster homes.

Critical Issue: Appropriate Use of Family Preservation Services

Family preservation was probably oversold at the outset of the current movement, when it was promoted as a way of almost universally preventing foster care placement. As time has gone on, controlled studies have raised questions about whether family preservation models actually lower the rates of foster care placement. Questions have also been raised about whether there has been too much emphasis on preserving families, at the cost of leaving children with or returning children to parents when their safety is at risk. The tension is an old one, but it is now framed both in terms of the rights of parents and in terms of the value of the biological family to the child.

Evaluation

A body of empirical data is emerging concerning the effectiveness of family preservation services in protecting children from further harm and preventing out-of-home placement. Intensive family preservation services were originally marketed as cost-effective because they would keep children out of foster care, so the outcome measure usually applied is the success of the program in preventing foster care placement. There are, however, difficulties with this approach. Placement is not frequent, even among high-risk families involved in the protective service system.[5] Although prevention of placement may be the policy goal of legislatures, it is not the ultimate goal of family preservation services. Rather, their goal is to stabilize families that will be safe and nurturing places for children.

The first evaluations, based on the criterion of lowering placement rates, reported the success of intensive family preservation programs. The crisis intervention programs reported that more than 90 percent of the families they served remained intact; other models that entailed longer contact with families reported somewhat lower percentages. However, the first controlled studies could not demonstrate that family preservation services lowered placement rates: the placement rates were low in control as well as experimental groups. In fact, the largest study of family preservation with a randomly assigned control group, carried out in Illinois, found that placement rates were slightly higher among those families receiving intensive family preservation services (Schuerman, Rzepnicki, et al. 1994).[6] If placement rates were not lowered, the cost-effectiveness of the programs could not be demonstrated, at least not in terms of the immediate outlay of funds.

If placement prevention cannot be demonstrated, and indeed may not be an appropriate outcome measure, improvement in family functioning becomes critical. McCroskey and Meezan (1997) carried out a large study with an experimental design in southern California. No one model was tested, but all interventions conformed to the basic principles of family preservation services. Families receiving family preservation services showed small but significant improvement on measures of family functioning, while the home environment improved for very young children, and school behavior improved for older children. In general, programs were more successful when physical abuse, rather than neglect, was present, and were less successful when there was substance abuse, domestic violence between adults, or a history of parental incarceration. Rates of placement were the same for control and treatment groups. This study also looked at reabuse rates and found them to be low in both groups.

Dore (1993) notes that family preservation services are less effective for families coping with extreme poverty, single-parent status, low educational attainment, and mental health problems. McCroskey and Meezan (1997) also report that the concrete needs of families had to be addressed before there was improvement in the interpersonal areas of family functioning. It is worth considering whether these are problems that would overwhelm any intervention. Most of the characteristics of the families less successful with family preservation services also apply disproportionately to families of color. Could it be that these services reflect a white, middle-class conception of how a family should function and thus are less effective for minority families?

McCroskey and Meezan (1997) also make note of a small group of families that was not able to complete services. These were families in which the caregiver was aggressive or violent and had severe emotional problems. They suggest that a different type of service, one that first addresses violence reduction, is needed by such families. They also note that these may be the very families that, because of the potential for violence against children, call the wisdom of family preservation into question.

Family preservation programs seek to empower families by creating opportunities for them to participate in assessing their difficulties and planning services. In this way they resemble the safety-focused assessments that have been introduced by some child protective service agencies. All of the studies cited here reveal that clients are enthusiastic about the services they receive. If empowerment is a goal; that is, if we truly believe that families are capable of judging what is in their own best interest, then their endorsement itself may be an important indicator of the effectiveness of family preservation services.

In their enthusiasm for a new model of working with troubled families, child welfare professionals and the public may have expected too much of intensive family preservation services. Most of the models are time-limited, whereas some family difficulties, such as substance abuse, require long-term support and protective monitoring and will probably continue to demand episodic intensive services. Family preservation services are but one part of the array of services that must be available to protective service workers. No service model will work for all families. One of the basic tenets of social work practice is the necessity of individualizing the needs of each client and designing an intervention package to meet those needs. All of the models of intensive family services described in this section are flexible. Nevertheless, it would be unrealistic to expect any service program to be equally effective for all families as each copes with a highly individual complex of difficulties and needs.

Do Attempts to Preserve Families Put Children at Risk?

When the media report on children who are injured or killed after being left in or returned to their homes, the public raises questions about the wisdom of family preservation services. The difficulty is in deciding when to try intensive family preservation services, when to remove a child from the family, and when it is safe to return a child home, in cases where—as in the majority of such situations—the child is currently safe from serious injury but the risk of future harm is unclear. Nelson (1994) points out that stories of bad decisions and child fatalities were in the newspapers long before the 1985 federal mandate that agencies attempt to preserve or reunify families.

The Adoption and Safe Families Act mandates that "reasonable efforts" be made to keep children in their own homes or, if they have been removed, to reunite them with their families. How extensive and intensive must reasonable efforts be? ASFA sets time limits, but they are increasingly called into question as it becomes evident that some family problems, such as substance abuse, can only rarely be remedied within the time frames provided. Intensive family preservation services present the opportunity to rebuild families, but their brief duration limits their potential to help families with multiple and complex problems, including substance abuse. Community-based family preservation services offer the promise of creating supportive networks and of utilizing existing networks, that can aid family functioning over the long term.

The publicized stories of injured children left with "bad" families are not often stories of the failure of intensive family preservation services. They are more likely to be the result of an unwise adherence to the idea that all families should be preserved. Most parents are protective of their children; but not all are capable of protecting them at all times. One can start with the proposition that children need to be rescued from bad families, or one can start with the idea that the "best way to protect children is to preserve as much of their families as possible" (Maluccio, Pine, et al. 1994:295). The latter is the philosophy behind family preservation services.

Intensive family preservation services and community-based services will enable some children to remain with their original families. Kinship foster care will enable others to remain within their extended families. Perhaps the most important contribution of the family preservation services movement is its affirmation that parents are concerned about their children and want to be good parents. The voices of parents—so crucial to planning and decision-making about their children—have been brought into the process and into the consciousness of professionals.

Conclusion

This chapter has reviewed the crisis services at the heart of the child welfare agency's mission. The agency assumes responsibility for the safety of the child receiving these services, calling upon the authority of the protective service system, including the courts. Although it can be argued that the community as a whole is responsible for its children, the community has delegated to the child welfare agency the responsibility for seeing that children are safe. This responsibility entails the most complex tasks that social workers undertake. It calls on all the social worker's skills of assessment, of clinical decision making, and of engaging families in working relationships. At the policy level and at the individual case level, tension arises continually between the child's need for the security of his own family and his need for safety from harm.

The power of the child welfare agency, and its use of authority, often creates fear and hostility in clients. Statistics indicate that many families that the agency encounters receive no services. Other families receive few or inappropriate services. We have looked at some techniques used to involve parents in defining family problems and deciding how to resolve them. These techniques can lead to more individualized and appropriate services; but their implementation demands flexible funding to pay for a wide variety of services, and it requires workers who have the time and training they need to help families find and use those services.

This chapter has noted current trends in child protective services that serve to involve families in planning for their children, and has focused on family preservation services as a means of resolving the tension between assuring safety and keeping the family intact. These services have made an important contribution in reminding us that most parents want the best for their children and want to be involved in their care. However, even the best of family preservation efforts will not be sufficient for every child. Some children need the safety of an out-of-home placement; some families need time to get their parenting skills in order. Kinship foster care is an important means of keeping the child within the extended family, but even this is not always possible. The next two chapters examine out-of-home care, the other major service delivered by child welfare agencies.

Notes

1. The National Incidence Study was described in chapter 3. A nationally representative sample of more than 5,600 professionals reported whether they had known of a child who had been harmed, or was at risk of harm; they also provided information about whether they had reported the incident.

2. An excellent example of this approach is presented in by Turnell and Edwards (1999:94–138), in a transcript of a practitioner's use of the model with a very serious incident of abuse.

3. The Edna McConnell Clark Foundation, which provided demonstration funding for many new Homebuilders programs, vigorously promoted the model as a revolutionary new way to work successfully with abusing and neglecting families while reducing the cost of maintaining children in foster care.

4. The original model was developed by Families, Inc., in Iowa. In cooperation with the School of University of Iowa Social Work and the University of Iowa Institute of Child Behavior and Development, Families, Inc., was an original sponsor of the Clearinghouse for Home-Based Services, which, with a grant from the Children's Bureau, became the National Resource Center on Family-Based Services in 1981. The yearly national conference sponsored by the National Resource Center has drawn increasing numbers of participants, and has been important in the development of family preservation services. The presence and voice of families themselves is a key aspect of that conference.

5. Families First, the largest randomized study of family preservation programs, conducted in Illinois in 1989–1992, found that the risk of placement in the control group was 7 percent in the first month of services, and after one year about 21 percent (Schuerman, Rzepnicki, et al. 1994:230).

6. This may be a positive finding. It could be that more intensive contact with the families who received family preservation services resulted in the detection of real threats to children's safety and thus to subsequent placements.

References

Adams, P., and K. Krauth. 1995. "Working with Families and Communities: The Patch Approach." In *Reinventing Human Services: Community and Family-Centered Practice,* edited by P. Adams and K. Nelson. New York: Aldine de Gruyter.

Adams, P., and K. Nelson. 1995. "Context of Community-and-Family-Centered Practice: Introduction." In *Reinventing Human Services: Community and Family-Centered Practice,* edited by P. Adams and K. Nelson. New York: Aldine de Gruyter.

Bartholet, E. 1999. *Nobody's Children: Abuse, Neglect, Foster Drift, and the Adoption Alternative.* Boston: Beacon Press.

Botsko, M., and T. Festinger. 1994. *Returning to Care.* Washington, D.C.: Child Welfare League of America.

Brace, C. L. 1872. *The Dangerous Classes of New York.* New York: Wynkoop and Hallenbeck.

Close, M. 1983. "Child Welfare and People of Color: Denial of Equal Access." *Social Work Research and Abstracts* 19(4): 13–30.

Costin, L. B. 1985. "The Historical Context of Child Welfare." In *A Handbook of Child Welfare,* edited by J. Laird and A. Hartman. New York: Free Press.

Costin, L. B., H. J. Karger, et al. 1996. *The Politics of Child Abuse in America.* New York: Oxford University Press.

Dore, M. M. 1993. "Family Preservation and Poor Families: When 'Homebuilding' Is Not Enough." *Families in Society* 74(8): 545–54.

Downs, S. W., E. Moore, et al. 2000. *Child Welfare and Family Services: Policies and Practice.* Boston: Allyn and Bacon.

English, D. 1998. "The Extent and Consequences of Child Maltreatment." *The Future of Children* 8(1): 39–53.

Faver, C. A., S. L. Crawford, et al. 1999. "Services for Child Maltreatment: Challenges for Research and Practice." *Children and Youth Services Review* 21(2): 89–109.

Gelles, R. J. 1996. *The Book of David.* New York: Basic Books.

Giovannoni, J. M. 1985. "Child Abuse and Neglect: An Overview." In *A Handbook of Child Welfare: Context, Knowledge, and Practice,* edited by J. Laird and A. Hartman. New York: Free Press.

Hanson, S. M. H., M. L. Heims, et al., eds. 1995. *Single Parent Families: Diversity, Myths and Realities.* Binghamton, N.Y.: Haworth Press.

Hayes-Bautista, D., A. Hurtado, et al. 1992. *No Longer a Minority: Latinos and Social Policy in California.* Los Angeles: UCLA Chicano Studies Research Center.

Inkelas, M., and N. Halfon. 1997. "Recidivism in Child Protective Services." *Children and Youth Services Review* 19(3): 139–61.

Kadushin, A., and J. Martin. 1981. *Child Abuse: An Interactional Event.* New York: Columbia University Press.

Kempe, H. C., F. N. Silverman, et al. 1962. "The Battered Child Syndrome." *Journal of the American Medical Association* 18(1): 17–24.

Kinney, J., D. Haapala, et al. 1990. "The Homebuilders Model." In *Reaching High Risk Families: Intensive Family Preservation in Human Services,* edited by J. K. Whittaker, J. Kinney, E. M. Tracy, and C. Booth. New York: Aldine de Gruyter.

Korbin, J. 1981. *Child Abuse and Neglect: Cross Cultural Perspectives.* Berkeley: University of California Press.

Lindsey, D. 1994. *The Welfare of Children.* New York: Oxford University Press.

Maluccio, A., B. Pine, et al. 1994. "Protecting Children by Preserving Their Families." *Children and Youth Services Review* 16(5/6): 295–307.

McCroskey, J., and W. Meezan. 1997. *Family Preservation and Family Functioning.* Washington, D.C.: Child Welfare League of America.

McGowan, B. G. 1983. "Historical Evolution of Child Welfare Services: An Examination of the Sources of Current Problems and Dilemmas." In *Child Welfare: Current Dilemmas, Future Directions,* edited by B. G. Mcgowan and W. Meezan. Itasca, Ill.: F. E. Peacock.

Nelson, K. E. 1994. "Do Services to Preserve the Family Place Children at Unnecessary Risk?" *Controversial Issues in Child Welfare,* edited by E. Gambrill and T. Stein. Boston: Allyn and Bacon.

Nelson, K. E., and M. J. Landsman. 1992. *Alternative Models of Family Preservation: Family Based Services in Context.* Springfield, Ill.: Charles C. Thomas.

Parnell, J., and G. Burford. 2000. "Family Group Decision Making: Protecting Children and Women." *Child Welfare* 89(2): 131–58.

Pecora, P. J., J. L. Whittaker, et al. 1992. *The Child Welfare Challenge: Policy, Practice, and Research.* New York: Aldine de Gruyter.

Pelton, L. 1989. *For Reasons of Poverty: A Critical Analysis of the Public Child Welfare System in the United States.* New York: Praeger.

Polansky, N., M. A. Chalmers, et al. 1981. *Damaged Parents: An Anatomy of Child Neglect.* Chicago: University of Chicago Press.

Rodgers, A. 2000. "Family Decision Meetings: A Profile of Average Use in Oregon's Child Welfare Agency." Child Welfare Partnership, Portland State University.

Schene, P. A. 1998. "Past, Present, and Future Roles of child Protective Services." *The Future of Children* 8(1): 23–38.

Schuerman, J. R., T. L. Rzepnicki, et al. 1994. *Putting Families First: An Experiment in Family Preservation.* New York: Aldine de Gruyter.

Shireman, J., S. Eggman, et al. 2000. "Strengths/Needs Based Services Evaluation: Interim Report, June 2000." Regional Research Institute for Human Services, Portland, Ore.

Stenho, S. M. 1982. "Differential Treatment of Minority Children in Service Systems." *Social Work* 17(1): 39–46.

Turnell, A., and S. Edwards. 1999. *Signs of Safety: A Solution and Safety Oriented Approach to Child Protection Casework.* New York: W. W. Norton.

U.S. Congress. 1998. "Green Book." U.S. House of Representatives, Washington, D.C. Available at http://aspe.os.dhhs.gov/98gb/intro.htm.

U.S. Department of Health and Human Services. 1999. *Blending Perspectives and Building Common Ground: A Report to Congress on Substance Abuse and Child Protection.* Washington, D.C.: U.S. Government Printing Office.

U.S. Department of Health and Human Services, Children's Bureau. 1997. *National Study of Protective, Preventive and Reunification Services Delivered to Children and Their Families. Washington, D.C.: U.S. Government Printing Office.*

———. 2000a. *Child Maltreatment 1997: Reports from the States to the National Child Abuse and Neglect Data System.* Washington, D.C.: U.S. Government Printing Office.

———. 2000b. *Child Welfare Outcomes 1998: Annual Report.* Washington, D.C.: U.S. Government Printing Office.

———. 2001. *Child Maltreatment 1999: Reports from the States to the National Child Abuse and Neglect Data System.* Washington, D.C.: U.S. Government Printing Office.

U.S. Department of Health and Human Services, National Center on Child Abuse and Neglect. 1996. *Third National Incidence Study of Child Abuse and Neglect.* Washington, D.C.: U.S. Government Printing Office.

Waldfogel, J. 1998. "Rethinking the Paradigm for Child Protection." *The Future of Children* 8(1): 104–20.

———. 2000. "Reforming Child Protective Services." *Child Welfare* 79(1): 43–57.

Wells, S. J., T. J. Stein, et al. 1989. "Screening in Child Protective Services." *Social Work* 34(1): 45–47.

Young, L. 1964. *Wednesday's Child*. New York: McGraw Hill.

CHAPTER 6

✦

Investment in Foster Care

"What's the matter, Eeyore?"

"Nothing, Christopher Robin. Nothing important. I suppose you haven't seen a house or whatnot anywhere about?"

"What sort of a house?"

"Just a house."

"Who lives there?"

"I do. At least I thought I did. But I suppose I don't. After all, we can't all have houses."

A. A. MILNE, *THE HOUSE AT POOH CORNER*

At the heart of the difficulties of the child welfare system are the difficulties of the foster care system: a shortage of foster homes, questions about the quality of care children are getting in some foster homes, the system's inability or unwillingness to provide needed support services to foster homes, and above all, uncertainty about the function of foster care within the child welfare system. Society's main response to difficulties with foster care has been an attempt to diminish its role; legislation and funding are targeted to promote family preservation and procedures that move children out of foster care and into permanent homes more quickly. Little attention has been paid to the improvement of foster care itself.

Demographic changes in the second half of the twentieth century have resulted in a severe shortage of foster homes. With more women in the workforce and more single-parent families, there are fewer families who wish to foster children. The shortage of foster homes has led to unacceptable compromises in foster care practice—compromises in the assessment and supervision of homes, in matching the needs of children with the capacities of foster homes, and in deciding how many children should be placed in a given foster home. As a result, children are too often placed in inappropriate homes, too often moved, and too often damaged by the foster care experience.

One approach to the shortage has been to try to limit the number of children who need foster care. Major policy thrusts have included the use of family preservation services, increased placement of children with relatives for fostering, and emphasis on shortening children's stays in foster care, either through reunification or adoption. Explicit federal legislation, including ASFA's requirements for periodic case review and its provisions for terminating parental rights, has also been directed at reducing the need for foster care. To date these efforts have not reduced the numbers of children in foster care. Martin (2000:35) notes "the clear association between economic and social stresses on the one hand, and the use of substitute care services on the other." Until the network of basic family support programs is better developed and funded, the need for foster care is unlikely to diminish.

If children are to be in foster care, the experience must help rather than harm them. Improving the experience of foster care has two facets. One is investment in the foster care system, so that foster homes are able to provide stable and good care for children. The other is development of alternative forms of out-of-home care, so that each child receives the care that best meets his or her needs. The first of those facets is the subject of this chapter; the next chapter concerns ways in which the foster care system has been expanded and might be further expanded.

This chapter begins with a brief look at the history of out-of-home care. The reader will note that themes of the needs of children, as perceived at different times, interplay with concerns about children becoming economically self-sufficient, and questions about the moral character of the homes of the poor. This history also, sadly, reflects a continuing reluctance of communities to be generous in meeting the needs of children. The chapter continues by developing of a picture of current foster care, both a statistical description, and an exploration of the experience of foster care. Finally, the dimensions of investment in foster care are considered.

Historical Perspective

Throughout the history of the United States—as in any society—there have always been some children who needed care outside their own homes. Until the mid-nineteenth century, children commonly became dependent on the community upon the death of their parents. Diseases claimed numerous lives; many women died in childbirth; the perils of western settlement and the hazardous conditions of early industry left children without parents. Others depended on the community for care because their families could not afford to house, feed, and clothe them, or because their families neglected them.[1]

Congregate Care

The almshouse In the eighteenth and early nineteenth centuries, the almshouse was the common institutional setting for the care of any member of society who could not live independently. There the poor, the mentally ill, and young children lived together. Conditions could be frightful. By the mid-1800s it was recognized that these large, mixed institutions were inappropriate for children.

> The high death rate, the outbreaks of contagious disease, the incompetent staff, and the generally neglected and unhappy condition of the children reported by individuals and special committees in one state after another led to the demand that this method of caring for dependent children be abandoned. Reform came slowly in view of the evidence of the serious conditions in the almshouses, because public funds had been invested in land and buildings and because of the fatal ease with which children and families could be placed in an almshouse. Moreover, as the number of children in almshouses was large, the problem of what to do with them if this form of care were abandoned was one not easily solved.
>
> (ABBOTT 1938B:7)

Orphanages Not until the middle of the nineteenth century were orphanages common enough to begin to replace almshouses for the care of children. Many were founded in response to specific crises. For example, the first orphanage in the United States was opened in New Orleans, in 1727, by the Ursuline Sisters to care for children orphaned after the Natchez Indian massacre. The Chicago Home for Unfortunates was founded to care for children orphaned by a cholera epidemic; the Parry Center in Portland, Oregon, to care for the children whose parents died as the wagon trains came westward.

Children were valued for their potential contributions in a rapidly expanding country, and work itself was valued as morally important. Thus it was thought important that children be taught a trade, or the skills of farming or housework. So when children in an almshouse or an orphanage, or sometimes in a poor family, reached an age at which their labor was considered valuable, they were indentured. Through indenture, children were "bound over" to a family for a period of years, with the expectation that they would be given room, board, and some education, and would be taught a useful trade. The following excerpt from the notes of a town meeting in 1726 in Watertown, Massachusetts, is illustrative:

> There having been Some complaints made to the selectmen of some families in Said Town That are under very Neady and Suffering Circumstances. . . . In which families there are Children of beth Sex's that are able to work in order to their Maintinance, and also of being Sent to School and brought to the Publick worship of God; But through the willfulness, Negligence & Indulgence of their parents they are brought up in Idleness Ignorance & Ereligion, and are more Likely to prove a Trouble and Charge, then blessings in their Day & Generation if not timely prevented. . . . The Selectmen . . . do therefore order that the Town Clerk . . . give notice to Such Families or the parents of them that they forth with take care and put out such their Children to Such Religious families where both Body and Soul may be taken good care of. . . . Also to Signifie unto such Persons that have a Desire to take Children or Servants to meet with the aboves Selectmen at their Meeting.
>
> (ABBOTT 1938A, 1:212–13)

An indenture contract provided that the children would receive food, shelter, and appropriate education in return for their labor. Indenture, although it was based on a reasonable concept and sometimes worked to a young person's advantage, was unsupervised and open to abuses.[2] It persisted until, in the middle of the nineteenth century, industrialization took labor out of the home and moved it into the factory. The abolition of slavery was doubtless also a factor in the demise of indenture, for the contract that bound apprentice to master had some characteristics of involuntary servitude and might be considered unconstitutional under the post–Civil War amendments (Kadushin and Martin 1988).

An entry from the 1850 ledger of the Chicago Orphan Asylum, a more or less standard form required of parents who could not care for their children, illustrates the use of the orphanage, and of indenture, to care for the children of the poor as well as those who were orphaned.

I, the subscriber, solicitous that my children, Christina Maria and Magnus Wilhelm shall receive the benefits and advantages of the Chicago Orphan Asylum, and the Trustees of said asylum being willing to receive and provide for them and also to place them out in a virtuous family until they are of age, agreeably to the provisions of the act of incorporation, and the rules and regulations of the said Asylum, provided I relinquish my children to them. I do, therefore, promise not to interfere in the management of them in any respect whatever, or visit them without their consent. And in consideration of their benevolence in thus rearing and providing for my children, I do relinquish all right and claim to them and their services, until they shall arrive of age. And I do engage that I will not ask or receive any compensation for the same, not take my children from, nor induce them to leave the families in which they may be placed by the Board of Trustees of the Asylum. Chicago, February 6, 1850.

(MCCAUSLAND 1976:23–24)

Foster Family Care

Foster care begins Orphanages sometimes placed children in homes for adoption, and homes were used for the indenture of children; but the idea of foster families as an alternative that might replace the orphanage had its beginning on a large scale when, in 1855, Charles Loring Brace sent a trainload of children from the streets of New York to the farms of the West. Brace was appalled by the neglect and destitution of homeless children on New York's streets. He believed that a family, much better than an orphanage, could provide a child a "normal" life and teach the skills required for a productive adulthood.[3] He was also aware of the consequences to society of neglecting its children.

It should be remembered that there are no dangers to the value of property, or to the permanency of our institutions, so great as those from the existence of such a class of vagabond, ignorant, ungoverned children. This "dangerous class" has not begun to show itself, as it will in eight or ten years, when these boys and girls are matured. Those who were too negligent, or too selfish, to notice them as children, will be fully aware of them as men. They will vote—they will have the same rights as we ourselves, though they have grown up ignorant of moral principle. . . . They will poison society. They will perhaps be embittered at the wealth and luxuries they never share. Then let society beware.

(BRACE 1872:321–22)

In the farming economy of the West, children's labor was needed on the farms, so foster homes were readily available. Brace's organization, the Children's Aid Society, collected children from the streets of New York City and from the city's institutions. Some were orphans; if a parent was living an attempt was made to get parental consent for the child's placement in a farm home. Large groups of these children would arrive in a community by train, and families would select the ones they wanted to take into their homes. The placement of the children was overseen by a committee of respected community members, but it may have been awkward for these citizens to object to a questionable placement. An early child welfare worker, Dr. Hastings Hart, described the placement procedure in a report to the National Conference of Charities and Corrections in 1894:

It was surprising how many happy selections were made under such circumstances. In a little more than three hours nearly all those forty children were disposed of. Some who had not previously applied selected children. There was little time for consultation, and refusal would be embarrassing, and I know that the committee consented to some assignments against their better judgment. . . . While the younger children are taken from motives of benevolence and are uniformly well treated, the older ones are, in the majority of cases, taken from motives of profit, and are expected to earn their way from the start.

(KADUSHIN AND MARTIN 1988:348)

Brace's program drew criticism because children were sent over such vast distances and because many children of Catholic immigrants were placed into Protestant homes.[4] Questions were also raised about inadequate supervision of the selection and placement of the children. Accused of sending children into unknown homes where they might be abused or neglected, Brace sent his own investigators to follow up on his placements. The reports were optimistic.

> The general results are similar. The boys and girls who were sent out when under fourteen are often heard from, and succeed remarkably well. In hundreds of instances, they cannot be distinguished from the young men and women natives in the villages. Large numbers have farms of their own, and are prospering reasonably well in the world. Some are in the professions, some are mechanics or shop-keepers, the girls are generally well married. . . . With the larger boys, exact results are more difficult to attain, as they leave their places frequently. Some few seem to drift into the Western cities and take up street trades again. Very few, indeed, get back to New York. The great mass become honest producers on the Western soil.
>
> (BRACE 1872:241–42)

These reports were never fully trusted; unfortunately, there was no independent investigation at the time. The orphan trains continued until 1929, by which time 31,081 children had been placed by the Children's Aid Society (Costin, Bell, et al. 1991). In the 1980s, interviews with about two hundred adults who had come west on the trains revealed the variety of experiences that one might expect. The uncertainty of the train trip and the hope that they could remain with siblings were common themes among those interviewed. They recalled continuing to wonder about, and to long for, their original families. Their experiences in their placements were mixed, ranging from being exploited and abused as laborers to feeling like part of the family and partaking of its joys and troubles. Some had several placements before finding a permanent home. The program was supervised in some respects; many adults remembered yearly visits by the agent of the Children's Aid Society. Probably the experiences of the younger children were better than those of the older children (Jackson 1986).

Whether the children sent west by Brace were rescued from an intolerable street life or were seized from their families, whether they had good or bad experiences, and whether they were provided opportunities that compensated for the loss of their original families are all subjects of continuing debate.

The development of foster care Brace's work stimulated the development of free foster homes at a more local level. As the child welfare field struggled with how to develop foster home services, the dominant issues were (1) how to provide adequate supervision to insure good care of children, (2) the temporary versus more permanent nature of foster homes, (3) whether foster parents should be paid, and (4) the nature of the partnership between foster parents and professionals. As foster homes began to be used more often, debate about the relative merits of the foster home and the orphanage emerged. Of course, each of these historical issues continues to be debated with respect to out-of-home care today.

Charles Birtwell had an early transforming idea about foster care. Massachusetts had, in the late 1860s, begun to pay for the board of children too young to be indentured (a move that roused the ire of Brace and others who thought that fostering a child was an act of charity and love, and should not be done for pay). As head of the Boston Children's Aid Society between 1886 and 1911, Birtwell conceptualized foster care as a temporary measure, to be used when it was the best way to meet a particular child's need. The Boston Children's Aid Society studied foster home applicants and supervised foster home placements after they were made. Careful records were kept. Kadushin characterizes the work as "an attempt to build a science of foster family care and to professionalize practice" (Kadushin and Martin 1988:350). Eventually these placements were made through one of a number of placing agencies. Because in Boston, as in other cities, there were an unlimited number of children whose condition could be improved, the demands on the agency, and the size of the network of homes that could be developed, were also unlimited (Crenson 1998). The potentially limitless nature of services to children continues to plague child welfare today.

The debate Thomas Mulry articulated the issues in the debate between proponents of orphanages and proponents of foster care.[5] He must have been a most interesting man. He was a Catholic, the son of an Irish immigrant, a prosperous businessman who spent much time in charity work, and, at the beginning of his work, a believer in orphanage care for children. In 1898, in an address to the National Conference of Charities and Corrections, Mulry spoke of the institution's role in the preservation of families; his arguments have a surprisingly current tenor. In the institution, he said, the "family bond" was kept intact through frequent visits, whereas children boarded out would be so scattered that visits would not be possible. The institution intended to return children to their homes, whereas families who took children usually intended to keep them until maturity (Crenson 1998:206).

Two years later in another address to the same conference, Mulry brought in a report from a committee of prominent child welfare workers. The report was a compromise between the supporters of institutions and those of foster care, a far-reaching document that laid the foundations of our current system of substitute care. It suggested that the important point was meeting the needs of individual children, and that as long as those needs were met either home or institution was appropriate. However, the report acknowledged that a family home was a more natural place for a child to grow up. The preservation of the child's own family was emphasized, and, in an idea far in advance of its time, day nurseries were suggested as a means to care for the children of single mothers and to avoid placements.

The momentum toward placement in foster care instead of institutional care carried into the White House Conference on the Care of Dependent Children in 1909. Urban areas were experiencing success with this method of caring for dependent children; that success was reported with enthusiasm. However, Crenson (1998) describes a little-noted speech, in which the different condition of the African American family in the rural South was described. Richard Carroll spoke of the difficulties of placing black children in South Carolina with black families, already poverty-stricken and with as many children as they could support. Carroll ran an institution that placed children in homes out of necessity; the meager resources of the institution did not allow it to keep children there, nor did the resources allow adequate supervision of children in the foster homes. A colleague from South Carolina suggested that the rural structure of a poor state made adequate supervision of placements for white children difficult as well. These reports apparently had no impact.

In 1909, "social reform on a grand scale was once again in favor, and the orphanage was not big enough to accommodate its aspirations" (Crenson 1998:255). The saving of large numbers of children could better be accomplished through a foster care system, theoretically unlimited in size. The White House Conference gave clear preference to foster home care in its recommendations. The stage was set for the widespread development of foster homes and for the eventual disappearance of large-scale institutional care of young children in the United States.

The advantages of foster care were apparent. Foster care was less expensive than the maintenance of large residential orphanages—especially as orphanage populations grew smaller because of the increasing use of foster care. And, in this era of high infant mortality, young children were more likely to survive in foster care. One institution reported a 98 percent death rate of infants in 1898; in 1904, when these infants were placed in foster care, the mortality rate was 10 percent (Crenson 1998:225). The unique needs of individual children could be better met in foster care. A family home seemed more "natural" for a child.

Many families were willing to take foster children, particularly when young children began to be placed and payment made for their care. Foster care fit well into a common American lifestyle in the first half of the twentieth century, when many families had a wage-earning father and a mother at home caring for several children. Adding a foster child was a way of adding to the family's income and providing a needed community service. As foster care became localized and professional services developed, it was possible to organize foster care so that placements would be adequately supervised.

The extended family, of course, has always been an important source of care for orphaned children and others whose parents cannot provide for them. Institutions dedicated solely to the care of children—orphanages—have usually been established either in response to disasters in which whole families have been lost, or in settings, such as the frontier West, where distance has separated extended families. Foster care, too, had its beginning and early growth under conditions—those of early industrial society with its large population of poor, immigrant factory workers—where extended family was either distant or unable to assume the burden of extra children.

Foster Care Today

Though national data are imprecise (as discussed in chapter 3), the data do provide a picture of the numbers of children involved in the foster care system, their young age and long placements, and the disproportionate representation of children of color. All of these factors have implications for the future of foster care.

Number of Children in Care

Foster care affects a large number of children. Changes in this number over time reflect social policy changes, economic cycles, and community conditions. The number of children in foster care declined sharply as a

result of the increased support available to families after the passage of
the Social Security Act in 1935, then began to rise in the 1960s. In 1977,
as the economic prosperity of the postwar years ebbed, it was estimated
that 395,000 children were in foster care. By the early 1980s some estimates were as high as 500,000 children (Kadushin and Martin 1988).

These alarming numbers, along with data demonstrating that once
children were in foster care they tended to remain for a long time, led to
nationwide efforts to move children out of foster care and into permanent homes (see chapter 2). Those efforts were quite successful. Some
programs, such as the Oregon Project, found that as many as a third of
the children in long-term foster care could be reunited with their families
(Emlen, Lahti, et al. 1976). With innovative recruitment and careful placement procedures, adoptive homes could be found for older children and
children with severe handicaps (Emlen, Lahti, et al. 1976; Unger, Dwarshusis, et al. 1977). By the late 1980s, it was estimated that there were
fewer than 300,000 children in foster care. Child welfare professionals
and policy makers hoped that before long, foster care would be a small
program, providing mainly for adolescents living in the foster homes
where they had grown up and for younger children needing very short
term crisis placements.

Then, in the last fifteen years of the century, the number of children in
foster care began to rise rapidly, coincidentally with the introduction of
crack cocaine into the nation's cities and with the increasing incidence of
family breakdown. Using data from the Adoption and Foster Care
Analysis and Reporting System (AFCARS) and the American Public
Human Services Association, the Children's Bureau reports that on September 30, 2000, there were 556,000 children in out-of-home care in the
United States (U.S. Department of Health and Human Services [hereafter,
U.S. HHS], Children's Bureau 2002a). Though complete and accurate
national statistics are not available, state statistics and trend data indicate
that the number of children in out-of-home care is rising (Martin 2000).

As table 6.1 displays, children and young people are placed in a variety of settings. Most children in out-of-home care are in nonrelative foster homes. Kinship or relative foster homes are next in importance.
Institutions are, generally, of two types: shelter or assessment facilities for
children just entering care; and residential treatment facilities for children
and adolescents with emotional disturbance. Some group homes are shelter facilities for assessment; most are group homes in the community

TABLE 6.1   Placement Settings of Children in Out-of-Home Care,
September 30, 2000

Setting	Percentage of Total	Number of Children
Preadoptive home	4	23,159
Foster family home (relative)	25	137,385
Foster family home (nonrelative)	47	260,636
Group home	8	43,893
Institution	10	56,512
Supervised independent living	1	5,108
Runaway	2	9,964
Trial home visit	3	19,343

SOURCE: U.S. Department of Health and Human Services, Children's Bureau 2002a.

where adolescents may live for considerable periods of time. These forms of care, and independent living programs, will be described in later chapters. Runaways, obviously, represent a failure of the child protective care system.

The data of the Child Welfare League in table 6.2 show the types of foster care. It is evident from both tables that nonrelative family foster care is by far the most common out-of-home placement.

Despite the large number of children in foster care, it should be recognized that placement in foster care is relatively rare. Working with the data of Illinois and Michigan, researchers at the Chapin Hall Center for Children at the University of Chicago discovered that in Illinois 7 percent of the first contacts with the child welfare system resulted in a placement; in Michigan only 4 percent resulted in a placement. Among cases in which maltreatment was substantiated, the placement rate rose to 14 percent in Illinois and 8.5 percent in Michigan. In both states the placement rate for neglected children was higher than for other types of maltreatment (Goerge, Voorhis, et al. 1996). The National Study of Service Delivery reported that 64 percent of the children served by the child welfare system over a one-year period received in-home services (U.S. Department of Health and Human Services, Children's Bureau 1997). It is difficult to tell how typical these figures are.

TABLE 6.2   Children in Foster Care: Types of Foster Care

Type of Foster Care	Percentage of Total	Number of Children
Nonrelative	56.7	184,074
Kinship (relative)	28.6	93,030
Therapeutic (treatment)	5.2	16,803
Preadoptive	2.2	7,013
Emergency shelter	1.7	5,360
Group home (eight or fewer children)	5.6	18,163
Total	100.0	324,443

* Total is less than the total number of children in foster care in 1996 because eight states did not report data in a way that could be displayed in these categories.

SOURCE: Child Welfare League of America 1996.

Characteristics of Children in Foster Care

Reasons for entry into care The basic reason that children enter foster care is, of course, that their families are, for a time, judged to be unable to care for them. The usual path of entry into foster care is the protective service system, but some children come into foster care at the request of their parents, either because illness, incarceration, or a similar circumstance makes them unable to care for a child, or because the child's difficulties have become so severe that the family cannot provide adequate care.

For the protective service placements, it appears that neglect is the most common reason (Goerge, Voorhis, et al., 1996). Oregon, using a research program based on extensive case reading, has developed data that demonstrate the prevalence of neglect, or situations of which neglect is a component, as a reason for entry into foster care (table 6.3). Although definitions may vary, it is likely that these data are reasonably representative of data from other state systems.

The rising proportion of children in out-of-home care because of neglect means that the percentage of children in care due to physical or sexual abuse has declined. When each of these types of abuse was first recognized as a problem calling for community intervention, the immediate

TABLE 6.3   Reasons for Entry into Foster Care in Oregon, 1995–1997

Reason	Percent*
Parental absence	21.5
Neglect	18.8
Threat of harm (including domestic violence)	16.5
Child's treatment needs (child requires extensive therapy or restrictive environment)	10.6
Parental treatment needs (parents require hospitalization or residential drug/alcohol treatment)	10.7
Physical abuse	9.2
Sexual abuse	6.6
Child's behavior issues (child is beyond parental control, dangerous, or delinquent)	4.4
Emotional abuse	0.9
Voluntary placement (child's care has overwhelmed parent)	0.5

* Percentages total 99.7 because of rounding.

source: Child Welfare Partnership 1999.

response was a tendency to rescue the child and place him or her in foster care. Gradually ways were found to work with families in many instances, stopping the abuse or removing the abuser and allowing the child to remain in the original home. Neglect is the most difficult of family problems to resolve, and (as described in chapter 5) does not yield to the short intervention modes of many family preservation programs. Neglect is also closely associated with extreme poverty, and the systemic economic changes that would alleviate poverty have yet to be effected.

Other family circumstances impact whether or not children enter foster care. Poor children, and children whose families do not have a steady source of income, are more likely to be placed (Lindsey 1994). Substance abuse is present in many of the families whose children are placed. The families are often involved in the criminal justice system, and domestic violence is common. In summary, if one were to sketch the "typical" family whose child is placed in foster care, it would be a poor family with no stable source of income. It would be headed by a single parent, usually the mother. There would probably be substance abuse and/or

TABLE 6.4   Comparison of Child Population and Foster Care Population

| | Race or Ethnic Group of Child | | | | |
	White	African American	Hispanic	Native American	Asian
As percentage of U.S population	66.0	14.7	14.5	1.0	3.8
As percentage of U.S. children in foster care	38.4	51.0	7.6	1.8	0.7

SOURCE: Child Welfare League of America 1996.

violence in the family. Neglect of the child, in some form, would have precipitated the removal of the child from the home.

Age of children in care Not only did the number of children in foster care increase in the last fifteen years, the age at which children were placed became much younger. By the late 1980s, the number of young children in foster care was decreasing, and most children in foster care were ten years of age or older (Kadushin and Martin 1988:356). Permanent homes had been found for many of the young children who had been found "drifting" in foster care. Foster care intake usually involved troubled adolescents. This trend changed abruptly in the 1990s. Suddenly, it was young families with young children who were experiencing difficulties and needing foster care for their children. In 2000, 38 percent of the children who entered out-of-home care were under five years of age, 21 percent between six and eleven years of age, and 40 percent eleven years and over (U.S. Department of Health and Human Services, Children's Bureau 2002a). Thus the children in foster care now are a young and vulnerable group, for whom prompt planning is particularly important. A year in foster care is a large proportion of their lives. And, if their own families cannot be rehabilitated, their options for permanent homes lessen with each year of age, as does their capacity to make firm new attachments.

Race of children in care Racism has always troubled programs providing out-of-home care. Thirty years ago, there were relatively few children of color in foster care, leading to speculation that these children were underserved by the public child welfare system. The suspicion that these children are underserved remains, for now there are many children of color in foster care, and they stay too long.

African American children are seriously overrepresented in the foster care system. As table 6.4 illustrates, although almost two-thirds of the children in the United States are white, only a little more than one-third of the children in foster care are white. At the same time, whereas only 15 percent of the children in the United States are African American, 51 percent of the children in foster care are African American. Native American children are also overrepresented in the foster care population, possibly reflecting the high poverty rate among Native Americans. Hispanic children and Asian children are underrepresented.

The reasons for the overrepresentation of African American children are many; poverty and racism are prominent among them. The stress of poverty, as we have seen in earlier chapters, makes it more difficult to raise a child without neglect or abuse, and poverty influences placement decisions. Poor families live in crowded conditions where they face scrutiny from neighbors. Poor families have limited access to services, and those they do access, such as large medical clinics, have no personal relationship with the family, may not expect to see a particular child again, and are quick to report to public child welfare agencies when there is any suspicion of maltreatment. And racism plays a role. The discussion in chapter 3 of racism in the child welfare system examines the statistics and points out that there is no evidence that the incidence of abuse and neglect differs by racial category. The National Study of Protective and Preventive Services (U.S. Department of Health and Human Services, Children's Bureau 1997) found that minority children, particularly African American children, were more likely to be in foster care—even when they had the same problems and characteristics as white children—than to be receiving services in their own homes.

Children of color remain longer in foster care than do white children. This in part explains their overrepresentation in the foster care system; any census of children at one point in time will overrepresent those in care for a long time. It is these long stays that raise the suspicion that family preservation services and adoption services are not being provided for, or adapted to, families of color—that these families are once again underserved by the child welfare system.

Characteristics of Foster Care

Length of stay Foster homes are meant to be temporary bridges to permanent homes. Since the 1950s, professionals and the public alike have been concerned about the length of time children stayed in foster homes. In 1959, Maas and Engler published a survey regarding children in foster care in six representative states, and the child welfare world was astounded. The study revealed that large numbers of children were drifting, without any planning for their future, in long-term foster care. Care that had been planned as temporary had become, by default, permanent (Maas and Engler 1959). Subsequent studies repeated the findings (Gruber 1978; Knitzer, Allen, et al. 1978). The problem has not been solved, despite focused efforts during the ensuing years to move children more quickly out of foster care. Research has shown that the longer children stay in foster care, the more likely they are to lose contact with birth families and to remain in care (Martin 2000:25). Long stays in foster care also exacerbate the shortage of foster homes.

Summarizing data on length of stay, Martin (2000:160—62) notes wide variability from one state to another and the consistent finding that African American children have longer stays in foster care than do white children. AFCARS data show that in 1999 more than half of the children in foster care had been in care two years or more, but these data overestimate the average length of stay, because any cross-sectional sample is overweighted with children in long-term care. Martin's analysis shows that about half of the children in foster care have short stays—six months or less—while "a substantial number" of children remain in foster care for more than two years. There is some evidence that younger children tend to have longer stays in foster care, which is unfortunate considering that the "time clock of the child" (Goldstein, Freud, et al. 1973) is ticking faster for young children.[6]

Data based on that submitted by twenty states to the AFCARS shows that in 1996 the goal for 54 percent of the children placed was reunification with their families; for another 6 percent the goal was a permanent home with relatives. This marks a significant change from 1982 VCIS data, which showed a plan of returning home for only 40 percent of the children (House Committee on Ways and Means 1998:790). Because there is no indication that family problems on the whole have diminished in the last ten years, one can only conclude that the emphasis on family preservation has had its impact not only in preventing placement, but in directing goal setting once a child is in out-of-home care.

The children who enter foster care are coming from families whose problems are serious, difficult to resolve, and often multiple. Poverty, erratic income, violence, substance abuse—none of these are easy to change. Their roots lie in behavior patterns laid down through a lifetime of limited opportunity to develop more functional coping skills. If the children in foster care are to go home, it is no wonder that it can take a very long time. If the problems of these families are so intractable, and if the goal is to have children return home, then one might think long stays in foster care are appropriate. Foster care, however, in the current environment of severely limited resources, is often a less than optimal environment for children's growth and development. It is still farther from ideal if children have to move from one foster home to another. The concept of the "time clock of the child" (Goldstein, Freud, et al. 1973) is an important one; two years is a long time in the life span of a child. Monumental developmental tasks are encompassed in two years. If children remain in a single home, critical attachments are developed. Additionally, should family reunification prove impossible, it becomes increasingly difficult to find adoptive homes for children as they grow older.

Number of placements The longer a child is in foster care, the more likely it is that he will be moved repeatedly from one home to another. Each move requires that the child deal with the loss of the attachments he has made and develop new attachments. Slowly children learn to believe that they will not be able to remain anywhere. To protect themselves against loss, they become wary about forming new attachments, and thus compromise their ability to develop a secure emotional base for development and learning.

Though it appears to many working in child welfare that foster care is a less stable form of care for children now than it was twenty years ago, statistics indicate that the picture is not very different. Twenty years ago, about half of the children placed in foster care had a single foster home, while 75 percent had just one or two homes (Kadushin and Martin 1988:41). VCIS data for 1990 indicate that 43 percent of the children in foster care had only one placement during the preceding three years, 27.5 percent had two placements, and 6 percent had six or more placements (House Committee on Ways and Means 1998:782–83).

A proportion of children in foster care are placed for a very short time, while a parent was found or a crisis resolved. When these short placements are not included, the data show more moves. In New York City in 1991, among a sample of 210 children who were in out-of-home care for at least sixty days, 52.4 percent had more than one placement; 12.9 percent were replaced twice, and 15 percent had four to ten placements (Botsko and Festinger 1994 pp. 17–18).

Could these multiple moves have been prevented? As efforts have increased to provide supportive services to families and to keep children in their own homes, it is possible that children are being left longer in difficult situations so that, when they do come into foster care, their problems have deepened and their behavior is harder to cope with. Meanwhile, the shortage of foster homes limits the child welfare agency's ability to match the specific behavioral difficulties of a child with the competencies of a foster home. If a foster parent has difficulties with a particular child and requests his removal, the agency may be tempted to preserve that foster home for future children by acting quickly to comply. All of these factors increase the number of moves that children experience.

Leaving foster care In the last decades of the twentieth century, an increasing number of children who left foster care returned to their families. VCIS data, available over a period of twenty years, indicate that two-thirds of the children who leave foster care are reunited with their families or go to relatives, an increase from 49.7 percent in 1982 (House Committee on Ways and Means 1998:796–99). AFCARS data indicate that 57 percent of the children who left out-of-home care in 2000 returned to their original families and an additional 10 percent went to relatives (U.S. HHS, Children's Bureau 2002a).

A relatively small proportion of foster children are adopted. Until the mid-1990s the percentage was fairly stable; about 10 percent of the children leaving foster care left for adoption between 1980 and 1996. In 1996, 28,000 children were adopted from the foster care system; by 2000 that number had increased 78 percent to 50,000 and accounted for 16 percent of the children leaving foster care (Evan B. Donaldson Adoption Institute 2002). Only 2 percent of the children adopted from foster care in 1998 were under one year of age; only 17 percent were over twelve. Nonrelative foster parents adopted 64 percent of those whose adoptions were finalized in 1999. Fourteen percent were adopted by relatives, some of whom were foster parents (U.S. HHS, Children's Bureau 1999). Thus recruitment of new adoptive homes was necessary for less than a third of the children who were adopted.

Of the children who exited out-of-home care in 2000, 7 percent, or 25,700 young people, "aged out"—became emancipated or reached the age of majority. Two percent ran away (U.S. HHS, Children's Bureau 2002a). Obviously, programs to teach the skills needed for independent living should be part of foster care programs. Currently only about a fifth of those "aging out" of foster care are served by independent living programs; the recent federal infusion of funds into these programs may provide an impetus to meet the needs of more young people. (Independent living programs are described in chapter 9.) However, even with the help of such programs, young people leaving foster care face a great challenge as they make their way into adult life without family to turn to for advice and help.

Reentry into foster care Not all of the children who leave foster care leave permanently. Most children who reenter foster care are children who have returned to their original homes, only to have the family again become unable to care for them. A smaller number reenter foster care after being placed for adoption. Of the children placed in foster care in 1998, 17 percent were reentering care (U.S. HHS 2000). The Oregon Project, the first project to demonstrate that permanent homes could be achieved for older children in long-term foster care, found 90 percent of its placements of children who had moved out of foster care to their own or adoptive homes to be intact eighteen months after the child moved (Lahti, Green, et al. 1978). A New York City longitudinal study, following the life course of a cohort of children placed in foster care for five years, found that 16 percent of the children who went home returned to foster care (Fanshel and Shinn 1978). Later studies in New York and Illinois showed a 22 percent rate of return to foster care (Goerge and Wulezy 1990, reported in Botsko and Festinger 1994). The rates of reentry found, of course, depend in part on the selection of the sample and the definitions of foster care used in each study. Whatever the rate, reentry into foster care represents another move for children and a failure of planning and services.

Studies based on samples and using case records or interviews with caseworkers as data sources have identified some factors associated with reentry into foster care. Children's behavior problems were an important factor, as was older age at discharge (Block and Libowitz 1983; Fein, Maluccio, et al. 1983). Children who had short stays in foster care are at risk for reentry (Goerge and Wulezy 1990, reported in Botsko and Festinger 1994). Older age at placement seems related to reentry in most studies. Families with a large number of problems were more likely to have a child reenter foster care. Not surprisingly, unmet service needs for the parents at the time of discharge, coupled with limited planning for services to meet those needs, were associated with reentry (Botsko and Festinger 1994).

Caseworkers were good predictors of which children might reenter foster care (Fanshel and Shinn 1978; Block and Libowitz 1983). This suggests that caseworkers are good judges of unmet service needs and that they must act to mobilize community supports for families, both while children are in foster care and after they return home. The fact that caseworkers can predict the return of some children to foster care may also indicate that they are willing to take some risk in an effort to give children every possible chance of growing up in their own families.

Maltreatment in Foster Care

Stories that appear in the media can create the impression that abuse and even fatalities of children in foster care are common. It is to be hoped that such publicity stirs public systems to action, for the number of children who do not find a safe haven in foster care should be zero. However, maltreatment in foster care, though a legitimate cause for great concern, is not common.

The extent of abuse and neglect in foster care is difficult to ascertain. Certainly maltreatment in foster care is a low-incidence event, as it is in the general population. Reports from the states to the NCANDS indicate that, in 1999, roughly 6 children out of every 1,000 in foster care were abused or neglected, compared with 12 out of every 1,000 in the general population. Of all substantiated incidents of maltreatment, 0.7 percent occurred in foster care (U.S. HHS, Children's Bureau 2002b). The data are incomplete, based on data submitted by 28 states. Underreporting is as likely to be reflected as in all data on child maltreatment.

There is relatively little literature on maltreatment in foster care. Ecological theory suggests that the interaction of many factors—pertaining to the foster family, the characteristics of the child, and the quality of support and supervision provided by the agency—underlies foster home maltreatment. A study of characteristics of foster families found few predictive attributes. Homes for which negative factors were noted at licensing, such as foster parent age, income, or health, were at greater risk, as were homes that were licensed only for a particular type of child. The authors suggest that these may be marginal homes, licensed because of the foster care shortage. Kinship foster homes were at less risk for maltreatment than regular homes. The authors note that the family bond may be protective, and that these homes are licensed for particular children and are not likely to be overcrowded (Zuravin, Benedict, et al. 1993). Media reports point to inadequate supervision of placements.

Careful selection and training of foster parents is the first step in protecting children in foster care. ASFA requires that foster homes meet certain safety standards, whether they are relative homes or nonrelated homes;

criminal background checks for foster parents are one example. When we know so little about the causes of maltreatment, however, it is difficult to know whether the most important elements are being targeted.

Child welfare agencies have been reluctant to acknowledge that the foster parents they select and supervise might maltreat children. Foster homes are scarce, and agencies understandably want to avoid bad publicity. Rather than conduct a formal investigation, sometimes an agency simply moves a child to another foster home and closes the offending home, or uses it more carefully and for a different type of child. Failure to investigate and document complaints not only puts children at risk, it obscures the picture of maltreatment in foster care. With less information, the problem is harder to remedy. On the other hand, an accusation of maltreatment is likely anger a foster family, and the fact that an agency investigates rather than taking their word may increase the anger. Unless the investigation is handled with great skill, the agency risks losing a foster home, and a potential recruiter of more foster homes, even if no maltreatment has occurred.

More study is needed of the important issue of maltreatment in foster care. We do not know how common it is, how great a proportion of resources should be devoted to it, or even how most effectively to address it. The caseworker's best safeguard is to maintain regular and frequent contact with foster parents, offering support and help as well as monitoring the placement.

The Foster Care Experience

When foster care is considered for a child, there are three parties whose interests are represented, and who must be considered as the experience unfolds. First, of course, is the child. The child is the person most directly impacted by foster care; his or her reactions and opinions should be assessed and attended to. Biological parents are critical, both for the role they can play while a child is in foster care, and because of the work they must do if the child is to return home. The foster family is the third party, assuming the daily care of the child but also taking into their home the child's representation of the original family as it is expressed verbally and in behavior. The social worker should be the glue that binds these three parties together in their common endeavor to make life better for the placed child.

> Ms. W. was a single parent with two boys, aged six and ten. At birth, her daughter tested positive for drugs in her system. Ms. W. had had prior contacts with child protective services; complaints had been made that the boys were neglected. Substance abuse had been identified as a problem in past contacts. The neglect was not considered serious enough for protective services to take authoritative action. The children had not been placed, and other than encouraging the mother to go to substance abuse treatment, the agency had offered no services to the family. The voice of the mother, the foster mother, and the child welfare worker appear in the following sections.

The Children's Original Families

One would expect that if family problems were identified as reasons for placement of a child in foster care, the system would make every effort to address these problems through services to the family prior to the child's return from foster care. We have seen that unmet service needs are associated with return to foster care (Botsko and Festinger 1994). However, there is evidence that services to a family actually decrease once a child is placed in foster care (Lindsey 1994:145). Once the child is safely placed, the crisis is over, and the intensity of work with the family diminishes. This is clearly a serious problem if the child is to return to the original home, as most children do.

Collaboration It might be supposed that a child would be relieved to be away from biological parents who have been so abusive or neglectful that the child has been removed from their care. However, as Judith Viorst (1986) writes, describing a frightened child in the burn unit of a hospital, crying for his mother who is responsible for his burns,

> It doesn't seem to matter what kind of a mother a child has lost, or how perilous it may be to dwell in her presence. It doesn't matter whether she hurts or hugs. Separation from mother is worse than being in her arms when the bombs are exploding. Separation from mother is sometimes worse than being with her when she is the bomb.
>
> (P. 10)

Children long for their absent parents and long to return home. Testimonies of foster children, such as those presented later in this chapter, document this longing. The actions of biological parents in using needed help and in continuing to visit the foster child are critical to the child's return home.

However, biological parents are often the least assisted of all the participants in the foster care of a child. They are often the victims of negative labeling and authoritarian treatment by social service agencies. Services often involve simply the removal of children when the parents are "bad" and their return when the parents are deemed "good" (Hubbell 1981). Workers confuse compliance with engagement in services.

THE MOTHER: I really didn't think they were going to take her, especially like they did. The worker walked in there and jerked her up off that bed and she wouldn't let me hold her, she wouldn't let her brother say good-bye to her. Nothing. She walked out with her. . . . Ten minutes and she was gone. I hate her, and I don't work well with her either. I didn't want to be honest with her, I didn't want to tell her nothing. I didn't feel like I could trust her. Everything I said and everything I did was used against me. I felt, with her . . . as a matter of fact, I knew, that as long as she was on the case, I would never get my kids back.

THE WORKER: We got a call from the hospital that mom had given birth to a drug-affected baby. She disclosed to hospital staff that she had prior contacts with the child welfare agency, and that she did not know who the father of the child was. . . . The decision was made to detain the child. . . . I had to do so much research into this one, because the information from the other state was so lengthy. . . . So at the very beginning, my concern was the safety of the baby. And I figured between extensive visitation and a lot of contacts with the mom and anybody she wanted to bring into the office. . . . Mom is a fighter. I consider that a strength. Sometimes it is frustrating, but it is a strength.

Child protective agencies have not always kept parents well informed regarding the status of their children, nor have parents always been allowed to be active participants in the decisions affecting the family. These problems have given rise to the adversarial juvenile or family court proceedings that are designed to protect the rights of parents. More recent practice, which involves parents in decision making, is viewed with alarm by some theorists who fear that families who have harmed their children are likely to make decisions that will subject the children to further harm

(Bartholet 1999). Family meetings have, however, proved a useful way of involving parents in joint decision making when the children are in foster care.

> THE MOTHER: That was good. We had two unity meetings; they were really good. As a matter of fact, my drug and alcohol counselor said that the first one was one of the best ones she's ever been to. . . . The second one, the caseworker was there. Myself was there. The facilitator was there. Nancy, my parenting teacher, was there, my drug and alcohol counseling was there, my mental health counselor was there. My bible study teacher was there. My aunt was there, my cousin was there. The paternal grandmother was there again. My oldest son's legal father, his girlfriend was there, and then his dad's brother's wife was there. So there were quite a few people there. I wanted my grandma there, but she had to work. . . . I basically said anything I wanted. . . . The second meeting was wonderful. I feel it is going to go a lot better now.

Crafting services Child welfare workers, on the whole, have not proved adept at identifying the individual needs of families and fitting services to those needs. Botsko and Festinger (1994), in a study of children returning to care, notes the large number of caseworker recommendations for counseling or therapy, coupled with notes describing families with multiple problems—such as poverty, poor housing, isolation, substance abuse—and few sources of support in the community. Counseling alone is unlikely to be sufficient to resolve these problems. Rather, an array of specific interventions is needed. This idea is reinforced by examination of the interaction of workers and families, which has revealed that it is difficult for caseworkers to identify the specific needs of children and families and to match services to those needs (Shireman, Yatchmenoff, et al. 1999).

Often when children enter foster care, the family's financial need is great. There may be many other complex problems. Some needs, such as financial support and housing, may be beyond the capacity of the child welfare worker to provide. Meeting those needs, however, may be critical to the children's safety and well-being, and the child welfare worker can link the family with social agencies that can help, and advocate for the family with those agencies. In the same way, the worker must be active in collaboration with agencies that provide treatment of substance abuse, support for victims of family violence, or any of the other services that may be needed.

Part of the reason for the gap between needs and services lies in the increasing use of managed care arrangements, with contracts for a specific number of clients to receive services. Workers are then expected to use the services there are contracts for, rather than develop services that will meet a specific family need. Part of the reason lies in the use of the scarce resource of child welfare workers' time: child welfare workers must spend so much time investigating maltreatment allegations that they do not have sufficient time available to work with families once the need is established. Part of the reason may be shortages of services in the community, and workers' consequent discouragement and frustration at their inability to meet needs associated with poverty. The gap also reflects inadequacies in the training of workers. But a major part of the problem is simply worker inattention to the unique needs of particular families, and a lack of creativity and energy for the task of developing services to meet those needs. All of these issues, of course, reflect the inadequacy of the resources society is willing to devote to child welfare.

Visiting Visitation with the biological family is very important for children in foster care. In a study of the long-term fate of 624 foster children in New York City; visiting was found to be the best predictor of return home (Fanshel and Shinn 1978). Research has also demonstrated a relationship between visiting and a child's sense of well-being and overall adjustment (Weinstein 1960; Fanshel and Shinn 1978). Furthermore, visiting appears to have positive benefits on parents' attitudes and behaviors (White 1981). The importance of active work to encourage and facilitate visiting is underscored by Fanshel's finding that of 23,051 children in placement in New York City for more than ninety days (who were not on trial visits home and not headed for adoption), only 13 percent saw their parents at least once a month, and half were not visited at all (Fanshel 1982).

The feelings of biological parents, particularly those of loss, anger, guilt, and shame (Jenkins 1981), may act as disincentives to visiting the children in foster care. Foster parents are not always gracious to parents whom they perceive as having maltreated their children; and they may experience the visits as a disruption. Children, too, are often upset by visits. Financial circumstances can make visits difficult. Foster homes are often far from original homes, and transportation can be difficult, costly, and time-consuming.

It is up to the social worker to stimulate in parents an interest in visiting, to help them work through the practical difficulties, and to help them deal with the emotions that make visits difficult. Fanshel writes that "passive agency acceptance of parental drop-outs should be considered violation of one of the criteria employed in utilization review procedures to monitor performance and lead to disciplinary action against the agency" (Fanshel 1982:101). Furthermore, planned visits with specific goals can help both parents and children to work through their feelings, thus becoming one of the therapeutic tools that move the family toward resolution of its problems.

Parents are able to provide essential information about the lives of their children. They can and should be active participants in the treatment planning, and especially in permanency planning. Even if parental rights are going to be terminated, parents should still have a place at the table where decisions that affect their children are made.

> THE MOTHER: I have made every one of them on time. I haven't missed one. The three that I have missed is because of the agency's problem with their timing and stuff. . . . It is fun to visit them. But when the boys were with me and we were going to see the baby at the office, we only got to see her two hours a week. But by the time the hour was up the boys were so bored, . . . and knowing that somebody was on the other side of that window watching us, it is not a very comfortable feeling. But now that we get to move to [a new visiting center] it is a lot better. And the worker lets us take them out to breakfast, as long as we pay. So it is a lot better. There are games there. It is clean, vacuumed. It is more of a living room type of setting.

Families whose children are in placement are not easy families to engage in remedial work. Their anger and defensiveness present obstacles. Once a child is out of the home, for both worker and family the crisis is resolved. It is too easy for the family to re-form without the absent child. The child's need for his parents is great, however, and the family's investment in the child is great. It is through their common recognition that the child's needs must be met that the worker and parent can come together and engage in a service plan that will truly meet the family's needs.

> THE MOTHER: It is not that I have a problem working with the agency, because I don't have a problem at all working with my new worker. She does tell me that I am doing good, keep up the good work, and stuff like that.

The Children

Though foster care has more impact on children than on anyone else, the voices of foster children are just beginning to appear in the literature. The reports of the children themselves reinforce our adult concerns about the impact of separation and the importance of maintaining attachment; at the same time they provide evidence that the safety and predictability of a good foster home are welcomed.

Separation from parents The work of Ner Littner, cited in chapter 2, brought to light the trauma children experience when moved from their own families into foster care and detailing the potential long-lasting effects of disrupted attachments. He noted that stable, consistent attachments are the foundation for healthy growth and development, and reviewed the potential hazards faced by children in foster care. Most notably, he described the process by which a child who has repeatedly formed relationships, only to see them broken, may develop an inability to trust people and thus an inability to form new attachments (Littner 1950).

The identity, or self-image, of children in foster care is formed through the interaction of their experiences in foster care and the bonds formed in their original home. Weinstein (1960) demonstrated that contact with original parents was an important factor in a foster child's positive self-image. Littner (1981) noted the responsibility of the worker to facilitate positive contact between children and their biological parents, listing the reasons. A child who has previously lived with his or her natural parents will likely identify with many of the parent's personality traits. The images a child carries of his or her parents become "in effect, a part of the child." As a consequence of this identification, any criticism of the parent may be perceived by the child as a personal attack. Children with emotional difficulties may develop an unrealistic picture of their biological parents. The child may overidealize the parents or may exaggerate their mistreatment in his or her mind. Children may deeply miss their biological family. A child may never really understand the circumstances resulting in separation, and thus may internalize feelings of rejection or even shame and guilt. The resulting unconscious feelings about separation can be "enormously exaggerated, irrationally fearful and completely illogical" (Littner 1981:271).

Separation from siblings Another important consideration is the impact of the separation from siblings experienced by a child in out-of-home placement. It is clear, both from common sense and from what children tell us, that the presence of siblings takes some of the fear and loneliness out of moves. Current policy is to place siblings together whenever possible; this can be difficult with large sibling groups, and can fail to happen if workers are not committed to keeping siblings together.

How professionals view sibling relationships in general, the priority joint sibling placement is given in practice, and how practitioners perceive conflict between siblings can all serve to undermine policy. Staff and Fein (1992) examined sibling placement for Casey Family Services, a private social service agency, at five different sites over a span of fourteen years. Because Casey Family Services relies on private rather than funding sources, the agency has access to substantially greater resources, and the authors surmised that "placements were based on diagnostic decisions rather than expedience" (p. 261). The results of this inquiry provide a dramatic demonstration of the impact of worker attitudes and workplace cultures on the way siblings are placed. "The Casey sites differed in their frequency of placing siblings together or separately, although the sites have no stated policy differences" (Staff and Fein 1992:265). In the five sites, placements of siblings together in the initial foster home varied from 25 percent to 81 percent of the time. Placements of siblings together where the siblings remained together throughout their time in foster care ranged from 0 percent at one agency to 69 percent at another.

What the children say Until very recently the literature has contained little testimony from children themselves about the foster care experience; for many years the best information came from theoretical writing and descriptions of best practice based on clinical work with children. A study published in 1960 provided about the only evidence about the experiences and opinions of typical children in foster care (Weinstein 1960). Suddenly, in very recent years, we are learning a great deal more—and it reinforces what we had already been told but had not really heard.

> THE WORKER: Then I came back and talked to the boys, and the response of the boys was, "Well, we told her if she didn't stop using we were going to be taken." So we sat there and I let them cry on my shoulder, and we talked. Then the foster parent came and picked them up. So we spent probably four hours with the boys that day, that afternoon, just trying to make things as calm as we could for them.

In 1960 Eugene Weinstein published a careful study, based on inter-views with sixty-one children in foster care. The children were between the ages of five and fourteen and had been in foster care for at least a year; sixteen were excluded by workers because of instability in the foster home situation or because of emotional instability (which of course meant that only children who were doing fairly well in stable placements were included in the sample). The interviews sought the children's answers to the questions "Who am I?" "Why am I here?" and "What is going to happen to me?" (pp. 22–23). Well-being was defined as "the development of per-sonality resources in the child" and was rated by the child's caseworker.

Weinstein found that visits from the child's natural parents were asso-ciated with well-being. Children who identified with their natural parents had the highest well-being ratings; children who were visited by natural parents and identified with foster parents also did well. Finally, an ade-quate conception of the meaning of foster care status and the reason for being in foster care were associated with well-being. (Weinstein 1960: 17–18). Though the study was never replicated, the findings make sense and have echoes in later research on outcomes for children in foster care.

In the late 1990s, additional information based on systematic interviews with children began to appear (Johnson, Yoken, et al. 1995; McAuley 1996; Toth 1997; Folman 1998; Wilson and Conroy 1999). All of the investigators inquired into the meaning of placement to a child, and many followed the children through their foster care experiences. The themes that emerge are remarkably consistent. Children feel tremendous anxiety and fear of abandonment when they are placed, and little is usually done to help them understand placement, to prepare them for placement, or to reassure them that they will see their parents again. [They should] "at least not take us away without our parents knowing. It seemed like we were going to jail," reported one child, who had apparently been placed from school (Johnson, Yoken, et al. 1995:970). Siblings become very important, both as supports during the frightening time of the placement process, and later as the people who help children maintain a sense of family. Children have and maintain an urgent wish to be reunited with their families, and most continue to identify themselves as members of their original families.

Relatives emerge as important in the lives of these children. Even when foster children are not living with relatives, they may visit them, spend holidays with them, or be visited by them. These contacts, of course, rein-force the children's identity as members of their own families. They also provide opportunities to see siblings and to maintain relationships with extended family. Additionally, Wilson and Conroy found that the 100 children in their sample who were living with relatives were more likely to feel "always" safe and "always" loved (Wilson and Conroy 1999:61).

Children's feelings that they have no control over plans for them emerge continually. Toth reports children deliberately being "bad" in order to get attention and get moved to what they hope will be a more favorable placement (Toth 1997). Wilson and Conroy found that only 29 percent of the 1,100 children they interviewed thought that they had had any voice in planning. One child said, "It was like I wasn't even there" (Wilson and Conroy 1999:63). For the most part children feel that the agency helps them, though many also can articulate unmet needs.

Somewhat unexpectedly in light of the current concerns about foster care, recent research is indicating that children in family foster care tend to evaluate their experiences positively, most feeling "loved" and "safe" and believing that their quality of life was improved by moving to out-of-home care (Wilson and Conroy 1999). Johnson reports that 60 percent of the children in her study thought it sometimes appropriate for a child to be in foster care, citing improvements in care and safety (Johnson, Yoken, et al. 1995). Evaluations are not as positive for institutional care, though the real unhappiness documented by Toth (1997) is not as evident in other investigations.

Overall then, the picture is one of the move itself as a terrible, traumatic time for children, especially if it is from home to foster care (Folman 1998), but also if it is from one foster home to another (McAuley 1996). Once in placement, children experience greater feelings of safety and often recognize that their quality of life has improved, although they remain identified with their original families and long to return. The many ways that workers could make placements easier for children—explaining what is happening, giving children some voice in plans, seeing that placements are stable—are evident. As, of course, is the importance of worker efforts to facilitate family contact and to rehabilitate the original home for the children's return.

> THE WORKER: I would say [that I am] pretty hopeful, because there is such a strong relationship [with the boys] there. This would be a case that even if the twelve months were up, it would need to be given consideration for extended time. With the baby, I don't know. It would depend strictly on what mom decides to do.

The Foster Parents

Who are foster parents? The short answer is that they are a group of people just about like everyone else. If the foster family is a two-parent family, as two-thirds are (Epstein 1999:58), it is usually the mother who is most intense in her interest and who will take the major responsibility for the care of the foster child. Cautley (1980), in a study of 115 new foster parents in the late 1970s, found most to have a high school education, and a quarter to have some college. Three-fourths of the fathers were employed in skilled or semiskilled jobs. Other studies have produced similar descriptions (Fanshel and Shinn 1978; Fein, Mallucio, and Kloser 1990, reported in Epstein 1999). Commonly expressed motivations include the enjoyment of children and the desire to be of use in the community (Hampson and Tavormina 1980). Foster parents often expect that a foster child will bring some specific benefit to the family, such as companionship for a child currently in the family, or additional income (Cautley 1980). Epstein, noting how close many foster parent incomes are to the poverty line, suggests that additional income from fostering may be very important to these families (Epstein 1999).

THE FOSTER MOTHER (WHO IS A MIDDLE-SCHOOL TEACHER AND HAS HAD TWELVE FOSTER CHILDREN BEFORE TAKING THIS BABY): Like we've said, the kids are great. The whole reason behind this, and we went to [foster parent training] classes before we were married, because I had a child [in my class] at school, a special-needs child, go into foster care, and I wanted to bring him home. I felt so bad for him, I wanted to bring him home. So when [my husband] and I were dating, I said, "How would you feel about being a foster parent?" And he said, "Tell me about it."

The role of the social worker The role of the social worker with the foster parent has a dual aspect, as is often the case in child welfare work. Once a child is placed in a foster home, the social worker is responsible for monitoring the placement and assuring that the child's needs are being met. At the same time, the social worker and the foster parents are partners in meeting those needs. The social worker is responsible for providing ongoing support and help to the foster parents as they care for the child, and for using their knowledge and including them in the planning for the child.

Caring for a foster child can be challenging—most are children who have been neglected or abused, whose developmental needs have not been met, and who evidence the anger that such treatment evokes. All foster children experience the stress of the placement and the need to make their way in a new home. Too often the foster care system fails to devote adequate attention to the mental health needs of its children.[7] Most children, after a time of seeming to adapt, will test the affection of the foster parents with a variety of acting-out behavior. Many children will, to some extent, attempt to recreate their own family systems, shaping foster parents by their behavior and provoking reactions similar to those of their own parents. Children are afraid of new attachments to foster parents, fearing they will be followed by rejection. Attachment to the foster parents also implies disloyalty to biological parents—a dilemma for the child. The child thus creates a complicated life within the foster family, and an important part of the social worker's role is to support the foster parent in understanding and coping with these issues in order to maintain the placement for the child.

To build a working relationship, it is vital that the worker and foster parent have continuing contact. Too often, the stress of heavy workloads cause workers neglect this contact. Foster fathers are often ignored, because the worker assumes that the mother is the caretaker. Most child welfare agencies have regulations that specify how often a foster home must be visited and a child seen; even these mandatory visits are sometimes skipped by busy workers responding to crises. This leaves foster parents without support.

Even more difficult for a foster parent is to be ignored by the child welfare worker when in need of help. Foster mothers report that they are unable to contact workers by telephone when they need advice, clothing, referrals for medical care, or other kinds of support. In a recent foster parent survey in Oregon, only half of the responding foster parents said that a worker would return their telephone calls the same day or the next day (Shireman and Alworth 1997).

> THE FOSTER MOTHER: I called the caseworker in one week's time, sixty-five times. Never got a return call, never got a message answered. Finally she did answer the phone; she wanted to know what the noise was when I explained to her what was going on with him about his screaming for days at a time. . . . He [an older foster child] was way out of control. He did a thousand dollars worth of damage to our home.

In the best of circumstances, the responsibility of the social worker to monitor the progress of the child is carried out in partnership with the foster parent. Foster parents grow wonderfully attached to children, and they are often persistent advocates with agencies, schools, and medical institutions to see that children get what they need. Workers should support this advocacy.

At the same time, as we have seen, sometimes children are neglected by overburdened foster parents or abused in foster homes. A great many of these tragic situations could be prevented by frequent interaction between foster parent and worker, which would allow the worker to be aware of stress as it developed in the foster home and to take corrective action. A delicate balance has to be maintained. The worker must make the foster parent a partner in caring for and planning for the child, while avoiding overidentification with the foster parent that might cause difficulties to be overlooked.

Foster parents and biological parents Increasingly, foster parents are being asked to have contact with the child's biological parents and to serve as role models or even mentors. According to Ryan, McFadden, et al. (1981), the relationships between foster parents and biological parents have traditionally been strained or nonexistent. The concept of foster care as "child rescue" focused the work of the foster family on the child alone. This focus was supported by the child welfare agency's usual assumption that the biological families of children in care were inadequate. It was also presumed that foster parents fostered children to meet their own family's needs and that interaction with the child's original family would interfere and complicate the relationships within the foster family. Foster families and biological families often ended up competing for a child's affection. Visits were often scheduled outside of the foster home. If visiting within the foster home was unavoidable, caseworkers would be present to supervise (Ryan, McFadden, et al. 1981). These ideas are very slowly changing.

> THE FOSTER MOTHER: We used to drop the baby off for visits and pick her up. We gave her [the mother] a high chair and a stroller; we would bring her formula. Because we didn't know how much assistance or help she was getting. And we wanted to make sure at least that the baby had formula while she was there.
>
> Right now the oldest boy's foster mother—he calls her his stepmom—and myself are doing the visits [of the siblings] between us. There is no

> caseworker in between that. And we are now trying to incorporate the
> younger brother, because he has been put in another foster home. He has
> been invited Saturday to the baby's birthday party. . . . [We worked this
> out because] the oldest boy was calling. He would say, "When can I see
> my little sister?" and that was fine with us. We were perfectly comfort-
> able with both families being together and playing together and stuff.

Styles of fostering can be thought of as lying along a continuum from
"exclusive" to "inclusive." Exclusive fostering, in which the foster family
attempts to exclude the child's biological family and the social worker, is
probably characteristic of long-term care and closed adoptions. Inclusive
fostering is characterized by a readiness to draw the child's original family
and the agency into the fostering constellation; this is the style of care that
has been most associated with the child's needs being met (Holman 1980).
Currently the child welfare system, geared toward family preservation
and recognizing how helpful foster parents can be to biological parents,
generally seeks inclusive foster parents. However, both styles of foster
home exist, and the needs of a particular child or family may be better met
by one or the other. Fostering style should be a consideration in placement
planning.

Davies and Bland (1981) present a four-stage model that illustrates the
complexity of developing a mentoring relationship between biological
parents and foster parents. Stage one is the beginning of the association, when hostilities, mistrust, and fear dominate the relationship. Social
workers act as mediators, negotiating the interaction so that the biological family is placed in the role of teacher and the foster family, seeking
information about the child, takes the role of learner. By asking about
the child's toys, routine, food preferences, and life in general, the foster
parents begin the process of modeling listening and acceptance. In stage
two, the social worker initiates a shift in roles: the foster parent begins to
teach the biological parent about parenting tools that will draw on the
biological parent's existing strengths. In stage three, the social worker
begins to withdraw from active involvement. This is usually two to three
months into the process. Although the social worker may continue to be
involved with each family individually, the foster family has now assumed
the therapeutic teaching role. In the final stage, the social worker is rein-
troduced into the relationship to facilitate termination of the foster family

placement when the child leaves and to help the parties process the feelings that the separation may evoke. The authors emphasize that the effective functioning of this model requires considerable skill on the part of social workers for the task of identifying appropriate foster parents and willing biological parents.

Other authors have had more radical ideas for expanding the roles and responsibilities of foster parents. Johnson and Gabor (1981) envision shifting the responsibility of counseling from caseworkers to trained "parent counselors," who would be regarded as temporary caregivers as well as overall family helpers. They believe that changing the foster parent paradigm to reflect this new role would allow biological parents to retain the perception of being the parent. Workers would be freed up for other assignments and would provide close supervision of the parent counselors while continuing to serve as mediators when necessary.

Foster parents and children We expect a great deal from foster parents. We expect them to give constant care over long time periods, and to be willing and helpful in facilitating the move of a child to whom they have become attached. We know that successfully nursing a child through an illness, or helping a child to overcome developmental or behavioral problems promotes a strong bond (Meezan and Shireman 1985). We expect foster parents to be interested in adoption if the child cannot go home, but not to be so attached to the child that they cannot let go if another plan is made. Too often, workers are too busy with current crises to help foster parents with their feelings of loss after children leave. And yet we expect them to continue to foster.

THE FOSTER MOTHER: So I packed up her baby book, her shot records. . . . I wrote down her sleeping habits and everything for them. And we went to court, and the judge said, "That child is not going anywhere. She will not be leaving that foster home." . . . We would like to keep her until they decide what they are going to do with her.

We have had twelve kids, and out of every set there is one kid that I would have loved to have kept. Just because I like the underdog. We had a little kid who couldn't crawl, he was so anemic, he was a sad little guy. I would have kept him in a heartbeat. Just because he busted my heart, you know. We had a little girl that couldn't talk, two years old and didn't talk, and she was here two weeks and she was talking. So every set. It is not that I want a house full, it is just, you know . . .

Outcomes

Foster Children as Adults

Over the years many researchers have examined how former foster children have fared as adults, beginning with Sophie VanTheis (1924) and continuing to the present. For the most part, the studies focus on adults who have experienced long-term foster care, usually with quite stable placements. Interest in the topic has waned in the 1990s, and we have little information from cohort studies about how children in our current system of foster care "turn out," though there are studies under way.

Adult functioning is the ultimate outcome of foster care—though, of course, multiple variables in addition to foster care affect how well an adult functions. VanTheis (1924) used the outcome variable of managing life in a "capable" way. Interviewing 235 adults twelve to eighteen years after placement, she found 88 percent to be "capable" and 12 percent "incapable." An interesting aspect of this study was that it did not distinguish between foster homes and adoptive homes. Later research has, of course, made this distinction.

In a recent and very comprehensive review of outcome studies of foster care, the variety of outcome measures used are grouped into four classifications: adult self-sufficiency, behavioral adjustment, family and social support, and sense of well-being (McDonald, Allen, et al. 1996).[8] This format provides a good way of illuminating the areas of competence and difficulty among former foster children.

Self-sufficiency Self-sufficiency begins with adequate education to compete in the job market, and in this regard those in foster care are at a disadvantage. While in foster care, a high proportion of foster children do poorly in school—quite probably as a result of disruptions in their lives, difficulties in establishing attachments, and anxiety. Consequently high school graduation rates are lower than for the general population, and only a small proportion, 2 to 5 percent (Festinger 1983), graduate from college. Fanshel's two longitudinal studies show that children enter foster care with school difficulties and that those difficulties continue while they are in foster care (Fanshel and Shinn 1978; Fanshel, Finch, et al. 1990).

Educational difficulties translate into low-paying unskilled or semi-skilled jobs in the young adult years. In a careful analysis of employment data, comparing it with census data for the same geographic area and year, McDonald, Allen, et al. (1996) show that, although the majority of graduates from foster care are employed, their employment rates seem to be somewhat lower than those of the comparison group. The various studies show about a quarter of those who have been in foster care to be receiving public assistance.

Follow-up studies show that most foster children have established independent living and have an adequate place to live. Meier (1965), whose 69 subjects were aged twenty-eight to thirty-two, found that two-thirds of the men were married and had homes; all of the women, whether married or not, had established independent homes. Studies of homeless populations, however, find a high proportion of former foster children among the homeless (Demcheck 1985; Pillavin et al. 1987, reported in McDonald, Allen, et al. 1996). Several explanations are offered; among them are that former foster children lack the family support networks that provide assistance in times of crisis and that the foster care system does not adequately prepare young people for independent living or give them the resources to get a start.

Antisocial behavior It appears that there is no strong link between the experience of foster care and adult antisocial behavior. McDonald's reporting of the behavioral indicators tracked in the various studies suggests that arrest rates are higher among former foster children than in the general population, but may not be when the comparisons are controlled for race and socioeconomic status. On the basis of arrest rates alone, contact with the family of origin is associated with negative behavior (Zimmerman 1982). Self-reports of drinking and use of illegal drugs present a mixed picture; the review found no clear evidence that substance use is any greater among those who have been in foster care (McDonald, Allen, et al. 1996).

Establishing families Adults who have been in foster care seem, in general, to be able to form social support networks that are satisfying. About a third have married or established a stable partnership. Of the adults interviewed while in their late twenties or early thirties, a higher proportion had married, but the rate of separation or divorce was also higher than in the general population (Meier 1965).

Most disturbing is the difficulty that may attend parenting. Festinger (1983) reported that most children of those studied were living with their mothers, "a few" parents having used foster care temporarily. Meier (1965), working with a sample of older adults, found that a fifth of the mothers had children in care. In a study of adults who had been in residential care, the presence of a supportive spouse or partner was associated with good parenting (McDonald, Allen, et al. 1996). It is not clear whether this is also true for those who have been in foster care. A fifth of those who had been in foster care reported doubts about their ability to meet the needs of their own children (Zimmerman 1982).

Foster children develop extended families as adults. A third to half are in touch with a biological parent; more than three-quarters with some member of the biological extended family. And more than three-quarters continued to be in touch with the foster family, finding in that family a source of support (McDonald, Allen, et al. 1996).

Well-being On the final dimension, personal well-being—assessed through measures of physical health, mental health, and satisfaction with life—the research is not conclusive. Individuals who have been in care seem more prone to mental health difficulties, but whether this is due to the separations and adaptations required in care or to the experiences that preceded care is, of course, unknown. The findings of Fanshel, Finch, et al. (1990) demonstrating the lifelong impact of traumatic events suggest that experiences prior to foster care are important.

Overall, studies of young adults have echoed the conclusion of Sophie VanTheis that a good proportion of them were managing their lives adequately and feeling quite satisfied with their lives (Meier 1965; Festinger 1983; Zimmerman 1982). Satisfaction is, of course, linked to overall ability to cope with the difficulties of life—linked to being "capable."

Facilitating Positive Outcomes

In an analysis of factors associated with better outcomes, McDonald and Allen (1996) isolated the following dimensions. Children in foster care fared better than those in group care. Admission to care for reasons of parental behavior, such as neglect, abandonment, or physical abuse, was associated with more negative outcomes than was placement due to circumstance. A lower number of placements while in care was, as expected, associated with better adult functioning. Surprisingly, a longer time in care, if the placement was stable, was also associated with better outcome. Contact with the original family while in care resulted in greater identification with that family, but this identification was not uniformly associated with outcome. Identification with the foster family tended to be associated with positive outcome.

Thus, it appears that foster care, when it is stable care that meets the needs of children, can lead to positive outcomes. The adult outcomes for former foster children are not as good as those for children who were never placed, but their experiences prior to entry into care are considerably more difficult. The factors associated with positive outcomes are, in general, those that would be expected. As adults, most of those who were in foster care are able to function as productive citizens and think of themselves as having a good quality of life. Foster care, it seems, helps children more than it hurts them, and is worth preserving and improving for those children who need it.

Ms. W.'s children are still in foster care. Her boys were home, and the baby was making weekend visits, when she relapsed in her recovery from substance abuse. She told the foster mother that she was "tired of it all." She missed court hearings and seemed resigned to losing her children. Relapse is part of the recovery process. The worker wondered if it had occurred because the responsibility for all of the children seemed too great. The uncertainty about eventual prognosis for the W. family is great.

The agency plans to ask the court to make an exception to the ASFA timelines for the boys, who have a long-term relationship with their mother, and allow her more time to establish a home for them. The baby is probably headed for adoption, perhaps with the current foster family; perhaps with another family.

Critical Issue: Establishing and Retaining Foster Homes to Meet the Needs of Children

If the foster care system is to be preserved it must be strengthened, and that will require renewed investment in every aspect of the system. It begins with improved recruitment, assessment, and retention of foster families, so that good homes will be available to meet the varied needs of the children who come into care. Supervision and support of the homes should be intensified so that children can receive excellent foster care. The system should differentiate its foster homes and provide training opportunities for foster parents who want to develop particular skills for working with children with special needs, or for working with parents. And the wisdom of foster parents should be respected, and their input valued, in the process of planning permanency for children.

Recruitment of Foster Parents

The process of recruitment involves reaching into communities to find people who might become foster parents. Agencies use a variety of means, including television ads, newspaper articles, billboards, and presentations to church congregations and civic groups, to raise general awareness of the need for foster homes. Targeted recruiting—which publicizes an agency's efforts to find care for specific children or for a particular category of children, sometimes using pictures of actual children who need foster homes—is often more successful in attracting the kinds of families that are needed. The most effective recruiting tool, however, is word of mouth—foster parents (usually foster mothers) sharing their experiences with the people they know.

A large, multistate study of foster care identified the recruitment of minority foster homes as a major area of need (U.S. HHS 1995). Fahlberg (1991) emphasized the importance of identifying systematic barriers to the development of culturally appropriate foster homes. The majority of foster parent recruiters are white, middle-class women. As they try to engage families in racially diverse communities, they may encounter resistance stemming from historically rooted distrust, both of white people and of social service agencies. African American recruiters have been significantly more successful in recruiting families in the black community. The issue is systemic; one long-term approach to the shortage of minority foster homes is to address the lack of ethnic diversity among workers throughout the child welfare system. Of course, the problem perpetuates itself because with relatively few foster families in a given cultural community, there are fewer opportunities for the most efficient form of recruiting—word of mouth.

Assessment

During the assessment process, the agency seeks to assure that a potential foster home meets minimal standards for health and safety and to engage the family in examining its own suitability for fostering. Criteria for selection of foster parents have traditionally been more relaxed than those for selection of adoptive parents; in this era when many foster homes provide care for several years and many foster parents adopt, this distinction must be questioned.

Some of the characteristics most commonly sought in foster parents are affinity for children, flexible expectations, the ability to view children as unique individuals, a realistic picture of the difficulties of children needing placement, and willingness to adapt to the needs and characteristics of such children. Other attributes include good enough health to have the energy to parent a sometimes difficult child, interest in learning—about the medical needs of a child, about behavioral problems, about ways to parent in response to particular difficulties—and, finally, a commitment to children and a demonstrated ability to use a variety of coping techniques to see difficult situations through to resolution.

States also require that prospective foster parents undergo criminal background checks. Although social workers may be accustomed to this routine, it may come a surprise to many applicants and can be seen as intrusive and demeaning. Workers must be prepared to present this requirement as a universal precaution taken for the safety of all children in the system. Agency policy should make clear how the results of such a check will be used and under what circumstances exceptions can be made to certain rules.

The requirements for licensure of foster homes in each state include certain minimal physical attributes of the dwelling. These requirements sometimes make it difficult to develop foster homes among poor communities—where, too often, minority foster homes are found—and can thus constitute a systemic barrier to finding culturally appropriate foster homes. If the home being considered is needed by the agency, and if the worker determines that the addition of foster children to the stresses of poverty will not overwhelm the family, the agency can often find uncommitted funds to help a family bring its home into compliance with certification standards. In such cases the flexible use of relatively small amounts of money can be of great benefit.

Philosophies and regulations regarding the discipline of children can present another impediment to the establishment of culturally diverse foster homes. Child welfare agencies have policies concerning acceptable methods of discipline to be used with foster children; their rules generally prohibit the use of physical punishment and certain other punitive forms of discipline. Some families are accustomed to using physical discipline; they will need to learn new methods and to see that those methods are effective before they are comfortable with agency policies. Acceptable methods of discipline vary among cultures, religions, and ethnic groups, therefore this issue will affect some populations more than others.

As they work to overcome the overall shortage of foster parents and the relative lack of diversity among them, policy makers must examine all of these factors. Triseliotis suggests that social workers must be open-minded, "looking at whether applicants will be able to meet a foster child's needs, not whether they will be able to meet them in a particular traditionally acceptable way, and looking at whether families function successfully, not whether they function in a way which might be expected from a Euro-centric perspective" (Triseliotis, Sellick, et al. 1995:80).

Training

Training of foster parents takes many forms. Initial training is often part of the assessment process, as worker and parents together decide whether the expectations and resources of the applicants meet the needs of the agency. Ongoing training involves periodic focus on specific aspects of foster parents' work; it is part of the package of support services that agencies provide for foster parents.

The initial training has two goals: (1) it is an opportunity for the prospective foster parents to complete the self-selection process, as they learn more about the characteristics of children who need foster homes and are encouraged to evaluate their own capacity to work with these children; and (2) it teaches foster parents new ways of thinking about foster children, their families, and the issues they bring to placement, as well as specific skills that will help them to manage problem behaviors.

Initial training starts foster parents on their adventure. As they gain experience, however, more advanced training can help them deal even more effectively with the complex needs of the children in their care. If foster parents decide to become "specialists" in one type of foster care, they will need specific training for that type of care in order to maximize their usefulness to children. For example,

- Foster parents who decide to operate shelter homes, taking children on an emergency basis for stays of less than two weeks, need advanced education concerning the impact of separation on children, and ideas about specific actions they can take to help children deal with the trauma.
- Foster parents who decide they are interested in parenting medically fragile children need specific training in techniques of nursing, use of medical equipment, and the meaning of illness and disability to children.
- Foster parents who decide they wish to parent older, troubled children and youth need help with understanding the dynamics of behavior and with behavior management techniques.

As the experiences of children in our society change over time, and as our understanding of child development is refined, new insights arise in the field of child welfare. For example, better understanding of the organic damage caused by prenatal exposure to alcohol has led to new ways of managing the resulting behaviors. Foster parents need ongoing training that enables them to share in these developing insights and to integrate the information they have with their new experiences.

Retention of Foster Homes

Retaining good foster parents is critical and should be a top priority of any child welfare agency. It is hard to recruit foster parents and expensive to assess and train them. A good foster home is a tremendously important resource for children who need care. A foster home that stays with the agency offers the possibility of a stable placement for the child currently in care, and the opportunity to provide for many other children. Too many foster parents withdraw from fostering after only a year or two. Kadushin reports a study in which a newly recruited group of foster parents was tracked; 47 percent had withdrawn by the end of two years, and 80 percent by the end of four years. Although some of the parents left after a mutual decision with the agency that fostering was not a good idea for them, and some left due to family circumstances, a substantial number stopped fostering because of difficulties with a particular child or because of stressful relationships with workers (Kadushin and Martin 1988:366). A multistate survey of 827 former foster parents found that 37 percent had stopped fostering because of specific agency policies, and 24 percent because of behavioral problems of children. Former foster parents also reported less satisfactory interactions with their caseworkers than did current foster parents. These findings point to the need for improvements in training, supervision, and support of foster parents (U.S. HHS 1995:vii).

The relationship between social worker and foster parent is without question a major factor in the retention of foster homes. Foster parents list other important factors, such as the availability of specialists' advice or counseling services, respite care, and support groups (Triseliotis, Sellick, et al. 1995:104; U.S. HHS 1995:vii). To these might be added fair compensation and recognition by the agency of foster parents as allies in the provision of services.

Foster parent support groups Foster parent support groups can be of great assistance in solving everyday problems. It is wonderful to experience a group of foster mothers together. Busy women who are largely tied to home by the demands of children, they do not see each other frequently. But they share an experience shared by no one else. As they

trade ideas about ways to handle problem children or problem social
workers, one can see ideas spark, new resolutions being formed, and new
paths of action opened. There is renewed energy, and a sense of mutual
support. The benefits are documented in a study of current and former
foster parents; 31 percent of those who continued to foster, but only 13
percent of former foster parents, had another foster parent on whom
they could call for support. Current foster parents were also more likely
to have joined a foster parent association (U.S. HHS 1995:85).

Compensation Payment for foster care has been subject of controversy since Charles Loring Brace reacted to the idea with the statement
that parents should foster out of "love and charity," and that introducing
the idea of payment would distort the foster parent–child relationship.
That argument, plus the budget-consciousness of legislatures, has kept
foster care payments pegged to the cost of feeding and clothing a child,
barely adequately, unless the child has particular problems that are deemed
to merit a supplement. Median board rates for children in the United
States in 1996 ranged from $340 for a two-year old to $422 for a sixteen-
year old. These medians conceal a wide range; Connecticut paid $621
per month for the care of a sixteen-year old, while Alabama paid $241
(Child Welfare League of America 1996). The cost of institutional care,
detailed in chapter 7, makes the inadequacy of foster care reimbursement
rates evident. Foster parents are still caring for children out of "love and
charity."

Caring for a child entails many expenses beyond food and shelter. Many
states do not pay for child care—an omission that will increasingly be a
disincentive to fostering as more women enter the labor market. Clothing
allowances are inadequate—particularly for teenagers, for whom issues
of self-esteem come into play. If a foster family sees as a necessity something the agency deems a luxury, the parents may resent the agency for
questioning their judgment as well as for failing to meet the child's needs.
Special lessons or experiences to enable children to develop their own talents are too often viewed as unnecessary by agencies concerned about
budgets, about equity, or about affording children advantages they would
not have in their own homes. The needs of particular children are too
often met out of the personal budgets of the foster parents.

There is no question, however, that generous policies for meeting the
child care expenses of foster parents, and generous compensation for
the skills required to deal with children's special needs, improves both
recruitment and retention of foster parents. In one imaginative program,

foster parents for delinquent adolescents were paid enough that if the family took two children, the amount equaled what one partner could earn in work outside the home. A thoughtfully developed payment scale was not the only reason for the program's success in recruiting and retaining foster parents, but it was an important component (Hazel 1981). Social workers, though they usually have altruistic motives for entering the profession, work for an income. Why should foster parents not also work for an income?

Almost as important as the rate of pay and the system's reluctance to fund special expenses is the manner in which foster parents are paid. Too often they must justify their expenses, plead with administrators, cope with rejected requests, or get paid months after the expense has occurred. This process creates a dynamic in which the foster parent begins to view the agency as an obstacle to the good care of the child—not a perspective that is conducive to partnership with the agency in planning.

Foster parents who take on difficult children, or many children, are customarily compensated with special rates. These rates are more commensurate with the expenses of raising a child and with the time the foster parent will spend with the child. The rates usually accompany added responsibilities, such as taking children to therapeutic appointments, advocating for children in special school settings, carrying out particular behavioral regimes at home, and/or working directly with biological parents. These foster parents become more truly partners with the agency in caring for the child. Such a combination of higher reimbursement rates and expanded responsibilities might be a better approach to all foster care.

The foster parent as colleague As they care for children day to day, foster parents learn a tremendous amount about the children and their needs. They often have opportunities to observe the child's interaction with family members. Sometimes they themselves have had extensive interaction with relatives of the child. When it is time to plan for the child, the foster parent has a great deal of useful information to share. Thus it is important that foster parents have ample opportunity to talk with workers and to express their ideas. It is important that they be invited to meetings where professionals are discussing plans, and to case status reviews by court-appointed reviewers. It is important that they be present as the information and perspectives they provide are discussed, evaluated, and woven into the perspectives of others.

Even so, it is not usually possible for foster parents to act as equal partners in the decision making about the child. They should be listened to, their information should be valued, and their perspectives should be given weight. However, if the child welfare worker and the foster parent disagree about planning for a child, the authority of the agency will back the child welfare worker. The court will, of course, be the final arbiter of any disagreements. But unless the foster parent is an actual party to a custody contest, foster parents seldom have the opportunity to speak directly to the court.

Conclusion

This chapter's review of the history of out-of-home care showed that the shortage of placements is not new. Early orphanages eased the pressure on their capacity by indenture. Cities sent children to rural areas. The advent of foster care created seemingly limitless family resources for the care of children, until demographic changes, increasingly high community standards for the treatment of children, and poverty and substance abuse all coincided to increase the number of children needing care while decreasing the number of available foster homes.

The consequences of the current shortage are many. Agencies place children in any available foster home rather than carefully matching their needs with the strengths of the home. Placement failures result, children are moved often, and each move damages the child's sense of trust and ability to form lasting relationships. The continual workload pressure on child welfare workers limits their capacity to supervise foster homes and to support foster parents who are caring for difficult children. In the worst of cases, the result can be abuse or neglect of the foster child.

In its response to the shortage of foster homes, the child welfare system's efforts have been focused on reducing its dependence on foster care—at best, through successful reunification of families or successful adoptive placements; when necessary, through the use of institutional or group care settings (discussed in chapter 7). Policy initiatives leading to increased placement of children with relatives in kinship foster care have also eased the pressure on foster homes. The crisis in foster care has also revived interest in congregate care, both a thoughtful consideration of which children might do better in a group setting rather than in family care, and a less thoughtful suggestion of wholesale return to the ease and control of orphanages. Missing is the work and investment needed to strengthen foster care.

That investment itself has the potential to relieve the shortage of placements. Too many foster parents leave the system after a very few years. Retention of foster parents is critical. Better supportive services are part of the solution, and adequate compensation would help. But probably the greatest need is for the creation of an atmosphere in which foster parents are treated with courtesy and respect, know their foster children's caseworkers and, if appropriate, the children's families, and are truly partners in decision making. Foster parents are remarkable people, and they deserve to be cherished.

Foster care is impermanent; it should be the long-term plan only in special circumstances and with special protections to ensure that children do not move. It is, however, a much-needed crisis service. Greater investment in foster care can promote the goal that each child will have only one placement, during which active work is done with both the biological family and the foster family while everyone, together, develops and implements a permanent plan for the child.

Notes

1. There is little record of children being removed from homes because of abuse, doubtless because of the severe physical punishment that was the norm.

2. Esther Forbes, in her novel *Johnny Tremain* (Boston: Houghton Mifflin, 1943), tells the story of an indenture that presents both its potential advantages and its dangers.

3. The reader should be careful not to judge the work of this reformer by the standards of the current century. Brace's own writing provides the context of the time.

4. The same relocation of children from cities to homes in the countryside took place over even greater distances through Barnardo's, a child welfare agency in Britain. Children from Great Britain were transported mainly to Canada and Australia. The last of these "shipments" of children occurred in the 1950s. The heartbreaking stories of many of these relocated children highlight the need for supervision of family homes by the placing agency. See P. Bean and J. Melville, *Lost Children of the Empire: The Untold Story of Britain's Child Migrants* (London: Unwin Hyman, 1989).

5. Throughout this section the historical background is drawn from Crenson 1998.

6. The Adoption and Safe Families Act, first discussed in chapter 1, sets a fifteen-month limit on the time a child is to be in foster care before termination

of parental rights is initiated. Although the provisions of the act have not been implemented long enough to allow any authoritative assessment of its impact, data from the AFCARS for the year 2000 does show that 61 percent of the children leaving foster care have had stays of seventeen months or less. The Evan B. Donaldson Adoption Institute reports that numbers of adoptions of children from foster care have increased 78 percent between 1998 and 2000; it is estimated that ASFA and adoption incentives resulted in 36,000 adoptions during this period that would not otherwise have occurred.

7. Martin (2000:143–46) presents an excellent table summarizing the research on the difficulties of children in foster care.

8. The findings of this excellent review should be read with caution, for it classifies all forms of out-of-home care as "foster care," including family foster homes, group homes, and residential facilities.

References

Abbott, G. 1938a. *The Child and the State: Apprenticeship and Child Labor.* Chicago, Ill.: University of Chicago Press.

———. 1938b. *The Child and the State: The Dependent and the Delinquent Child.* Chicago, Ill.: University of Chicago.

Bartholet, E. 1999. *Nobody's Children: Abuse, Neglect, Foster Drift, and the Adoption Alternative.* Boston: Beacon Press.

Block, N. M., and A. S. Libowitz. 1983. *Recidivism in Foster Care.* New York: Child Welfare League of America.

Botsko, M., and T. Festinger. 1994. *Returning to Care.* Washington, D.C.: Child Welfare League of America.

Brace, C. L. 1872. *The Dangerous Classes of New York.* New York: Wynkoop and Hallenbeck.

Cautley, P. W. 1980. *New Foster Parents.* New York: Human Sciences Press.

Child Welfare League of America. 1996. "National Data Analysis System." Washington, D.C. Available at http://www.cwla.org.

Child Welfare Partnership. 1999. *Children Entering Foster Care, 1995–1997: Report for the State of Oregon.* Salem: Oregon Department of Human Resources.

Costin, L. B., C. J. Bell, et al. 1991. *Child Welfare: Policies and Practice.* New York: Longman.

Crenson, M. W. 1998. *Building the Invisible Orphanage: A Prehistory of the American Welfare System.* Cambridge, Mass.: Harvard University Press.

Davies, L., and D. Bland. 1981. "The Use of Foster Parents as Role Models for Parents." In *Parents of Children in Placement: Perspectives and Programs,* edited by P. A. Sinanoglu and A. N. Maluccio. New York: Child Welfare League of America.

Emlen, A., J. Lahti, et al. 1976. *Overcoming Barriers to Planning for Children in Foster Care.* Portland, Ore.: Regional Research Institute for Human Services.

Epstein, W. M. 1999. *Children Who Could Have Been.* Madison: University of Wisconsin Press.

Evan B. Donaldson Adoption Institute. 2002. "Foster Care Facts." Evan B. Donaldson Adoption Institute, Washington, D.C. Available at http://www.adoptioninstitute.org.

Fahlberg, V. I. 1991. *A Child's Journey Through Placement.* Indianapolis: Perspectives Press.

Fanshel, D. 1982. *On the Road to Permanency.* New York: Columbia University Press.

Fanshel, D., S. J. Finch, et al. 1990. *Foster Children in Life Course Perspective.* New York: Columbia University Press.

Fanshel, D., and E. B. Shinn. 1978. *Children in Foster Care: A Longitudinal Investigation.* New York: Columbia University Press.

Fein, E., A. N. Maluccio, et al. 1983. "After Foster Care: Outcomes of Permanency Planning for Children." *Child Welfare* 62(6): 485–557.

Festinger, T. 1983. *No One Ever Asked Us—A Postscript to Foster Care.* New York: Columbia University Press.

Folman, R. D. 1998. " 'I Was Tooken': How Children Experience Removal from Their Parents Prior to Placement in Foster Care." *Adoption Quarterly* 2(2): 7–35.

Goerge, R., J. V. Voorhis, et al. 1996. "Core Dataset Project: Child Welfare Service Histories." Chapin Hall Center for Children, University of Chicago. Available at http://www.chapinhall.org

Goldstein, H., A. Freud, et al. 1973. *Beyond the Best Interests of the Child.* New York: Free Press.

Gruber, A. A. 1978. *Children in Foster Care: Destitute, Neglected, Betrayed.* New York: Human Sciences Press.

Hampson, R. B., and J. B. Tavormina. 1980. "Feedback from the Experts: A Study of Foster Mothers." *Social Work* 25 (March): 108–13.

Hazel, N. 1981. *A Bridge to Independence.* Oxford: Basil Blackwell.

Holman, R. 1980. "Exclusive and Inclusive Concepts of Fostering." In *New Developments in Foster Care and Adoption,* edited by J. Triseliotis. London: Routledge and Kegan Paul.

House Committee on Ways and Means. 1998. *1998 Green Book: Section 11. Child Protection, Foster Care, and Adoption Assistance.* Washington, D.C.: U.S. Government Printing Office.

Hubbell, R. 1981. *Foster Care and Families.* Philadelphia: Temple University Press.

Jackson, D. D. 1986. "It Took Trains to Put the Kids on the Right Track out of the Slums." *Smithsonian* 17:95–102.

Jenkins, S. 1981. "The Separation Experiences of Parents Whose Children Are in Foster Care." In *Parents of Children in Placement: Perspectives and Programs,* edited by P. A. Sinanoglu and A. N. Maluccio. New York: Child Welfare League of America.

Johnson, E., and P. Gabor. 1981. "Parent Counselors: A Foster Care Program with New Roles for Major Participants." In *The Challenge of Partnership: Working with Parents of Children in Foster Care,* edited by A. N. Maluccio and P. A. Sinanoglu. New York: Child Welfare League of America.

Johnson, P. R., C. Yoken, et al. 1995. "Family Foster Care Placement: The Child's Perspective." *Child Welfare* 74(5): 959–74.

Kadushin, A., and J. Martin. 1988. *Child Welfare Services.* New York: Macmillan.

Knitzer, J., M. L. Allen, et al. 1978. *Children Without Homes.* Washington, D.C.: Children's Defense Fund.

Lahti, J., K. Green, et al. 1978. "A Follow-up Study of the Oregon Project." Regional Research Institute for Human Services, Portland State University.

Lindsey, D. 1994. *The Welfare of Children.* New York: Oxford University Press.

Littner, N. 1950. *Some Traumatic Effects of Separation and Placement.* New York: Child Welfare League of America.

———. 1981. "The Importance of Natural Parents to the Child in Placement." In *Parents of Children in Placement,* edited by P. A. Sinanoglu and A. N. Maluccio. New York: Child Welfare League of America.

Maas, H., and R. Engler. 1959. *Children in Need of Parents.* New York: Columbia University Press.

Martin, J. A. 2000. *Foster Family Care: Theory and Practice.* Boston: Allyn and Bacon.

McAuley, C. 1996. *Children in Long-Term Foster Care: Emotional and Social Development.* Avebury, England: Aldershot.

McCausland, C. L. 1976. *Children of Circumstance.* Chicago: Chicago Child Care Society.

McDonald, T. P., R. I. Allen, et al. 1996. *Assessing the Long Term Effects of Foster Care.* Washington, D.C.: Child Welfare League of America.

Meezan, W., and J. Shireman. 1985. *Care and Commitment.* Albany: State University of New York Press.

Meier, E. 1965. "Current Circumstances of Former Foster Children." *Child Welfare* 44 (April): 196–206.

Ryan, P., E. J. McFadden, et al. 1981. "Foster Families: A Resource for Helping Parents." In *The Challenge of Partnership: Working with Parents of Children in Foster Care,* edited by A. N. Maluccio and P. A. Sinanoglu. New York: Child Welfare League of America.

Shireman, J., and J. Alworth. 1997. "Foster Parent Survey." Regional Research Institute for Human Services and Child Welfare Partnership, Portland State University, Portland, Ore.

Shireman, J., D. Yatchmenoff, et al. 1999. "Strengths/Needs Based Services Evaluation: Biennial Report." Regional Research Institute for Human Services, Portland, Ore.

Staff, I., and E. Fein. 1992. "Together or Separate: A Study of Siblings in Foster Care." *Child Welfare* 71(3): 257–70.

Toth, J. 1997. *Orphans of the Living; Stories of America's Children in Foster Care.* New York: Simon and Schuster.

Triseliotis, J., C. Sellick, et al. 1995. *Foster Care: Theory and Practice.* London, B. T. Batsford.

Unger, C., G. Dwarshusis, et al. 1977. *Chaos, Madness, and Unpredictability: Placing the Child with Ears Like Uncle Harry's.* Chelsea, Mich.: Spaulding for Children.

U.S. Department of Health and Human Services. 1995. *The National Survey of Current and Former Foster Parents.* Washington, D.C.: U.S. Department of Health and Human Services, Administration on Children, Youth, and Families.

———. 2000. *Child Welfare Outcomes 1998: Annual Report.* Washington, D.C.: U.S. Government Printing Office.

U.S. Department of Health and Human Services, Children's Bureau. 1997. *National Study of Protective, Preventive and Reunification Services Delivered to Children and Their Families.* Washington, D.C.: U.S. Government Printing Office.

———. 1999. AFCARS Report No. 1. Available at http://www.acf.hhs.gov/programs/cb/publications/afcars/report1.htm.

———. 2002a. AFCARS Report No. 7. Available at http://www.acf.hhs.gov/programs/cb/publications/afcars/report7.htm.

———. 2002b. "Child Maltreatment 2000: Reports from the States to the National Child Abuse and Neglect Data System." Available at http://www.acf.hhs.gov/programs/cb/publications/cm00.index/htm.

VanTheis, S. 1924. *How Foster Children Turn Out.* New York: State Charities Aid Association.

Viorst, J. 1986. *Necessary Losses.* New York: Fawcett Gold Medal.

Weinstein, E. 1960. *The Self Image of the Foster Child.* New York: Russell Sage Foundation.

White, M. S. 1981. "Promoting Visiting of Children in Foster Care." In *Parents of Children in Placement: Perspectives and Programs,* edited by P. A. Sinanoglu and A. N. Maluccio. New York: Child Welfare League of America.

Wilson, L., and J. Conroy. 1999. "Satisfaction of Children in Out of Home Care." *Child Welfare* 78 (January/February 1999): 53–69.

Zimmerman, R. 1982. *Foster Care in Retrospect.* New Orleans: Tulane University.

Zuravin, S. J., M. Benedict, et al. 1993. "Child Maltreatment in Foster Care." *American Journal of Orthopsychiatry* 63(4): 589–96.

CHAPTER 7

——— ✦ ———

Expanding the Foster Care System: Other Types of Out-of-Home Care

I am often asked by my friends, who think the child is little more than half-witted, why I do not "send her back and get a brighter one." My answer is, that she is just the one who needs the care and kindness which Providence has put it into my power to bestow. We love her dearly.

A FOSTER MOTHER IN OHIO, 1859

Traditional family foster care is the most frequently used type of out-of-home placement. Homes of relatives have become an important resource. Some children need extra help to manage family living, and some require the structure of group care.

Out-of-home care settings should encompass kinship care, family foster care, treatment foster care, emergency shelter care, apartments, community based group homes, campus style facilities, self-contained group care settings, and secure facilities. Within these settings children and their families should be able to obtain an appropriate mix of services, including counseling, education, health, nutrition, daily living experiences, independent living skills, reunification services, aftercare services, and advocacy.

(CHILD WELFARE LEAGUE OF AMERICA 1991:5)

Relative or kinship foster care is a relatively new adaptation of a long-used resource for children who cannot remain within their own homes but whose extended families have the capacity to care for them. Whole-family foster care, in which parents and their children live together in supervised settings, is even newer. These forms of care keep families involved in the lives of children and empower them to be part of the decision-making process; they are expressions of a new view of out-of-home care as a form of family preservation. Kinship foster care also plays a role in addressing the issue of cultural competence in the delivery of out-of-home care to minority children. We have noted that disproportionate numbers of African American and Native American children are in foster care, and that foster families are disproportionately white. Kinship foster care is one way of assuring that children of color remain in culturally appropriate homes; however, since kinship homes tend to receive fewer supportive services, the question of systemic racism must once again be considered.

Many children in out-of-home care have extensive behavioral difficulties and/or serious emotional disturbance. Some children are physically fragile, with medical needs that can best be met in a specialized setting. Children with developmental delays need specialized family care, with providers who are trained to meet their special needs and competent to work with the systems that serve such children.

There are also children who are, for a time, emotionally and behaviorally unable to benefit from family life. The reason may be serious emotional disturbance or pervasive developmental delay; or, older children may simply be at a developmental stage where they are moving away from family toward independence and not ready to form bonds with a new family. For these children and young people, group care can be appropriate and even therapeutic, and it is important that they experience the continuity of group care rather than moving from one failed foster home placement to another.

Finally, a new issue on the horizon in child welfare is the question of group care for children who do not have special needs. Group care is attractive, with its promise of standardized education and training for children. It is expensive, and the deinstitutionalization movement has focused us on the benefits of families for children. But many children are in group care, largely because of the shortage of foster homes; and proposals for increasing the role of group care have recently gained political attention. Thus the subject warrants examination here.

This chapter explores the child welfare system's attempts to expand and diversify its out-of-home care resources, creating a continuum of care so that each individual child's needs can be met. It attempts to illuminate the complexity of the task of matching these children, with their many needs, to appropriate resources and assuring that any moves from one type of care to another are appropriate and backed by adequate community support.

Shelter Foster Care and Assessment Centers

Child welfare agencies continually face emergency situations in which children need immediate placement. It can be very difficult to find a regular foster family willing to take a child within an hour or two, and even harder to find one that has the capacity to absorb a sibling group. The shortage of foster homes has compounded this problem, and one solution is the creation of shelter foster homes or group shelter facilities. However, aside from those relatively rare occasions when a child is discovered to be in real danger in the current home, emergency placement is likely to be an indication of the system's failure to work productively with parents or foster parents so that a placement can be avoided or, if necessary, made in a planned way. Whether the existence of shelter facilities increases the number of emergency placements is an interesting, and unanswered, policy question.

Shelter foster homes are family homes that are ready to take a child at any time of day or night and to care for the child for a brief time. Usually the placements are intended to last no longer than two weeks. Shelter foster homes are often salaried, since their beds will of necessity be empty at times if they are to retain the capacity for emergency placements. Usually they are licensed for up to five children.

Foster parents who take in children for emergency shelter care must be ready to recognize and comfort the fear and anxiety of children who have been removed from their homes abruptly and thrust into a strange environment. Children removed in emergency situations often show signs of severe neglect or abuse; foster parents can be very angry that parents would allow such things to happen to children. One of the tasks of the social worker is to recognize this anger and help the foster parents deal with it, because it will be important for the children to have visits with their parents or former caretakers very soon. Another task of the worker, carried out in conjunction with the foster parents, is the assessment of the child's needs. When children come into shelter care, very little may be known about them. A great deal must be learned in a brief time, in order to maximize the possibility that the next placement will be the last out-of-home placement a child will experience.

Group shelters, or assessment centers, of varied sizes exist in many communities. Usually they are isolated from the community, providing care and schooling within their own walls. One advantage of group shelter homes is that they can usually take sibling groups, thus providing some support and continuity for children. They are staffed by rotating shifts, so that there is little continuity of caregivers, a particular liability for young children if the stay is longer than a matter of days.

Assessment of the child's needs takes place during these weeks. A multidisciplinary staff provides medical examination, psychological testing and consultation with a psychologist, an educational evaluation, and assessment of social skills made through observation of children's behavior. The thoroughness of this assessment is one of the advantages of group shelter care.

Shelter care is controversial, in part because it means that every child will have more than one placement. Its advocates point to the advantages of a thorough assessment of each child so that a long-term placement can be planned that will meet the child's needs. Opponents point out that with foster homes so scarce, such careful matching is unlikely to occur, and instead the shelter facility may become the setting for a long stay. Indeed, one of the findings of a study of children in group care in California was that, although shelter placements for young children were designed to be brief and for the purpose of assessment, the median length of stay was more than a year (Berrick, Needell, et al. 1998).

Expanded Resources for Children Within Their Families

Kinship Foster Care

Kinship care has been defined by the Child Welfare League of America as "the full-time nurturing and protection of children who must be separated from their parents by relatives, members of their tribes or clans, godparents, stepparents, or other adults who have a kinship bond with the child" (Child Welfare League of America 1994:2). This is a broad definition, recognizing both blood ties and relationships more akin to the "psychological" family of the child. In 1996, only nineteen states were using this broad definition; in all but two of the remaining states, policies promote placement of children with biological family members if possible (U.S. Department of Health and Human Services [hereafter, U.S. HHS] 2000). Forty-eight states, and the District of Columbia, give preference to relatives when placing children in foster care (U.S. HHS 2000).

> *Nora is now eleven. At age seven she was removed from her mother, who was living in an abusive relationship and having problems with drugs. She has lived with her aunt in kinship foster care for four years, and is soon to return to her mother. Her aunt is her foster parent, speaking throughout this section:*
>
> > Well, my sister had a bad habit of leaving her . . . leave her for a week-end, come back in a week. Leave her for a week, come back in a month. . . . [Family friends took Nora, age seven, to the beach for a week.] It had been five weeks and no contact with her mother and they couldn't find her. She [called me] and said, "I have had Nora for five weeks and I don't know what to do." I said, "I'll be there in twenty minutes." I picked up Nora with the clothes on her back, got in the phone book, hired an attorney, and took her to court. . . . I literally saw this kid who was angry, nightmares, didn't want to sleep in a room by herself, had no clothes on her back, poor hygiene, no manners. I just thought, "Oh, my God, oh, my God. Literally, I don't know if I can do this." Then I just, thought, "Well, somebody has got to do it." And that's how it sort of happened. Then we just became a team.

Kinship foster care has grown rapidly. In part this is due to the shortage of foster homes, as kinship homes are used to augment the supply of regular foster homes. In part it is due to the family preservation movement, with its expanded definition of family and its emphasis on the importance of keeping children within their families. Advocacy by grandparents and other relatives has also been important; they have sought continued contact with children who have entered the child welfare system.

Formal and informal kinship care can be distinguished. Informal care is far more common. In 1998 there were 2.13 million children in the United States living apart from their parents with relatives; 1.4 million children were living with grandparents without a parent present (U.S.

HHS 2000). Some portion of these children have had contact with the child welfare system and have been "diverted" from that system into the homes of family members. About 200,000 children are living in formal kinship foster homes—homes that are part of the child welfare system (U.S. HHS 2000).

Informal, or private, kinship care may be an arrangement made among relatives. Such arrangements have been common practice for generations, particularly in certain cultural communities. It may be suggested or encouraged by workers in the child welfare system.[1] Financial support for private kinship care placements is provided, if the family applies for it and qualifies, through the state's income maintenance programs. These TANF grants amount to much less than foster care payments. Scannapieco (1999:72) suggests that if "family circumstances are such that they need an income transfer but not services, a diversion program is appropriate." Under the welfare reform initiative, this support has become more uncertain. It is up to states to decide whether their block grants will be used for the support of children in relative foster care, and whether any time limits apply to these children.

If an assessment of the child's and the family's needs, and of risk, suggests that services will be needed, a formal kinship care placement is more appropriate (Scannapieco 1999). In formal kinship care, the relative's home is held to foster care licensing standards; is under the supervision of the child welfare agency, which retains the ultimate decision-making authority for the child; and receives the same level of payments for the child's maintenance as an unrelated foster family would.[2]

Questions have been raised about the appropriate assessment and licensing requirements for relative homes, and many states use expedited procedures for such placements. The Adoption and Safe Families Act requires that all foster parents undergo a criminal background check and a check against the child abuse registry. Other requirements for foster homes, particularly those regarding space and income, are not considered essential for safety and are often waived for relatives. Ability to care for the child, ability to meet any special needs, and willingness to work with the child welfare agency are necessary. The standards for relative foster care must be continually examined, because the pressure of scarcity may tempt agencies to use relative homes that are only marginally equipped to add a child.

Relative foster parents receive fewer services from child welfare agencies than do regular foster parents (Dubowitz, Feigelman, et al. 1993; Berrick,

Barth, et al. 1994; Ingram 1996). Because situations requiring the placement of a child often unfold rapidly, they often receive no formal training
about the responsibilities of fostering, or about what the foster parent
has a right to expect from the agency. Because relatives usually know the
child, the agency tends to spend less time preparing them to meet the
needs of the particular child. How much supervision do kinship foster
homes need? According to a 1999 study done in Illinois, the incidence of
child maltreatment in relative foster homes, at 19 per 1,000, is lower than
in most other types of out-of-home care (Poertner, Bussey, et al. 1999).

How much should the child welfare agency invest in services to relative foster homes? If the state has assumed custody of a child, it is
responsible for that child's welfare; regular foster home visits to assure
that the needs of the child are being met should certainly be required.
The level of additional services needed is as varied as the case situations.
The social worker has to assess many factors—including the competence
of the relatives, their knowledge of the child and comfort with his or her
behaviors, the degree of emotional and/or behavioral disturbance the
child exhibits, the relationship between the foster family and the child's
own parents, and the degree of stress caused in the household by the
addition of the foster child—and then plan supervision and support
activities accordingly.

> I think that the behavioral displays and me not having even been a parent
> before, and having been a single person with a complete life of my own
> prior to having her, I think that I wanted assistance also in how to deal
> with getting her back on track. . . . I was looking for practical ways to
> resolve the outbursts and the mood swings and the anger quickly, with-
> out getting frustrated myself. And I was looking for tools. So I would say
> between the school counselor, her teacher, and our counselor [provided
> through the child welfare agency] . . . and then a lot of the people I work
> with are grandparents their own selves and they have a lot of practical
> parenting skills. I read books . . .

It must be recognized that the child is still within the family. The
agency must avoid being needlessly intrusive, respecting the family's
desire to make decisions about its own members. Kinship foster homes
tend to be stable; there is less need for contact to preserve the placements. However, it is necessary to recognize that these caregivers have

responded to a family crisis by taking in a child, and that they may experience intense feelings of "disappointment, helplessness, uncertainty, grief, loss, guilt, obligation, pride, or anxiety" (Jackson 1999:108). These feelings are different from those of nonrelated foster parents; training and support must also differ.

> I have had her for quite some time, and there are attachments there. And there are concerns. I have had many misgivings about having her go home, and worry spells. So how do I neutralize and detach and let go my own self, and encourage the fruitful relationship between she and her mom, when I am still in disagreement or discord with how that family unit operates. So I've really had to learn, and [the therapist] has really, she is a wonderful woman, we work on different skills. . . .
>
> But I think that there is a special history that follows a biological placement and I think that the caseworkers would benefit from having some specialty training there, as well. In other words, there are just different attachments and there are different histories of how a grandparent or a sister or a mother will deal with the history of the biological parent, and making it more like a divorce.

Kinship foster homes are most common among communities of color, where extended families are traditionally involved in the rearing of children (Berrick, Barth, et al. 1994). This suggests that assessment, training, and support activities need to be tailored to the practices of these communities, recognizing their traditions and the natural helping networks that exist. The fact that kinship foster homes receive fewer services than do non-kin foster homes must be viewed with the suspicion that it may be another example of racism in the child welfare system.

Descriptions of relative caregivers suggest that most are African American and many are single women with little education. Poverty is common among them. Many are grandparents (Dubowitz, Feigelman, et al. 1993; Berrick, Barth, et al. 1994; Ingram 1996). These characteristics suggest that concrete services are important; attention must be given to ensuring adequacy of income, to helping relatives to bring homes into conformity with state standards for the safety and health of children, and to providing day care and after-school care. Help with transportation to appointments can be greatly appreciated. When placements continue for long periods, relatives may experience exhaustion and a sense of helplessness. Their sense of family obligation and attachment to the children may seem to preclude any future change in circumstances. Respite care can be vital, as can support groups.

The children coming into kinship foster care have had the same difficult experiences as those coming into regular foster care. Their move to foster care may be less traumatic if they are go to the home of a relative they know. Their parents usually have more access to them in relatives' homes, so that visits can be frequent and informal. However, children in kinship foster care suffer from the same mental health and behavioral problems evident in other foster children. Relatives need expert help in managing their behaviors and providing the most therapeutic environment possible.

Kinship foster care is different from regular foster care. In some ways it seems more natural, an extension of the long tradition of extended family care of children, and thus to be an easier service to administer than regular foster care. Agencies may expect it to require fewer services and less attention. In some ways, though, it is much more complex. Kinship foster care incorporates the tensions of a family that has had difficulty with its children, with caretaker and parent roles shifting. Additionally, relatives are often motivated by affection and family obligation, and may take on the care of children without sufficient resources of either finances or energy to handle the task easily.

> But I really felt all along that I wanted to stay separate from my sister and Nora's relationship, whatever that might be. . . . But I could see [the child welfare agency] kind of wanting me to be in it when they wanted me to, and wanted me to stay out . . . when they wanted me to. . . . It was very strange. So I chose to stay out and try to neutralize myself. Other than my love for Nora, but to try to stay at a distance. Like a foster parent.

There is debate about how to interpret the outcomes of relative placements. They are longer than placements in regular foster care, and they are usually exempted by the courts from the provisions of ASFA that mandate a permanent home within fifteen months. Though relatively lengthy, kinship foster placements are usually stable (U.S. HHS 2000). Parents often have considerable access to their children when they are placed with relatives, and because they are with "family," returning children to a more problematic life with their original parents may not seem very important to the agency. On the other hand, adoption is often of little interest to relatives because of the family disruption they believe it would create. Has permanency, within the extended family, been achieved for these children?

> You want to help the kid, but I've gotten to the point where I don't feel like I can deal with my sister or [the child welfare agency] together. They are on the same pathway of reunification. I really feel that they always have been, and that's great. But after four years the kid needs to, be it good or bad, have some permanency.

Certainly kinship foster care has grown rapidly, both in response to the child welfare system's emphasis on preserving families and in response to the shortage of foster homes. It demands a new way of thinking about families and about foster care.

Whole-Family Care

Whole-family care programs are those that allow parents (usually mothers) and children to live together in supervised living arrangements for extended periods. The programs provide comprehensive services to both parents and children, tailored to meet the individual needs of the family. The Children's Defense Fund describes family care as "an important component of the service continuum for some families for which in-home services will not work because the family is homeless, the children's or the mother's safety is at risk in the home, or for other reasons" (Allen and Larson 1998:ix).

Family care programs serve families with complex problems that might, without this opportunity, necessitate long separations between parents and children. Families that have made use of these programs include teens who are parenting, single parents in difficult financial circumstances, parents in substance abuse treatment programs, families with developmental delays or mental illness, and families where violence or homelessness are present.

Ryan, McFadden, et al. (1981) have identified foster parents as having unique contributions to make to biological parents. They are knowledgeable about community resources, agency policy and practice, and legal processes. To make fuller use of such a valuable resource, the authors suggest expanding their role from one that focuses only on the child to one that focuses on the child's family as a whole. This requires a shift in thinking, not only about the relationship between the foster family and the biological family but also about that of the foster family and the agency. With appropriate training, foster parents can become an essential part of the professional team.

Maluccio (1981) describes several programs that exemplify the changing roles of foster parents. One program places single mothers and their abused children together in a specialized foster home. Within the home, both the parent and the children are "fostered." Nelson describes similar programs that bring services to homeless parents and their children. She writes of the need for cultural diversity among the providers, in order that families in need can be matched with families who are not too different. She also notes that the care providers in these programs are people who believe that "homes and possessions are meant to be shared," and come from backgrounds that have left them "used to negotiating with peers for what they need" (Nelson 1992:582).

Barth (1994) reviews the range of programs in which parents live with children in out-of-home care, and notes that many forms of treatment already exist that are designed for work with whole families. Many of these, such as substance abuse programs, are in the mental health rather than the child welfare system, and some, in which services are intensive, use residential care rather than family foster care as the framework for services. Residential care, with staff members who work rotating shifts and serve multiple clients, does not add another intense personal relationship to the family mix, and indeed may be an easier way to implement whole-family care. Gibson and Noble (1991) write of such a program, developed for single mothers and their children, that has experienced success in helping the mothers resume self-sufficient lives in the community.

Obviously, taking on the care of a whole family has different dimensions than caring for children only. Foster parents must be recruited and trained with this service in mind; they have to be "inclusive" foster families (Triseliotis, Sellick et al. 1995). They will act as negotiators and mediators and teachers, so they should be people who enjoy those processes. The support services needed for foster family care will be different, too; they will involve facilitating communication and mediating among adults, calling for some of the same social work skills that promote successful family respite services. To date little has been written about whole-family foster care. It is an exciting concept with possible wide application, particularly

in circumstances where it can avert long and potentially damaging separations between parents and children.

Care for Children with Special Difficulties in the Child Welfare System

Children are placed in specialized foster homes or in group settings for a
number of reasons, usually because they have needs that cannot be met
in a regular family foster home. The nature of the child's needs dictates
the appropriate placement. The child may require the therapeutic intervention or skilled medical care available in a specialized foster home or a
residential treatment setting. An adolescent moving toward independence,
whose prior experiences make him or her unable to sustain the demands
of a family, may need to live in a group setting that provides consistency
and safety while fostering the development of the skills necessary for
independence. The special needs of such children may be apparent at the
time the child moves from the original home, or they may become evident
through a series of failed foster home placements. Children are sometimes
placed in group care for their own protection, or for the protection of the
community.

Children in specialized foster care and in group care are disproportionately African American, reflecting the situation in all out-of-home care.
They tend to come from poor families. Often there is a history of removal
from the original home after abuse or neglect, followed by foster home
placements that have failed due to the children's behavioral disturbance,
and then placement in group care. Group settings that provide extensive
control and treatment are often relatively short-term placements, primarily
because of their high cost. Children often move back into the community
from these settings, either as residents of group homes or as members of
specialized foster families.

Specialized Foster Homes

Specialized foster homes, or therapeutic foster homes, or professional
foster homes, are homes that care for children with special difficulties.
They are a relatively recent service development. These are interesting
homes, with special training and support needs. They receive high board
rates for the difficult children they serve. The foster parents' relationship

to the child welfare system is usually different from that of regular foster parents, containing more elements of partnership with the agency.

One foster mother we know described her medically fragile foster child:

> We are just beginning to look at are we dealing with some autism or something else going on. Even if he is severely hearing impaired, I was just talking with the pediatrician yesterday, he should break out in a big grin when he at least sees me, even if he is not hearing me. He makes very little, very short eye contact. . . . So we are beginning to wonder about his capacity to respond that way.

Definitions Specialized foster homes create a community-based alternative for children with serious emotional disturbance, medical needs, or developmental delays who might otherwise be placed in group care, and are part of the continuum of care. They are defined by the following characteristics.

1. Children are placed with families selected and trained to work with children with special needs who would otherwise be admitted to an institutional setting.
2. The home is a part of a program explicitly identified as a specialist or treatment foster care program with a name and budget, and operates within an identifiable theoretical model.
3. Typically, only one or two children are placed at a time.
4. Payments are made to caregivers at rates above those provided for regular foster care.
5. Specialized training and multiple support services are provided to the specialized foster parents.
6. The treatment foster parent is considered a member of a service or treatment team. (adapted from Hudson, Nutter, et al. 1992; Jivanjee, Severin-Held, et al. 1999)

A child may need a group setting to stabilize behavior or a medical condition, then be able to function in a specialized foster home. Or the foster home may be a point of transition from a residential setting back to the original home. Or the foster home may itself be the sole placement a child needs. As always, this type of out-of-home care is accompanied by services to strengthen the family and follow-up services to help child and family live together again, or, if reunification is not possible, services to move the child toward adoption.

Although the use of terminology is not consistent, authors tend to distinguish among forms of specialized foster care. In specialized foster care, foster parents are provided training "to create a nurturing therapeutic environment" in their home; they carry out interventions designed by professionals (Reddy and Pfeiffer 1997:518). In treatment foster care, the foster parents are viewed as the primary change agents; they are trained and supported as they design and carry out interventions. Professional foster parents may follow either of these models, and are distinguished by receiving a salary, usually between $15,000 and $25,000 (in addition to board payments), and being viewed as agency employees. It is not clear which of these models gives the foster parent the strongest voice in decisions regarding children in their care. The term "therapeutic foster care" is generally reserved for families caring for children with mental health problems; families caring for children with serious medical problems are usually designated as medical foster homes.

Characteristics of youth served The most notable characteristics of children in specialized foster care are their serious emotional and behavioral problems. Dore (2001), in a qualitative study of children in specialized foster care, noted traumatic histories of abuse and neglect and frequent changes of caregivers, followed by behavior problems that were extremely difficult for foster parents to manage. This often led to children being moved from foster home to foster home, and often into residential care for a time— a series of moves that, of course, exacerbated emotional and behavioral difficulties. Berrick found similar characteristics in a study of children in specialized foster homes in California (Berrick, Courtney, et al. 1993). She also noted educational difficulties—about 30 percent of the children had repeated a grade in school; 40 percent were enrolled in some type of special education class.

The youngsters in specialized foster care share characteristics with all children in foster care. African American children are overrepresented. Most children come from impoverished families and have histories of abuse and neglect (Schneiderman, Connors, et al. 1998). And, as we have seen in earlier chapters, emotional and behavioral problems are common among foster children; Schneiderman and colleagues (1998) concluded that half of the children in foster care had serious emotional and behavioral disturbances.

What distinguishes children in specialized foster care is, in part, the extent and form of their behavioral disturbance—behavior so difficult that the children cannot be maintained in regular foster care. And, as Dore (2001) noted in her examples of children's histories, the other thing that distinguishes them is the plain good fortune of having had a child welfare worker who recognized their need for specialized help, and who was working in a system with the resources to provide it.

Treatment interventions Specialized foster care programs have developed from varied theoretical bases, and those origins are reflected in the training and interventions characteristic of each program. The common dimensions are the nurturing and supportive environment that the foster home is expected to provide, the close cooperation with professional staff, and the extensive training and professional support the foster parent can expect. In a review of outcome studies of treatment foster care, Reddy and Pfeiffer (1997) point out that to be more useful the studies should include more description of the training and support services offered, delineate the critical dimensions of the interventions used, and link these elements to outcomes.

Qualitative research, detailing the experiences of the foster parent in interaction with caseworkers, other professional personnel, and the child's own parents, has provided valuable insight into the context of specialized foster care. Foster parents noted difficulties they faced as treatment foster parents. They lamented the absence of complete information about children coming into their homes, they noted their need for support and guidance as they dealt with difficult children, and they talked of the grief they felt when children left their homes. Inconsistencies in the definition of roles emerged; they saw themselves both in a parent role and in a provider role, and they received mixed messages from the professionals guiding the programs (Wells and D'Angelo 1994).

THE FOSTER MOTHER: Well, my major concern right now is the caseworker's determination to place him for adoption as soon as possible. And his attorney and my medical people and I all believe he is not ready. So I don't know. She keeps telling me she is not going to place him before he is ready, but she is recruiting families. I don't know how patient she will be. . . . By the time you have been through a lot of medical crises and you are not sure the kid is going to come out the other end and they have, you have a lot of attachment. I am trying to balance that out and make sure that it is not coloring my "Oh, I don't want him to go for another year."

Interaction with the child's biological parents emerges as a major theme. Jivanjee (1999) concludes that "relationships and practices with parents were shaped by professionals' values regarding family involvement and their attitudes toward specific parents, and by TFC [treatment foster care] providers' willingness to communicate with parents and facilitate parent-child contact" (p. 333). All professionals and most foster parents expressed favorable attitudes about family involvement in foster care. If the foster parents think that the child's family members are "trying," foster parents will encourage contact, create opportunities for parents to interact with children, and work with child and parent toward reunion (Wells and D'Angelo 1994; Jivanjee 1999). Negative attitudes toward children's families seem related to foster parents' past experiences, and are expressed as dislike or fear. Because the attitudes of providers largely determine the amount of contact, these attitudes can present a significant barrier to family involvement (Jivanjee 1999).

> THE FOSTER MOTHER: I get so frustrated seeing moms come in at eleven months and they have had eleven months to get into drug treatment and clean up their lives. Two weeks before the court hearing they go into drug treatment, and "Now I am going to get my life squared away." And so they put the kid on hold for another year. Not O.K. . . . I've had several kids where I have had lots of visitation here at my house. I am not real excited about doing that. I am no longer willing to do that at the outset of a placement.

The voice of the parents is heard in Jivanjee's (1999) study of parent perspectives about specialized foster care. The author conducted a qualitative study of ten families who were involved in their children's lives although the children were in placement. The families were typical of those described in larger, quantitative studies—struggling with the stresses of poverty, mental illness, and substance abuse, as well as having children with serious emotional or behavioral disorders. The attitudes of professionals, and to a lesser degree those of foster parents, were known to the parents and emerged as either barriers or facilitators of contact with children. Time spent by professionals in getting to know them, involving them in planning for their children, and assisting them with arrangements for contact with their children was deeply appreciated by these families, as was the sharing of information by foster parents. More convenient scheduling of visits and assistance with transportation to visits were noted as some concrete ways that professionals could help facilitate family involvement.

> THE MOTHER: So what if I don't get to see him at this present time because I am not in [substance abuse] treatment? That still don't give you the right to deprive me of at least keeping me up on what's going on. Because the more you keep a parent away from what's going on with a child, the more you have them constantly thinking, What is going on? It kind of sends them into a lot of chaos, a lot of stress.

Outcomes Reddy and Pfeiffer (1997) in a review of research on specialized foster care, consider the outcomes of placement permanency, remediation of behavior problems, and discharge status. Forty studies were reviewed. The authors report that treatment foster care increased the stability of placements for children and that it had positive effects in improving social skills and reducing behavior problems. Data were mixed on whether placements ended with discharge to less restrictive placements. Hudson, Nutter, et al. (1992) report that two-thirds of the 1,738 children sampled in their survey were discharged to living arrangements less restrictive than specialist foster family care. Fanshel, Finch, et al. (1990) found only about a fifth of the 585 youths from the Casey Family Program returning home, but one of the criteria of admission to the program is that return home is unlikely; almost 60 percent were emancipated from the program, an outcome considered positive.

Testa and Rolock (1999) address the question of the role of specialized foster care in the child welfare system, and make the point that specialized foster homes are expected to meet the criteria of all foster homes: (1) community-based care, (2) maintaining family integrity through keeping sibling groups together, (3) continuity of care in the same foster home, (4) caring for children in the least restrictive setting, and (5) moving children toward permanent homes. Comparing specialized foster homes with regular foster homes and with kinship foster homes, they found that kinship foster homes and specialized foster homes performed better than regular foster homes according to these criteria.

Because therapeutic foster homes work with very disturbed young people, most of whom have been unable to live successfully in their own families or in regular foster care, many outcome studies are designed to compare their outcomes with those of youngsters in residential care. The common finding is that specialized foster care "is less expensive, offers comparable behavioral improvements, and offers a less restrictive treatment setting" (Reddy and Pfeiffer 1997:581). Studies that have used control groups to compare treatment foster care with group care find that it costs about half as much and is as effective as group care at changing behavior and maintaining youth in a community setting. (Rubenstein, Armentrout, et al. 1978; Chamberlain 1998).[3] Berrick, Courtney, et al. (1993) compared children in specialized foster homes with children in group homes; they found those in group homes to be older and to have more severe behavior problems—factors that could partially explain the more favorable outcomes of treatment foster homes.

Finally, there are descriptive studies that report on positive behavioral changes shown by children in the programs. For example, Hazel (1981) reports positive change on a variety of social and psychological measures for adolescents in the Kent Project.[4] Similarly, Fanshel's longitudinal study of the Casey Family Program notes positive behavioral changes, although the results confirmed that study's hypothesis that the children who had had more adversarial experiences prior to placement and showed more distress at placement would have the poorest outcomes (Fanshel, Finch, et al. 1990).

Group Care: Meeting a Range of Needs

Group care for children consists of a number of types of services, some of which have already been discussed. Some are clearly crisis services; some might become substitute families for children. The Child Welfare League of America (1991) identifies a continuum of group care settings. Community-based group homes, housing twelve or fewer children and using community services, are at one end of the continuum. Campus-based facilities consist of a cluster of separate living units, each housing twenty or fewer children. The units are usually self-contained, though they may use some community facilities. Self-contained group care settings house up to forty children, often in one building, and are usually therapeutic environments that provide a high level of child supervision. Finally, secure facilities have the features of self-contained settings, but maintain intensive supervision and may be locked facilities. The outdoor programs currently popular for troubled youth also represent a type of group care. One other form of group care is that provided in residential educational facilities, including private boarding schools used by families who can afford them, as well as the thirty or so residential schools for disadvantaged youth that exist in the United States.

A wide variety of systems are involved in the group care of children. The most intensive therapeutic settings are often under the auspices of the mental health system; the outdoor programs are run by nonprofit or for-profit organizations. Any residential setting that cares for children who are developmentally delayed will have to follow the guidelines of the developmental disability services system for the care of children. Residential settings that house delinquents are usually part of the criminal justice system. And those that market themselves as schools are, obviously, part of the educational system. Each type of institution must also cooperate with other systems to obtain the specialized help that children need.

The most recent census of group care facilities was conducted in 1981, and the authors of that study compare their findings with those of a 1966 census. The changes are interesting, demonstrating trends that may well have continued. During the fifteen-year interval the total number of residential facilities increased, but as smaller group facilities became more common, the number of children in residential care declined. Only in juvenile corrections did large numbers of children remain in big facilities. Overall the average length of stay decreased, facilities reported a higher proportion of children attending school in the community, and involvement with families was a component of the program for more facilities. The authors point out that these changes reflect the ability of residential care programs to respond to the increasingly complex situations of the children they serve; the changes also attest to the programs' recognition of the importance of family and community. Finally, it should be noted that the 2000 AFCARS data show that 8 percent of the children in out-of-home care are in group homes and 10 percent in institutions—though a small percentage, it represents more than 100,000 children and youth (U.S. HHS, Children's Bureau 2002). Pecora, Whittaker, et al. (1992) raise the fundamental policy question about group care: "Is it best seen as a substitute for a family that has failed, or as a support for a family in crisis?" (p. 410).

Group Homes

There are two principal types of group homes. One type is staffed by child care workers, sometimes rotating as institutional personnel do, sometimes supplementing and giving relief time to a couple who are the parent figures in the home. The second category is the group foster homes, which are licensed for several children, usually between the ages of eight and twelve. They differ from small institutions in that they are homes, with parents who are there twenty-four hours a day.

Group placements are particularly appropriate for adolescents who are at a developmental stage where they thrive in a group culture. They can, however, be useful for any child who cannot tolerate the intense parent-child relationships of a more traditional home. Based on incomplete reporting from the states, the Child Welfare League database estimates that 18,613 children were living in group homes in 1996, about 5 percent of the children in out-of-home care.

Group homes are established in the community, usually in a large house or apartment. Children placed in them must be capable of maintaining reasonable social relationships with the neighbors, and of attending public school. Interactions with schools, police, parents of the children placed there, and neighbors are frequent. One problem for foster parents is maintaining good relationships with the neighborhood, particularly if there are several active adolescents in the home.

Residential Treatment Centers

Residential treatment placements are designed so that therapeutic interventions can be woven into the structure of the child's day, and thus can be constant and intensive. They were developed for the most seriously compromised of the children with mental health or developmental difficulties. The definition of "residential treatment centers" varies; here the term refers to twenty-four hour care that includes on-site mental health treatment outside of the hospital. Residential care encompasses a continuum of restrictiveness, ranging from locked facilities that provide intensive treatment, through more open facilities that encourage interaction with the community through special projects or trips as children are ready, to facilities from which some children attend community schools.

Although treatment efforts may be based on differing theoretical orientation, a common thread is the development of a "holding environment," in which the quality of the youth's life in the treatment milieu is the focus of intervention. Attention is paid to relationships with staff members and other residents, and the child's day is programmed in such a way that his or her therapeutic needs can be met (O'Malley 1993).

Characteristics of children Wells and Whittington (1993) studied the characteristics of children admitted to one residential care facility in considerable depth. They found that the youths tended to come from impoverished families. In many families the parents had separated, and most children had no contact with the absent parent. Youths displayed "diverse, severe, and diffuse behavioral problems and significant deficits in their social competencies" (p. 213). Problems had emerged at an early age, and 93 percent had had prior out-of-home placements. These characteristics echo the findings of other studies (U.S. General Accounting Office 1994). Yelton (1993) notes that the overall policy shift in child welfare and mental health services toward family preservation and community-based care means that the children who do come into residential care are more difficult and at greater risk than in prior years. An example drawn from our interviews illustrates the complex problems presented:

> *When John was seven, a psychiatrist told his mother that he was homicidal and needed care in a locked facility. His behavior has continued to be frightening to his family. The family lives in a poor community; John has been involved in thefts and drugs. He is now thirteen and, for the last six months, has been in a residential care facility three hundred miles from his home.*
>
> JOHN'S MOTHER: It is scary. . . . Because he has hallucinations. . . . He was hearing voices tell him, "Go ahead. You can jump over this fence [a fence topped with razor wire] and it won't hurt you." He still has them. [The residential care facility] seems to think his psychotic episodes aren't as severe because he is not talking about them. He learned that if he didn't talk about them, and this is what he told me, "If I don't talk about them, then people won't think that they are bad." . . . I mean, when he comes home, I don't want him to have voices tell him to kill . . . his sister or somebody else.

Numbers There are far more children in family foster care than in residential care; the latter is an expensive option for a small group of children who need intensive therapeutic services. The AFCARS estimate (9 percent of the children and youth in out-of-home care are in institutions) is probably most accurate with respect to those children who enter residential care from the child welfare system. But residential care is both publicly and privately financed, and most states do not maintain central registries of children in residential care. Children and adolescents enter residential care from the mental health system (for example, after a stay at an acute-care psychiatric hospital, from the child welfare system (after other foster home or group home placements), from the juvenile justice system, from the educational system, or through referral by a primary physician. In many cases these young people are simultaneously involved with several systems (Wells 1993).

The continuum of care Residential care is one option in a continuum of care for children. With the current emphasis on deinstitutionalization, it is often considered a last resort, and used when it has proved impossible to manage a child's behavior in a family or community setting. Yelton's research suggests that the movement from institution-based care to community-based, family-focused care has been spurred by changes in the mental health system, by a general emphasis on fiscal responsibility in the provision of social services, by the development of managed care, and by the findings of various pilot projects that have demonstrated the feasibility of providing intensive services within the community (Yelton 1993).

In this light residential care is seen as a short-term option, to be used until the child's behavior is stabilized and he is moved back to the community. For some children brief treatment in residential care may work well; O'Malley (1993) suggests that if the youth has a supportive family, if the child and family have at least a moderate ability to collaborate in treatment, if there is at least moderate control of impulses, and if treatment goals are limited, brief residential care may be effective. Community resources for aftercare must, of course, be in place.

Other youths, who have serious difficulties and have failed in other treatment programs, need extended care for their own safety and for the protection of the community. A policy mandating brief stays ignores the fact that most of these children have suffered from numerous prior broken relationships, and that relationships are of central importance in the treatment of many of their difficulties. "The issue for this population is not how to prevent placement but, rather, how to prevent successive placements and to allow a safe passage through adolescence, with a half decent chance for adequate functioning as a young adult" (Wells and Whittington 1993:214).

JOHN'S MOTHER: He didn't want to come home to see us, and he was very honest about that. He said he wanted to come back to the area where his friends are so he could hang out with his friends and do drugs that he likes to do and just be on his own. . . . He is thirteen. He will be fourteen in December. So that's why I finally got it through my thick skull that he may not be able to come home. . . . I am still working toward that goal. I

> haven't given up the goal. But I am more realistic that I don't think he will be able to come home and actually be a functioning member of the family. It is finally sinking in.

In recent years, the trend throughout the field of child welfare has been toward enhancing the role of family. This trend is paralleled in the area of residential treatment. Residential treatment centers have historically been notorious for excluding the family. In the residential program, the child is the focal point of service; in recent history, not only was therapy generally reserved entirely for the child but a separation from parents was often considered therapeutic. However, gradually it was recognized that children do go home to their families, and that the child was best served if family ties were maintained and the family was prepared to further the child's progress on his return.

Even though efforts at reform have been made, theoretical and logistical impediments to the inclusion of family in treatment remain. Parents are sometimes viewed as part of the "problem," and providers may believe that parental involvement will exacerbate or interfere with treatment. This is particularly true when parents have been neglectful or abusive toward the child. A logistical problem arises when the residential treatment center is located many miles from the child's home. This creates difficulties if the child is in short-term placement and the participation of the family is needed to achieve treatment goals. If the child needs long-term residential treatment, out-of state placement is often necessary because there are so few such facilities. Technology has improved access for some parents, however; most practitioners in residential treatment centers today are well acquainted with "phone therapy."

> JOHN'S MOTHER: I try to talk to him at least once a week on the phone. . . .
> If they would at least meet me halfway on visits. Make it a little more flexible for our face-to-face counseling, do it on the weekends, because when I work, and my husband works full time, that would be the time we could get over there. . . . Also we were supposed to be able to do it on the phone, just kind of talk on the phone. . . . They would call me at eleven. And they knew that my lunch hour was eleven-thirty. . . . I lost one of my recent jobs because I would have to leave my desk and go take these phone calls.

Management of cost Length of stay in residential treatment centers has been decreasing not only because of emphasis on community-based services, but also because of cost. Managed care has had a considerable impact on the policies and practices in residential care. Residential treatment is expensive. Bradshaw, developing an argument in favor of group care and basing his data on a single residential care institution that provided few therapeutic services, estimated it at $32,350 per child in 1995 (Bradshaw, Wyant, et al. 1999:273). Berrick and colleagues, in an article comparing specialized foster care and group care, estimated that group care in California of any type cost an average of $35,892 per year (Berrick, Courtney, et al. 1993:464). As such, the relatively small number of children and youths who need residential care consume a high proportion of any child welfare budget.

> JOHN'S MOTHER: The last time we talked [to the residential care facility] my son was on the run. I think a day or two after we talked, my husband and I went out and tracked him down and found him. . . . He was kicking and hitting and trying to bite, spitting on us. It was really bad. So we got him to the [hospital] triage center. They kept him for twenty-four hours. Then I went back to the child welfare agency and requested that I place him in their custody, because I couldn't afford to get him placed anywhere. They were talking about five hundred dollars a day to place him in a private hospital.

Outcome data regarding the benefits of long-term care have been inconclusive, although methodological issues greatly complicate the analysis of such data. Many insurance plans cover only a preset amount of acute care and residential treatment days (O'Malley 1993). Many of the benefit packages offer sixty or fewer days of residential treatment per year. Managed care relies on utilization reviews, which require that the practitioner be able to demonstrate need and progress on a weekly or daily basis. For behaviors that typically occur at a low rate, such as assaults or suicide attempts, it may be difficult to show that behavioral change has not yet occurred. Risk is always difficult to assess and to demonstrate.

Cost, and cost containment through managed care, raise an additional issue for parents. When insurance companies will no longer pick up the cost of stays in residential care, many families have to turn to state assistance. When a child is placed for care by the state at the state's expense, the child welfare placement procedures take effect. In many states this means that parents lose custody of their children, either when they are placed or after only a brief period of placement. This loss of parental rights and control, of course, is contrary to the goals of a system that is trying to build family strength to support these children.

Under managed care, lengths of stay in psychiatric hospitals have significantly declined (O'Malley 1993); the trend is toward provision of less treatment. What were settings for acute psychiatric care have become settings for brief assessments; what was long-term residential treatment is becoming a hybrid of more extensive assessment and stabilization. It remains to be seen whether the patients who formerly would have had access to long-term residential services are finding the resources they need, or whether these trends will eventually result in another increase in adolescent state hospital populations.

Abuse and neglect in residential care As is the case with foster care, the professional community has been reluctant to examine, or even to admit the existence of, abuse or neglect in residential care settings. Therefore there is relatively little literature concerning maltreatment in either family care or group care. Before the mid-1970s, complaints were usually treated as licensing difficulties, and were handled internally by whatever authority licensed the child care facility. In 1977 the National Center on Child Abuse and Neglect stipulated that, if a state wished to receive federal grant funds, it must conduct independent investigations of any reports of abuse or neglect in a child care facility. The word *independent* has been variously interpreted; in many states the usual child protective investigations are viewed as being independent, whereas in some states another state agency investigates the complaint (Reindfleisch and Hicho 1987).

Abuse of children seems to be more of a problem in institutional care than in foster care. Investigations in the 1980s indicated a rate of abuse or neglect more than twice as great in institutions as in foster homes (Merkel-Holguin and Sobel 1993), and twice as high as for children living with their own families (Rabb and Reindfleisch 1985). In 1980, Reindfleisch and Rabb estimated an incidence rate of 39 per 1,000 residents; they note that the number is based on self-reporting and so may be an underestimate (Reindfleisch and Rabb 1984). In 1992, Spencer and Knudsen analyzed data from the state of Indiana and found a rate of 120 incidents per 1,000; the authors note that this rate is higher than for any other type of out-of-home care, and significantly higher than that found by Reindfleisch and Rabb. Sexual abuse was the most commonly reported form of maltreatment. Physical abuse was more common in foster care; sexual abuse more common in residential care. The authors note that other residents were perpetrators in 70 percent of the residential instances of sexual abuse (Spencer and Knudsen 1992). Using a sample of data from thirteen states, Merkel-Holguin and Sobel (1993) estimated a maltreatment rate of 51 per 1,000 institutionalized children. Poertner and colleagues reported from the state of Illinois in 1999. They report the lowest rate, a rate of 15 per 1,000 over a five-year period. Again, sexual abuse was the most commonly reported form of maltreatment (Poertner, Bussey, et al. 1999). Together these studies give some idea of the incidence of abuse and neglect. The latest study is by far the most optimistic, reporting an abuse rate about the same as that for children in their own homes, while the rates found in the other studies are markedly higher. One hopes that this reflects improved awareness and monitoring, rather than differences in study methods.

More reliable data on the maltreatment of children in out-of-home care will soon be available. The Adoption and Safe Families Act mandates that the U.S. Department of Health and Human Services develop a common set of outcome indicators, including reports of maltreatment in out-of-home care. And the data systems being developed (see chapter 3) will allow tracking and reporting of statewide outcomes, including child safety.

Outcomes Few residential care programs have measured the adjustment achieved by their graduates over the long term. Whittaker, in an extensive review of outcome studies of residential care up to 1985, noted the complexity of interacting variables and the difficulties of carrying out evaluations with rigorous designs. He concluded that "the most powerful determining factor of the child's post-discharge adjustment is the status of the post-discharge environment. Central in this environment is, most generally, the family" (Whittaker 1985:635).

Later studies that have followed graduates for a year generally find positive outcomes in some areas, such as education, employment, or lack of contact with the juvenile justice system (U.S. General Accounting Office 1994). Information is limited concerning the characteristics of those who require long-term residential treatment, and their outcomes, and those who can benefit from shorter terms of residential care (O'Malley 1993). McDonald, in his review of research, concluded that those who had been in foster care had generally better outcomes than those who had spent time in residential care. However, those in residential care had arrived more troubled, and after more placement failures, than those in foster care, so that poorer outcomes might be expected (McDonald, Allen, et al. 1996).

Many residential care programs provide support after discharge. Wells, Wyatt, et al. (1991), in a follow-up study of youth one to three years after their discharge from residential treatment, found family support to be positively related to self-esteem, mastery of life tasks, and absence of psychopathology, while stability in a single home was related to absence of substance abuse and antisocial behavior. Stress was, as would be expected, associated with time spent in restrictive mental health settings since discharge. These findings support the idea that residential treatment constitutes a continuum of care that must extend beyond discharge.

> What is different today is that we no longer expect residential treatment centers to replace a family and community. But we do expect them to be part of the community and for the communities to link with the treatment the centers provide. As residential treatment centers adapt to the policy changes, we are seeing them individualize service plans, include families in a more meaningful way, network with their community and provide for more linkage with other services that children need.
>
> (YELTON 1993:188)

The larger community's ability to pick up where residential treatment leaves off is certainly in question, especially when it comes to providing services to extremely troubled youth (Yelton 1993). Parents and social service agencies are witnessing the frustration of an underfunded community system unable to offer needed services.

Critical Issue: Institutional Care for Dependent Children as a Supplement to Foster Care

What about group care for children who do not have special needs? The community's evaluation of the relative merits of institutional care and foster care has varied over time, as reviewed at the beginning of chapter 6. Pecora, Whittaker, and colleagues suggest that the events in the development of residential care cluster in four stages: (1) a period in which the goal was to extricate children from the almshouse and provide separate institutions for them; (2) a move, in the late nineteenth century, from large institutions to large, family-style "cottages" staffed by house parents; (3) a "psychological phase" in the mid-twentieth century, during which the therapeutic milieu and group dynamics were considered important, and (4) a time of increasing attention to work with families and community supports (Pecora, Whittaker, et al. 1992:404). The last ten years of the century added a fifth stage, during which group care for children with special needs was, conceptually, sharply separated from group care for dependent children, and during which there was increasing debate about the appropriateness of such care for both populations.

The debate about orphanages reemerged in the context of the welfare reform movement of the 1990s. Prominent conservatives proposed a return to group care for poor children. Newt Gingrich, for example, suggested that the states should be allowed to end cash assistance to welfare recipients whether or not they participated in work programs. According to the *New York Times*, Gingrich "would use some of the money to build orphanages or group homes for the children of those families rendered destitute" (London 1999:87). The vision of reviving the orphanages did not survive public scrutiny, especially after its potential costs were better understood, but the ideas brought forth in the debate remained part of the discussion in the child welfare literature.

Institutional care is used for dependent children in other parts of the world. It is more widely used in Western Europe than in the United States, and it is the primary mode of care for dependent children in less developed countries. Societal attitudes toward institutional care are varied. In Great Britain, for example, there has been a concerted movement to move children from institutions to homes, and by the end of the twentieth century very few children remained in institutions. In Germany, where parents' rights remain an unusually strong value, institutional care has been more accepted because parents preferred it. In less developed countries, where nonrelative family care is not the tradition, institutions are common; and they are generally considered acceptable because they provide food and shelter for children. Recognizing the damage that institutional care can do to young children, many international child welfare agencies are striving to build foster care systems, and to encourage adoption, in the less developed world.

Appropriate Uses

For many adolescents, who are at a developmental stage of moving away from home, to be asked to form an attachment to foster parents is not appropriate. Such young people do better in group settings. Another group of children for whom institutional care may be appropriate are children who have close ties to biological families, but whose families over time demonstrate that they cannot manage to care for the children. Institutional care can provide a stable living situation for these children, allow sibling groups to remain together, and allow parents to maintain contact without the complications of interacting with a competing set of parents. When it is evident that families are not going to be reunited, but the family ties make adoption unrealistic, institutional care might well be considered. A third group are those identified earlier who have serious problems, have experienced repeated treatment failures, and need the stability of institutional care through adolescence Some require a therapeutic setting; others may be able to manage with the structure of an educational setting.

Young Children

As was noted in chapter 2, scholars agree that institutional care carries a developmental risk for very young children (Bowlby 1951; Goldfarb 1955). The opening of Romania to the world, following the collapse of the Communist regime in 1989, brought to the world's attention the impact of poor institutional care on young children. The infants in Romanian orphanages suffered profound neglect, spending almost all of their time in cribs; they were fed with propped bottles and handled only briskly and occasionally for changing. Observation of these children revealed major developmental delays, inappropriate and aggressive responses to other children once mobility was attained, and a disturbing lack of interest in contact with caretakers.[5]

In a longitudinal study of children who spent the first two years of their lives in institutions that provided good quality care, less serious developmental delays of about two months during the first two years were found, as well as difficulties in attachment to adults and peers throughout the sixteen-year follow-up (Hodges and Tizzard 1989).

Despite our knowledge of its effects, group care is too often used for young children, usually because foster homes are in short supply or because a foster home cannot be found for a sibling group. Berrick reported that about 14 percent of the children in group care in California were placed before age six; 996 children under age six were placed in group care settings in California in 1994. There did not appear to be any advantage to group care for these children; it did not facilitate reunion with their families or shorten their stays in out-of-home care. Furthermore, children in group care were less likely to be adopted than those in foster care (Berrick, Barth, et al. 1997). Given these findings and the developmental needs of very young children, the authors question the appropriateness of group care for young children.

Those who advocate the return of the institution as a means of caring for children often forget that in the era when orphanages were popular, they cared for young children who were relatively easy to manage. When children became adolescent, they were either indentured, sent to work homes, or returned to their families to work and contribute to family income (Smith 1995). Orphanages controlled their intake, accepting only children who were well behaved and whose parents (most children had one living parent) were "worthy" (McCausland 1976; Smith 1995). Many of the children who are removed from their homes and need out-of-home care today are young and thus developmentally at risk in group care; and they come from backgrounds that have engendered behavioral difficulties, and thus will not be easy to manage in group care.

Cost

The cost of group care is not easy to assess; estimates vary widely. Berrick, Barth, et al. (1997) report that the median monthly payment for group care of children under six in California, in 1994, was $4,091, while the median rate for a young child in foster family care was $360. This is $49,092 for a year's care in a group setting. Bradshaw compares the long-term cost of care for a disadvantaged child and the cost of temporary residential care for a severely troubled child. Studying the records of two institutions, he concludes that the cost of care in a group setting for a child who does not need therapeutic intervention is $30,000 per year, roughly the same as the cost of care for the child within his own family, when the "opportunity value" of parental time is included in the cost of family care.[6] The cost of care for severely troubled children is, Bradshaw estimates, about twice as great (Bradshaw, Wyant, et al. 1999).

The cost of family care was developed through addition of the direct costs of maintaining a child, an allowance for housing and utilities, and a computation of parental time based on wages. Computations were completed for three different wage levels. The direct out-of-pocket costs of raising a child for a family in a $32,000 to $55,000 household income range were $5,282 per year. Addition of housing, utilities, repairs, and maintenance brings the yearly family figure to $7,814; the remainder is the value of parental time, bringing the yearly cost of caring for a child to $28,029. The cost of caring for each child in the institution caring for disadvantaged children was $32,350. This was a large institution (118 children) that did not employ specialized personnel for therapeutic purposes and used the community schools (Bradshaw, Wyant, et al. 1999: 279–81).

This analysis confirms that group care is far more expensive than foster care. Apparently, as a society, while we expected families to take in children for charitable reasons, we decided that institutional care was impersonal and could be paid for at full value. It is doubtful that the public will want to fund institutions at this rate when they are accustomed to the bargain of foster care. The above figures show that a large proportion of the cost of care is for staff. The most effective way to lower the cost of institutional care is through changes in staffing. Employing fewer people to care for more children will lower cost. Employing staff with less training will lower costs. Lowering wages will lower costs. All of these approaches of course compromise the quality of care for children, and increase staff turnover. Staff turnover is difficult for institutionalized children, because it prevents them from making any lasting attachments.

Bradshaw advocates the deregulation of institutional care. With regulations gone (mainly those that pertain to staff/child ratios, space, and child labor within the institution) he believes that institutions could again thrive (Bradshaw, Wyant, et al. 1999). Smith (1995) reminds us that costs would be borne almost completely by the government; private philanthropy does not contribute substantially to child welfare now, and the children who need care come from impoverished families who could not contribute to the costs of their care. Government reimbursement schedules are not generous. Without regulation, large institutions with poorly paid, poorly qualified staffs would doubtless develop. But is this the care we want for our children?

Maltreatment

If children are removed from their own homes because of abuse or neglect, it is indeed tragic if they have the same experiences while in care. Prevention of maltreatment through high program quality, thorough training and consistent, supportive supervision of workers, and citizen oversight is, of course, the best route to children's safety.

The literature on maltreatment in residential care, reported earlier in the chapter, contains the best data available about maltreatment in institutions caring for dependent children. The only survey found of institutions for dependent children without special needs was a mailed survey of 4,000 alumni of nine institutions for dependent children, with about a 50 percent response rate. Ten percent of those who responded reported having been physically abused at some time during their stay, 9 percent reported mental abuse, and 5 percent sexual abuse. The definitions used were "loose," the author reports (McKenzie 1999). The survey respondents reported long stays in the institutions (the mean stay was nine years), which means that the abuse could have happened at any time during those years, or could have been repetitive.

Reporting is a problem in institutional settings, for residents may fear retribution and are relatively powerless to prevent it. In an earlier time, when children received long-term care in "orphanages" parents were very much involved; one mother wrote that she "felt sorry for the boys and girls there who have no one to defend them" (Smith 1995:130). Perhaps the involvement of families in residential treatment can serve as a corrective in those settings. But for the children whose long-term care is to be in institutions for dependent children, families may be too distant to be of much help.

Outcomes

The information concerning outcomes for children who have spent a good part of their childhood in institutional care is conflicting. Careful outcome studies, such as those done for residential treatment, do not exist. There are, however, indicators of their experiences from the residents themselves.

The most recent of these is McKenzie's mailed survey of the alumni of nine institutions that cared for dependent children who did not have special needs. The author acknowledges the impossibility of knowing much about the nonrespondents. All respondents were white and, at the time of the survey, forty-five years of age or older. Comparisons with census data indicate that in education, employment, and income the orphanage alumni did better than the general population. Interestingly, however, they had higher divorce rates. Seventy-six percent of the respondents gave a "very favorable" rating to their orphanage experience. The positive attributes of the orphanage experience cited most often were personal values and direction (60%) and a sense of self-worth (59%). The most common negative attributes were separation from families and siblings (34%) and lack of love and emotional support from institutional staff (31%) (McKenzie 1999).

The feelings of other children who have grown up in institutions are reported in varied literature. The condemnation of the system reported by Toth (1997) and Epstein (1999) are based on the vastly unhappy experiences of children in institutional care. Bush (1980) asked children actually residing in various forms of out-of-home care for their evaluation of the experience. He reports that the children did not like living in institutions, finding them to be the least supportive and therapeutic of the forms of care.

> At home, people don't just walk out of your life and you don't see them again. You always have some kind of connection with the person. They'll stick by you. But here maybe about ten people have come and left since I've been here. Maybe five of them were super close.
>
> (BUSH 1980:250)

Conclusion

We do have options for relieving the current pressure on the foster care system, once again providing children the stability and care that foster care once offered. Of these options, kinship foster care and group care are of most interest; both promise stability, both promise care. They are, of course, at opposite ends of the continuum of "least restrictive" placements, one being in the family and community, the other striving to keep those bridges intact. Again, we are circling back in time. In the institution, as Thomas Mulry said in 1898, the "family bond" was kept intact through frequent visits, but children boarded out would be so scattered that visits would not be possible. The institution intended to return children to their homes, whereas families who took children usually intended to keep them until maturity (Crenson 1998:206).

Perhaps it is unfortunate that in the early twentieth century, when the relative merits of foster family and institutional care were debated, foster care won out so definitively, limiting the options for group care. Certainly it is unfortunate that the deinstitutionalization movement of the late twentieth century was not accompanied by greater investment in services for children within their communities. The key, of course, lies in the availability of a full array of out-of-home care possibilities, and the careful matching of each child to the type of placement that will best meet his or her needs.

Notes

1. The children we followed through a protective service experience in chapter 5 spent a brief time in an informal foster placement with their grandparents.

2. The appropriateness of paying relatives to care for children has, of course, been debated; some observers contend that relatives should care for children out of family obligation alone. In Illinois, a class action suit was brought by relative foster parents, who sought the much higher maintenance payments available to regular foster families. In 1979 the Supreme Court ruled in *Miller v. Youakim* that Congress intended relatives to receive the same maintenance as nonrelatives, and that states are obligated to make these payments and, for Title IV-E eligible children, are entitled to federal reimbursement.

3. Chamberlain (1998) describes a series of studies, using control and comparison groups, in which the behavioral approach of the Social Learning Center in Eugene, Oregon, has been demonstrated to be effective. In this program, foster parents receive intensive training in behavior management, after which they are expected to have extensive, regular contact with professionals (in some programs, as often as a daily telephone call) to assure that behavioral management is occurring. This is one of the programs being highlighted by the federal Office of Juvenile Justice and Delinquency Prevention as having been demonstrated effective through controlled studies and at least three replications.

4. The Kent Project was an early specialist foster care project in Kent, England. Intervention structure was based on "task-centered casework." Contracts outlining specific goals and tasks to reach those goals were developed for each youth. The time frame was a two-year commitment by parent and youth to the placement. Foster parents were paid a salary such that, if they cared for two children, the amount was equivalent to what a parent would have earned if working outside the home. The homes were successful in retaining very difficult adolescents.

5. Deborah Towner, personal communication, 1998. Towner was, in 1998, Director of Romanian Services for the Romanian Children's Relief Society. Her work in Romania began with her doctoral studies of attachment theory, and since her first visits there in 1996 she has dedicated many months of her life to the development of policy and programs to open the orphanages to the community and to bring caretaker nurturing and stimulation to the infants and toddlers

in the orphanages. Currently Romanian efforts are focused on the development of a foster care system, with the hope that the orphanages for very young children can be closed.

6. This is another piece of clear evidence that payments to foster parents are extremely low, being based on maintenance of the child without taking into account the time of the foster parent. The foster care payments multiply to $4,320 per year, enough to cover only the most basic out-of-pocket costs.

References

Allen, M. L., and J. Larson. 1998. *Healing the Whole Family: A Look at Family Care Programs*. Washington, D.C.: Children's Defense Fund.

Barth, R. P. 1994. "Shared Family Care: Child Protection and Family Preservation." *Social Work* 39(5): 515–24.

Berrick, J. C., R. P. Barth, et al. 1994. "A Comparison of Kinship Foster Homes and Foster Family Homes: Implications for Kinship Foster Care as Family Preservation." *Children and Youth Services Review* 16:34–50.

———. 1997. "Group Care and Young Children." *Social Service Review* 71 (June): 257–74.

Berrick, J. D., M. Courtney, et al. 1993. "Specialized Foster Care and Group Home Care: Similarities and Differences in the Characteristics of Children." *Children and Youth Services Review* 15(6): 453–73.

Berrick, J. D., B. Needell, et al. 1998. *The Tender Years: Toward Developmentally Sensitive Child Welfare Services for Very Young Children*. New York: Oxford University Press.

Bowlby, J. 1951. *Maternal Care and Mental Health*. Geneva: World Health Organization.

Bradshaw, D., D. Wyant, et al. 1999. "The Cost of Care in Institutions and Families." In *Rethinking Orphanages for the 21st Century*, edited by R. B. McKenzie. Thousand Oaks, Calif.: Sage.

Bush, M. 1980. "Institutions for Dependent and Neglected Children: Therapeutic Option of Choice or Last Resort?" *American Journal of Orthopsychiatry* 50(2): 239–55.

Chamberlain, P. 1998. "Treatment Foster Care." *Juvenile Justice Bulletin*. Washington, D.C.: Office of Juvenile Justice and Delinquency Prevention.

Child Welfare League of America. 1991. *Standards of Excellence for Residential Group Care Services*. Washington, D.C.: Child Welfare League of America.

———. 1994. *Kinship Care: A Natural Bridge*. Washington, D.C.: Child Welfare League of America.

Crenson, M. W. 1998. *Building the Invisible Orphanage: A Prehistory of the American Welfare System*. Cambridge, Mass.: Harvard University Press.

Dore, M. M. 2001. "Treatment Foster Care: A Qualitative Study." Casey Family Services, Baltimore, Md.

Dubowitz, H., S. Feigelman, et al. 1993. "A Profile of Kinship Care." *Child Welfare* 72:153–69.

Epstein, W. M. 1999. *Children Who Could Have Been*. Madison: University of Wisconsin Press.

Fanshel, D., S. J. Finch, et al. 1990. *Foster Children in Life Course Perspective*. New York: Columbia University Press.

Gibson, D., and D. N. Noble. 1991. "Creative Permanency Planning: Residential Services for Families." *Child Welfare* 70(3): 371–83.

Goldfarb, W. 1955. "Emotional and Intellectual Consequences of Psychological Deprivation in Infancy: A Revaluation." In *Psychology of Childhood*, edited by P. Hoch and J. Zubin. New York: Grune and Stratton.

Hazel, N. 1981. *A Bridge to Independence*. Oxford: Basil Blackwell.

Hodges, J., and B. Tizzard. 1989. "Social and Family Relationships of Ex-institutionalized Adolescents." *Journal of Child Psychology and Psychiatry* 30(1): 77–97.

Hudson, J., R. Nutter, et al. 1992. "A Survey of North American Specialist Foster Family Care Programs." *Social Service Review* 66(1): 51–63.

Ingram, C. 1996. "Kinship Care; From Last Resort to First Choice." *Child Welfare* 75 (September/October): 550–66.

Jackson, S. M. 1999. "Paradigm Shift: Training Staff to Provide Services to the Kinship Triad." In *Kinship Foster Care: Policy, Practice, and Research*, edited by R. L. Hagar and M. Scannapieco. New York: Oxford University Press.

Jivanjee, P. 1999. "Parent and Provider Perspectives on Family Involvement in Therapeutic Foster Care." *Journal of Child and Family Studies* 8(3): 239–341.

Jivanjee, P., D. Severin-Held, et al. 1999. "Family Participation in Therapeutic Foster Care: Multiple Perspectives." Research and Training Center on Family Support and Children's Mental Health, Portland, Ore.

London, R. D. 1999. "The 1994 Orphanage Debate." In *Rethinking Orphanages for the 21st Century*, edited by R. B. McKenzie. Thousand Oaks, Calif.: Sage.

Maluccio, A. 1981. "Casework with Parents of Children in Foster Care." In *Parents of Children in Placement: Perspectives and Programs*. New York: Child Welfare League of America.

McCausland, C. L. 1976. *Children of Circumstance*. Chicago: Chicago Child Care Society.

McDonald, T. P., R. I. Allen, et al. 1996. *Assessing the Long Term Effects of Foster Care*. Washington, D.C.: Child Welfare League of America.

McKenzie, R. B. 1999. "Orphanage Alumni: How They Have Done, and How They Evaluate Their Experience." In *Rethinking Orphanages for the 21st Century*, edited by R. B. McKenzie. Thousand Oaks, Calif.: Sage.

Merkel-Holguin, L. A., and A. Sobel. 1993. *The Child Welfare Stat Book, 1993*. Washington, D.C.: Child Welfare League of America.

Nelson, K. M. 1992. "Fostering Homeless Children and Their Parents Too: The Emergence of Whole Family Foster Care." *Child Welfare* 71(6): 575–84.

O'Malley, F. 1993. "Short-term Residential Treatment of Disturbed Adolescents in a Continuum of Care." *Children and Youth Services Review* 15(3): 245–60.

Pecora, P. J., J. K. Whittaker, et al. 1992. *The Child Welfare Challenge: Policy, Practice, and Research*. New York: Aldine de Gruyter.

Poertner, J., M. Bussey, et al. 1999. "How Safe Are Out of Home Placements?" *Children and Youth Services Review* 21(7): 549–63.

Rabb, J., and N. Reindfleisch. 1985. "A Study to Define and Assess Severity of Institutional Abuse and Neglect." *Child Abuse and Neglect* 9:285–94.

Reddy, L. A., and S. O. Pfeiffer. 1997. "Effectiveness of Treatment Foster Care with Children and Adolescents: A Review of Outcome Studies." *Journal of the American Academy of Child and Adolescent Psychiatry* 36(5): 581–88.

Reindfleisch, N., and D. Hicho. 1987. "Institutional Child Protection: Issues in Program Development and Implementation." *Child Welfare* 66 (July/August): 329–42.

Reindfleisch, N., and J. Rabb. 1984. "How Much of a Problem Is Resident Mistreatment in Child Welfare Institutions?" *Child Abuse and Neglect* 8:33–40.

Rubenstein, J. S., J. A. Armentrout, et al. 1978. "The Parent-Therapist Program: Alternate Care for Emotionally Disturbed Children." *American Journal of Orthopsychiatry* 48(4): 654–62.

Ryan, P., E. J. McFadden, et al. 1981. "Foster Families: A Resource for Helping Parents." In *The Challenge of Partnership: Working with Parents of Children in Foster Care*, edited by A. N. Maluccio and P. A. Sinanoglu. New York: Child Welfare League of America.

Scannapieco, M. 1999. "Formal Kinship Care Practice Models." In *Kinship Foster Care: Policy, Practice, and Research*, edited by R. L. Hegar and M. Scannapieco. New York: Oxford University Press.

Schneiderman, M., M. Connors, et al. 1998. "Mental Health Services for Children in Out-of-Home Care." *Child Welfare* 77(1): 29–41.

Smith, E. P. 1995. "Bring Back the Orphanages? What Policymakers of Today Can Learn from the Past." *Child Welfare* 74, no. 1(January/February), 115–42.

Spencer, J. W., and D. D. Knudsen. 1992. "Out of Home Maltreatment: An Analysis of Risk in Various Settings for Children." *Children and Youth Services Review* 14(6): 485–92.

Testa, M., and N. Rolock. 1999. "Professional Foster Care: A Future Worth Pursuing?" *Child Welfare* 78(1): 108–24.

Toth, J. 1997. *Orphans of the Living: Stories of America's Children in Foster Care*. New York: Simon and Schuster.

Triseliotis, J., C. Sellick, et al. 1995. *Foster Care: Theory and Practice*. London, B. T. Batsford.

U.S. Department of Health and Human Services. 2000. "Report to the Congress on Kinship Foster Care, Part I." U.S Department of Health and Human Services, Administration on Children, Youth, and Families, Washington, D.C.

U.S. Department of Health and Human Services, Children's Bureau. 2002. AFCARS Report No. 7. Available at http://www.acf.hhs.gov/programs/cb/publications/afcars/report7.htm.

U.S. General Accounting Office. 1994. Letter to the Honorable Carl M. Levin, Chairman, Subcommittee on Oversight of Government Management, Committee on Governmental Affairs, United States Senate. U.S. General Accounting Office, Health, Education, and Human Services Division, Washington, D.C.

Wells, K., and L. D'Angelo. 1994. "Specialized Foster Care: Voices from the Field." *Social Service Review* 68(1): 127–44.

Wells, K., and D. Whittington. 1993. "Characteristics of Youths Referred to Residential Treatment: Implications for Program Design." *Children and Youth Services Review* 15(3): 195–217.

Wells, K., E. Wyatt, et al. 1991. "Factors Associated with Adaptation of Youths Discharged from Residential Treatment." *Children and Youth Services Review* 13(3): 199–216.

Whittaker, J. K. 1985. "Group and Institutional Care: An Overview." In *A Handbook of Child Welfare: Context, Knowledge, and Practice*, edited by J. Laird and A. Hartman. New York: Free Press.

Yelton, S. 1993. "Children in Residential Treatment: Policies for the 90's." *Children and Youth Services Review* 15(3): 173–93.

CHAPTER 8

✦

Adoption

For whither thou goest I will go; and where thou lodgest I will lodge: Thy people shall be my people, and thy God my God.

RUTH 1:16

Adoption is a legal procedure by which a permanent family is created for a child. Adoptive parents assume all the rights and responsibilities of natural parents. Although there are three parties to every adoption—the child, the birth parents, and the adoptive parents—adoption is child-centered, focused on meeting the needs of the child. At its best, it also meets the needs of adopting parents who have wanted a child, and the needs of the original parents who are relieved of responsibilities they were not in a position to assume. Reitz and Watson (1992) have defined adoption as

> a means of providing some children with security and meeting their developmental needs by legally transferring ongoing parental responsibilities from their birth parents to their adoptive parents; recognizing that in so doing we have created a new kinship network that forever links those two families together through the child, who is shared by both.
>
> (P. 11)

Most people have some acquaintance with adoption. Many of us have an adopted child, have an adopted parent or other relative, or know well someone who is adopted. Adoption is widely accepted in the United States—a cultural belief in the power of individuals to create their own future makes bringing a child into a family and giving him or her the resources to create a good life seem like a natural step. In some other countries adoption is not looked on as favorably. Ties of heredity and biological family are considered more important than the social ties created by adoption.

There is a new focus on adoption as the twenty-first century begins, and a renewed public and professional interest in such issues such as

- ensuring that adoption policy and practice become fully child-centered;
- determining the circumstances under which it is justifiable to permanently separate children from their families;
- finding adoptive families, particularly for older children, for some very psychologically damaged children, and for some children with severe physical handicaps, and insuring that those families will be able to meet the needs of the children they adopt;
- resolving policy dilemmas surrounding adoptive placements that form nontraditional families, such as placement with single parents, transracial placement, and placement of children in homes with gay or lesbian parents;
- regulating and managing independent adoption and intercountry adoption, as well as resolving the related policy dilemmas.
- recognizing the possibilities and limitations of open adoption and developing mediation skills to help manage possible conflict; and
- recognizing that children's needs for special services do not end with adoption, and developing more uniform and higher-quality postplacement support services to all those affected by adoption.

(ADAPTED FROM TRISELIOTIS, SHIREMAN, ET AL. 1997:IX–X)

Many of these issues, particularly those regarding termination of parental rights, have been discussed in earlier chapters. This chapter focuses on the controversial issues of current adoption policy. A brief look at the history of adoption will help ground the reader in the basic philosophy and practice of adoption.

The Framework of Adoption

A Brief History of Adoption

The first recorded adoption in Western tradition was that of Moses. It was an adoption in which the child of a subjugated people was adopted by a member of the dominant class—a transcultural and possibly transracial adoption, in which a single parent independently adopted an infant whose birth parent's identity was concealed. We are told that the motive of the adopting mother was compassion, and the motive of the birth parent, to find a home in which the life of her infant would be preserved. (From the birth mother's point of view, it was an open adoption; the birth mother volunteered to act as nurse to the infant.) Many of the policy issues we face today are reflected in that adoption.

Adoption in the United States began rather informally, as children placed in family homes for fostering remained and grew up in those homes. This occurred when children were placed from orphanages (McCausland 1976), and to an even greater extent among the children moved to distant, free foster homes. If the placement worked, children came to be considered part of the family, and an informal adoption had taken place (Brace 1872). If the adoption was legalized, it was done through a specific act of the legislature; these adoptions became quite common during the nineteenth century (Witmer 1963).

Adoption in the United States has always been regulated by the states. The first adoption statute, passed in Massachusetts in 1851, became the model for subsequent adoption legislation; it outlines the basic provisions of adoption. It provided for

1. The written consent of the child's biological parent(s),
2. Joint petition by both the adoptive mother and father,
3. A decree by the judge, who had to be satisfied that the adoption was "fit and proper," and
4. Legal and complete severance of the relationship between child and biological parents.

(KADUSHIN AND MARTIN 1988:535)

Only this last provision has, with the advent of open adoptions in recent years, been modified. In open adoptions, though the legal relationship between child and biological parents is severed, a social relationship may remain.

In the years between the two world wars, infant adoptions gained increasing popularity. The development of infant formulas made it possible for young infants to thrive in adoptive families. The openness and opportunity of a fluid American lifestyle, in which the frontier was not far in the past, contributed to the perception that environment was as important as heredity, and helped make adoption seem a good option.

The first agencies whose purpose was adoption were founded during this period, and adoption legislation was enacted in the remainder of the states, so that by 1929 all states had adoption legislation. An increasing number of regulations were developed to require investigations of adoptive homes and to establish trial periods in adoptive homes (Sokoloff 1993).

During this time, the provision that adoptive records be "sealed" became common. In order to protect the child from the stigma of illegitimacy, the birth parent from public knowledge that she had surrendered a child for adoption, and the adopting parents from possible interference by the birth parent, the original birth record was sealed by the court and an amended birth certificate was issued. It read as though the child had been born to the adoptive parents. The effect of these laws was, of course, to present the adoptive family to the community as indistinguishable from a family formed through the birth of children.

During this same period, the growth of a so-called black market, in which unregulated "baby brokers" required large fees to procure infants for infertile couples, prompted concern about the welfare of the children thus placed. In the 1920s, many states passed laws requiring an investigation of a prospective adoptive home, and specialized adoption agencies were founded to handle adoptions. These agencies almost exclusively placed healthy white infants with white couples. Some agencies charged fees to adopting parents on a sliding scale based on income; others charged very large adoption fees.

Following World War II, adoption became a recognized solution to the problem of infertility. This was an era of "the perfect baby for the perfect couple" (Triseliotis, Shireman, et al. 1997:7). The adoptable child was an infant or toddler, white, in good health, and developing at an average or better pace. Infants, even if adoption was planned from the time of their birth, were kept in foster care for at least six months to be sure that they had no problems. And as adopting couples were guaranteed perfect infants, an attempt was also made to guarantee infants perfect parents. The requirements that a husband and wife had to meet grew increasingly restrictive; adopting couples had to have a marriage of some duration, be within a specific age range (usually between twenty-five and forty-five), have steady and adequate income, and have comfortable housing spacious enough to add a child. Children and families were matched for religion, ethnic background, educational background, and appearance. With this careful matching, a family was created that was assumed to be "just like any other family." Once the adoption was finalized, it was not expected that the family would need any special community services. These traditional, infant adoptions still form the image that many people have of adoption. However, the adoption world continued to evolve.

The 1960s brought startling changes in adoption. Adoptive parents themselves provoked the first change, insisting that they wanted to parent their infants from the time of birth onward. In a cautious beginning, placements of infants directly from the hospital were carefully monitored, and indeed adoptive parents proved able to cope with any unexpected developmental problems. The opportunity to parent very young infants made the families even more "like any other family."

David Kirk's *Shared Fate* appeared in 1964, presenting a new framework for adoption in which the difference from other families was acknowledged and viewed as an asset to the family. Although *Shared Fate* is now recognized as a landmark book, Kirk's ideas were little noticed until the 1980s, when the struggles of adopted adults began to be publicized and new forms of adoption became prominent.

By the 1970s, fewer infants were available for adoption. In part this was due to new and more effective contraceptive methods and the increasing availability of abortion. In part it was due to changing sexual mores and society's increasing acceptance of a single woman raising a child. Traditional adoption agencies began to experience long waiting lists for white infants.

At about this same time, a series of studies documented that many children were growing up in foster care. Planning for permanent homes for these children became important. Early research demonstrated that many children could return to their own families when efforts were made to locate the families and provide needed services (Emlen, Lahti, et al. 1976). This research also demonstrated that it was possible to find adoptive homes for children with physical handicaps and for older children (e.g., Hargrave, Shireman, et al. 1975; Emlen, Lahti, et al. 1976; Unger, Dwarshusis, et al. 1977). These families were no longer limited to the traditional adoptive families, however; they included single-parent families, families with older parents, and families who could afford to take in an additional child only if provided an income subsidy. Also lingering in hospital nurseries, or in foster care, were African American infants. Transracial adoptions began in the late 1960s and early 1970s, as adoption agencies realized that there were many white families eager to adopt these children. It was an exciting time, as adoption became truly child-centered, and as adoption agencies reported success after success in placing children with special needs. The slogan was "No child is unadoptable."

Another result of the scarcity of white infants was the empowerment of unwed mothers who chose adoption for their unborn babies. Women now had a real choice, knowing that society would permit them either to raise their children or release them for adoption. "Social workers began to listen more carefully to birth mothers' requests to be included in the decision of who would parent their children" (Carp 1998:202). Experimentation with open adoptions began.

All of this, of course, changed the very nature of adoption. No longer were adoptive families "just like any other." Older children had memories of their own parents and of their experiences prior to adoption. Infants often arrived through open adoption arrangements, in which the birth family remained linked to the adoptive family. Transracially adopted children did not look like their parents. Adoptive parents began to ask for continuing professional support to cope with these complex issues.

As families who wanted to parent very young children sought adoptable infants, part of the adoption world became more willing to compromise the protections that careful agencies had built around children, birth parents, and the adoptive parents themselves. Some families adopted directly from lawyers or doctors; these independent adoptions take place without the protection of the child-placing agency. Others adopted from foreign countries, usually less developed countries with few child welfare or family support services, where large institutions housed many very young children. Many of the foreign adoptions were independent adoptions. Gradually states began to regulate these adoptions, mainly through insistence on a study of the adoptive home by a licensed agency.

The emphasis that Americans have begun to place on family heritage and "blood ties" has had an impact on the way adoption is viewed, raising questions about its effect on children's identities. In recent years Americans have been increasingly interested in their "roots"—their origins, culture, and genealogy. Along with that has come a celebration of the diverse cultures that make up the United States. Is the social and legal family created by adoption really enough? Some have argued that children actually need contact with their biological families to thrive. Publicity surrounding the attempts of adopted adults to find their birth parents has reinforced that idea. Open adoptions have been one answer. Another has been the strengthening of efforts to preserve families of origin and make adoption unnecessary. Federal funds were directed toward foster care and toward extensive efforts to reunite children with their parents.

In 1996, however, the federal stance changed. Responding to the large numbers of children spending long periods in foster care, President Clinton established "Adoption 2002," an initiative designed to double the number of children placed in permanent homes each year (U.S. Department of Health and Human Services [hereafter, U.S. HHS] 1997). The Adoption and Safe Families Act (ASFA) passed in 1997 (discussed in detail in chapter 2) pushes the child welfare system to work toward adoption as a solution for children who cannot be quickly reunited with family. As part of these federal initiatives, bonuses have been established for states that substantially increase the number of children who move from foster care to adoption each year.

Despite the growing interest in biological family histories, the public has remained supportive of adoptions. In 2002 the Dave Thomas Foundation for Adoption, in cooperation with the Evan B. Donaldson Adoption Institute, sponsored a national survey of public attitudes toward adoption (Evan B. Donaldson Adoption Institute 2002e). This second survey provides current information and allows tracking of changes from the 1997 Benchmark Survey, also sponsored by the Evan B. Donaldson Adoption Institute, the first national survey of public attitudes (Evan B. Donaldson Adoption Institute 1997). Responses to the 2002 survey reinforce the perception that many of us have personal contact with adoptions: 64 percent reported that a family member or close friend had been adopted, had adopted, or had placed a child for adoption. Most respondents, 94 percent, had a favorable opinion of adoption. Both percentages were slightly higher than in the 1997 survey.

As we have seen with regard to many other aspects of child welfare policy, changes in the society are reflected in the development of adoption policy and practice. Thus we can be sure that the evolution will continue.

Major Adoption Legislation

This section briefly reviews the major acts of child welfare legislation that were introduced in chapter 2, focusing on their impact on adoption policy and practice.

The Indian Child Welfare Act The Indian Child Welfare Act of 1978 (ICWA) followed a long history of attempts to assimilate Native American peoples into mainstream culture through boarding schools and transracial adoption for their children. The goal of ICWA is to protect tribal communities and institutions. The out-of-home placement of children born to members of a tribe is controlled by the tribe. The act's provisions specific to adoption specify a very high standard of proof—"beyond a reasonable doubt"—that a child will be harmed by remaining in the custody of the parent or tribal custodian before parental rights can be terminated. This provision, coupled with the low level of funding for tribal child welfare services, may compromise the safety of children. After termination of parental rights, ICWA directs that preference be given to placement with (1) a member of the child's extended family, (2) other members of the child's tribe, or (3) other Native American families (Pecora, Whittaker, et al. 1992).

Controversy about ICWA has centered on the extent to which children may be denied permanency because of the difficulty of terminating parental rights, on concern about children's safety, and on the lack of understanding in the mainstream culture of the concept of decision-making power residing in the tribe. To a fair extent, the act has made Native American children who are tribal members unavailable for adoption, offering them the embrace of the extended family and tribe instead of adoptive families.

The Adoption Assistance and Child Welfare Act of 1980 The Adoption Assistance and Child Welfare Act of 1980 provided for services to prevent placement, programs to reunify children with their families, periodic case reviews for children in foster care, and subsidies to remove financial barriers to adoption. The emphasis of the act is on permanency; and the mandated periodic case reviews have been important in ensuring that continual attention is paid to permanency planning for children in foster care. Adoption is viewed in this legislation as one route to permanency, and the adoption subsidy legislation has opened the possibility of adoption to an increased number of families.

The Multiethnic Placement Act of 1994 and the Interethnic Adoption Provisions Amendment of 1996 The Multiethnic Placement Act (MEPA) and the Interethnic Adoption Provisions Amendment (IEPA) can be viewed either as legislative efforts to increase the numbers of adoptive homes for children of color or as attempts to increase the number of children available to white couples who wish to adopt. MEPA forbids discrimination on the basis of race, color, or national origin and encourages the recruitment of culturally diverse foster and adoptive homes. IEPA strengthened these provisions by explicitly prohibiting denial of the opportunity to become a foster or adoptive parent on the basis of the race of the applicants or the race of the child.

Native American children are exempt from the provisions of MEPA and IEPA, which are superseded by ICWA. However, the new legislation may create confusion for adoption workers unsure about whether the provisions of the earlier ICWA still apply.

The Adoption and Safe Families Act The provisions of the Adoption and Safe Families Act of 1997 (ASFA) have more to do with limiting the time during which an agency must make "reasonable efforts" to reunite a child with the original family than they do with the completion of adoptions. However, the provision that when a child has spent fifteen of the last twenty-two months in nonrelative foster care, the agency must move to terminate the rights of the parents and free the child for adoption will have major impact on the numbers of children available for adoption and on the number of adoptive homes that must be found. Also important is the mandate for concurrent planning—that is, planning for adoption at the same time that attempts are being made to reunite children with their original families.

The practice implications of ASFA are just beginning to be examined. Will too many children now be rushed toward adoption whose families might have been able, given more time, to take them back? What is the impact on a family's hope and motivation for change when the caseworker is simultaneously supporting their efforts and making a "back-up" adoption plan? Will enough adoptive families with the capacities to meet the needs of these children be found? And can child welfare services stretch to make additional adoptive placements and provide the post-adoption support that will be needed? These questions will be answered in the early years of the twenty-first century. It may be that the challenge of ASFA will be to develop new forms of adoption adapted to older children who have ties to their birth homes—open adoptions, adoptions with respite care in homes they know, permanent guardianship by foster parents, or other creative solutions.

The Paths to Adoption

Public child welfare agencies Public child welfare agencies are concerned primarily about the children already in their care. When the home of a child who has been abused or neglected cannot be made safe, adoption offers the opportunity for a permanent family and a "home of one's own." It is a vitally important part of public child welfare service. Adoption for these agencies is a child-centered process, focused on finding homes for children. Usually children are beyond infancy, and many of them have very special needs. Adoption tax credits and government subsidies for children's care may partially offset costs for the adoptive families.

It is time-consuming to plan for these children, and while plans are being made children wait in foster care. McKenzie's (1993) analysis showed that the average time a child spends in foster care before moving to adoption is between 3.5 and 5.5 years. A child with special needs may wait much longer.

The first part of this time is spent in extended work with birth parents to ascertain and support their ability to parent. A second phase is planning with the parent for adoption. A parent may decide that adoption is the best option and voluntarily surrender parental rights, but more often the parent contests the ending of their rights. The complexity of the legal process that leads to termination of parental rights (see chapters 2 and 3) extends the child's time in foster care; however, the legal procedure is vital for the protection of the rights of birth parents. A third phase of the work is time spent in finding an adoptive home, preparing a child for a move, effecting the move, and helping the child adjust to a new home.

Concern about the length of time children spend in foster care is pervasive. ASFA was a response to this concern, and it aims to shorten this time by exempting agencies in certain aggravated situations from the requirement to make "reasonable efforts" to reunite families. (Such situations include the child being abandoned, a parent having caused the death of another child, and a parent having seriously injured, starved, or tortured the child.) It also mandates that at the same time that efforts to reunite the child with birth parents are being made, an adoptive home is to be found for the child. Within fifteen months of placement in out-of-home care, if the child cannot return home, legal procedures to terminate parental rights and place the child in an adoptive home are to take place. Overall, to date, there has been little evidence that these procedures have materially shortened the time that children are in foster care prior to adoption.

Some practice changes also work to shorten the time in foster care. Mediation has been used to help birth parents decide on voluntary surrender of parental rights, thus avoiding the lengthy and often distressing legal termination proceedings. Usually one part of a mediation agreement is that the birth parents and/or extended family retain some contact with the child. Another practice change is the use of foster families that are interested in adoption, either relative foster homes or unrelated foster homes. These are usually used when the worker believes that there is little chance that the child will return to the original home. This is a special kind of foster home, for the foster parent must be willing to risk losing the child in order to have its care from an early age.

The situation is particularly serious for children of color. We have noted the disproportionate numbers of African American children in foster care.

More than half the children waiting for adoption are children of color (McKenzie 1993). Historically child welfare services have not been able to find sufficient same-race adoptive homes for children of color. Providing adoptive homes for these children will require creative and intensive home-finding efforts, willingness to consider nontraditional forms of adoption, and adherence to the tenets of MEPA.

Private agency adoptions Private adoption agencies have a variety of origins. Some are long-established organizations, many of which were founded by churches but are now nondenominational; some began as orphanages and have turned to the delivery of the services needed today. Some are religious agencies, firmly allied with a particular denomination or religion.

Some private agencies are large and offer a range of services including adoption. Some are smaller agencies, founded solely to provide adoption services. Some were founded to provide only a single type of adoption service, such as adoption of children with special needs, or international adoptions, or open adoptions. The children and families served by voluntary agencies are as varied as the agencies. The common thread is that in an agency adoption the child is surrendered to the agency, which takes responsibility for placing the child in an adoptive home.

Voluntary adoption agencies have, over time, provided the best and the worst of adoption services. A few have become notorious for providing "perfect" babies for film stars and celebrities without, it is suspected, sufficiently rigorous examination of the prospective adoptive homes. More have done groundbreaking work, pioneering adoptions that the big public agencies would not attempt, then evaluating and publicizing their work. The first single-parent adoptions were made through the Los Angeles County Bureau of Adoptions, but all of the other new and sometimes controversial forms of adoption were first developed in the private sector. Most notable at the end of the twentieth century was the activity of private agencies in international adoption and in open adoptions.

Though not all private agencies charge fees for adoption, in general the cost of adoption through a nondenominational private agency is $10,000 to $20,000. The cost of adoption through religious agencies is a few hundred dollars to $8,000 or more. The costs of international adoption vary by country, and they are usually higher than the cost of domestic adoption (Evan B. Donaldson Adoption Institute 2000). The cost of adoption would be a concern for half of the National Adoption Attitudes Survey respondents (Evan B. Donaldson Adoption Institute 2002e).

Independent adoption Independent adoptions are those in which the birth parents give their consent to the adoption directly to the adopting parents rather than to an adoption agency. The process emphasizes the right of adults to adopt, but offers little protection to the birth parents and even less to the child.[1] Independent adoptions are legal in all but six states and have become increasingly important in the adoption of white infants. Recent estimates are that half to two-thirds of adoptions of white infants are independent adoptions (Evan B. Donaldson Adoption Institute 2002d). McDermott (1993) notes that the reason for the popularity of independent adoptions is that many birth parents seek this route because they distrust agencies, desire to play an active role in the selection of the home for their child, and want the child to go directly into an adoptive home.

Independent adoption can be conceptualized as a means through which families can adopt the type of infant they want. Adopting parents like the autonomy and decision-making capacity they have in these adoptions (Meezan, Katz, et al. 1978; McDermott 1993). They have the opportunity to adopt without a long waiting period and, although state laws mandate a home study at some point in the process, the home study will not be extensive and will be to corroborate that the mother has chosen an adequate home. There are risks; if a birth parent changes her mind about consenting to the adoption, the adopting parents will suffer emotionally and probably also financially. Although very limited, the research in existence suggests that most independent adoptions are satisfactory (Witmer, Herzog et al. 1963; Meezan, Katz et al. 1978).

In independent adoptions, the adopting family customarily pays the mother's medical expenses and contributes toward her living expenses during the pregnancy. These adoptions cost up to $15,000, or perhaps more if there are extremely high medical bills.

In independent adoption the baby really has very little protection. A doctor or attorney is probably not experienced in helping families think through the implications of adoption, and the home study is often perfunctory and meant only to detect gross unsuitability to parent. Finally, should the baby be born handicapped in any way, the family may refuse to adopt the child, leaving the mother with a responsibility she is not prepared to handle.

Black-market adoptions Adoptions that involve the purchase of a child are illegal around the world. They involve payment for a child, either to an intermediary or directly to the child's mother, that is not for medical care, lodging during pregnancy, or legal services. "The community and professional consensus is that such efforts to obtain children by making outright payments compromise the mother's integrity and endanger the child's well-being (Pecora, Whittaker, et al. 1992:376).

Numbers of Children Involved in Adoption

As was noted in chapter 3, the data systems through which the United States keeps track of the number of children in all types of care are flawed. Until 1975 adoption statistics were kept by the National Center for Social Statistics; after that time there has been no federal attempt to develop adoption statistics. The new AFCARS system will, in time, give us much better data about adoptions from public agencies and from private agencies that contract with the public system. The latest attempt to develop national statistics was in 1992, when the National Center for State Courts gathered data from a variety of sources in an attempt to get a picture of private agency and independent adoptions, as well as adoptions from the foster care system. From this incomplete data, estimates can be made and trends noted.

Adoption is fairly common; ask a group of people how many are adopted, have adopted children, or know someone who is adopted, and most will answer affirmatively. About 1.5 million children in the United States are living with adoptive parents—more than 2 percent of our children (Evan B. Donaldson Adoption Institute 2002d). Forty-two percent of adoptions are relative adoptions, mainly adoptions by stepparents (Evan B. Donaldson Adoption Institute 2000d).

Adoptions from foster care have increased steadily in recent years as a result of state projects and federal incentives. Twenty thousand children were adopted from the foster care system in 1996; by 2000 this number had increased 78 percent to 50,000. Reflecting the disproportionate number of African American children in the foster care system, 42 percent of these adopted children were African American; 32 percent were white (Evan B. Donaldson Adoption Institute 2002a).

There has been a long-term trend toward adoption of older children. At one time, almost all adoptions were those of infants or very young children. In 1989, only about a quarter of adoptions were of children under two years of age (National Committee for Adoption 1989). Only 2 percent of the children adopted from public agency foster care in 1998 were under one year of age; 44 percent were between one and five. As children grow older in foster care, they are less likely to be adopted; only 17 percent of adoptions in 1998 were of children over twelve (U.S. HHS, Children's Bureau 1999).

The National Adoption Attitudes Survey showed that 73 percent of the respondents would be willing to consider adopting a child who had been in foster care for several years. Medical and behavioral problems were of greater concern; 47 percent would consider adopting a child with behavioral problems and 56 percent a child with medical problems (Evan B. Donaldson Adoption Institute 2002e). The high prevalence of physical and mental health problems among foster children suggests that it may not be easy to find homes for these youngsters; the survey data suggest that, particularly with the development of postadoption support services, it should be possible.

The importance of foster parents as an adoptive resource for the children in their care is underscored by the AFCARS data. Of the children adopted from the public child welfare system, 64 percent were adopted by their nonrelative foster parents, and 14 percent were adopted by relatives, some of whom were also foster parents to the children (U.S. HHS, Children's Bureau 1999). The continuity of care achieved for these children is a great accomplishment of the child welfare system.

Protecting the Adoption Triad

In adoption, as in all child welfare services, the primary focus is the welfare of the child. As we have seen, however, during some periods and in some types of adoption the concerns of the adoptive parents have been preeminent. Most likely to be forgotten are the interests of the birth parents. But an adoption that is carefully accomplished in a way that protects the interests of each of the parties can be a very positive solution for all three.[2]

The Birth Parents

Though we acknowledge, intellectually, the benefit that adoption can bestow on a child, as a society we tend to be critical of birth parents who plan adoption for their children. A national survey of opinions about adoption, conducted by Princeton Survey Research Associates for the Evan B. Donaldson Adoption Institute, found that "many Americans support birth parents' decisions to place children for adoption, but a substantial minority disapproves of decisions to do so, and some even see it as irresponsible or hard-hearted" (Evan B. Donaldson Adoption Institute 1997:1–2). The attitude is reflected in our language. Rather than saying that adoption was planned for a child, often people say the child was "adopted out." Does the expression mean placed outside the family? Or are there echoes of "thrown out"?

Infant adoptions The rate at which women relinquish infants for adoption has declined dramatically, from 19 percent in 1965–72 to 1.7 percent in 1989–95 (Evan B. Donaldson Adoption Institute 2000). The decline, of course, reflects changes in society; better contraception and the availability of abortion have decreased the number of unwanted pregnancies, and changing social norms have enabled more single women to keep and raise their children. As a result, many fewer white infants are available for adoption, and considerably more attention is paid to the needs and wishes of birth parents.

Birth parents have told us for a long time that giving up a child was not an event from which one easily moved on with life (Bouchier, Lambert, et al. 1991; Howe, Sawbridge, et al. 1992; Wells 1993; Gritter 1997; Christian, McRoy, et al. 1997).

> The studies . . . tell us that some of the lasting feelings carried by birth parents who give up children for adoption include continued guilt and anger and feelings of loss and grief. . . . Some relinquishing mothers' sense of loss, far from diminishing with time, seems to intensify and is particularly high at certain of the child's milestones such as birthdays or starting school. . . . In summary, a positive resolution seems to be associated with:
>
> - Experiencing understanding, care, and support from all those around her (mothers who experience hostility from social workers, hospital staff, relatives, and friends appear less likely to come to terms with the experience);
> - Owning the decision; that is, feeling in control through having a real choice;
> - Having opportunities, if desired, to select the adoptive parents and keep in touch;
> - Having opportunities to talk through feelings about the relinquishment, to reflect on it, and to anticipate future pain and possibly remorse; and

- Continuing opportunities, when required, for subsequent exploration and reflection.

  (TRISELIOTIS, SHIREMAN, ET AL. 1997:99–100)

In earlier years the birth mother—often young, often poor—was the least powerful of the figures in the adoption triad, the most likely to be exploited, and the least likely to receive sensitive social work services; but the situation has to some degree changed. The shortage of infants available for adoption has given birth mothers who want to plan adoption for expected infants a great deal of power in the adoption triad.

One outcome of this shift in status has been the development of open adoptions, in which the birth mother has a voice in the selection of the adopting family and can negotiate with the adopting family concerning continued contact. Another outcome has been increased recognition of the responsibility of social workers, and other professionals who have contact with the mother, to recognize her feelings and provide the support she needs as she makes her decision. At the same time, exploitation of birth mothers remains a danger: the lack of strict laws and practice guidelines for independent adoptions has allowed children to be treated as a commodity by some "independent adoption enablers."

Birth mothers sometimes want to find and get to know the children they released long ago; aside from stories in the media about successful reunions, we have relatively little information about their motivations or experiences. Sorosky, Baran, et al. (1978) report numerous letters received from birth mothers, many expressing deep feelings of loss and continuing affection for the child released.

> I was a mother who gave up her rights but not her feelings, about the daughter she gave up for adoption. I would like her to know that I didn't give her up because I didn't want her, or love her. I wanted her to have something I couldn't give her at the time that she needed it most.
>
> (P. 62)

Other letters, fewer in number, expressed fears about the disruption a reunion would cause and hope that the child they had released would not attempt to find them. Almost all the letter writers were appreciative of the opportunity to share feelings that had long been impossible to express.

So far our discussion has concerned birth mothers only, and indeed most of the extant literature is about birth mothers. Birth fathers have become increasingly important in the adoption triad since, as a result of Supreme Court decisions in the 1970s, courts have begun to mandate that they consent to adoptions whether or not they are married to the mother. We still, however, have little information about birth fathers' reactions to the surrender of a child for adoption.

Nor is very much known about the parents in other countries who surrender infants and young children for adoption. Many of these are countries where poverty is extreme and where income supports or other supports for family living are minimal. Reports from Romania, for example, suggest that many families gave up infants to the orphanages, and then to adoption, because they were simply unable to support additional children. These are the conditions that can lead to the development of a "black market" for young children; tempted by cash payments that are large in proportion to their incomes, families may release infants, to their later regret. And the middlemen who procure those infants may accept extremely large fees from prospective adoptive parents. Such selling and buying of children is morally abhorrent and offers little protection to birth parents and none to children.

Parents of older children Another area in which research has been scant is the reactions of families who release older children to adoption or who have their parental rights terminated by the courts. Most of these parents have abused or neglected their children, have later made attempts to create a home to which the children could return, and have been unable to do so. Some release children voluntarily when skilled social work or mediation helps them to recognize that this is a way they can plan responsibly for their children. Some fight bitterly to retain custody and lose the children in court. Once satisfactory plans have been implemented for the children, the case is closed in the child welfare system. There has been remarkably little interest in studying how these parents handle the loss of their children.

An ethical dilemma The changes in American society that have led to the development of open adoptions have posed another dilemma for birth mothers of the past. For many years, birth mothers entered into confidential adoption arrangements and were promised that (1) the adoption records would be sealed by the court and (2) only those whom the birth mother told would ever need to know about the child released for adoption. As adopted adults have increasingly pressed to learn more about their biological heritage, and perhaps even to get to know their biological families, a terrible ethical dilemma has arisen. In the context of our current society, adoptees have a right to this knowledge. On the other hand, agencies made contracts with birth mothers in the context of the time, and to many those agreements remain enormously important.

Twenty-four states have dealt with this dilemma by establishing mutual consent registries, in which an adopted adult can indicate a wish to find a birth mother, or a birth mother can indicate a wish to find an adopted child. If parent and child are matched in this way, there is no problem. But often there is no match. Twenty-four states also have "search and consent" statutes, which provide that a birth parent may be contacted by a "confidential intermediary" and, if the birth parent consents to disclosure of identity, the disclosure may be authorized by the court (Evan B. Donaldson Adoption Institute 2000).

In the fall of 1986 the Child Welfare League, in its role as a leader in policy development, passed resolutions at its biennial conference for executives of member agencies recommending that, "starting with children adopted in 1986, confidentiality shall no longer be in effect once the adopted child reaches eighteen or the age of majority," and that "agencies should advocate the development of state and provincial laws to allow adopted individuals who have reached the age of majority to be given all identifying information, with the consent of the birth parents, or after posting an appeal for their consent (Watson and Strom 1986).

Currently in only six states can adopted adults obtain copies of their original birth certificates. A few other states allow access to the original birth certificate under certain conditions, mostly limiting access to more recent adoptions and to those in which there is no certificate of non-disclosure (Evan B. Donaldson Adoption Institute 2000). Two factors now lessen the relevance of the debate: the increasing numbers of adoptions of older children, and the fact that the use of the Internet and private investigators have made it almost certain that those searching will find the information they seek, if they have persistence and financial resources. Nevertheless, the debate surrounding proposed statutes is intense, as it should be. The ethical dilemma is real.

The Adopting Parents

Adopting parents, like foster parents, come in all shapes and sizes, with talents and circumstances as varied as the general population. A profile of adopters in California provides data that are probably typical; most adoptive parents are married couples in their thirties, though a growing number are in their forties. Most adopting parents have attended or completed college. Nearly two-thirds of those adopting outside the public child welfare system earn $50,000 or more. Those adopting from the public child welfare agency tended to be younger and to have lower levels of education and less income (Barth, Brooks, et al. 1995, reported by National Adoption Information Clearinghouse 2000).

Recruitment, preparation, and support In their efforts to place older children who have specific needs, public agencies recruit adoptive parents. Many of the practices and policies concerning the selection and preparation of foster parents (discussed in chapter 6) apply also to adoptive parents; in fact, in many places, those interested in long-term foster care and those interested in adoption go through the same processes. In contrast to earlier practices of selecting the "perfect family" (based on social workers' standards of family living), the preparation process is now considered to be collaborative. The agency prepares prospective parents for the available children while prospective adopters decide whether they have the capacity to undertake such challenges as behavior problems, disabilities, or continuing contact with the birth family.

In the past it was thought that no further services would be called for once an adoption was finalized. However, the voices of adopted adults have made us aware that all adoption is complicated. The adoption of older, more difficult children has made the need for postadoption services even more evident. These children carry legacies of loss and trauma, and it may be difficult for adoptive parents to provide the necessary support and nurture and to establish a close relationship with them. The provision of postadoption services is the critical issue examined at the end of this chapter.

Foster-parent adoptions With almost two-thirds of the children adopted from public child welfare agencies being adopted by their foster parents, it is apparent that foster parents are a major adoption resource. Some are foster parents who have wanted to adopt and have accepted a "legal risk" child—a child that the social worker believes will need to be adopted, although parental rights have not yet been terminated. These are interesting families, and there is little literature about them. They are willing to invest in a child in the hope it will be theirs, yet are expected to work with biological parents toward return of the child, as long as that is the plan. It is a fine plan for the child, who avoids a move, but a difficult role for the foster-adoptive parents.

Other foster-parent adoptions are made by foster parents who have cared for a child for a number of years and, when that child becomes available for adoption, decide to adopt rather than have the child moved. These homes are likely to be successful adoptive homes, for the foster parents know the child well prior to adoption. It has gradually been recognized, however, that the transition from foster home to adoptive home is not simple, and that the child, in particular, may test out his new permanent status with difficult behavior (Meezan and Shireman 1985).

Not all foster parents want to adopt the children they are caring for, even if they have been together for some time. Some are reluctant to take on the responsibility of the child without the support of the agency. Some are caring for children so developmentally delayed or so handicapped that they do not wish to burden themselves and their other children with the full responsibility of parenthood, though they are quite willing to continue fostering the children. Most question about whether the adoption subsidy they are offered will actually continue after the adoption is final. Unfortunately, some foster parents feel pushed to adopt by the social worker's determination to find a permanent home for a child, which can come across to the foster parents as a threat to move the child unless they adopt (Meezan and Shireman 1985).

The Children

Adopted children also come in all varieties. Traditionally we think of adoption as involving healthy infants, but increasingly children with special needs are being placed in adoption. Older children who often have a history of difficult experiences, and consequently present difficult behaviors, are also adopted.

Placement The most important protection for children in adoption is the study of the prospective adoptive home, which is mandated in most states. Adoptive home studies, like foster home studies, have increasingly taken the form of mutual decision making between social worker and parents about the appropriateness of adoption—or of the adoption of a particular child or the use of a particular form of adoption—for the family. Many of the dimensions of the home study were discussed in chapter 6; the basic characteristics sought in adoptive homes are the same as those of desirable foster homes.[3] If possible, the home study should take place prior to the placement of a child in the home, but this is not always possible when a relative or a foster parent is adopting a child, or when a child has been placed independently. Once a child is in a home, the child's need for continuity of care makes it difficult for social workers to decide that the home is not suitable.

Children who are beyond infancy need preparation for adoption. They need to work through the loss of their original families. They need to understand the reasons for their removal from their original homes. If possible, they should have the opportunity to discuss the impending adoption with members of their own family, either to formally end the relationship or to plan continuing contacts. They need permission, time, and help to mourn losses.[4] Preadoptive preparation also offers the child the opportunity to explore the idea of a new family and his or her own child's wishes, desires, and possible fantasies. This direct work with children is time-consuming and professionally challenging. It requires skilled supervision and is resource intensive.

Another source of protection for the child is the social worker's careful work in preparing the family for the particular characteristics of they child they adopt, and in the provision of ongoing postplacement services. One of the great concerns about independent adoptions, and many international adoptions, is that this postadoption support is not provided.

During the adoption The primary purpose of services for the adoptive family after the placement of the child in the home is to support the family, so that it will remain a permanent placement for the child and will meet the child's needs as he or she develops. These services customarily are provided through fairly frequent contacts with the adoption worker in the months immediately following the placement. After the adoption is final, the adoption agency has a responsibility to see that the family has access to a range of postadoption services as they feel the need, and to inform the family about those services. Adoption is truly a lifelong process.

Adopted adults A growing number of adopted adults are insisting that they have a constitutionally based civil right to know the identity of their birth parents. The adoption rights movement has been active since the 1970s and has garnered extensive political and media attention.[5] By the end of the twentieth century many states had developed mutual consent registries and six states had opened previously sealed adoption records. In the process of achieving this openness, the adoption rights movement has emphasized the importance of biological connections, and has depicted adoption as an artificial contrivance that results in psychological distress for adopted children. To evaluate these ideas, we need to know (1) what proportion of adopted adults want to find birth parents, (2) what drives adopted adults to search for birth parents, and (3) how satisfying reunions are for all parties. Only after all these questions are answered will it be possible to develop sensible policy.

Although media publicity sometimes gives the impression that all adopted adults want information about their birth families, the data are scarce as to how many actually do want it. Triseliotis (1973) reviewed the British statistics concerning adoptees' inquiries about birth families after the 1975 Children's Act gave them access to their birth records. He found that only a limited number applied for information, and his statistical calculations suggested that about 21 percent of adopted adults might pursue this information. Kadushin and Martin's (1988) review suggests that this proportion is similar to that found in a number of studies using various methodologies in the United States. The proportion may have grown in recent years as adult adoptees' searches for and reunions with birth parents have been publicized.

Adopted adults say they are searching to resolve "genealogical bewilderment," to fill in gaps in their sense of self, and to find a "cohesive identity" (Sachdev 1992). There is mixed evidence concerning whether those who search have more psychological difficulties than those who do not, and mixed evidence about the association of experiences in the adoptive home with the decision to search. It should be noted that those who were adopted after infancy may also wish to reunite with people they remember who were once important in their lives, or to fill in gaps in their memories. One difficulty in determining how many have the desire to learn about their origins is that most studies have used samples of adults who were already interested in searching, rather than diverse samples of people who had been adopted (Haugaard, Schustack, et al. 1998).

Accounts of those who have searched for birth parents, and newsletters of support groups formed to help adopted adults search, suggest that barriers simply intensify the determination to discover information. Secrets arouse curiosity; anything denied is all the more wanted. This human trait is perhaps the strongest argument for open records! When searches are successful, adopted adults generally report that the experience was positive—in this respect the data supports current media representations (Haugaard, Schustack, et al. 1998).

Adoption Outcomes

Discussion of adopted adults, and of searching for birth parents, gives immediate rise to questions about the outcome of adoption. It is difficult to discuss adoption overall, for there are many special circumstances. Any discussion of adoption outcomes tends to become segmented, as this one is, with data on infant adoptions, data on adoptions of children with special needs, and data on special forms of adoption. The literature is vast. Perhaps a good introduction is the National Survey of Adoption Attitudes, which revealed that in the last five years respondents have increasingly viewed adopted children no differently from children being raised by biological parents, a shift from about a quarter (Evan B. Donaldson Adoption Institute 1997) to about half of the respondents. However, significant minorities of respondents (more than a third) think that adopted children (particularly children adopted from foster care) are more likely than biological children to have emotional, behavioral, and school problems (Evan B. Donaldson Adoption Institute 2002e). And these mixed results are reflective of the findings of other research.

If adoption is viewed as a child-centered institution, the key question is, Is it a good solution for children who cannot remain with their own families? The short answer is yes, with qualifications.

Infant adoptions Over the years, outcome studies of infant adoptions have documented parental satisfaction and satisfactory adjustment of adopted children. Kadushin and Martin (1988:614–17) present a review of these studies in tabular form. Of the 2,645 adoptions involved in these studies, two-thirds were found to be fully satisfactory adoptions with few or no problems, and another 18.2 percent to be fairly successful. Disruption rates—the rates at which adoptions fail and the child is removed from the home—for infant adoptions are below 2 percent (Kadushin and Martin 1988:588). Children adopted as infants do tend to have more school problems, both in terms of behavior and school achievement, than other children, but these problems are not extreme (Brodzinsky 1984).

Theoretical literature suggests that adolescents will have difficulties as the fact of adoption complicates their development of self-identity. This idea is supported by data indicating that adoptees, who comprise 2 percent of the under-eighteen population, comprise 5 percent of mental health referrals and 10 to 15 percent of those in residential care settings (Sharma 1997). However, studies of nonclinical populations have not found such identity problems. The largest of these studies was that of the Search

Institute, which used survey methodology and gathered responses from 715 families with 881 adoptees and 78 (younger) nonadopted siblings. Both adopted adolescents and their parents expressed attachment to each other and viewed their families as essentially like any other family. Sixty-five percent said they would like to meet their birth parents. The measure of mental health status showed adopted adolescents to be more vulnerable than nonadopted adolescents, but only 15 percent scored in the clinical range on the scale (compared with a normative 11%) (Benson, Sharma, et al. 1994). A much smaller study using interview methodology confirmed these conclusions, finding adopted adolescents to be similar to nonadopted adolescents on measures of identity (Stein and Hoopes 1985).

These studies are significant; they indicate that adoption in itself does not present insurmountable obstacles to child development. Of greater interest for the child welfare field today are the growing number of studies of the outcomes of adoptions of children with special needs.

Infants and young children with special needs Early in the movement to find adoptive homes for "all children who could use a home" it became apparent that it was not going to be difficult to place infants with developmental delays such as Down syndrome or handicaps such as cerebral palsy. Outcome studies of these placements are scarce but generally suggest that families are content with the adoptions and that there are few disruptions. Many are pleased that the children have exceeded their expectations. Families do need continuing support from the placing agency.[6]

Many infants who come into the child welfare system have experienced prenatal drug or alcohol exposure. Because so little is known about their prognosis, many people are hesitant to adopt them. Thus the results of the first long-term outcome study are of great interest. Barth and Brooks (2000) report a comparison of adoption outcomes of 112 drug-exposed and 112 non-drug-exposed infants. The drug-exposed infants were slightly older at adoptive placement, and more had a history of neglect. Nevertheless, in their adjustment eight years after adoption, "according to their adoptive parents, children who are prenatally exposed to drugs appear to function very much like other adopted children on educational attainment and emotional or behavioral adjustment" (Barth and Brooks 2000:46).

Older children Kadushin's (1967) follow-up study of children older at adoption was groundbreaking, indicating that it was possible for children who had early experiences of abuse or neglect to function well in adoptive homes, and it opened the door to the idea that older children might succeed in adoption.

As older children have been placed, overall rates of adoption disruption have increased. Reviews of existing studies of special needs adoption estimate that the adoption disruption rate for children placed when older is between 10 percent and 15 percent (Rosenthal 1993; Barth, Gibbs, et al. 2001). The resounding finding from these and similar studies is that the younger a child is at adoptive placement, the more likely it is that the adoption will be successful. This, of course, makes sense, for the older a child is, the more years there have been for the accumulation of experiences of maltreatment and moves from one home to another. It is a powerful argument for moving children as rapidly as possible into permanent homes.

Rosenthal (1993:81—82) identifies key predictors of adoption disruption as

- older age of child at time of adoptive placement
- inadequate background information or unrealistic parental expectations
- rigidity in family functioning patterns, in particular the father's non-involvement in parenting tasks
- low levels of support from relatives or friends
- history of physical, and particularly sexual, abuse prior to adoption
- psychiatric hospitalization prior to adoption
- externalized behavioral problems, including sexual acting-out
- adoptive placement with "new" parents rather than with foster parents.

In many ways a review of factors associated with failed adoptions gives a misleading picture, for most adoptions of with special needs are successful. And often a child or a family who has participated in an adoption that did not work can move on to another adoption that will be successful. Finally, it should be noted that families of lower socioeconomic status, minority families, and families with nontraditional family structure are particularly positive about the success of their special needs adoptions.[7]

Nontraditional Adoptive Homes

As adoption has changed in recent years, the image of the perfect family for the perfect baby, resulting in a family just like any other, has been replaced by adoption that takes many different forms and results in many kinds of families. The healthy baby has been replaced by older children, children with physical and mental disabilities, and children with serious behavioral disturbances. The traditional family has been replaced by parents of all kinds, including single parents, gay and lesbian parents, and working-class parents who need subsidy to be able to afford the addition of a child to their homes. The "family just like any other" has been replaced by families with children and parents of different races, and from different countries, and by families that include the birth parents and extended family of the adopted child.

Controversy remains about many of these types of adoption. Each must be examined with consideration of the extent to which it affords the child the conditions for optimal growth and development, and then of the degree to which it protects the rights of the birth parents and the adopting parents.

Adoption is very much in the public eye. Children are helpless, and the decision to place a child in a particular adoptive home has life-shaping implications. This recognition was behind the search for the "perfect family" of earlier times. As family structures change across the nation and children with diverse needs wait for adoptive homes, new forms of adoption constantly arise. Some, such as foster-parent adoption, or subsidized adoption, become common and are no longer subject to controversy. Other forms are watched by the community or by adoption professionals with skepticism and concern. As the provisions of ASFA continue to be implemented, many more adoptive homes will be needed, for children with many different needs. Careful thought about the strengths and difficulties of different types of homes, and evaluation of the success of children in each of these types of homes, is imperative.

Single-Parent Adoption

Adoptions by single parents are not as controversial today as they once were. In 1965, when single-parent placements began, adoption practice was heavily influenced by psychoanalytic theory, which postulated that both a mother and father figure were necessary for a child's intrapsychic development. The public has always been comfortable with single-parent adoptions, because this form of family has "worked" for children over the centuries. Gradually, professionals became more certain that single parents were capable of providing good adoptive homes. However, it remains "difficult, but not impossible, for a single person to become an adoptive parent," a handbook for single adoptive parents begins (Marindin 1992:1).

Characteristics It is difficult to know the number of single-parent adoptions; it is known that they have grown rapidly. The National Adoption Information Clearinghouse (2002) estimates that between 8 percent and 34 percent of nonrelative adoptions may be by single parents, and a third of the children adopted from foster care are adopted by single parents. Some of these adoptions are not, however, true single-parent adoptions, but rather adoptions in which, in order to meet legal requirements, one partner in a gay or lesbian couple has adopted the child, purporting to be a single parent (Shireman 1995).

The evidence suggests that nontraditional applicants, such as single parents, find it difficult to adopt healthy young children and often receive children who are more difficult to place (Groze and Rosenthal 1991). Thus they face the complex tasks of managing the economic and logistical strain of parenting without a partner, difficulties of all single parents, and in addition the stress of parenting children with special needs and of handling all the issues presented by adoption. If the child is from another country, (many single parents adopt internationally), issues of ethnic and cultural identity must be considered, and if the placement is transracial, then racial identity becomes an issue.

Outcomes The evidence suggests that single parents manage these difficulties well. A longitudinal study, which followed adoptions of young children by single parents over, eventually, sixteen years, noted these strengths: (1) commitment to the child and the adoption, creating a close and nurturing bond; (2) strength and capacity to handle crisis; (3) a relatively simple family structure, which meets the needs of some children; and (4) self-confidence, independence, and ability to develop and use supportive networks (Shireman and Johnson 1985). Whether these results can be generalized to the adoption of older, more troubled children has just begun to be answered. Fiegelman and Silverman (1983) reported that, when controlling for the age of children at placement, "direct and indirect assessments of children's overall adjustments show fundamentally corresponding patterns among single parents and adoptive couples" (p. 191). Groze and Rosenthal's (1991) follow-up of special needs placements showed that, at all ages, children adopted by single parents had the lowest percentage of scores in the problematic range. Studies of adoptions that disrupt provide additional evidence. In those studies that reported data concerning single parents, single and two-parent families were equally represented; other factors, such as age at placement or a child's prior experiences were associated with disruptions (Kagan and Reid 1986; Barth and Berry 1988).

Single-parent homes are not homes in which to place a child for whom no two-parent home can be found. Rather, they are homes with unique strengths (Shireman 1995). They are homes in which to place children whose background and experiences are such that they can benefit from those strengths.

Adoption by Gay and Lesbian Parents

For many years, adoptions of children by gay and lesbian parents were hidden in the statistics of single-parent adoptions. Those who wanted to adopt did so as single parents; if agencies knew they were placing children in gay or lesbian homes, it was easier to "look the other way." This reluctance of gay and lesbian parents to identify themselves has probably increased their opportunities to adopt, even as it has made it difficult to estimate the numbers or evaluate the adoptions.

In recent years, gay and lesbian individuals and couples have been less willing to adopt in this covert way. Many, in committed relationships, are seeking to adopt as couples. At the same time agencies, seeking homes for the children in the foster care system, have become more willing to place youngsters with a variety of families. Gay and lesbian adopters are the most recent group to join other nontraditional adopters who need a subsidy to adopt. It has become imperative that agencies take a position on the subject, develop relevant policy, and publicize that policy.

> Agencies must recognize the complexities and politics that accompany this issue as they develop their policies. Adoption by gay men and lesbians is an intensely emotional topic that polarizes groups of people on the basis of their values and beliefs. No matter what position is taken, it will not be possible to please everyone with a stake in the issue. For agency board members, administrators, and staff, then, the challenge is to develop a rational position based on professional values and experience and that can be defended when challenged.
>
> (SULLIVAN 1995:1)

Public fears Sullivan (1995), in a review of policy issues, identifies three "myths" that lead to public reluctance to place children in gay or lesbian adoptive homes. The first is the fear that children might be molested, a fear that stems from the failure to distinguish homosexuality from pedophilia. In fact, most pedophiles are heterosexual males (Finkelhor 1984). The second fear is that children will become homosexual, or be pressured to become homosexual, if they are placed in these adoptive families. In fact, sexual orientation does not seem to be determined by family, but it was this belief that made agencies willing, as they took their first tentative steps toward open placements in gay or lesbian households, to place adolescents who had "clearly developed homosexual identity" in gay or lesbian homes. The third concern is that children adopted by gay or lesbian parents will be growing up in an "immoral" environment. Morality, Sullivan points out, is a very personal issue, and whether one is more outraged by children growing up without families, or in homosexual families, is personal.

Outcomes The adoption of children by openly gay or lesbian parents is new enough that there is no body of research on the skills of these parents in raising children or on the special issues they face. Flaks (1995), in a thorough review of research concerning gay and lesbian parenting, concludes that "to date, no evidence has emerged that suggests that homosexual parents are inferior to their heterosexual counterparts, or that their children are in any regard compromised" (p. 33). Logic suggests, however, that these homes may raise some special issues for children. One is "differentness," which all children abhor. There seems to be agreement that the children of gay or lesbian parents have to learn to be discreet in selecting those friends to whom they will explain the true nature of their household (Flaks 1995). However, the issue does not seem to overwhelm children, and we have a growing body of evidence that foster care status has its own negative impact on self-esteem and that group home status can be very troubling (Kools 1997; Toth 1997; Mallon 1998, for example).

Legal and professional barriers Despite these findings, it remains difficult for gay or lesbian applicants to adopt a child. Two states (New Hampshire and Florida) explicitly prohibit the adoption of children by gay or lesbian parents. States may or may not allow joint petitions for adoption by a gay or lesbian couple (Horwitz and Maruyama 1995). A joint adoption is obviously preferable. It confers on both parents joint authority, easing potential household tensions. And it confers on the child the protection of the surviving parent should one parent die, as well as securing social security, medical, and inheritance rights for the child.

Adoption must be seen as a changing area of social work practice. Today children are placed in adoption who would not have been considered adoptable fifteen years ago, and they are successfully adopted by families who would not have been considered suitable at that time. Adoption agencies, private or public, are dependent on the support of their communities, and it is understandable that they are reluctant to commit openly to policies of placing children in gay and lesbian households. However, if all available resources are to be used for children this commitment must be made. If it is not, gay and lesbian adopters will increasingly turn to independent adoption, with all its risks.[8]

Transracial Adoption

Transracial adoption refers to the adoption of a child of one race by parents of another. It is another subject that arouses strong passions.[9] People who are concerned about social justice question whether it is morally acceptable for people of a dominant race to be responsible for the socialization of the children of oppressed races; this is the issue behind the Indian Child Welfare Act, reviewed in chapter 2 and again earlier in this chapter. Transracial adoption looks toward a society in which races are integrated; those who value cultural and racial separatism oppose such adoptions. Finally, there are those who point out that individual children cannot wait for the injustices of society to be remedied, and that children of color, waiting in foster homes, need permanent homes now.

Divided public opinion is one reason these adoptions remain so controversial. The National Adoption Attitudes Survey asked questions about the adoption of African American children by white families, the most common domestic transracial adoption in the United States. Survey respondents believe that there is substantial opposition to interracial adoption; the perception is that 47 percent of whites and 61 percent of African Americans would oppose such adoptions. A subsample of African American respondents, however, thought that only 49 percent of each racial group would disapprove. Despite these perceptions, 77 percent of the respondents said that they would be at least somewhat likely to consider the adoption of a child of a different race (Evan B. Donaldson Adoption Institute 2002e).

There is no good source of information on the number of transracial adoptions of children currently in foster care. It is estimated that 117,000 children in foster care need adoptive homes. The Child Welfare League estimates that 4 percent of adoptions in a year are transracial; other estimates are somewhat lower or higher (Evan B. Donaldson Adoption Institute 2000).

History When transracial adoption began, cautiously, in the 1960s, it was a "fit" with the civil rights movement and the spirit of a society moving toward racial integration. The pace of such adoptions was accelerated by the reduction in the number of white infants available for adoption, the increase in the number of African American children in the foster care system, and the new commitment to finding a permanent home for every child. Transracial adoptive placements increased in number until the early 1970s. But in the 1970s, as the richness of minority cultures became more widely celebrated, the goal of many concerned with race relations became cultural integrity rather than integration. There was also the concern that white families could not teach children of color to protect themselves effectively from racism. In 1972 the Black Association of Social Workers issued a statement condemning transracial adoption. Sensitive to the political climate and to the concerns being raised, adoption agencies, both public and private, almost universally ceased making transracial placements. Despite attempts to recruit ethnically diverse adoptive homes, the numbers of African American children in foster care continued to grow.

By 1994 there were almost 500,000 children in foster homes, of whom many thousands needed adoptive homes. Children were waiting a median of two years and eight months to be adopted, and African American children waited longer than other children. When the Multiethnic Placement Act was passed, forbidding denial of adoption because of the race of the child or family, it was expected that removing the barrier to transracial placement would open more homes to African American children and increase the numbers adopted (Brooks, Barth, et al. 1999). This hope was enhanced by the vocal support of advocacy groups composed of parents who were interested in transracial adoption.

The real effects of the implementation of the MEPA remain uncertain. There has been confusion about which practices are permissible and which forbidden under the law. Additionally, categorical assumptions about the benefit of same-race placements have been part of the policy, written or unwritten, of child-placing agencies for the last twenty years. Changing practice, when the beliefs on which that practice are based have not changed, is difficult. "MEPA may someday have a significant impact, but for now race matching by the state is alive and well" (Bartholet 1999:140).

Outcomes Because of the controversy surrounding them, transracial adoptions have been subject to extensive evaluation.[10] The findings of the studies are broadly similar. Repeatedly they find that about 20 to 25 percent of the transracially adopted children experience moderate to severe problems in family, school, or community. This is about the same percentage found in same-race adoptions. Transracially adopted children appear similar to other adopted children on measures of self-esteem. In spite of the fact that many have been raised in predominantly white communities, measures of racial identity elicit pride in their racial heritage. They appear comfortable in the white world and in the world of their ethnic origin.

These findings are puzzling. Adoption is complicated; when racial difference is added one would expect to find additional difficulties. There is also some anecdotal information about very serious difficulties experienced by transracially adopted individuals who seem unable to find a place in either the world of their adoptive families or the world of their birth families.

The findings are also subject to varied interpretation. On the one hand, they provide evidence that transracially adopted children adjust well and, for the most part, do not experience overt problems in adolescence or young adulthood. The adjustment measured is, of course, adjustment to the mainstream society. It is also possible, however, that the findings are reflecting a superficial adjustment that young people maintain in order to conceal from themselves the depth of their own concern about racial identity, and that this adjustment will break down under the stress of adult life. Empirical work provides a good deal of information about childhood, less about adolescence, and to date very little about the adult lives of these adoptees. It is a line of research that will be interesting to follow.

Policy implications So where should the child welfare profession stand on transracial adoption? Probably most practitioners would agree that transracial placement adds a complication to a child's development, and that same-race placement is preferable. The MEPA recognizes this by its emphasis on recruitment of diverse homes; extensive and creative efforts are certainly critical. At the same time, the empirical evidence shows that no demonstrable harm comes to children who are transracially placed. Evidence clearly shows that great harm comes to many children who spend long periods in foster care. As long as we believe that the purpose of adoption is finding homes for children, transracial adoption is an option we are obligated to use.

Transracial adoption has implications for the society we are trying to build. Of course, we must commit resources so that all groups in our society, and world, have equal capacity to raise their children. But transracial adoption also helps us build a world in which differing peoples interact. It may be that these youngsters, with their identity based in two cultures, will grow into adults who build bridges toward better understanding.

International Adoption

International adoptions also raise political, moral, and policy questions. The political and moral issues stem from the removal of children from poor countries to more wealthy countries; until all countries can provide the family support and child welfare services to provide birth parents with real choices, these adoptions will continue to be questioned. Theorists who are family oriented write movingly on this point, emphasizing that international adoptions "find children for parents" rather than finding the most appropriate resources for children. Triseliotis, Shireman, et al. (1997) cite evidence that "many intercountry adopted children are neither orphaned nor abandoned. The reason that many of them are given up is their parents' extreme poverty which makes the lure of money irresistible" (p. 205).

However, there is little doubt that international adoptions provide vastly improved opportunities for those children whose parents are unable to care for them, particularly if the best option their own country provides is institutional care. From this perspective, Bartholet writes:

> In the poorer countries of the world, war, political turmoil, and economic circumstances contribute to a situation in which there are very few prospective adopters in comparison with the vast numbers of children in need of homes. . . . The benefits of international adoption far outweigh any negatives and . . . international adoption should be encouraged with appropriate protections against abuses.
>
> (BARTHOLET 1993:90–91)

Both authors quoted here would agree that the key words are "appropriate protections." It is important that family support services (including income maintenance) be so developed that in all countries parents have real choices about raising children themselves or planning adoption. It is important that adopting parents have orderly access to the adoption process without facing unreasonable barriers, so that any family interested in international adoption has the opportunity. And, most of all, it is important that the interests of children be protected, both in the country of origin and in the country to which they move.

The scope and nature of international adoption It is estimated that there were almost 20,000 international adoptions in 2001; this is more than double the number in 1991 (Evan B. Donaldson Adoption Institute 2002b). War and upheavals have left many countries unable to provide for their own children, as has poverty; in China, population control policies have led to many girls being abandoned to state care. The countries that "sent" the most children to adoption in 2001 were China (4,723 children) and Russia (4,279 children). Korea, in the years since the Korean War a major sender of children, sent only 1,870, and Guatemala 1,609 (U.S. Immigration and Naturalization Service and U.S. Department of State statistics, from Evan B. Donaldson Adoption Institute 2002b). These adoptions have taken place primarily in the United States, the Netherlands, Germany, and Denmark.

International adoption is expensive, and some of the expense may be questionable. Fees charged by agencies in the United States range from $3,000 to $14,000 (Evan B. Donaldson Adoption Institute 2000). In addition, depending on the laws of the country in which the child lives, there may be costs for air travel for the adopting parents, as well as living expenses and legal fees in the foreign country while the adoption is processed. A recent survey by the Evan B. Donaldson Adoption Institute found that 14 percent of the adopting families said the adoption cost more than the agency had told them it would cost, and 11 percent said overseas agency facilitators had asked for additional fees that had not been disclosed by the agency (Evan B. Donaldson Adoption Institute 2002c). The survey also revealed that almost three-quarters of the adopting families were asked to carry cash, usually $3,000 or more, for anticipated fees and expenses. Whenever undocumented expenses are required for adoption, suspicion arises about whether children are being purchased.

Independent adoptions have accounted for a large proportion of international adoptions, and this lack of regulation has drawn much criticism.[11] Many adoption agencies specialize in international adoption; some have a long tradition of excellent service, but others have more questionable practices. The survey cited in the previous paragraph found that 14 percent of the adopting families felt that the agency had given them inaccurate information about the child, 14 percent had received inaccurate information about the adopting process, and 13 percent would not recommend their agency to other families (Evan B. Donaldson Adoption Institute 2002c).

Despite this troubling background, the sound and innovative work of many nonprofit adoption agencies should be recognized. For example,

Holt International Adoption Services began its work by bringing over children left destitute by the Korean War, and has since specialized in international adoption and in providing consultation to "sending" countries about the development of child welfare and family support services within those countries. Holt makes postadoption services available to adopting parents and children, including a developing program of visits to the country of origin for adolescent children. Two good indicators of the professional responsibility of an international adoption agency are the degree to which it is involved in the development of child welfare services in the sending country, and the extent to which it provides postadoption services to support the adoptions it has arranged.

Outcomes One of the interesting things about the controversy concerning international adoptions is that there is little debate about the outcomes of these adoptions. Studies in the United States have consistently shown that children adopted as infants or very young children had adjustments as good as children adopted from the United States, with, as is true of domestic adoptions, somewhat more problematic adjustments for children adopted when older (Kim 1976; Fiegelman and Silverman 1983; Altstein and Simon 1991; Bagley, Young, et al. 1993; Benson, Sharma, et al. 1994). Concern is rising over the experiences of families who have adopted more recently from the orphanages in Romania and other Eastern European countries, where children often experienced profound neglect as young infants. It will be interesting to follow the course of these adoptions and see whether Kadushin's optimism about the reversal of early trauma is sustained, or whether Bowlby's earlier, more pessimistic formulations about the lasting impact of inadequate infant-caretaker interaction are upheld.

Most families who adopt internationally are white and live fairly mainstream cultural lives in the United States. If the children are of a different race, they face the dual challenge of establishing a cultural identity different from that of their community and a racial identity different from that of their family. The degree to which such children are accepted by the communities in which they live is doubtless an important factor in the success of international adoptions.

Creating international order Both supporters and critics of international adoption stress the importance of bringing order to this relatively unregulated enterprise. Those who think of international adoption as a resource for homeless children focus on the barriers adoptive parents face: different procedures for adoption in each country, immigration restrictions, the need to repeat the adoption in the United States, and the need for the child to become a naturalized citizen. Those who are concerned about the rights of birth parents emphasize the need to prohibit independent adoptions and thus exclude unscrupulous intermediaries who seek to profit from adoption.

The lack of regulation has been addressed by the Convention on the Protection of Children and Cooperation in Respect of Intercountry Adoption (the Hague Convention). This convention requires each country to designate a central authority to coordinate international adoptions and to develop some system of accreditation for intercountry adoption practitioners. These provisions have been troublesome for the United States, where adoptions are generally regulated by state law. However, the United States signed the Convention in 1993, and in 2000 the Intercountry Adoption Act was passed to implement the convention. The State Department will become the central coordinating authority, and one or more organizations will assume an accrediting function with the goal of improving agency services. The Hague Treaty makes the sending country responsible for assuring that the child is legally freed for adoption and that adoption is appropriate for the child. It gives the receiving country the responsibility to ensure that the applicants are eligible and suitable as adoptive parents. Other provisions of the act require that medical and other records be preserved and that only reasonable costs and expenses be charged for adoption. Additionally, the Child Citizen Act of 2000 was signed into law in November of 2000. It amends the Immigration and Nationality Act to grant automatic citizenship to children born abroad who are in the legal and physical custody of at least one parent who is a U.S. citizen; this eliminates the need for adoptive parents to have children naturalized in a separate proceeding.

The United States was fairly late in agreeing to the Hague Convention; it has been accepted by many other countries. One disappointment is that the treaty does not eliminate the possibility of independent adoptions, though the provisions do require that any agency or person facilitating the adoption "meet standards of competence, financial soundness, and ethical behavior" (Evan B. Donaldson Adoption Institute 2000c). The authority of the accrediting body, whatever it is, will be critical. Despite questions about how effective the convention can be, it is hoped that this framework will stimulate countries to work more cooperatively and that duplicative processes will be eliminated. However, the trust between countries and the agreements between agencies that will be needed to make it work are things that cannot be legislated.

Open Adoption

Open adoptions are relatively new, having been common in the United States only since the mid-1980s. Professionals, sensitive to the need of many adopted adolescents and adults to know their own families, have generally thought open adoption a good idea as long as both the birth and adoptive parents are comfortable with the arrangement. The public, generally accepting of different forms of adoption, is more conservative on this subject. In 1997 and 2002 survey respondents were ambivalent about open adoptions, though more favorable in 2002 than in 1997. In 2002 only 21 percent said it is a good idea in most situations, while 47 percent thought it a good idea in some cases, believing decisions should be made on a case-by-case basis (Evan B. Donaldson Adoption Institute 1997, 2002a).

Several streams of adoption work came together to foster the development of open adoptions. Perhaps most important, agencies heard adopted adults and adolescents saying emphatically that they wanted to know their birth families, and saw the distress that closed birth records could cause. At the same time, the growing scarcity of white infants available for adoption put more power in the hands of birth mothers, many of whom felt more comfortable if they knew where their child was going and could keep some contact through the years. Older children were being placed in adoption; many knew their original families and had some contact with relatives; it became evident that this contact could be absorbed into the adoption experience. Adopting parents were aware of all of these trends, recognized that their best hope of adopting the child they wanted was through accepting the wishes of birth mothers, and saw that open adoption might be good for their adopted children and workable for their families.

A continuum of openness Open adoption is an umbrella term, used to cover a variety of arrangements ranging from minimal sharing of identifying information to continuing contact between birth parents and adopting families. It is distinguished from confidential adoption, in which the identity of the birth parents and adoptive parents are concealed from each other. Though for many years the identity of adopting parents was not disclosed to birth parents, it was not until after World War II that adoption "secrecy became pervasive, preventing everyone directly involved in adoption from gaining access to family information about their own lives" (Carp 1998:102). Change began to occur in the late 1970s, and by the end of the 1980s open adoptions were common.

Open adoptions form a continuum of openness, from simple exchange of identifying information before the adoption to continued contact and meetings.

> There is great variation in open adoption today. Adoptions can be open prior to placement, for a set period of time after placement, or for the duration of the child's life. Openness can involve a sharing of identifiable or nonidentifiable information during the preplacement period, a meeting of both sets of parents, and agreements concerning ongoing contact and/or sharing information after adoption.
>
> (BERRY 1993:126)

Decisions about the degree of openness are made at the time of placement, but the degree of openness desired by birth or adoptive parents, or by the child, can of course change over time. The literature stresses that any of these degrees of openness is acceptable if it meets the needs of all parties. Etter (1993) suggests that openness is such an important dimension of adoption that participants should discuss it thoroughly prior to any matching.

Open adoptions are new enough, and there are enough differences of opinion about them, that everyone is eager to know how they work out. Unfortunately, they are so new that there is not yet a body of empirical evidence about their outcomes. An examination of what we do know, however, can give us an idea of the known and anticipated benefits and risks to each of the members of the adoption triad.

Birth mothers Studies of open adoptions have included small samples, and few have used comparison groups. However, some knowledge about the way in which open adoption affects birth mothers is beginning to emerge.[12] Birth mothers may believe that adoption will be the best plan for the child but may be unwilling to relinquish the opportunity to know about the child as he or she grows (Kallen, Griffore, et al. 1990, reported in Berry 1993). Often they are more willing to plan adoption if they can select the family and have some continuing contact. Grotevant (2000), in a brief review of the empirical literature, concludes that birth mothers who have continuing contact with their adopted children experience more successful resolution of grief. Grotevant and McRoy (1998) report a study with a national sample that included confidential, mediated, and fully disclosed adoptions. The birth mothers in their study who had open adoptions tended to feel positive about the adoption and said they felt better about the adoption because they could see that the child was happy.

Adoptive parents Open adoption was expected to be more difficult for adoptive parents than for other members of the adoption triad. It was thought that the presence of birth parents would have a negative impact on their sense of entitlement to the child, and that it would enhance their fears that the birth parents might reclaim the child. These fears have not been borne out. In fact, increasing levels of openness seem to be associated with lessening of fears about losing the child. Although some adoptive parents report that they chose open adoption because it was the only way they could adopt a child, most seem satisfied with the open adoption (Berry 1993; Grotevant and McRoy 1998).

The adoptive parents' satisfaction with open adoption is related to their sense of control over the frequency and nature of contacts (Berry 1993). An occasional difficulty is the birth parent who becomes overly dependent on the adoptive family, using them for support in her own life struggles (Siegel 1990, reported in Berry 1993). The other source of disappointment for some adoptive families who value the birth mother's role in the adoptive family's life is the birth mother who, over time, maintains less contact and may eventually disappear (Reitz and Watson 1992). Etter (1993) notes the importance of a written contract in making both of these situations less likely, and Reitz and Watson (1992) suggest that the placing agency has some responsibility to provide services to help families with these difficulties.

Adopted children Most adopting parents, birth parents, and professionals who participate in open adoption believe that the arrangement will be good for the children. It is expected that knowing the birth parent will resolve children's questions, enable them to incorporate both the social heritage of their adoptive family and their biological heritage, and enable them to locate biological family without searching. The openness should promote healthy interactions within the adoptive family; and the child who knows all the parties to the adoption should be better able to develop a positive sense of identity.[13]

Open adoptions are so new that few studies have been completed on children beyond the very early childhood years. Grotevant and McRoy (1998), in their national study, interviewed 163 children between the ages of four and twelve in confidential, mediated, and fully open adoptions. Their conclusion was that knowing the birth parents neither enhanced nor damaged the child's adjustment and self-esteem. They note that many of the children they interviewed were still very young, and they looked forward to interviewing them again as adolescents.

Open adoptions of older children have certainly occurred for a long time—almost all children placed when older know their parents, siblings, and extended family. The impact of this knowledge has not been systematically studied, however. Meezan and Shireman (1985) found that foster parents were more willing to adopt when they knew the birth parents; this would imply that such placements were going well. In a California study of 1,396 adoptions of children ranging in age from infants to sixteen years, Berry (1991) found that adoptive parents rated the behavior of children who had contact with birth parents more positively. On a more negative note, Partridge, Hornby, et al. (1986) found that in 14 percent of the disruptions in her study, adoptive parents blamed the disruption on contact with birth parents. Just as more time is needed to attain information about the impact of openness on children adopted as infants, more attention is needed to the question of its impact of children adopted when they are older.

Critical Issue: Continuing Support for Postadoption Services

We have come a long way in time and sophistication from the belief that adoption creates a family "just like any other," and that after adoption the family will continue through life without needing any special support or services. This section draws together material about the adoptive family's need for services after adoption is finalized, and examines the types of postadoption services offered and some of the controversies surrounding them.

The Need for Postadoption Services

As long as most adoptions involved the placement of infants and very young children, disruption rates were low, and it was easy to view adoptive families as ordinary families. But older children who had been adopted as infants appeared in mental health treatment settings in disproportionate numbers, and adult adoptees expressed a powerful need to explore their

biologic origins. As the philosophy developed that adoption was appropriate for any child who needed a home, older children and children
with serious disabilities began to be adopted. Children adopted from the
foster care system had often endured abuse or neglect in their early years,
as well as having experienced the trauma of many moves. The behavior
these children presented in their adoptive homes was often difficult. Some
of these adoptions disrupted, but many others remained intact, despite the
challenges brought into the home by the adopted child. Rosenthal and
Groze (1992), in a follow-up study of older-child adoptions, document
the difficulties these families face, and their strengths.

Most adoptive families would benefit from post-adoption support services at some time. The traditional adoption of a same-race infant may
bring a few problems during childhood, but many families could use help
in sorting through feelings about the role of the biological parents as the
adopted child reaches adolescence and thinks about searching for them.
Open adoptions bring with them continual interaction with biological
parents, with all the potential for differences around child-rearing practices, as well as around amount of contact. Transracially adopting parents
and parents who adopt children with medical needs have long sought
support in groups of families facing similar issues. Adoption agencies have
recently been fairly active in the development of support groups around
issues of adoption itself, and various inquiries and agency reports indicate
that adoptive parents find them helpful. Families that adopt older children with a history of abuse and neglect may face the greatest difficulties.
Their needs for therapeutic services have received the most attention in
adoption literature, both around appropriate therapeutic techniques for
adoptive faimiles and around the difficulties and expense of obtaining
such services. Families of many special-needs chidren need respite care in
order to sustain family energy and need adoption subsidies to meet the
needs of those children.

In response to federal initiatives, as we have seen, increasing numbers
of children are being adopted from foster care. Permanent homes are
vitally important for these children, many of whom have experienced
multiple changes in their lives. It is thus critical that the necessary services be provided to support the adoptions and insure that these children's homes are, indeed, permanent.[14]

Continued funding and support for postadoption services is becoming
a critical issue. For many years adoption has been "sold" to legislators as

both good for children and economical for state budgets—because after adoption, the new parents are responsible for the care of their children. However, some postadoption services, such as adoption subsidies, grow each year as new subsidies are added to existing ones, and they are an increasing item in state and federal budgets. In general, legislators still believe that adoption is a good plan for children, as evidenced by the emphasis on adoption in ASFA. But the expense of postadoption services means that stronger public policies will be needed if their continuation is to be assured.

The Range of Postadoption Services

There are many types of postadoption services, and they are so new that, beyond the reports of adopting parents themselves, there is little empirical evidence to indicate how effective the various services are. Barth, Gibbs, et al. (2001:10) classify postadoption services according to four categories: (1) educational and informational services, (2) clinical services, (3) material services, such as adoption subsidies, and (4) support networks. This section discusses these four kinds of services, plus respite care and advocacy, starting with the type that is simplest and most commonly used.

Adoption subsidies As agencies began to focus on the needs of older children and children with special needs for permanent homes, it became evident that one of the barriers to adoption was family income sufficient to meet these children's needs. Foster families who had been caring for children emerged as a good source of adoptive homes for these children, but many of these families had marginal financial resources and would be unable to adopt if they faced the loss of income from foster care payments (Shireman 1969). A few private agencies developed adoption subsidy programs to make it possible for families to adopt children with serious, and expensive, problems. In 1968 New York became the first state to enact legislation making adoption subsidies widely available. Other states rapidly followed. In 1980 Congress passed the Adoption Assistance and Child Welfare Act, which—among its many provisions—encouraged states to make subsidies available to families who adopted children with special needs, provided a 50 percent federal match for state adoption subsidies, and guaranteed Medicaid insurance coverage for those children. Most state laws provide that in order for a child to be eligible for a subsidy, (1) the child must have "special needs"—that is, must be older, a member of a minority group, part of a sibling group, or handicapped in some way; and (2) an attempt must have been made to find a home that does not need subsidy.

Subsidies can be geared to meet the needs created by a specific disability, or they can be payments to supplement income for the daily care of the child. The amount is based on the child's need and the family's resources, and yearly review is required.

The legislative debates over the provision of subsidies echoed earlier debates concerning payment to foster parents. Senators decried the idea of adoption subsidies, believing that desire for a child and affection for a child should be the motivations to adopt, and wondering how a child would feel knowing that his parents were paid to take him. Early demonstration projects showed the positive impact of subsidies in finding homes for older, African American children drifting in foster care (Hargrave, Shireman, et al. 1975); concerns about financial incentives receded as it became evident that subsidies could remove a barrier to adoption, both for foster families and for newly found families.

The policy issue that has plagued the implementation of adoption subsidies is the question of whether the subsidy is part of the placement planning for a specific child, in recognition of special needs, or whether it is dependent on the economic resources of the family. In the early days of subsidized adoption it was hoped that the subsidy could be attached to the child, whatever the circumstances of the adoptive home. But this approach did not meet the needs of budget-conscious administrators or legislators. What has evolved is a formula, which varies by state, in which both needs of the child and the economic resources of the family are factored in. Unfortunately, workers are sometimes required to search for homes that will not need subsidy; this has resulted in some children having to move from foster homes that could have kept them, and in some foster parents not being informed of available subsidies (Meezan and Shireman 1985).

Adoption assistance has been particularly important in increasing the number of homes available for minority children who are proportionately overrepresented in the foster care system and underrepresented in adoption statistics. Although African Americans adopt children at a rate 4.5 times greater than whites when income, family composition, and age are held constant (Gershenson 1984), it has remained difficult to find a sufficient number of African American adoptive homes; cultural biases in home-finding probably play a role, but poverty plays a major role.

For this historically disadvantaged segment of the population, and their children, adoption assistance seems a logical and uncomplicated way to increase adoptions.

Educational and informational services Used by many adoptive families, educational and informational services are often thought so basic that they receive little attention. However, if a difficulty can be solved, or prevented, through the cognitive work of gaining additional information and thus greater understanding of a child's needs and how to meet them, it is by far the most efficient approach.

Educational and informational services include books and articles, lectures, workshops. Many books and articles have been written for adopting families and are widely available. Books and articles are the most frequently used postadoption resource, used by 82 percent of families in one recent large survey (Brooks, Allen, et al. 2002). However, the same survey found that for families adopting from public agencies, who in general had less formal education and had adopted older children with more behavioral problems, reading was not as helpful (p. 232–33).

In a recent survey, 82 percent of 873 adoptive parents reported reading books or articles on adoption, and 43 percent reported attending lectures or workshops, while less than 30 percent used other postadoption services (Brooks, Allen, et al. 2002). Informational sources may be preferred by adoptive parents, or they may simply be the most readily available resource.

Support networks Many adoptive parents utilize support groups, or contacts with other adoptive families, and find them among the most helpful postadoption services available. Asked how they would design postadoption support services, more than 60 percent of adoptive families in a recent survey included support groups, and 60 percent included classes, which are educational but have a social component (Brooks, Allen, et al. 2002).

Many local groups are specific to those adoptions particularly likely to raise difficult issues, such as transracial adoption, open adoption, or single-parent adoption. Other support groups are organized around the difficulties of adopted children who have special needs. Support groups may be initiated by adoptive parents, sponsored by adoption agencies, or supported by state agencies. Several national organizations that focus on adoption, such as the North American Council on Adoptable Children, have Web pages with information on finding or starting a support group.

A support group can be especially important to a family formed through adoption, for adoptive families do not always enjoy the level of extended family and community support available to most families. A support group reduces the sense of isolation, in addition to providing practical, parent-tested ideas for problem solving. One responsibility of an adoption agency is to help the family to find a support system, either in adoption-focused support groups or in the wider community (Tilbor 1988).[15]

Barth, Gibbs, et al. (2001) note in their review of the effectiveness of postadoption services that contact with support groups, or with other adoptive parents, is one of the elements of service that has proved useful (p. 16). Brooks, Allen, et al. (2002) report, from their survey of 873 adoptive parents, that 70 percent found support groups helpful (p. 224). This is one of the least intrusive and probably least expensive of the postadoption support services, and the energy that has gone into establishing support groups is testimony to the wide recognition of their usefulness.

Clinical services In keeping with the philosophy that adoptive families were "just like any other family," for a long time adoption agencies refused to provide services after the adoption was finalized. Families who turned to community mental health services were often frustrated by providers' lack of understanding of the issues raised by adoption and by their tendency to attribute any difficulties to the interactions of the current family. Bourguignon and Watson (1987) identified for mental health professionals the issues faced by adopting families (whether they adopt an infant or an older child). Chief among them were the grief and loss felt by the child, and the need for resolution of those feelings before the child could truly become part of a new family. The authors argued that these families need a combination of support for the adoptive parents and direct help for the child.

Recognizing that these concepts are unfamiliar to most mental health service providers, adoption agencies have increasingly assumed responsibility for providing postadoption services directly or contracting with mental health service providers with expertise in adoption. In this way a broad range of services can be provided, including family counseling, brief crisis interventions with the family, intrusive interventions such as holding therapy for adopted youth, and residential care.

Postadoption clinical services take many forms. Family therapy approaches are based in theories, such as those put forward by Bourguignon and Watson (1987), that emphasize the uniqueness of the adoption process, in which children (of any age) bring their family ties and history into the new family and in which both children and adoptive parents experience feelings of loss that must be worked through. Behavioral theory informs many of the crisis-oriented, brief family preservation models that have been used when adoptions are close to disruption. Intrusive therapies—direct work with the adopted child in which regression to earlier stages of development is encouraged—are based on the idea that the child's experiences prior to adoption have damaged the ability to attach to the adoptive family and that the child does not have the sense of trust necessary for the therapeutic relationships of traditional therapy. Approaches that focus on organic difficulties, such as fetal alcohol syndrome, as the basis of child behavior will emphasize educating parents in behavioral techniques to help children learn to better manage their behavior.

To date we have no empirical evidence that any one approach is superior to the others. Barth, Gibbs, et al. (2001) note that few postadoption support programs have conducted formal evaluations of their own effectiveness. Based on their review, they suggest that brief family preservation models do not fit the needs of adoptive families as well as more extensive, family-focused treatment models.

Residential care Residential care is the most intensive of the clinical services that make up the continuum of postadoption support services. Residential care (discussed more fully in chapter 7) involves immersion of the child full time in an environment designed to meet his or her needs and to modify behaviors that are interfering with the child's ability to live in the adoptive family. There are a variety of treatment modalities with different theoretical bases, but a common thread is the development of the "holding environment," in which the quality of the youth's life in the treatment milieu is considered the key to successful intervention. Attention is paid to relationships with staff members and with other residents, and the day is programmed in such a way as to meet the individual child's therapeutic needs (O'Malley 1993). The most progressive residential care programs increasingly involve adoptive families in their children's treatment programs.

More than half the states say that they provide residential treatment as a postadoption service (Barth, Gibbs, et al. 2001). Residential treatment is a very expensive service, and funding mechanisms vary among the states. Current Title IV-E regulations prohibit using that program's funds for children who are already receiving adoption subsidies, making a high proportion of such special-needs children ineligible for this source of funding. A few states have specific programs that allot funds for residential care to children if the purpose is reunification with the adoptive family. Too often, however, the state will pay for residential treatment only if the adoptive parents surrender custody of their children so that foster care funds can be used. This requirement would be devastating to any family, but it is especially hard on the adopting family at a time when the child is very troubled and the family structure may be fragile. A recent Casey Family Services white paper on postadoption services recommends that "states should be encouraged to use a mix of existing community-based mental health services funding to maintain adoptive families' legal responsibility for and involvement in their children's treatment" (Casey Family Services 2002:5).

Respite services Discussed in more detail in chapter 4, respite care is another part of the continuum of postadoption services. In the context of adoption as in other settings, it is a temporary service, focused on enhancing and stabilizing the relationship between parent and child. As such, respite services can facilitate the formation of strong adoptive families. For example, respite care can be critical in enabling a family to continue to care for an adopted child with serious disabilities or with severe behavioral problems. The constant demand of the care of such children can exhaust parents, leaving them with the feeling that the only solution is to ask the placing agency to take back custody of the adopted child. Respite care can provide just what its name promises—a time for parents to regroup, to regain energy and commitment, and to attend to other family business.

Respite care providers should be trained to work with the adoptive family, supporting the customs and rules of that family and easing the child's return to that family. Unlike the therapeutic nursery or respite foster care provider, the respite care provider for an adoptive family is not expected to effect change in the child or the family. Rather, the task is to provide care within the framework of the child's permanent family.

Reflecting its origins in the care of children with disabilities, respite care is offered under a variety of agency auspices. Respite service work requires special skills in assessing the needs of the child and family, matching the child to a respite provider that can meet those needs, and then mediating the demands of the family and of the provider. Well supported, the same respite home can remain available to a child and family, as needed, over a long time period.

Advocacy Like foster parents, adoptive parents tend to be forceful and effective advocates for their children. However, as do many families who have needs that are unusual, adoptive families may need help in finding adoption-competent community services, and help in seeing that the educational, medical, and mental health systems meet the needs of their children. Advocacy for these families should be a part of the continuum of postadoption services.

Policy Implications

This brief review of adoptive families' needs, and the resources available, makes clear that a continuum of postadoption services should be available to any adoptive family that needs them, whenever the need arises. If adoption is truly a child-centered process, it is the responsibility of placing agency to use all the available resources to make sure that services are in place for adoptive families. And it is the responsibility of the community, through legislation and assignment of funds, to see that such services are continuously supported.

Ideally, adoption agencies would work with the families who have adopted, and with young people who have been adopted, to design optimal adoption support services. What would the service design look like? The "home" of such services might be an adoption agency, which would maintain contractual arrangements with community mental health service providers. Some states are experimenting with family resource centers as the "home" for postadoption services; others are setting up special agencies solely to provide the continuum of postadoption services (Barth, Gibbs, et al. 2001). The planners should listen to adoptive families: the Brooks and Allen survey (2002), for example, suggests that most adoptive families want, and will use, informational and support services, while a relatively small proportion want therapeutic services.

However, such surveys should be read with care. It is not certain whether nonuse of a service really indicates that adoptive families do not need the service, or whether it means the service is not available. Mental health services are notoriously scarce and hard to access; the data do not tell us whether this is why adoptive families use them infrequently.

The Casey Family Services white paper, recommending that flexible federal funding be made available to states to develop a comprehensive array of postadoption support services (Casey Family Services 2002:5), certainly makes a critical point. Also critical is stability of funding for adoption subsidies. As expenses for subsidies grow, legislatures are beginning to consider limiting their duration or capping the amount allowed. Such action would destroy a program that has been instrumental in enabling families to adopt, and that often provides the means for children to receive the special services they need.

Adoption is not an event, it is a process. The process continues throughout the life of the adoptive family. Support for adoption must also continue throughout the life of the family.

Conclusion

This is an exciting time for those involved in adoption. Earlier reservations seem to be disappearing. Almost all Americans agree that adoption serves a useful purpose in our society, and most have a favorable opinion of it, though they may harbor doubts about certain aspects. A new openness pervades adoption, and adoptive families recognize their uniqueness and build on their strengths.

Adoption is a child-centered institution. The most exciting development of the last thirty years is, without question, the realization that a permanent home should be found for every child, and that one can be found for almost every child. This philosophy has guided the increasing number of adoptions of children from the foster care system—still a small proportion of all adoptions. This quest has stretched the thinking of professionals working in adoption, and opened the public mind as it reacts to adoption. The challenge is to extend this child-centered philosophy to all adoption.

The ability of nontraditional families to embrace children with unusual needs and to meet those needs has been demonstrated over and over again. The controversies are real, and the policy questions are difficult. However, if we have learned anything in these years, it is that we should greet each new form of adoptive family with warmth and support, and learn which children they can best parent. This is, indeed, the route to finding a home for every child who needs one.

As children with increasingly complex needs are placed in a variety of adoptive homes, and as a new openness pervades adoptions, the need for skilled professionals to work with all parties to the adoption becomes increasingly evident. It is to be hoped that the recent federal emphasis on adoption, including federal bonuses to agencies for completed adoptions, is an indication that this service will continue to be adequately funded. It is also to be hoped that public policy will support the integrity of the adoptive family, not by neglecting the rights of birth parents but by recognizing that adoption is a good plan for children; and that public policy will support the development and delivery of postadoption services. Certainly the United States, with its historic emphasis on opportunity tied to individual effort rather than inheritance, is a country that can increasingly support adoption for children.

Notes

1. Independent adoptions are illegal in countries such as Great Britain in which adoptions are more tightly regulated. In the words of one British observer, they result in "high fees, competitive business practices, clinical services of declining quality, litigation, distrust, and a sense of uneasiness" (Davis 1995).

2. Michael Shapiro's *Solomon's Sword* (New York: Random House, 1999) provides a thought-provoking examination of the protection of all three parties to adoption. One of the book's central subjects is the attempt of a couple to adopt a child who is later reclaimed by her birth mother.

3. Although the basic characteristics are the same, foster homes that are becoming adoptive homes need an adoptive home study. The study, however, focuses on the transition to adoption and its expected impact on all of the family members.

4. It is in this work that the "life book" can be of great use. This is a scrapbook, developed with the participation of the child, that documents as much as is known of the child's past. It is a place for pictures and documents, and creates order from a fragmented past.

5. Carp (1998:138–95) provides a thoughtful history of this movement from the perspective of one apparently sympathetic to the value in traditional adoptions.

6. These conclusions are drawn from Hockey 1980; Coyne and Brown 1986; MacCaskill 1988; Pine 1991; and Glidden 1991 as reported in Rosenthal 1993.

7. The major studies on which these findings are based are Triseliotis and Russell 1984; Nelson 1985; Festinger 1986; Kagan and Reid 1986; Partridge, Hornby, et al. 1986; Reid, Kagan, et al. 1987; Barth and Berry 1988; and Rosenthal and Groze 1992.

8. The experiences of gay and lesbian adolescents who grow up in foster care and group care are movingly described in Gerald P. Mallon's *We Don't Exactly Get the Welcome Wagon* (New York: Columbia University Press, 1998). The book makes clear how important it is to think creatively and imaginatively about the needs of children and youth, and to work to develop all possible appropriate resources.

9. Indeed, in a recent book on adoption the three authors were unable to agree, and present their separate positions (Triseliotis, Shireman, et al. 1997).

10. There have been longitudinal studies through adolescence (Shireman 1988; Shireman and Johnson 1975, 1986; Shireman, Johnson, et al. 1987; Simon and Altstein 1977, 1981, 1987, 1992; Vroegh 1997), and "snapshots" taken during childhood (Falk 1970; Fanshel 1972; Grow and Shapiro 1972; Ladner 1977; Zastrow 1977; Fiegelman and Silverman 1983) and during adolescence (McRoy and Zurcher 1983).

11. For a well-written account of the difficulties of independent adoption of a child from a Central American country, and an analysis of policy issues, see Elizabeth Bartholet's *Family Bonds: Adoption and the Politics of Parenting* (New York: Houghton Mifflin, 1993).

12. Grotevant and McRoy (1998:18–20) present a table outlining the existing studies of open adoption that provides a good overview of the existing research.

13. In *Shared Fate* (1964), David Kirk developed the idea that adoptive families were different from families created through birth and that they got in trouble when they pretended they were the same. The ideas presented were startling, and they moved adoption professionals toward a new way of thinking.

14. Many of the services described in this section are, of course, also useful for children in foster care, who share the difficulties that result from repeated losses and broken attachments, and the resultant behaviors that create strain in foster as well as adoptive homes.

15. Informal social support groups have been important also for adoptees searching for their birth parents and birth parents searching for their adopted children. Because such searches took place, at least in the early years, outside professional agency channels, these support networks were vital to many; they were also important in the advocacy for changes in law and agency practice detailed earlier in the chapter. Although face-to-face groups were helpful in supporting the efforts of some searchers, this particular support network operated mainly over distances, and the Internet has become an important tool. Like support groups for adoptive parents, the network combines the provision of information and the encouragement to persist.

References

Altstein, H., and R. Simon. 1991. *Intercountry Adoption: A Multinational Perspective*. New York: Praeger.
Bagley, C., L. Young, et al. 1993. *International and Transracial Adoptions*. Aldershot, Avebury.

Barth, R. P., and M. Berry. 1988. *Adoption and Disruption: Rates, Risks, and Responses*. Hawthorne, N.Y.: Aldine de Gruyter.

Barth, R. P., and D. Brooks. 2000. "Outcomes for Drug-Exposed Children Eight Years Postadoption." In *Adoption and Prenatal Alcohol and Drug Exposure*, edited by R. P. Barth, M. Freundlich, and D. Brodzinsky. Washington, D.C.: Child Welfare League of America and Evan B. Donaldson Adoption Institute.

Barth, R. P., D. A. Gibbs, et al. 2001. "Assessing the Field of Post-Adoption Service: Family Needs, Program Models, and Evaluation Issues—Literature Review." University of North Carolina School of Social Work, Jordan Institute for Families, and Research Triangle Institute, Chapel Hill and Research Triangle Park.

Bartholet, E. 1993. "International Adoption: Current Status and Future Prospects." *The Future of Children* 3(1): 89–103.

———. 1999. *Nobody's Children: Abuse, Neglect, Foster Drift, and the Adoption Alternative*. Boston: Beacon Press.

Benson, P. L., A. Sharma, et al. 1994. "Growing Up Adopted: A Portrait of Adolescents and Their Families." Search Insitute, Minneapolis.

Berry, M. 1991. "The Practice of Open Adoption: Findings from a Study of 1,306 Adoptive Families." *Children and Youth Services Review* 13:379–95.

———. 1993. "Risks and Benefits of Open Adoption." *The Future of Children* 3(1): 125–38.

Bouchier, P., L. Lambert, et al. 1991. "Parting with a Child for Adoption." British Agencies for Adoption and Fostering, London.

Bourguignon, J. P., and K. W. Watson. 1987. *After Adoption: A Manual for Professionals Working with Adoptive Families*. Springfield: Illinois Department of Children and Family Services.

Brace, C. L. 1872. *The Dangerous Classes of New York*. New York: Wynkoop and Hallenbeck.

Brodzinsky, D. M. 1984. "Psychological and Academic Adjustment in Adopted Children." *Journal of Consulting and Clinical Psychology* 52(4): 582–90.

Brooks, D., J. Allen, et al. 2002. "Adoption Services Use, Helpfulness, and Need: A Comparison of Public and Private Agency and Independent Adoptive Families." *Children and Youth Service Review* 24(4): 213–38.

Brooks, D., R. P. Barth, et al. 1999. "Adoption and Race: Implementing the Multiethnic Placement and the Interethnic Adoption Provisions." *Social Work* 44(2): 167–78.

Carp, E. W. 1998. *Family Matters: Secrecy and Disclosure in the History of Adoption*. Cambridge, Mass.: Harvard University Press.

Casey Family Services. 2002. *Strengthening Families and Communities: Post Adoption Services. A White Paper*. Shelton, Conn.: Casey Family Services.

Christian, C., R. G. McRoy, et al. 1997. "Grief Resolution of Birth Mothers in Confidential, Time-Limited Mediated, Ongoing Mediated, and Fully Disclosed Adoptions." *Adoption Quarterly* 2(3): 35–58.

Coyne, A., and M. E. Brown. 1986. "Relationship Between Foster Care and Adoption Units Serving Developmentally Disabled Children." *Child Welfare* 65(2): 189–98.

Davis, D. F. 1995. "Capitalizing on Adoption." *Adoption and Fostering* 19(2): 25–30.

Emlen, A., J. Lahti, et al. 1976. *Overcoming Barriers to Planning for Children in Foster Care.* Portland, Ore.: Regional Research Institute for Human Services.

Etter, J. 1993. "Levels of Cooperation and Satisfaction in 56 Open Adoptions." *Child Welfare* 72(3): 257–67.

Evan B. Donaldson Adoption Institute. 1997. "Benchmark Survey: Executive Summary." Evan B. Donaldson Adoption Institute. Available at http://www .adoptioninstitute.org.

———. 2000. "Adoption in the United States." Evan B. Donaldson Adoption Institute. Available at http://www.adoptioninstitute.org.

———. 2002a. "Foster Care Facts." Evan B. Donaldson Adoption Institute. Available at http://www.adoptioninstitute.org.

———. 2002b. "International Adoption Facts." Evan B. Donaldson Adoption Institute. Available at http://www.adoptioninstitute.org.

———. 2002c. Testimony of Cindy Friedmutter, Esq., on International Adoptions, Problems and Solutions, Before the House Committee on International Relations, May 22, 2002. Evan B. Donaldson Adoption Institute. Available at http://www.adoptioninstitute.org.

———. 2002d. "Overview of Adoption in the United States." Evan B. Donaldson Adoption Institute. Available at http://www.adoptioninstitute.org.

———. 2002e. "National Adoption Attitudes Survey: Research Report." Evan B. Donaldson Adoption Institute. Available at http://www.adoptioninstitute.org.

Falk, L. 1970. "A Comparative Study of Transracial and Inracial Adoptions." *Child Welfare* 49:82–88.

Fanshel, D. 1972. *Far From the Reservation.* Metuchen, N.J.: Scarecrow Press.

Festinger, T. 1986. *Necessary Risk: A Study of Adoptions and Disrupted Adoptive Placements.* New York: Child Welfare League of America.

Fiegelman, W., and A. Silverman. 1983. *Chosen Children: New Patterns of Adoptive Relationships.* New York: Praeger.

Finkelhor, D. 1984. *Child Sexual Abuse: New Theory and Research.* New York: Free Press.

Flaks, D. K. 1995. "Research Issues." In *Issues in Gay and Lesbian Adoption,* edited by A. Sullivan. Washington, D.C.: Child Welfare League of America.

Gershenson, C. P. 1984. "Community Response to Children Free for Adoption." Child Welfare Research Note No. 3. U.S. Children's Bureau, Administration on Children, Youth, and Families, Washington, D.C.

Glidden, I. M. 1991. "Adopted Children with Developmental Disabilities: Post-adoptive Family Functioning." *Children and Youth Service Review* 13:363–78.

Gritter, J. L. 1997. *The Spirit of Open Adoption.* Washington, D.C.: Child Welfare League of America.

Grotevant, H. D. 2000. "Openness in Adoption: Research with the Adoption Kinship Network. *Adoption Quarterly* 4(1): 45–65.

Grotevant, H. D., and R. G. McRoy. 1998. *Openness in Adoption: Exploring Family Connections.* Thousand Oaks, Calif.: Sage.

Grow, L., and D. Shapiro. 1972. *Black Children, White Parents: A Study of Transracial Adoption.* New York: Child Welfare League of America.

Groze, V., and J. A. Rosenthal. 1991. "Single Parents and Their Adopted Children: A Psychosocial Analysis." *Families in Society: The Journal of Contemporary Human Services* 9(2): 67–77.

Hargrave, V., J. Shireman, et al. 1975. *Where Love and Need Are One.* Chicago: Illinois Department of Children and Family Services.

Haugaard, J. J., A. Schustack, et al. 1998. "Searching for Birth Parents by Adult Adoptees." *Adoption Quarterly* 1(3): 77–83.

Hockey, A. 1980. "Evaluation of Adoption of the Intellectually Handicapped: A Retrospective Analysis of 137 Cases." *Journal of Mental Deficiency Research* 24(3): 187–200.

Horwitz, R., and H. Maruyama. 1995. "Legal Issues." In I*ssues in Gay and Lesbian Adoption,* edited by A. Sullivan. Washington, D.C.: Child Welfare League of America.

Howe, C., P. Sawbridge, et al. 1992. *Half a Million Women.* London: Penguin.

Kadushin, A. 1967. "Reversibility of Trauma: A Follow-up Study of Children Adopted When Older." *Social Work* 12(4): 22–33.

Kadushin, A., and J. Martin. 1988. *Child Welfare Services.* New York: Macmillan.

Kagan, R. M., and W. J. Reid. 1986. "Critical Factors in the Adoption of Emotionally Disturbed Youth." *Child Welfare* 65(1): 62–82.

Kallen, D. J., R. J. Griffore, et al. 1990. "Adolescent Mothers and Their Mothers View Adoption." *Family Relations* 39:311–16.

Kim, D. S. 1976. "Inter-country Adoptions." Ph.D. diss., School of Social Service Administration, University of Chicago.

Kirk, D. 1964. *Shared Fate.* Port Angeles, Wash.: Ben Simon Publications.

Kools, S. 1997. "Adolescent Identity Development in Foster Care." *Family Relations* 46:263–71.

Ladner, J. 1977. *Mixed Families.* New York: Doubleday.

MacCaskill, C. 1988. "'It's a Bonus': Families' Experiences of Adopting Children with Disabilities." *Adoption and Fostering* 12(2): 24–28.

Mallon, G. P. 1998. *We Don't Exactly Get the Welcome Wagon: The Experiences of Gay and Lesbian Adolescents in Child Welfare Systems.* New York: Columbia University Press.

Marindin, H. 1992. *Handbook for Single Adoptive Parents.* Chevy Chase, Md.: Committee for Single Adoptive Parents.

McCausland, C. L. 1976. *Children of Circumstance*. Chicago: Chicago Child Care Society.

McDermott, M. T. 1993. "Agency Versus Independent Adoption: The Case for Independent Adoption." *The Future of Children* 3(1): 146–52.

McKenzie, J. 1993. "Adoption of Children with Special Needs." *The Future of Children* 3(1): 62–76.

McRoy, R. G., and L. Zurcher. 1983. *Transracial and Inracial Adoptees: The Adolescent Years*. Springfield, Ill.: Charles C. Thomas.

Meezan, W., S. Katz, et al. 1978. *Adoptions Without Agencies: A Study of Independent Adoptions*. New York: Child Welfare League of America.

Meezan, W., and J. Shireman. 1985. *Care and Commitment*. Albany: State University of New York Press.

National Adoption Information Clearinghouse. 2000. "Persons Seeking to Adopt." National Adoption Information Clearinghouse, Washington, D.C. Available at http://www.calib.com/naic.

———. 2002. "Adoption: Statistics." National Adoption Information Clearinghouse, Washington, D.C. Available at http://www.calib.com/naic.

National Committee for Adoption. 1989. *Adoption Factbook: United States Data Issues, Regulations, and Resources*. Washington, D.C.: National Committee for Adoption.

Nelson, K. A. 1985. *On the Frontier of Adoption: A Study of Special-Needs Adoptive Families*. New York: Child Welfare League of America.

O'Malley, F. 1993. "Short-Term Residential Treatment of Disturbed Adolescents in a Continuum of Care." *Children and Youth Services Review* 15(3): 245–60.

Partridge, S., H. Hornby, et al. 1986. *Legacies of Loss, Visions of Gain: An Inside Look at Adoption Disruption*. Portland: University of Southern Maine, Human Services Development Institute.

Pecora, P. J., J. L. Whittaker, et al. 1992. *The Child Welfare Challenge: Policy, Practice, and Research*. New York: Aldine de Gruyter.

Pine, B. A. 1991. "Special Families for Special Children: The Adoption of Children with Developmental Disabilities." Ph.D. diss., Florence Heller School for Advanced Studies in Social Welfare, Brandeis University, Waltham, Mass.

Reid, W. J., R. M. Kagan, et al. 1987. "Adoptions of Older Institutionalized Youth." *Social Casework* 68:140–49.

Reitz, M., and K. Watson. 1992. *Adoption and the Family System*. New York: Guilford.

Rosenthal, J. A. 1993. "Outcomes of Adoption of Children with Special Needs." *The Future of Children* 3(1): 77–88.

Rosenthal, J. A., and V. K. Groze. 1992. *Special-Needs Adoption: A Study of Intact Families*. New York: Praeger.

Sachdev, P. 1992. "Adoption Reunion and After: A Study of the Search Process and Experience of Adoptees." *Child Welfare* 71(1): 53–68.

Sharma, A. 1997. "Growing Up Adopted: The Search Institute Study, Updated." Search Institute, Minneapolis.

Shireman, J. 1969. *Subsidized Adoption: A Study of Use and Need in Four Agencies.* Chicago: Child Care Association of Illinois.

———. 1988. "Growing Up Adopted: An Examination of Major Issues." Regional Research Institute, Portland State University, Portland, Ore.

———. 1995. "Adoptions by Single Parents." In *Single Parent Families: Diversity, Myths and Realities,* edited by S. M. H. Hanson, M. L. Heims, D. J. Julian, and M. B. Sussman. Binghamton, N.Y.: Haworth Press.

Shireman, J., and P. Johnson. 1975. "Adoption—Three Alternatives: A Comparative Study of Three Forms of Adoptive Placement." Chicago Child Care Society, Chicago.

———. 1985. "Single Parent Adoptions: A Longitudinal Study." *Children and Youth Services Review* 7(4): 321–24.

———. 1986. "A Longitudinal Study of Black Adoptions: Single Parent, Transracial, and Traditional." *Social Work* 31:172–76.

Shireman, J., P. Johnson, et al. 1987. "Transracial Adoption and the Development of Identity at Age Eight." *Child Welfare* 66:45–55.

Siegel, D. 1990. *Open Adoption of Infants: Adoptive Parents Perceptions of Advantages and Disadvantages.* Philadelphia: National Conference of the National Association of Social Workers.

Simon, R., and H. Altstein. 1977. *Transracial Adoption.* New York: John Wiley.

———. 1981. *Transracial Adoption: A Follow-Up.* Lexington, Mass.: Lexington Books.

———. 1987. *Transracial Adoptees and Their Families: A Study of Identity and Commitment.* New York: Praeger.

———. 1992. *Adoption, Race, and Identity: From Infancy Through Adolescence.* New York: Praeger.

Sokoloff, B. Z. 1993. "Antecedents of American Adoption." *The Future of Children* 3(1):17–25.

Sorosky, A., A. Baran, et al. 1978. *The Adoption Triangle.* San Antonio, Tex.: Corona.

Stein, L., and J. Hoopes. 1985. *Identity Formation in the Adopted Adolescent.* New York: Child Welfare League of America.

Sullivan, A. 1995. "Policy Issues." In *Issues in Gay and Lesbian Adoption,* edited by A. Sullivan. Washington, D.C.: Child Welfare League of America.

Tilbor, K. 1988. "Educational and Social Support Groups and Events." In *Working with Older Adoptees: A Sourcebook of Innovative Models,* edited by L. Coleman, K. Tilbor, H. Hornby, and C. Boggis. Portland: University of Southern Maine.

Toth, J. 1997. *Orphans of the Living: Stories of America's Children in Foster Care.* New York: Simon and Schuster.

Triseliotis, J. 1973. *In Search of Origins*. London: Routledge and Kegan Paul.

Triseliotis, J., and J. Russell. 1984. Hard to Place: The Outcome of Adoption and Residential Care. London: Gower.

Triseliotis, J., J. Shireman, et al. 1997. *Adoption: Theory, Policy and Practice*. London: Cassell.

Unger, C., G. Dwarshusis, et al. 1977. *Chaos, Madness, and Unpredictability: Placing the Child with Ears Like Uncle Harry's*. Chelsea, Mich.: Spaulding for Children.

U.S. Department of Health and Human Services. 1997. "Adoption 2002: A Response to the Presidential Executive Memorandum on Adoption." U.S. Department of Health and Human Services, Washington, D.C.

U.S. Department of Health and Human Services, Children's Bureau. 1999. AFCARS Report No. 1. Available at http://www.acf.hhs.gov/programs/cb/publications/afcars/report1.htm.

Vroegh, K. 1997. "Transracial Adoption: How It Is Seventeen Years Later." *American Journal of Orthopsychiatry* 67(4): 568–75.

Watson, K. W., and J. Strom. 1986. "Report of the Child Welfare League of America National Adoption Task Force." Child Welfare League of America, Washington, D.C.

Wells, S. 1993. "What do Birth Mothers Want?" *Adoption and Fostering* 17(4): 22–32.

Witmer, H., E. Herzog, et al. 1963. *Independent Adoptions*. New York: Russell Sage Foundation.

Witmer, R. T. 1963. "The Purpose of American Adoption Laws." In *Independent Adoptions: A Follow-up Study*, edited by H. Witmer, E. Herzog, E. Weinstein, and M. Sullivan. New York: Russell Sage Foundation.

Zastrow, C. 1977. *Outcome of Black Children/White Parents Adoptions*. San Francisco: R and E Research Associates.

CHAPTER 9
✦

At-Risk Youth

with Charles Shireman

It is not enough just to open the gates of opportunity. All our children
must have the ability to walk through the gates.

LYNDON B. JOHNSON

The child welfare system historically worked with young people until
they were established as adults. As a consequence of narrowing its
mission, that is, focusing on protective services for vulnerable young
children, public child welfare now offers relatively little in the way of
services to adolescents, unless they have been taken into care in earlier
years. However, adolescents are also at a vulnerable point in their lives,
at a point of transition from the relatively protected status of childhood
toward the independence of adult life. This is a difficult transition. It is a
time when decisions can have lifelong consequences.

Part of this transition is experimenting with independence, which entails
risk taking. Most adolescents, of course, manage their growing independence and the risks involved in such a way that they need no support and
guidance other than that provided by their families and communities.
Some adolescents, however, engage in such a degree of risky behavior that
they are themselves at risk of what Schorr (1988) calls "rotten outcomes."
The decisions they make, the risks they assume, may commit them to
adult lives of poverty, substance abuse, ill health, or involvement in the
criminal justice system. Services to this population have been to a great
degree relegated to assorted private community services, and, when the
law is broken, to the juvenile justice system.

The public has been relatively acquiescent about the shifting of responsibility for troubled adolescents away from the child welfare system. The

adolescent population is not, after all, an easy population to serve, nor attractive to market as a group worthy of services. There are no heart-warming and photogenic endings, as there is when a toddler goes home, or a first-grader is adopted. Most often, youths who pose problems for society are attempting to find their own way, sometimes making themselves as different as possible from the community at large, and, by their very difference, provoking anxiety. And it is perhaps this anxiety that has kept in place what few services there are.

What defines a youth as being at risk? Identifying this trait is challenging because being "at risk" is a process of escalating conditions and actions. Burt, Resnick, et al. (1992) provide a conceptual framework for understanding risk, with the idea that if risk itself can be identified, intervention might be provided to avert negative outcomes. "Risk antecedents" are defined by these researchers as environmental factors that impact the development of individuals and place them at greater vulnerability for future problems with their families, their communities, or their schools; they suggest that critical risk antecedents for younger adolescents are poverty, neighborhood environment, and family environment. "Risk markers" are visible behaviors that may be found in public records, such as involvement with child protective services and poor school performance. The authors found risk antecedents and risk markers to be consistently related to all the defined problem behaviors of adolescence: early sexual behavior; truancy; running away from home; use of tobacco, alcohol, or other drugs; and associating with delinquent peers—all activities that lead to negative outcomes in later societal functioning.

Being disconnected from major institutions of society is emerging as a primary indicator of the potential for behavior that may have negative consequences. Besharov and Gardiner (1998) define disconnectedness, which they view as a significant indicator, as "not being enrolled in school, not gainfully employed, not in the military, and not married to someone who was 'connected' in one of these ways" (p. 799). *The Kids Count Data Book: 2000* (Annie E. Casey Foundation 2000) explores the same issue, focusing on the disconnectedness of the nation's poorest children and using indicators such as access to computers or having a telephone at home. The work notes both family and community isolation from opportunities, networks, and services that might help them prosper.

The issue can also be framed this way: protective factors that serve to connect youth to family and to larger society have been identified, and research has begun to demonstrate that the more these factors are in place, the less likely it is that youth will engage in negative behavior (Institute for Youth Development 2000). The Forty Assets, developed by the Search Institute (1997), consist of external assets for youth such as family and community support and guidance, and internal assets such as commitment to learning, positive values, and social competencies. They are commonly referred to in educational programs and programs that work with troubled adolescents. The positive youth development movement, which builds on strengths in the way espoused also by family support services, moves in the direction of a promising practice (Batavick 1997). These approaches suggest that the targeting of communities and families in order to create the conditions for youth "connectedness" may be promising ideas.

What proportion of adolescents engage in behavior that may lead to unfortunate outcomes? Burt, Resnick, et al. (1992) suggest that as many as half of today's youth run a moderate to high risk of adopting problem behaviors. A recent Urban Institute study concluded that the majority of adolescent problem behaviors pertain to a minority of youth who, in turn, engage in multiple risks (Limberg, Bogess, et al. 2000).

Some young people are more vulnerable to risky behavior than are others. Burt, Resnick, et al. (1992) identify disadvantaged homes and communities as risk antecedents. Not only does poverty increase the chances that youth will not be connected to the opportunities of mainstream society; violence in these communities generates fear and resultant aggressive behavior, and the adolescents there are often surrounded by peers and role models who have themselves engaged in negative behavior. Most vulnerable are children without families: those who have grown up in nonrelative out-of-home care, those who have found it impossible to continue to live with their families and have run away, or those who have been turned out of their homes. Sexual minority and ethnic/racial minority youth are disproportionately represented in many risk categories, including homeless youth (Stephens 1997).

This chapter focuses on the potential for risk behavior that seems most directly connected with the responsibilities and knowledge of child welfare: young people without families. It explores the ability of programs to smooth the transition to adult life. The chapter then examines the risk behavior of all youth that has the potential for lifelong negative consequences, with the intent of giving the reader a sense of the vulnerability of all adolescents and leading to a few ideas about ways to strengthen the connectedness of young people to their communities. Finally the chapter discusses the impact of the juvenile justice system on those youths whose behavior leads them into criminal activity.

The reader must recognize that each of this chapter's topics could easily be expanded and has been expanded by others, into articles, research reports, and books. Nonetheless, it seems important to include at least an overview of the difficulties of these individuals, for they are part of our country's child population and, as such, part of the charge of child welfare.

Youth Without Homes

Independent Living Programs

When adolescents reach eighteen years of age, they are generally no longer eligible for foster care. Too many of these young people are left without resources. They are expected to join the adult world as productive citizens but are given little help in attaining that status. Some have been fortunate enough to spend their growing years in a stable foster home that will continue to provide support, but these cases are the minority. Independent living programs provide an array of services to these young people, including assistance with continuing education and finding employment; subsidies for housing; instruction in basic skills such as money management, housekeeping, and nutrition; and supervised practice living arrangements. All these programs are designed to give these individuals the skills they need to become productive members of the adult world.

The need Studies in the 1990s demonstrated the need for increased help for these young people. They found that 46 percent of former foster children dropped out of school after "aging out" of foster care. Between one-third and one-half were unemployed. Affordable housing was also shown to be a problem for former foster youth; 25 percent had been homeless at least once. Also, 32 percent had been on public assistance at some time, and 27 percent of the males and 10 percent of the females had been incarcerated (Courtney and Piliavan 1995; Edmund S. Muskie School of Public Service and National Child Welfare Resource Center for Organizational Improvement 1998; Westat 1991; U.S. General Accounting Office 1999). Obviously, these youths are at risk of making decisions that lead to negative outcomes.

Of the approximately 25,000 youths who "age out" of foster care annually, about one-fifth are in independent living programs. About a quarter return to their biological families for whatever support the families can give. The remainder manage on their own. Given these facts, interest developed in augmenting the capacity of programs specifically designed to help youth make the transition from foster care to independent living.

The federal role In 1985 Congress created a pilot program to help youth make the transition from foster care to independent living. Funding rose to $70 million and became permanent in 1993. It was divided into two categories: $45 million was available to states without any matching funds, and $25 million was available to states with a dollar-to-dollar state match. Funding remained at that level, though the number of youths leaving foster care increased. Youths who were sixteen and over, and for whom foster care payments were being made, were eligible for independent living programs. Thus, California and New York, the states with the largest populations of children in foster care, spent the most for independent living programs (U.S. Department of Health and Human Services [hereafter, U.S. HHS] 1999). Other federal programs provide some assistance to this population, such as Transitional Living Services for Homeless Youth and Job Corps, which enrolls economically disadvantaged youths in need of education or training. Independent living programs are, however, the only federal program targeted at helping adolescents make the transition from foster care to adult living.

Funding for independent living programs expanded once again in December 1999, when President Clinton signed into law a bill that doubled the Title IV-E Independent Living Program from $70 million to $140 million and allowed states to extend Medicaid coverage for young people until they are age twenty-one. The outcome measures states are required to implement include education, employment status, avoidance of dependency on public welfare, homelessness, nonmarital childbirth, high-risk behaviors, and incarceration.

The process that resulted in the expansion of independent living programs, as reported by Boyle (2000), involved advocacy by youths themselves; professional organizations prepared to provide data, share meaningful experiences, arrange visits, and present ideas to senators and representatives and their staffs; and a series of circumstances that brought independent living programs into the national spotlight. Early in the process, in 1997, a group of young people who had been in foster care had the opportunity to talk with Hillary Clinton as part of a recognition ceremony for passage of the Adoption and Safe Families Act.

"They told me about being forced out of their homes on their birth-days, about staying in a cold dorm room alone during the holidays because they had nowhere to go, about getting sick and having no insurance to get any medical care." Particularly striking to her was a young woman who said, "You know, it's almost Thanksgiving and I have no one to call and ask how to bake a turkey."

(BOYLE 2000:52)

It was a bill that appealed to almost everyone. Democrats saw it as pro-moting positive youth development, and Republicans saw it as promoting self-sufficiency. The major opponents of the bill were, interestingly, those who were lobbying for increased resources for adoption under the new provisions of ASFA and feared that expansion of independent living pro-grams would be viewed as an indicator that older adolescents should not be adopted.

The programs Independent living programs have served an increasing number of youths in the ten years of their existence; although with funds remaining fixed, the amount spent on each youth has declined. Surpris-ingly, half the youths served had been in foster care less than two years. Not surprisingly, about one-quarter of those served were described as hav-ing special needs, and 9 percent either were parents or were pregnant (U.S. HHS 1999).

Most independent living programs offer education and employment assistance, providing tutoring and remedial work to help participants graduate from high school or receive a GED; many of the programs offer aid for college or vocational training. Difficulties exist in developing appropriate employment opportunities to teach skills and appropriate work habits, and funding limits the ability to provide needed vocational training. Almost all programs offer training in daily living skills and report that these skills are best developed through experiential learning. The programs also report the benefits of teaching interpersonal skills such as conflict management, communication, and decision making. There is a demand for transitional living arrangements, supported by services to help youths deal with issues that arise, but transitional living facilities are limited, serving only a fraction of the young people who could benefit from them (U.S. General Accounting Office 1999).

Cook (1988) conceptualizes the learning process that occurs as adoles-cents make the transition from dependence to autonomous and independent living. Programs that support each phase of learning are available to some

extent through public community service agencies. Not all of these services are aware of the learning process, and often phases are skipped or
opportunities for practice are denied. Cook recommends assessing each
youth individually as well as assessing programs for matches between
need and opportunity. She notes that youth who need services may (1)
have obtained some basic skills and only require minimal assistance in
making the transition to independence; (2) have had inconsistencies in
their lives that impaired their opportunities for informal learning, or
have behavioral or emotional problems that interfere with their ability to
learn informally in family-style environments; or (3) have multiple handicaps and need pervasive support. As always, the services should be tailored
to the individual learner's situation.

Outcomes Independent living programs meet an obvious need, make
sense, and are popular. However, the evidence of their success is mixed.
A General Accounting Office review located six studies at the state or local
level that, albeit with very small numbers of subjects, evaluate independent
living programs and link participation with positive outcomes in education
and housing. Many participants, however, felt that the programs did not
fully meet their needs (U.S. General Accounting Office 1999).

In the Department of Health and Human Services review of the programs, tracking data were insufficient to evaluate outcomes, though the
authors note that "several supplementary state ILP outcome studies suggest
that after exiting care, many youth had difficulties completing educational
goals, maintaining jobs, achieving financial self-sufficiency, paying for
housing expenses, and accessing health care" (U.S. HHS 1999:v). However,
the authors also note that states have placed emphasis on serving youths
with special needs.

Another approach to evaluation, which provides illustrative program
detail, is covered in one of the small state studies mentioned above.
Twenty-five former consumers of independent living services were surveyed in focus groups to describe aging out of foster care, to evaluate the
usefulness of the programs they participated in, and to offer suggestions
for improving the effectiveness of independent living services in general
(McMillen, Rideout, et al. 1997). All the youths surveyed had participated
in at least six months of weekly independent living skill classes in various
locations within the state of Missouri. Other services that were provided
varied; they included subsidized independent living in apartments or
dormitories, conferences and seminars on specific topics, wilderness rope
courses, youth advisory boards, aftercare groups, and paid opportunities to

teach independent living skills to other youths in the process of emancipating from foster care.

The most consistently reported benefit of independent living services in general was the opportunity to socialize with other youths transitioning out of foster care. The youths reported that being in care was difficult and that services lessened the stigmatization and isolation of being in care. The youths valued instruction on financial matters such as budgeting, using checking accounts, comparison-shopping tactics, money-saving strategies, and methods of building credit. In general, they found the skill classes helpful, particularly classes on apartment-hunting, changing tires, birth control, cooking, building healthy relationships, and finding community resources. Stipends to support independent living efforts were considered helpful, but the youths had reservations about the stipulations for receiving this service. Some felt that the requirements were excessive and that social service professionals were intrusive.

Foster parents in this study were reported as providing the most assistance in the transition to independent living. They were able to provide both material and emotional resources to the youths, and when the family was actively involved in this role the youths reported the transition as being much smoother. The least helpful individuals, as reported by the youths, were the child welfare caseworkers assigned to assist in the transition.

These results support the commonsense notion that what is beneficial to most youth as they leave home is also essential for youth transitioning out of foster care. Whether foster, biological, or otherwise, a supportive and loving family available to model the skills and values necessary for successful independent living is a valuable resource. Having regular peer interaction with others who share some common experiences will provide a sense of community and identity that decreases the isolation and loneliness that can occur when living independently. Having general knowledge of the daily skills required for independence along with both a financial and emotional safety net, for use when difficulties emerge, are of course necessities in transitioning to independent living.

In some cases, it would be helpful for program builders to rethink their expectations for independent living programs. Youths in these programs have experienced family problems of sufficient intensity that they could not remain at home. They have lived through the instability of foster care. At least a quarter have special needs, including disabilities, substance abuse, and involvement in the juvenile justice system. Nine percent are, or expect to be, parents in the near future. In general, this group of adolescents has had few consistent opportunities for learning the skills of independent living. Certainly, programs should have both intensity and duration to support learning. However, one must ask what impact is reasonable to expect from a single program, however positive, in the context of life experiences. It may be that the modest gains and trends that the studies report constitute outcomes as good as can be expected. And, of course, it is important that these programs not become a substitute for the quest to find stable homes for foster children, so they do have families to help them progress toward adult life.

Runaway and Homeless Youth

Legally, youths without families are the responsibility of the state. Sometimes they are considered juvenile delinquents; more often they are remanded to the responsibility of the child welfare system or to a network of private agencies that contract to serve this age group. The most common service response is to attempt to reunite the runaway with his or her family. If it is not possible for a youth to go home, foster care or group home care may be tried, but the youth may also leave these settings. If an individual is not legally emancipated, parental permission may still be required for medical care.

Studies of homeless youth indicate that they represent all socioeconomic, racial, and ethnic groups and types of families. Homeless youth are at greater risk for health problems, including sexually transmitted diseases (STDs) and AIDS; substance abuse; mental health problems, including suicide attempts; illegal behaviors, including prostitution; and other forms of victimization (Shane 1989; Robertson 1992; Ringwalt, Greene, et al. 1998). Most have left home due to conflict with parents. Many have histories of physical or sexual abuse and have fled that situation; others have been ordered out of parental homes due to unacceptable behavior. A strikingly high proportion (20% to 35%) seem to have been in the foster care system (Rothman 1991). Estimates of the number of youths who run away range from 450,000 to as many as 2.8 million every year (Greene, Ringwalt, et al. 1997). A national probability sample estimates that in a given year 5 percent of adolescents spend at least one night away from home in a public place, in an abandoned building, outside, or in a stranger's home (Ringwalt, Greene, et al. 1998). However, the number of adolescents who are homeless for more than a few days is unknown.

There have been several attempts to clarify and classify the differences between being homeless, a runaway, or a street kid. The U.S. Department of Health and Human Services in 1983 differentiated between the three as follows:

> Runaways (are) youth away from home at least overnight without parent or caretaker permission; homeless (are) those with no parental, foster or institutional home, including pushouts (urged to leave) and throwaways (left home with parental knowledge or approval without an alternative place to stay); street kids (are) youth who believe they belong on the street and have become accustomed to fending for themselves.
>
> (ROBERTSON 1992:288)

In a survey of 640 youths in shelters and 600 youths on the street, it was documented that just under half of the two samples reported either being asked to leave by their parents or leaving with their parent's knowledge but without their concern (Greene, Ringwalt, et al. 1995).

A population at risk Powers, Eckenrode, et al. (1990) document several studies that indicate youth who have run away or are homeless have experienced an "alarming incidence of abuse and neglect" (p. 87). For example, within a sample of 223 adolescents receiving services from runaway/homeless youth programs in New York State (1986–87) who also reported having a history of maltreatment, 60 percent alleged physical abuse, 42 percent emotional abuse, 48 percent neglect, and 21 percent sexual abuse. The majority of the youths in the sample were female and between the ages of fifteen and sixteen. More than one-third were "push-outs." Those who reported being abused or neglected were more likely to have attempted suicide and more likely to be female.

Greene, Ringwalt, et al. (1995), working with a large, national sample, found that 45 percent of street youths and 31 percent of youths in shelters reported substance use by a family member in the thirty days before leaving home. The majority of the street and shelter sample reported that when family members used substances, they were more likely to neglect, abuse, ignore, or engage in conflict with the young persons. There was a strong connection between family substance use and youth substance use in the shelter sample. In both the street and shelter samples, youths from families with substance use were twice as likely to have attempted suicide. Family substance use was also associated with delinquency and weapon carrying once the youth was on the street.

The sample of this study contained not only street youths and youths in shelters but also a sample of 6,496 adolescents living with their families. Comparisons are informative. Although estimates of youth in poverty range from 22 percent to 25 percent, about 40 percent of youth in shelters or on the street come from families that were on public assistance or received housing subsidies. Substance abuse is more prevalent among youth not living at home. Thirteen percent of males with runaway experience report having gotten a girl pregnant compared with 2 percent of males who had no runaway experience. One-half of the females in the street sample reported having been pregnant at least once, and one-tenth of both the street and shelter sample were pregnant at the time of interview (Greene, Ringwalt, et al. 1995).

A total of 58 percent of shelter youths and 71 percent of street youths reported having spent time in institutional settings (foster care, group home, psychiatric or mental hospital, juvenile detention, or jail). Twenty-six percent of the shelter sample and 32 percent of the street youths reported a suicide attempt. While on the street, young people are also at significant risk for being victimized or engaging in illegal or dangerous behaviors. Abuse of marijuana was six times more likely, and use of cocaine thirty-five times more likely, in youths with runaway experiences compared to those without. One-third of the street sample and one-sixth of the shelter sample reported having been robbed, assaulted, or both while on the streets. One-half of the shelter sample and two-thirds of the street sample reported that they carry a weapon; two-thirds of the shelter sample and four-fifths of the street sample admitted to having committed theft-related activity (Greene, Ringwalt, et al. 1995).

Service needs Youth who have acted out their rejection of success in mainstream culture, and of parental values, constitute one of the most difficult populations to serve. They are also one of the most vulnerable populations. They need safe housing, which means an adequate number of shelter beds to allow for flexibility in length of stay, as well as a continuum of living accommodations including residential housing and transitional housing. Trained staff members and case managers should assess the needs of each individual youth and have the capacity to provide an array of services. Necessary services include both individual and group counseling to attend to mental health needs, family therapy or other interventions to help if reconnecting with family is an option, and independent living programs to assist in moving into adult living in a way that will bring some stability, success, and rewards (Robertson 1992). However, these youths are not actively seeking to make their living patterns

more conventional. They are often suspicious of mainstream service providers, fearing that these providers will either attempt to send them back
to their families or back into the child welfare system.

Of the services available, homeless youth made the greatest use of
health services, although the hospital emergency room was often their
provider (Greene, Ringwalt, et al. 1995). The health risks these young
people face, and the percentage who are pregnant or parenting, make it
imperative that health clinics be readily available. This has been a service
that youth drop-in centers have used to attract youth.

Shelters, transitional living programs, and daytime drop-in centers are
all programs that provide central services from which to meet the needs
of these young people. Outreach is an important part of shelter programming. Greene, Ringwalt, et al. (1995) found that 56 percent of youths
sampled while living on the street had never used a youth shelter. About
a third perceived them as dangerous and a third thought of them as too
restrictive. Almost two-thirds thought shelter programs could be helpful,
but they were wary. Barriers to the use of shelters need analysis; it is
probable that an emphasis on reuniting youths with their families and
relatively short time limits for stays are disincentives to youths who have
run from bad family situations. The rules that a shelter must enforce to
maintain a semblance of order may seem restrictive to youths who have
come from neglectful and chaotic homes.

Transitional living programs and easy access to substance abuse treatment emerge as important in these studies, as they did in the studies of
independent living programs. Access to ways of finishing secondary education, probably in a nontraditional manner, gives these youths more
opportunities. Links to employment options are necessary as youth become
ready to begin the process of leaving the streets and assuming more conventional lifestyles. Homeless youth and youth in independent living programs share, after all, many background experiences and current needs.
The expansion of federal funding for independent living programs, so
that they could be offered to youth who do not qualify for IV-E foster
care funding, would make the resources available to more youth. The
current state of funding is, of course, another example of the way that
categorical funding limits the capacity of developed services to meet the
needs of a larger group.

This discussion has focused on the needs of youth in the framework of
child welfare services. This kind of discussion is most productive within
the framework of building on the strengths of youth, as articulated in the

positive youth development model (Batavick 1997). Two fundamental dimensions of services for all at-risk young people are coordination of services for those already engaged in problem behaviors and direction of funds toward community programs to target risk antecedents. After briefly exploring other dimensions of adolescent risk, we will return to these ideas.

Youth with Special Needs

Sexual Minority Youth

Quite recently, concern has arisen about the additional risk to which gay and lesbian youth may be exposed. In convenience samples (drop-in centers, health clinics, gay-identified youth shelters, etc.), gay, lesbian, and bisexual youths have been documented to have higher rates of suicide, up to three times the rate of heterosexual youths (Lock and Steiner 1999); greater incidence of health problems; and higher rates of substance abuse, homelessness, family discord, sexual risk-taking behaviors, and dropping out of school (Proctor and Groze 1994; Lock and Steiner 1999).

In their self-report study of 1,769 high school students in an upper-middle-class school district, Lock and Steiner (1999) found that 6 percent reported being gay, lesbian, or bisexual, and 13 percent reported being unsure of their sexual orientation. Some of the stresses identified as contributing to the increased physical, emotional, and behavioral problems associated with sexual minority youth are (1) managing social intolerance, (2) physical injury experienced as a result of that intolerance, and (3) self-identification with negative opinions of homosexuality (Lock and Steiner 1999:298). For youth whose families remain supportive, these stresses are easier to manage than they are for youth whose families abandon them.

Gay and lesbian youth have recently documented for us their experiences in the child welfare system (Mallon 1998). A sample of fifty-four self-identified gay and lesbian youths, living in three cities, were interviewed. Their stories are those of verbal and physical harassment, in their own homes (from which they were often ejected), in foster homes, in group homes, and in the community. They searched for a "good fit," and "when they found a responsive environment, they suspended the search and got on with their lives. Conversely, when and if they found themselves to be negotiating a life with a stress-filled, unnurturing, and hostile environment, they either tried to adapt to that inhospitable environment or moved on to the next level" (Mallon 1998:119). Many had spent time on the streets as they searched.

The policy recommendations from this study are not those of more services or greater access to services but those of changed services. "A system designed to serve gay and lesbian youth must have . . . a historical and social perspective on sexual orientation as well as on race and ethnicity. The gay or lesbian young person must be the central focus of the system rather than the incidental or accidental recipient of services designed and operated for other people" (Mallon 1998:120). The environment must affirm the gay or lesbian identity and provide protection. This, the author points out, means recognizing the presence of gay and lesbian youth, listening to their ideas, and reeducating society to eradicate myths about gay and lesbian identity. It means recognizing the heterosexual orientation of existing child welfare organizations, bureaucracies, and staffs and creating separate programs designed around the needs of gay and lesbian youth.

Youth of Color

The evidence of racism in the child welfare system has been presented throughout this book. The disproportionate numbers of African American youths in foster care, and the relatively low rate of adoption for African American children, suggests that a disproportionate number of those aging out of foster care without the support of families are African American. Thirty-eight percent of youths served in independent living programs are African American (U.S. HHS 1999). This is a somewhat smaller percentage than one might expect.

Communities in which African American young people grow up can be poor and violent. Forty percent of homeless youths are from homes that are poor enough to receive public assistance or publicly assisted housing, and families of color are disproportionately represented among the poor. Although homicide rates declined between 1993 and 1997, homicide remains a leading cause of death for young people. Juvenile victims between twelve and seventeen in 1997 were more likely to be male (81%) and African American (70%) (*Juvenile Justice Bulletin* 2000:3). Most victims of juvenile violence are other juveniles, including children uninvolved in the underlying conflict (Stephens 1997).

Data from the juvenile justice system (in the last section of this chapter) show the disproportionate number of youths of color in this system. Yet, despite these concerns, there is little literature about the experiences of young persons of color within the child welfare system. Documentation of these experiences exists, hidden in studies indexed under other topics. For example, all seventeen of the adolescents in Kools's (1997) qualitative study of identity development belonged to a minority group. Her findings of stigmatized self-identity (as a foster child), low self-esteem, social isolation, and lack of family connections paint a disturbing picture of the experience of these adolescents in group care. In speaking of the future, the youths emphasized what they could not do, not opportunities. Kools attributes this to foster care status, but it is quite possible that these negative findings stem from the interaction of minority status and foster care status.

It is beyond the scope of this book to attempt to explore the detailed experiences of adolescents of color, the extent to which racism puts them at additional risk, and the protective strategies they adopt. To explore this, the reader is referred to the vast literature on racism in the United States. However, the needs of youth of color are integral to an extensive examination of services for at-risk youth. The ideas concerning unique services, centered in knowledge of the history and experiences of particular peoples, which were put forth in the discussion of services to gay and lesbian youth, are worth applying to an evaluation of this group. It is also interesting to take these ideas a step further and recognize the success that African American, Hispanic, Asian, and Native American child welfare organizations have had working with their own people. Such organizations affirm the history and unique needs of a vulnerable people. Within this framework, services are designed to address special concerns. The public policy question for child welfare is whether the development of such unique organizations should be nurtured, whether this competence should be or can be incorporated into all child welfare services, or whether both approaches are possible.

If we take the analysis of risk and the prediction of later difficulties seriously, as Burt, Resnick, et al. (1992) have proposed, we cannot help but realize that youngsters who grow up in communities beset by poverty, violence, and lack of opportunity are at risk. If we believe in prevention, targeting these communities for intensive intervention is a long-overdue initiative.

All Youth: At Risk

Although youth without families, youth who perceive themselves as different, and disadvantaged youth are at risk, all youth take more chances during adolescence. The remainder of this chapter will briefly examine behavior that stems from the usual developmental processes and activities of youth and that, if poor choices are made, puts youth at risk.

Sexual Behavior

The sexual behavior issues of great concern facing teenagers today are the consequences of early sexual activity and of "unsafe," or unprotected, sexual activity resulting in STDs or unplanned teenage pregnancy.

Early sexual activity Early sexual activity is apparently prevalent among our youth. Patterns of sexual activity vary according to community and class standards, yet certain consequences seem inevitable. Smith (1997) collected data from a longitudinal study of more than eight hundred urban youths of color in relation to early sexual behavior. She found that adolescents who had sex at an earlier age were more likely to practice unsafe sex and to have more than one partner. Smith found that 54 percent of the girls who had intercourse at age fifteen or younger had a child during the four-year study. For girls, having two biological parents in the home was statistically related to delaying sexual activity. Substance abuse, low educational goals, and depression were significant correlates of early sexual activity.

Boys who had sex at a younger age were less likely to report using condoms and reported having multiple sexual partners. Also, boys who became sexually active at earlier ages were more likely to report impregnating a girl and were more likely to be fathers than boys who became sexually active later. The strongest predictors relating to boys' early sexual activity were maltreatment as a child and substance use (Smith 1997).

Teenage pregnancy One in ten teenage females becomes pregnant every year. Out of four teenage mothers, one will have a second child within a year of her first child's birth. The majority of teenage mothers are single parents and receive no financial support from the father. Only two out of ten teenage mothers finish high school (Stephens 1997). As noted in chapter 1, young families headed by single mothers are the group with the highest rate of poverty.

Teen parents are the focus of many services. Abuse and neglect prevention programs often target them, teaching and supporting parenting skills. Welfare reform targets them, providing disincentives to early parenting and offering child care while the parent becomes self-supporting. Many school health curriculums and other community programs emphasize the risks of early parenting and the rewards of waiting. Birthrates for teen mothers are falling; the national rate dropped by 14 percent between 1990 and 1997 (Annie E. Casey Foundation 2000:24). It is not clear whether this improvement is in response to these programs or is simply a change in teen culture.

Sexually Transmitted Diseases and AIDS *Newsweek* reports that one in four sexually experienced teens acquires an STD every year, equivalent to nearly 3 million teens each year (*Newsweek* 2000). Adolescents account for more than 10 percent of reported primary and secondary syphilis cases. Teenagers have higher rates of gonorrhea than sexually active women and men between the ages of twenty and forty-four. Almost one-fifth of all reported AIDS cases are young people between the ages of thirteen and twenty-nine. Although STDs are more preventable than most infectious diseases and exposure can be greatly reduced by condom use and by having fewer partners, sexually active adolescents may heighten their risk by using drugs and alcohol. Furthermore, many teenagers are unaware of having contracted an STD and may continue to infect others before receiving treatment.

Buzi, Wineman, et al. (1998) report ethnic differences in STD rates among female adolescents who received care from two family-planning clinics in Houston, Texas. In their study of 205 teenage girls, they found African American teens to have a higher rate of past STDs than white or Hispanic teens; Hispanic teens were least likely to be represented. The authors call for STD prevention and treatment programs to specifically address cultural, ethnic, and gender issues that may place minority females as greater risk.

Policy and programmatic issues Just as the shelter is an accessible site in encouraging homeless adolescents to use services, the school is an accessible site for those in school. Policy makers, health care professionals, educators, active community members, and social service practitioners have participated in the movement toward utilizing the school site as an accessible setting for preventive health care service delivery. Components of a comprehensive school health program include not only health services but also psychological services and health education, all of which can work toward preventing the behaviors that place teens at risk (Koprowitz 1999).

Although early sexual activity, unplanned pregnancies, and STDs have been recognized as interfering with a youth's ability to succeed academically, there remains controversy about the extent to which public institutions, such as schools, should become involved. Issues that in particular trigger debate among parents and other community members are birth control, STDs, and homosexuality. Many individuals feel strongly that the school is not an appropriate place to discuss sexual activity and that parents have a responsibility and the right to educate their children about sexuality in accordance with the family's value system. Others hold the strong belief that society has a vested interest in preventing early pregnancy and sexually transmitted diseases and therefore must ensure that education about such health concerns extends beyond the family. Controversies such as these can interfere, sometimes terminally, with efforts to educate or to provide student-requested health treatment for adolescents.

Another strategy for discouraging early and risky sexual behavior has been to look at young persons who are not engaging in such behaviors and to find out what factors contribute to their success in avoiding risk. These factors can be considered when programs are developed. For example, teenagers who are goal-oriented have demonstrated less risky sexual behavior. A program in West Virginia has attempted to increase goal setting, as well as to improve communication skills and problem-solving abilities, among their adolescents as a means to combat risk factors (Koprowitz 1999).

Substance Abuse

Incidence and attitudes Bruner and Fishman (1998) reviewed the literature to identify selected trends among adolescents in substance use. They concluded that drug use among teenagers has risen since 1992. Although tobacco, alcohol, and marijuana remain the most widely abused substances, the use of drugs such as heroin, amphetamines, methamphetamines, and LSD has increased dramatically. In 1997, almost three times as many eighth-graders reported using marijuana in the past year (17.7%) as had reported doing so in 1991. Only 58.1 percent of twelfth-graders in 1997 felt that smoking marijuana regularly is harmful, down from 78.6 percent in 1991. A study of 650 adolescents and their perceived risk to self and others relating to a range of topics including drug/alcohol use and being in a car with someone under the influence of drugs or alcohol was conducted over a four-year time span. Disturbingly, as the age of students surveyed increased, they rated drinking alcohol, drinking five or more alcoholic beverages on a single occasion, and using marijuana as less risky (Smith and Rosenthal 1995). According to Bruner and Fishman (1998), approximately 76 percent of high school students say that drugs are stored, used, or sold on school grounds, and 85 percent of adolescents cite drugs as the most important issue they face.

Policy considerations There are many substance abuse treatment programs and many models of treatment. However, there are not enough programs to meet the demand, the efficacy of programs is limited, and relapse is part of eventual recovery (U.S. HHS 1999). Substance abuse can ruin young lives, incapacitating youth at a time of important decisions and major learning.

Prevention is, of course, the approach that can rescue these young lives. If the community can be convinced that there is a problem, community action is a promising approach. An example is the success that Mothers Against Drunk Driving has had in turning an action once condoned into a serious offense. Drug education programs through the schools may be having some effect. The University of Michigan's Institute for Social Research has, with an annual self-report survey, tracked illicit drug use among twelfth-graders since 1975; in 1991 eighth- and tenth-graders were added to the study. Drug usage increased through the 1990s until it leveled off in 1996. In 2001, usage of newer drugs (such as ecstasy and steroids) increased, while declines were found in the use of drugs that had been popular in earlier years. The overall percentages of teens who use any drug seem to be holding steady since 1996 (Johnston, O'Malley, et al. 2002).

Politics and economics can influence the problem's definition, however. The drugs that receive community attention are subject to the climate of the community. Although alcohol is widely regarded as the teenager's drug of choice, serves as a "gateway" to other drug use, and is the drug most associated with other risky behaviors (National Center on Addiction and Substance Abuse 1997), alcohol usually does not provoke as much community alarm as do the illegal drugs. Koprowitz (1999) describes a substance abuse prevention program that the American Medical Association attempted to implement in a community where many people were employed by the local brewery. The effort was unsuccessful because community members were unwilling to identify alcohol as an "abused substance."

Solutions for Problem Behaviors

The preceding section has taken a brief look at the problems and problem behaviors of adolescents most commonly targeted for intervention by the social services community.[1] Policy considerations pertaining to remediation of these difficulties have been briefly examined. This section draws together three threads that run through the intervention ideas.

The first is that services must be comprehensive and integrated so that they are readily available to adolescents in risk situations. This requires the development of procedures and structures that enable several service agencies to coordinate their responses in a helpful and holistic manner. Burt, Resnick, et al. (1992) identify the steps to integrating services, noting that the target population must be specified, goals must be clear, and a variety in breadth and depth of services must be offered in order to have comprehensive services. Beyond that, systems for delivery of services should be identified (several models have been developed), and there must be administrative agreements to share resources. Pooled funding sources that can be used flexibly provide true service integration. The authors note the need for effective use of program evaluations. All of these steps seem almost self-evident, and all are very difficult to implement, requiring the adoption of new modes of thinking and the willingness of staff members at all levels to think beyond traditional agency boundaries. In my experience, shared resources and pooled funding are the most difficult steps to accomplish in practice.

A second requirement that emerges in all of the ideas for working with adolescent problems is that of individualized services, delivered within a framework of building on the strengths of the adolescent and tailored to meet the individual needs of the adolescent. Most important, they must be tailored to meet the needs of the adolescent as the adolescent perceives those needs and to build on the strengths of the adolescent as he or she is ready to use those strengths. Independence is a critical component of adolescence. If an adolescent is to stay with a service provider, the provider must be ready to work at the adolescent's pace. This is the prescription for working with any individual, of course. The problem arises when the risk to which an adolescent is exposing him or herself, or to which he or she is exposing another, is so great that intervention is necessary. At that point, the social worker will have to use all of the complex skills of the child protective service worker.

The third theme that emerges is the focus on community. Current research indicates that if risk antecedents could be modified, adolescent problem behaviors would be lessened. This speaks first, of course, to intervention in poor and violent communities, at many levels, to increase safety and to increase opportunity. It speaks to the provision of the family support services outlined in chapter 4. But examination of these adolescent problem behaviors also suggests that changes in community attitudes and community willingness to target problems, and to devote resources to solutions, can have a significant impact. Social work turned its back on the community as a target of intervention after the 1960s. It seems to be turning back.

Critical Issue: Juvenile Law Violations and Violators

For somewhat more than a century, debate has continued about whether the societal response to law violations by juveniles should reflect child welfare or criminal justice philosophy. For the greater part of the history of the United States (and of the industrialized Western world), the confrontation with the offender has rested on what is usually termed *classical criminology*. The offenders were seen as rational human beings, capable of making decisions and controlling their behavior. They were to be held responsible for decisions. The state's major function was to detect violations and to administer punishment to wrongdoers. Almost universal opinion held that both the offender and citizens generally would thus be impressed by the painful consequences of offending and would be deterred from it. Persistent and dangerous offenders would be incapacitated and prevented from further offenses by imprisonment, watchful probation or parole supervision, or other means, including capital punishment.

For much of our history, only children under the age of seven were presumed incapable of criminal intent. Those seven or older could be tried in criminal court and, if found guilty, could be sentenced to prison or even to death. Beginning with the nineteenth century, however, a new philosophy began to emerge. The new perspective came to be termed *positive criminology*. It was based on a belief that human behavior, whether it violated the law or not, was the natural consequence of antecedent causes, many external to the individual. These causes could be determined and understood, which made intervention in causal trains possible. Such intervention was seen as a societal imperative, particularly with respect to juveniles.

Thus the "era of the rehabilitative ideal" emerged, and with it the concept of the state's employing services to better promote societal welfare in general and child and youth welfare in particular. The most notable step toward putting this new philosophy into practice took place in Chicago, Illinois, with the founding in 1899 of the Cook County Juvenile Court. This was the first statutorily created juvenile court in the United States and possibly in the world. It came about as a result of the joint efforts of the Chicago Bar Association and major social work pioneers and educators of the time (see chapter 2). By 1925 all but two states had juvenile courts and most had probation services.[2] Generally, such courts had original and inclusive jurisdiction (meaning that all cases involving juveniles come first to the juvenile court) over persons younger than eighteen charged with violation of the law.

The juvenile court employed the doctrine of *parens patriae*, the state as the ultimate parent. Because children did not have full legal capacity, the state had the responsibility to intervene for the welfare of the child when the parents failed in, or were incapable of, carrying out their responsibilities. Thus the court also had jurisdiction over status offenses (actions constituting law violations when committed by children, though not when committed by adults, such as running away, truancy, failure to obey parents, and a myriad of other "nuisance offenses" thought to be possible precursors of serious difficulties). The juvenile court was obviously a child welfare agency as well as one charged with carrying out for children, when necessary, the punishment, incapacitation, and societal protection functions of criminal law. This late-nineteenth- and early-twentieth-century turn toward positive criminological thinking about juvenile offenders was a true revolution in delinquency philosophy and practice, and it was widely hailed as such.

However, the last two decades of the twentieth century saw a counter-revolution. The juvenile court and justice systems came under bitter attack as instruments for supposed coddling and protecting of young criminals. Public perception has been of a "juvenile crime wave" demanding an increasingly "get tough" approach. This approach emphasizes higher rates of arrest, the use of more secure and punitive institutions, and longer sentences. If after such tactics are employed, delinquency rates fail to decline, the public perception tends to be that we must get tougher still, whether or not there is any research substantiating the presumed capacity to solve the "juvenile crime problem" through get-tough measures. These contrasting points of view demand careful, thoughtful scrutiny of the extent and nature of juvenile delinquency and of the efforts being made to cope with it.

Extent of the Problem

Available data sources The most voluminous and most quoted source of data on crime (juvenile and adult) and official efforts to cope with it is the annual publication of the Federal Bureau of Investigation, *Crime in the United States,* also known as the Uniform Crime Reports (UCRs). For this annual publication, the FBI compiles data from carefully structured reports from some 17,000 American law enforcement agencies on the number and nature of their arrests of supposed offenders and their other activities regarding crime and criminals. From these police reports, the FBI assembles an annual index of the number of crimes known to the police in eight categories, which can be grouped under two main headings: (1) four serious violent crimes: murder and manslaughter, rape, aggravated assault, and robbery; and (2) four property crimes: burglary, larceny theft, motor vehicle theft, and arson. (Arson has only recently been added to the list and is frequently not included in tables recording crime trends over time.) This index is intended to provide a rough assessment of the annual extent, nature, and levels of serious crime.

The next major source of information concerning the extent of and trends in crime is the data compiled by the U.S. Department of Justice, Bureau of Justice Statistics, from its national Crime Victim Surveys. These surveys are conducted at regular intervals. In 2000, 159,000 people aged twelve or older from 86,000 households were interviewed (U.S. Bureau of Justice, Bureau of Justice Statistics 2001). These persons constitute a national stratified sample. They are asked to report every criminal victimization they personally experienced during the preceding year. From these interviews, data reports are compiled that estimate total criminal victimization each year. (Murders are not included because victims cannot be interviewed, but it is assumed that most murders, unlike other crimes, do come to the attention of police.)

What we know From these varied and rich data, we know that in 1996 interviewees often did not report victimization to the police. Only 47 percent of violent crimes were so reported (Snyder and Sickmund 1999). We also know that of all crimes reported to the police, only 21 percent result in an arrest (Federal Bureau of Investigation 1999:201). In other words, less than half of crimes committed are reported to police, and less than a quarter of those reports result in arrests. *The seldom-realized fact is that we know nothing at all about the perpetrators of most crimes.* Our pronouncements about them are largely the result of impressions and estimates drawn from a far-from-random sample.

We do know a great deal (though not as much as we wish and often believe) about offenders who are actually arrested and thus drawn into the toils of the criminal justice system. From these data, we know that in 1997 law enforcement agencies made 2.8 million arrests of persons under eighteen years of age.[3] One of every five arrests made by U.S. law enforcement agencies involved a juvenile. Some 123,400 of these arrests were for violent index crimes (including 2,500 for murder), and 701,500 were for property index crimes (Snyder and Sickmund 1999:115–116).

These data also tell us that the recent decade has seen considerable fluctuation in the numbers of juvenile arrests. That number rose from 1,166,000 in 1990 to 1,489,461 in 1995. But from 1995 to 1999 juvenile arrests showed patterns of meaningful reductions in serious crime: 23 percent reduction for violent crimes and 24 percent for property crimes.[4] Snyder and Sickmund (1999) present data that even more dramatically illustrate changing numbers of arrests of juveniles for serious crimes. They focus on the juveniles in the age range most likely to engage in serious crimes and to contribute to public resentment and alarm, ages ten to seventeen. For that group, the researchers provide data on the rate of arrests per 100,000 juveniles of that age in the population. They note that from the early 1970s through 1988, the number of juvenile arrests for violent crime index offenses varied with the size of the juvenile population. Thus the arrest rate remained constant. But a rapid surge in that rate began in 1988, with an increase from about 300 arrests per 100,000 juveniles in 1987 to about 529 per 100,000 in 1994. Then, perhaps even more dramatically, the earlier rapid increase was followed by an even more rapid decline, by 1997 reaching a rate of 400 arrests per 100,000 youths aged ten through seventeen, its lowest during the 1990s (but still 25 percent above the figure for 1988). The rates for property crimes, always much more frequent (but less likely to produce public outrage), remained fairly steady during the period in question, varying from about 2,500 in 1980 to about 2,400 in 1997.[5]

Prediction of future rates of crime and delinquency remains speculative at best, however. In particular, one cannot be confident that recent rates will continue into the future. The beginning of the twenty-first century has seen, on the basis of preliminary FBI data, some resurgence of urban violent crime rates, possibly related to a faltering economy and resulting higher unemployment among youth (Savage 2001).

Societal Response

Obviously, the United States does not possess a unitary law enforcement and justice system for either juveniles or adults. Indeed, there may be as many as 20,000 such systems, federal, state, and local. Although in their general makeup, policies, and resources they may vary widely, they have in common the responsibility of ensuring both that the safety of individuals and the property of the citizenry are protected and that alleged offenders' rights are also protected through due process of the law.

The systems for discharging these responsibilities are, generally, a set of interrelated mechanisms for coping with offenders. These mechanisms focus on two major endeavors: the apprehension of alleged offenders and attempts to curb their offense behaviors. Such responsibilities demand a series of interdependent processes that screen alleged offenders entering and exiting the various stages of the system:

- Detection and arrest. This is more generally a local law enforcement function but also frequently a state or federal responsibility.
- Screening out of or referral to court. This is used where indicated and is generally a law enforcement function.
- Detention. This refers to temporary placement in a secure facility pending court decisions regarding proper final disposition of charges. It is usually a local government function.
- Adjudication by the courts. Here two major sorts of decisions must be made: (1) Did the accused actually commit a chargeable offense that brings him or her into the purview of the law (the jurisdictional decision); and (2) if so, what should be the consequences of the behavior that has brought the accused into the law's jurisdiction (the dispositional decision)?
- Disposition. The major resources available for the disposition of individuals found within the jurisdiction of the juvenile or criminal justice system are of two basic sorts, field and institutional: (1) Field services are also of two types, probation and parole. Probation involves providing supervision and guidance to persons not committed to institutions,

and parole (aftercare) involves services to those released from institutions. (2) Institutional services provide care to those ordered removed from their homes and communities. Usually this is in a juvenile correctional institution.

Among the most notable aspects of this overall system is that although its individual elements often appear to be separately functioning units, they are extremely interdependent. Variation at any point in the system will affect the total system. Thus, for example, any changes in the number, nature, or gender or racial distribution of arrests, or any change in seriousness ratios of arrests and referrals by police, will necessitate shifts in resources and practices at all succeeding points.

The System's Clientele

Although youth from all sectors of American life can become involved in juvenile crime, there are major variations. As in the child welfare system, one finds in the juvenile justice system overrepresentation of poor youth, youth of color, and disturbingly young boys and girls.

Ethnic and racial disproportion Building Blocks for Youth (2000) provides valuable data on the overrepresentation of people of color in the juvenile justice system. The authors note that of the total population of persons under eighteen in 1998, 79 percent were white, 15 percent African American, 1 percent Native American, and 4 percent Asian.[6] Whereas white youths constituted 71 percent of all juvenile arrests, the African American 15 percent of the juvenile population contributed 26 percent of all such arrests, including a startling 59 percent of those for index violent crimes. (Unfortunately, many justice system agencies do not disaggregate Hispanic youth, so their representation in the various stages of the system is unknown.)

Major imbalances continue at each step of the juvenile justice system: referral to juvenile court, detention pending disposition, formal court processing, and incarceration. At this final step, African Americans represent 41 percent of all youth adjudicated delinquent and ordered to residential placement and 37 percent of those placed on probation. Of those sent to residential placement for drug offenses, 45 percent were African American (Snyder and Sickmund 1999).

Youth and guns Among the most alarming of youth crime phenomena are the rates of juvenile gun homicide. Between 1980 and 1987, nearly

38,000 juveniles were murdered. In 26 percent of those crimes, a juvenile offender was identified. Seventy-seven percent of murders by juveniles under age fifteen were carried out with firearms (Snyder and Sickmund 1999:20).

According to the *Kids Count Data Book* (Annie E. Casey Foundation 2000), every two hours a child dies of a gunshot wound. The Children's Defense Fund has targeted the easy availability of guns as a prime reason for the high homicide rate. However, to date the various programs to reduce access to guns have not been markedly successful (Krajicek 2000). The problem arises from deep and explosively contentious responses both from gun control proponents and from those opponents represented, for example, by the National Rifle Association. That association's members assert a long historical and constitutional basis for "firearms freedom" and often seem able to muster powerful support for their cause.

Effectively meeting the issues that stem from the presence and ready availability of an estimated 60 million handguns throughout our population has proved difficult. However, Zimring (1998) points out that programs aimed at the problem of gun possession by juveniles are beginning to seem more acceptable to opponents of gun control than are those that apply to the population at large. There are three different targets for preventing juveniles from obtaining unlicensed or unregulated guns. The first is the legally regulated control of the sale of guns by licensed retail suppliers. The second is the difficult task posed by the unregulated exchange of used guns in the "hand-to-hand market." The third is the legal purchase of guns by adults followed by their sale to persons who the seller knows are not legally entitled to them.

As daunting as these challenges appear, there are indications that they may (at least occasionally) be approached with considerable success. The most often cited example is a tactic carried out in Boston. There, a vigorously aggressive law enforcement approach targeted at high-crime neighborhoods, and involving the coordinated efforts of all law enforcement and some related agencies, seems to have been a promising means of placing restrictions on the sale or transfer of guns to youth and on the carrying of guns by youth. Data indicate a reduction in those neighborhoods of some 80 percent in juvenile homicides from 1990 to 1995, as well as a reduction in other violent juvenile behaviors (Howell and Hawkins 1998).

Variations by gender Juvenile delinquency and crime have generally been considered to be largely male problems. Thus in the areas of popular concern, research interest, and provision of resources, female offenders have received little attention. Historically, given the expectations surrounding the roles of men and women, this oversight may have seemed inevitable and even reflective of crime statistics. But in recent years, comparative arrest rates have shown us that new assumptions are warranted. In 1981 female juvenile violent crime index arrest rates were 12 percent of the male rate. But by 1997 that figure had increased to 20 percent of the male rate. Similarly, in 1981 the female property crime index arrest rate was 24 percent of the male rate; it increased by 1997 to 40 percent of the male rate (Snyder and Sickmund 1999:121).

The insights to date into the problems of juvenile delinquency have largely been developed through observations of delinquent boys. Such data as girls' definitions of their own choices, solutions, and behavior rarely occurs in the literature. Further research is needed on the family, school, and community settings of delinquent girls. More complete understanding is needed of how poverty and racism, as well as the actions of official agencies, tend to shape girls' lives. New conceptualizations of juvenile female psychology must emerge and find their way into society's policy development processes (Chesney-Lind 1989).

Age Arrest rates for both violent and property index crimes for younger individuals (between ages ten and twelve, inclusive) have in recent years tended to rise and fall at rates paralleling those of older juveniles. In 1997 they represented some 8 percent of all juvenile violent index crime arrests and 12 percent of those for index property crimes (Snyder and Sickmund 1999:138).

The need for social welfare, educational, family counseling, psychotherapeutic, and in some instances out-of-home services tailored to the needs of this younger group becomes obvious. Whether these services are best delivered within the juvenile justice system, with its increasingly punitive orientation, or whether they would be better delivered through child welfare or mental health systems, is open to question. These young offenders are probably one group that fits none of the systems very well, may almost by happenstance be served by one system rather than another, and too often "falls through the cracks."

Drugs and delinquency Among the most disturbing reports contained in year trends on delinquency rates are those on juvenile arrests for drug violations. In 1990 there were 43,213 such arrests. By 1999 that figure had risen to 100,352, an increase of 132 percent. This growth occurred during a period in which the rate of increase for all other crimes combined was 11 percent and the rate of index juvenile crimes *decreased* by 20.5 percent (U.S. Department of Justice 2000).

The policy implications of these data are pressing. We have by now learned a good deal about treating drug abuse and addiction. But this information tends to be applied to adults and to be clinical in nature. Work with juvenile drug offenders may well demand different approaches, requiring integration of the efforts of a variety of resources and orientation toward a community-based approach. The strengths of family and community may offer a basis for meaningful help.

Presently, for example, juvenile courts and other services for youth tend to work apart from each other. Neither may emphasize seeking out broad community thinking and leadership. Or, to the extent that they do, they often seem focused on pumping into the community an array of resources to meet existing needs. But the state of the art in juvenile justice, as in working with youth who have other problem behaviors, involves changing patterns of competitive and isolated programs to patterns emphasizing partnership among programs working toward coordinated goals. Such coordination is yet in the developmental stages, requires the policy and management actions discussed earlier in the chapter, and is too rarely employed (Burt, Resnick, et al. 1992).

Prevention and Treatment

The great debate pervading all juvenile delinquency and criminal justice theory and practice is between the proponents of a "war on crime," get-tough philosophy, on the one side, and on the other side those who urge the necessity of understanding the causal roots of violative behavior, intervening in such causes, and bringing about behaviors that satisfy common human needs in licit ways. We have in this chapter previously referred to the debate as the clash between classical and positive criminology. We have also referred to the debate in discussing attacks upon the rehabilitative ideal.

The get-tough approach The proponents of the get-tough school of thought urge action to more surely and severely punish juvenile offenders or to imprison them in order to prevent them from committing further offenses. Their rallying calls are dramatic:

- "Juveniles mature enough to commit an adult crime are mature enough to face adult-level consequences for their behavior."
- "Honest sentencing." The offender, the victim, and the general public should know that announced sentences will be carried out. Thus parole (early and supervised release and return to the community) or

"good time" release for desirable behavior should be eliminated. Inmate behaviors such as participation in education, various forms of therapy, or prison work should have no effect on the time of release.[7]

- "Just deserts." The offenders, juvenile or adult, should receive sentences of severity commensurate with the seriousness of their offenses and their records of past offenses, if any. Such policy frequently results in legislative or other action calculated to remove sentencing authority from judges by mandating fixed terms prescribed by statute. At the sentencing stage of the juvenile or criminal justice procedure, social or psychological studies of youth and their family or community backgrounds become irrelevant. Sentencing guides that bring together data on the seriousness of present or past violations prescribe the nature and length of penalties to be imposed. (It should be noted that many proponents of mandated sentences agree that once the juvenile is committed to an institution, all possible means to help him or her move toward a constructive life should be employed during the period of custody.)

The most usually employed method for the accomplishment of the get-tough goals is the transfer to the adult criminal justice system of many juveniles who until recently would have been retained in the juvenile system. Most of the time since their founding, the juvenile courts have had jurisdiction over all offenders under the age of eighteen. But by the end of the twentieth century, almost all states had made provisions for waiving to the adult criminal justice system those juveniles considered to be dangerous or too resistant to programs of juvenile institutions. Howell (1997) provides a thoughtful review of the rich and fairly extensive literature concerning the nature and consequences of such waivers.

The extent of the fervor in recent years for expanding the criminal court's jurisdiction over juveniles may be appreciated in the fact that in 1996 some 27,000 juveniles were proceeded against in criminal court. Some statutes call for transfer to adult criminal jurisdiction and mandate specific punishments for specific offenses. Extreme examples are too common. For, example, in Oregon, as a result of an election initiative in 1995, youths fifteen and over found guilty of any one of twenty-one specified crimes are to be given long prison sentences, whether they are first offenders or not. A pamphlet distributed by Oregon's Multnomah County juvenile agencies to warn youth of the new law makes its impact vivid (see figure 9.1). It must be noted, however, that any system calling for mandated

FIGURE 9.1   Doing a Crime Means Big Time

Robbery II: You alone or with a friend want someone's baseball cap. You either pretend to have a weapon or threaten to beat the owner up.

You and your friend go to prison for 5 years and 10 months.

Assault II: You and a friend get into a fight with another person. Your friend pokes the other person in the eye with the handle of a hairbrush, a stick, etc. The eye is injured.

You and your friend go to prison for 5 years and 10 months.

Sexual Abuse I: You and a date are at a movie. You touch your date's buttocks, crotch, or breast. Your date tells you to stop. You ignore this and touch your date there again.

You go to prison for 6 years and 3 months.

Kidnapping II: You hear that someone is messing with your friend. You go to their house and force them outside to beat them up.

You go to prison for 5 years and 10 months.

Manslaughter I: You are driving under the influence of alcohol and/or drugs. You cause an accident and someone dies.

You go to prison for 10 years.

Measure 11, *New Oregon Law: One Strike and You're Out!*

Multnomah County Department of Juvenile Justice Services; Portland Public Schools; Oregon Attorney General's Office; and Multnomah County District Attorney's Office, 1995.

sentences for designated crimes removes decision-making authority from the judiciary. In practice, prosecuting attorneys have enormous discretion as to what charges will be filed against a defendant.

Precise data are not always available on the number of juveniles under age eighteen who actually reach detention or imprisonment in adult jails and lockups (the latter of which are generally institutions that hold individuals awaiting court trial or those convicted and sentenced to confinement for terms not exceeding one year). However, in 1997 a one-day national count was made of juveniles present in adult jails or lockups. On that day, there were 9,100 youths in custody in these institutions. Data on young people in adult prisons (usually expected to hold persons committed for periods of confinement of more than one year) are also neither complete nor precise. However, in one study thirty-eight states contributed data showing approximately 5,600 new prison commitments of youths under eighteen in 1996, down from 6,000 in 1992. Of all our nation's offenses (adult and juvenile) leading to conviction in 1996, 2 percent were committed by youths under age eighteen (Snyder and Sickmund 1999:209).

The efficacy of the various increasingly punitive trends resulting from adherence to the get-tough model is difficult to assess. Nonetheless, some research programs have attempted to compare recidivism rates of seemingly comparable groups of youth waived to the criminal justice system compared with those treated as juveniles. In a major research effort carried out in Florida, nearly 3,000 juveniles who were transferred to criminal court were followed and their recidivism rates compared with those remaining in the juvenile system. The two groups were matched on several dimensions, including offense category, prior offenses, age, sex, and race. Although wholly satisfactory matching may have been difficult to achieve, it is interesting to note that the transferred group had higher rates of rearrest, more serious recent offenses, and shorter times before rearrest (Snyder and Sickmund 1999).

Somewhat similarly, J. A. Fagan (1995) reported on a cross-state comparison of the handling of serious and violent juveniles in New York and an apparently socioeconomically similar group from New Jersey. New York requires that felony cases involving persons aged fifteen through seventeen be referred to criminal court. New Jersey juvenile felony offenders are normally handled by juvenile court. For the study reported by Howell, samples of randomly selected felony offenders from New York and New Jersey were selected and followed for four years. Recidivism rates were higher for the criminal court than for the juvenile court cases. Criminal court youth reoffended more quickly and were more likely to be returned to confinement. Fagan suggests that the more severe criminal court sanctions "may enhance the likelihood of recidivism" (p. 254).

Positive criminology and the rehabilitative ideal The proponents of positive criminology tend to rest their approaches upon assumptions that the roots of juvenile violative behavior are different than those for adults. Juveniles are presumed to have less capacity than adults to perceive and act upon clear perceptions of the consequences of their behavior, either to themselves or to others and either immediate or long term. Their behavioral choices are more powerfully shaped by peer group affiliations. Their conceptions of their relationships with broader society are still tentative. They remain in the process of "becoming," and may at some times seem quite different persons than at other times.

Volumes have been written over the past hundred years concerning the methodologies for the prevention and treatment of juvenile delinquency. In the earlier decades of the twentieth century, scholars and practitioners emphasized the use of professional skills to bring about change on the part of individuals. Later emphasis was on securing "partnerships in problem solving" with youth. In both, the goal was to produce change in the individual, frequently with little regard to the possible role of the world in which the individual lived. Broad environmental change seemed beyond available skills or resources. The effort was to enlarge the coping capacity of the individual.

The last two decades of the twentieth and the beginning of the twenty-first century, however, have seen—and are seeing at the time of this writing—major change in much of the thinking of scholars, some practitioners, and many leaders in policy formulation. Previous theory and practice tends to be criticized as based upon a "medical model" in which the goal is for the professional expert to do something to, or for, or even with, the individual in order to "fix" him or her. In the field of social work, new emphases are being developed that describe the necessary target for intervention as the transaction field where the individual personality and the environment meet and within which they must be seen as an interacting whole. Person, problem, and environment become one.

In keeping with this so-called ecological approach, the current models for efforts to prevent behaviors harmful to the individual, to others, or to societal well-being are frequently termed the "balanced model," the "restorative justice model," and the "community-based model."[8]

Proponents of the balanced model have developed a triadic approach that features accountability, community safety, and competence development.

The restorative model emphasizes the necessity of understanding by the parties involved (including the victim, the victim's family, the offender, the offender's family, and the community) that all are harmed by offense behavior and must be involved in restorative efforts. Activities to that end may include

- victim-offender mediation and dialogue leading to recognition of the harm done to the various parties and the development of a plan to make amends;

- family group counseling coordinated by a trained facilitator and directed toward issues of how the harm has affected lives and how it will be repaired;
- peacemaking circles, in which all interested persons—victim, victim supporters, judge, defense and prosecuting counsel, and court workers—share in the search for what has gone wrong in the community and what each can do to remedy it;
- financial or personal restitution to the victim;
- community programs in which juvenile offenders undertake to contribute to community life by agreed-upon projects; and
  victim empathy groups.

The community-based model underlies both the balanced and restorative models and is the core of much of today's thinking about juvenile offense behavior. This model is built on intense awareness of the degree to which behavior is shaped by the world in which the juvenile must live. Thus attempts to achieve long-term change in the behaviors of individual youths solely by coercive methodologies are doomed to failure. The more reasonable goal is facilitated rather than coerced change. Societal acceptance, opportunity ladders, and participation are necessary if the youth are to seek and achieve behaviors that contribute to society rather than rejecting and attacking it. Poverty, impoverished family life, discrimination, absence of role models that embody success rather than failure—all are barriers. According to this model, young people must be shown opportunities for success in civic participation if they are to overcome the barriers that have resulted in their turning away in rebellion from conventional society.

It is evident that these and similar programs are rich outgrowths of the positive approach to dealing with juvenile offenses. The programs have grown rapidly in numbers, although probably only a small proportion of possible target youth are as yet involved. But their growing impact upon current value systems, theory, philosophy, and practice may promote renewed movement toward positive criminology.

Conclusion

A consequence of analyses such as those in this chapter is recognition that our society needs more than a theory of delinquency or of any other problem behavior. We need a theory of youth in society and a determination to move toward enhancing the opportunity structure for all youth. The risk analysis with which the chapter began emphasized the risk antecedents of poor and violent communities and families without the resources to nurture their children. Intervention in these communities, support to these families, and recognition of how essential it is that youth have the opportunity to develop and use their strengths, should provide the practice base for the next decade. Because such a strategy is the route to social justice, it must become the great adventure of social welfare planning and striving in our day.

Notes

1. Other problem behaviors are equally serious but are usually thought of as in the domain of other systems. For example, see Besharov and Gardiner (1998).

2. Probation services are used instead of incarceration when it is thought that the community does not need protection from the offender and that the offender will benefit from staying in the community. They consist of community supervision by a probation officer, who monitors the activities of the offender to the extent reasonable by policy, provides guidance and counsel, and endeavors to see that the offender has opportunities to function in law-conforming ways.

3. It must be noted that this figure is the number of juvenile arrests, not necessarily the number of juveniles arrested. Some juveniles may well have been arrested more than once during the period at issue.

4. Percentages were drawn from the Uniform Crime Reports (Federal Bureau of Investigation 1999), tables 32 and 34, pp. 216–218.

5. Figures estimated from the trend-time tables provided by Snyder and Sickmund (1999:120, 126).

6. Note that these population proportions differ from those presented in chapter 6, in which a disproportionate representation of African American children in foster care was examined. The difference occurs because these justice system statistics combine white and Hispanic youth into a single category.

7. Correctional institutions' administrators and workers find that these policies create serious problems in the management of inmates when they lead inmates to lose hope that there is anything they can do to affect their release date.

8. Thoughtful analyses of the balanced and the restorative models are provided by the U.S. Department of Justice, Office of Juvenile Justice and Delinquency Prevention, in its *OJJDP Report: Guide for Implementing the Balanced and Restorative Model* (December 1998).

References

Annie E. Casey Foundation. 2000. *Kids Count Data Book: 2000.* Washington, D.C.: Annie E. Casey Foundation.

Batavick, L. 1997. "Community-Based Family Support and Youth Development: Two Movements, One Philosophy." *Child Welfare* 75(5): 639–63.

Besharov, D. J., and K. N. Gardiner. 1998. "Preventing Youthful Disconnectedness." *Children and Youth Services Review* 20(9/10): 797–818.

Boyle, P. 2000. "Young Advocates Sway Washington." *Youth Today* 1:52–57.

Bruner, A., and M. Fishman. 1998. "Adolescents and Illicit Drug Use." *Journal of the American Medical Association* 280:597.

Building Blocks for Youth. 2000. "And Justice for Some." Available at http://www.buildingblocksforyouth.org/justiceforsome.

Burt, M., G. Resnick, et al. 1992. "Comprehensive Service Integration Programs for At-Risk Youth." Department of Health and Human Services, Washington, D.C. Available at http://aspe.os.dhhs.gov/hsp/cyp/atrisky.htm.

Buzi, M., M. Wineman, et al. 1998. "Ethnic Differences in STD Among Female Adolescents." *Adolescence* 33:313–19.

Chesney-Lind, M. 1989. "Girls' Crime and Women's Place: Toward a Feminist Model." *Crime and Delinquency* 35(1): 5–29.

Cook, R. 1988. "Trends and Needs in Programming for Independent Living." *Child Welfare* 67(6):497–514.

Courtney, M. E., and I. Piliavin. 1995. "The Wisconsin Study of Youth Aging Out of Out-of-Home Care." School of Social Work and Institute for Research on Poverty, University of Wisconsin, Madison.

Edmund S. Muskie School of Public Service and National Child Welfare Resource Center for Organizational Improvement. 1998. "Opportunities for Foster Care Youth in Transition: Three Views of the Path to Independent Living." Annie E. Casey Foundation, Baltimore.

Fagan, J. A. 1995. "Separating the Men from the Boys: The Comparative Advantage of Juvenile Versus Criminal Court Sanctions on Recidivism Among Adolescent Felony Offenders." In *A Sourcebook: Serious, Violent, and Chronic Juvenile Offenders,* edited by J. C. Howell, B. Krisberg, et al. Thousand Oaks, Calif.: Sage.

Federal Bureau of Investigation. 1999. *Crime in the United States.* Washington, D.C.: Federal Bureau of Investigation.

Greene, J., C. Ringwalt, et al. 1995. "Youth with Runaway, Throwaway, and Homeless Experience: Prevalence, Drug Use, and Other At-Risk Behaviors." U.S. Department of Health and Human Services, Administration on Children, Youth, and Families, Washington, D.C.

———. 1997. "Shelters for Runaway and Homeless Youths: Capacity and Occupancy." *Child Welfare* 76(4): 549–61.

Howell, J. C. 1997. *Juvenile Justice and Youth Violence.* Thousand Oaks, Calif.: Sage.

Howell, J. C., and D. Hawkins. 1998. "Prevention of Youth Violence." In *Youth Violence, Crime, and Justice: A Review of Research,* edited by M. Tonry and M. H. Moore. Chicago: University of Chicago Press.

Institute for Youth Development. 2000. "Protecting Adolescents from Risk." Institute for Youth Development, Washington, D.C.

Johnston, L. D., P. M. O'Malley, et al. 2002. "Monitoring the Future: National Results on Adolescent Drug Use: Overview of Key Findings, 2001." National Institute on Drug Abuse, Bethesda, Md.

Juvenile Justice Bulletin. 2000. "Children as Victims." U.S. Department of Justice, Washington, D.C.

Kools, S. 1997. "Adolescent Identity Development in Foster Care." *Family Relations* 46:263–71.

Koprowitz, C. 1999. "An A+ for Adolescent Health." *State Legislatures* 25: 30–34.

Krajicek, D. J. 2000. "Anti-gun Youth Programs Shoot Blanks: Funder Seeks New Tactics." *Youth Today* 1:43–44.

Limberg, L. D., S. Bogess, et al. 2000. "Teen Risk-Taking: A Statistical Report." Urban Institute, Washington, D.C.

Lock, J., and H. Steiner. 1999. "Gay, Lesbian and Bisexual Youth Risks for Emotional, Physical, and Social Problems: Results from a Community-based Survey." *Journal of the American Academy of Child and Adolescent Psychiatry* 38:297–305.

Mallon, G. P. 1998. *We Don't Exactly Get the Welcome Wagon: The Experiences of Gay and Lesbian Adolescents in Child Welfare Systems.* New York: Columbia University Press.

McMillen, J., G. Rideout, et al. 1997. "Independent-Living Services: The Views of Former Foster Youth." *Families in Society: The Journal of Contemporary Human Services* (September/October): 471–79.

National Center on Addiction and Substance Abuse. 1997. "Substance Abuse and the American Adolescent: Highlights." National Center on Addiction and Substance Abuse, Washington, D.C.

Newsweek. 2000. "The Teen Years: A Special Report." *Newsweek* 135, no. 19 (May 8): 52–75.

Powers, J., J. Eckenrode, et al. 1990. "Maltreatment Among Runaway and Homeless Youth." *Child Abuse and Neglect* 14:97–98.

Proctor, C., and V. Groze. 1994. "Risk Factors for Suicide Among Gay, Lesbian, and Bisexual Youths." *Social Work* 39:504–12.

Ringwalt, C. L., J. M. Greene, et al. 1998. "The Prevalence of Homelessness Among Adolescents in the United States." *American Journal of Public Health* 88(9): 1325–29.

Robertson, J. 1992. "Homeless and Runaway Youths." In *Homelessness: A National Perspective,* edited by M. Robertson and M. Greenblatt. New York: Plenum Press.

Rothman, J. 1991. *Runaway and Homeless Youth: Strengthening Services to Families and Children.* New York: Longman.

Savage, D. 2001. "Urban Crime Resurges After Decade Drop." *Los Angeles Times,* Nov. 25, A13.

Schorr, L. B. 1988. *Within Our Reach: Breaking the Cycle of Disadvantage.* New York: Anchor, Doubleday.

Search Institute. 1997. *Forty Assets.* Minneapolis: Search Institute.

Shane, P. 1989. "Changing Patterns Among Homeless and Runaway Youth." *American Journal of Orthopsychiatry* 59:208–14.

Smith, A., and D. Rosenthal. 1995. "Adolescents' Perception of Their Risk Environment." *Journal of Adolescence* 18:229–45.

Smith, C. 1997. "Factors Associated with Early Sexual Activity Among Urban Adolescents." *Social Work* 42:334–46.

Snyder, H., and M. Sickmund. 1999. *Juvenile Offenders and Victims: 1999, National Report.* Washington, D.C.: Office of Juvenile Justice and Delinquency Prevention.

Stephens, G. 1997. "Youth at Risk: Saving the World's Most Precious Resource." *Futurist* 31:31–38.

U.S. Department of Health and Human Services. 1999. *Blending Perspectives and Building Common Ground: A Report to Congress on Substance Abuse and Child Protection.* Washington, D.C.: U.S. Government Printing Office.

U.S. Department of Justice. 2000. *Crime in the United States 1999: Uniform Crime Reports.* Washington, D.C.: U.S. Government Printing Office.

U.S. Department of Justice, Bureau of Justice Statistics. 2001. "National Crime Victimization Survey." Available at http://www.ojp.usdoj.gov/bjs/

U.S. General Accounting Office. 1999. "Foster Care: Effectiveness of Independent Living Services Unknown." Report to the Honorable Nancy L. Johnson, U.S. House of Representatives, Washington, D.C.

Westat, I. 1991. "A National Evaluation of Title IV-E Foster Care Independent Living Programs for Youth, Phase I, Final Report." U.S. Department of Health and Human Services, Administration for Children and Families, Washington, D.C.

Zimring, F. E. 1998. *American Youth Violence.* New York: Oxford University Press.

CHAPTER 10

◆

Concluding Thoughts

We define our horizons by the decisions we make. Acting collectively we can build a fundamentally better future for our children.

LINDSEY 1994

In this book I have sought to outline the policy framework of child welfare services. A broad conception of child welfare has been used; having worked and studied in the field for more than four decades, I am reluctant to see the older, traditional definition of child welfare pass away. I have tried to describe the policy initiatives and services that make up the child welfare system, and to place them in a historical context and in the context of our current communities. The review of research is reasonably thorough, for I believe that empirical data provide the best means of determining the state of a field of practice. I have sketched an outline of the laws and judicial decisions that are important in framing child welfare policy. The formal part of this policy is contained in the laws and federal funding structures that have been identified, as well as in the regulations and policy manuals of the many agencies that deliver services. But unwritten policy is almost as important. Informed by the worldview of our society, by practice wisdom, by ethics and values, and by personal commitments, it is a powerful force that shapes all the services described throughout the book.

Probably child welfare's greatest strength as we move into a new millennium is the movement toward reprofessionalization of the field, based on the recognition of the complexity of child welfare practice and on a determination to give children the best possible help. Also exciting are the new techniques developing in the attempt to support parents in their care of their own children. Ideas about the empowerment of parents and participatory decision making are familiar to social work, but are new and more controversial in protective services. Adoption is also an exciting part of child welfare practice, which continues to develop and incorporate new ideas—continuity of care for the child, empowerment of birth parents to participate in children's lives, expansion into new forms of adoptive homes, and continuing support for adoptive parents. Also notable is the new effort, triggered by a federal funding initiative, to develop networks of community partners to provide a safety net for children and families.

Protective services and foster care have emerged as the troubled spots in child welfare. At its core, the child welfare system deals with the protection of children. From that responsibility flows the responsibility to provide care that will meet the needs of the child—either by enabling the family to continue to care for its children or by providing appropriate care outside the original home. Thus the problems in these areas strike at the core of the field. They are especially difficult for the child welfare profession to surmount because their roots lie in pervasive community conditions such as poverty, the deterioration of supportive family structures, and substance abuse.

In chapter 5 the difficulties of the protective services system were reviewed. We noted the great amount of worker time spent investigating complaints that were not substantiated, and the shockingly small percentage of those families involved in abuse or neglect who received appropriate services. Waldfogel (1998) summarizes the problems that overwhelm protective services this way:

1. Overinclusion—families involved in the system that should not be.
2. Underinclusion—families who should receive protective services and are not being served.
3. Capacity—the number of families involved far exceeds the capacity of the system.
4. Service delivery—families do not necessarily get appropriate services, and
5. Service orientation—protective services has had difficulty in finding a balance between protecting children and preserving families.

(PP. 107–8)

Foster care also has been overwhelmed with an increasing number of children who need placement. At the same time demographic changes have reduced the number of foster homes, and the complexity of parents' problems has lengthened children's stays in foster care. Efforts to preserve families and avoid foster placements for children, and the increasing use of kinship foster care, have not been adequate to solve the problem of capacity. And foster parents are not receiving the training and support that they need if they are to be successful in caring for the troubled children who come to them.

This chapter brings together the major policy issues in child welfare as I see them. It briefly reviews some of the new ideas for solving the structural problems of child welfare services, and finally, returns to where the book began, discussing the education and retention of child welfare workers and the role of social work.

Major Policy Issues

In the preceding chapters, nine critical issues of child welfare practice were identified and explored. They are: (1) the child welfare system's response to community concerns about the impact of family violence on children, (2) planning to insure that children have a stable and permanent home in which to grow up, (3) evidence and impacts of racism in the child welfare system, (4) child care for all children who need it, (5) determining the appropriate use of family preservation services, (6) establishing and retaining foster homes to meet the needs of children, (7) the potential of institutional care as a resource for dependent children, (8) postadoption support services, and (9) the child welfare system's interface with the juvenile justice system. At the conclusion of this chapter we will examine a final critical issue, the retention of qualified workers in the child welfare profession.

There are, however, larger issues equally critical to child welfare and to the families who receive services. The largest of these is poverty and the impact of welfare reform, discussed in chapters 2 and 4. Another critical issue that runs through many of the discussions is that of substance abuse—both its impact on children and families, and the question of how policies can be crafted to simultaneously protect children and allow parents the time necessary for recovery. The way in which our society provides mental health services, and the ways in which the child welfare

and mental health services systems interact, are important because many
of the children who enter the child welfare system have extensive mental
health needs, as do their parents. Space limitations have prevented deeper
exploration of these and many other larger social issues that are critical
to child welfare.

This section explores a set of major policy questions that affect not
only the child welfare field but also many other areas of social service.
The approaches to these issues reflect broad social policy trends whose
impact extends far beyond the child welfare system.

Comprehensive and Universally Available Services

Child welfare services should be comprehensive, including any of the
services described in chapter 4 that a family needs; and, to be truly effective in preventing problems as well as helping to resolve them, they should
be universally available to families. Historically, these services have been
provided for a small group of families and children, after difficulties have
developed. This approach conceptualized families as able to handle their
own affairs, needing help only when they fail. The approach has been
labeled "residual," meaning that families must prove their need for the
service before it is available to them. It is the same approach that the United
States has taken to income maintenance, providing assistance only to those
families that cannot support themselves.

When the child welfare system dealt with relatively few children—
children who came to the attention of the community because they needed
care and shelter, or because they were maltreated, or because they had
behavior problems—it was able to provide comprehensive services. Imaginative work was done, innovations in care were developed, and child
welfare workers could take pride in their accomplishments.

With the advent of mandatory reporting of child maltreatment, and the
accompanying public education campaigns, the numbers of children and
families that the community identified as needing child welfare services
suddenly grew large. At the same time, changes in society brought to the
child welfare agencies families with complex sets of problems. New cases
came in great numbers; ongoing cases needed comprehensive services. The
child welfare system was overwhelmed.

Impoverished families who are unable to meet the needs of their
children are, in overwhelming numbers, relying on the child welfare

system for help. Yet the child welfare system has been transformed and is no longer able to cope with the problems of child poverty. From its inception the child welfare system has focused on the children left out. . . . In recent decades, the economic hardship and social changes experienced by so many families has unraveled that system. As a consequence, the residual approach within which child welfare operates no longer makes sense.

(LINDSEY 1994:4)

The burden of investigating these many reports of suspected abuse or neglect has taken over the child welfare system, leaving few resources for services to actually provide help to children and families. In an attempt to control their intake and keep the numbers of investigations manageable, agencies often use increasingly stringent definitions of child maltreatment to limit the number of reports to which they will respond. This approach does nothing to free child welfare workers from the responsibility of conducting investigations, does not guarantee the protection of children, and satisfies no one.

As public child welfare agencies narrow the scope of the services they deliver, the system becomes increasingly dependent on the community to provide the comprehensive services that families need. Some of these services, such as substance abuse treatment or mental health services, clearly demand specific training and expert delivery, and will be accomplished through cooperative arrangements between child welfare and other service systems. Other services, such as regulation of child care, parent training, family preservation, and juvenile detention, were once, in many places, part of the public child welfare system; now they are most commonly provided through cooperative relationships with community agencies. Ensuring that such ancillary services receive adequate support from public funds, that they are managed for the benefit of children and families, and that they are so closely linked with child welfare services that there is indeed an integrated system of care for each child, becomes a major policy consideration for child welfare.

If we are truly to support families in their care of children, services must be comprehensive and they must be available to all families. Among children's services, only education is funded as a universal rather than a residual service. In most other industrialized nations, universal health care services are provided and there are children's allowances or other mechanisms of providing every family with a basic income. The United

States has taken a first and very limited step in this direction with the Earned Income Tax Credit (described in chapter 2).[1] Most programs that affect children are residual, targeted to children and families whose problems have become acute. If we are to prevent maltreatment of children, and if we really believe that parents should be supported so that they can raise their own children, we must seriously consider the provision of basic child welfare services to all families.

Shifting of Program Responsibility to the Local Level

As we have seen in earlier chapters, for many years new programs have been developed at the federal level, standards set, and states enticed by the promise of federal money to adopt these programs. This approach has been credited with raising standards for children's services throughout the country, particularly in the poorer states.

We are now seeing the beginnings of a different pattern. The federal government is increasingly giving states block grants of funds, with few requirements attached, so that the states can develop their own programs. The rationale is that the community knows best what it needs, and indeed there is probably some truth to this. But the block grants are set amounts that do not change according to the number of people needing services. Thus the result will be to shift the funding of children's programs increasingly to state funds as the states try to make up the shortfall when demand increases. To date children's advocates have managed to prevent the "block granting" of the basic core of child welfare services, thus insuring continuous funding for protective services and out-of-home care despite changes in demand.

The strength of block grants is that the money can be used for innovative programming. Thus we should begin to see differences in some child welfare services among the states. Careful evaluation of programs and good communication among states will be increasingly important; the developing comprehensive data systems should help. As responsibility is devolved to the states, however, it must be remembered that the federal initiatives came about partly as a remedy for inadequate services in some states.

The Impact of Welfare Reform

It is not clear what will be the long-term impact of 1990s welfare reform on child welfare, but without doubt this is one of the major policy issues of the field. Families are no longer entitled to basic income support. It is difficult to envision how it will be possible to implement the goals of protecting children and preserving families without this basic support. Certainly the goal of the worker who administers Temporary Assistance to Needy Families (TANF)—to get the parent into full employment—will often conflict with the goal of the child welfare worker, to enable the parent to provide adequate child care. With parents in the workforce, it will be difficult to arrange home visits, parenting classes, interventions in which child care is modeled, or almost any other family support service. It will be difficult to arrange parent-child visits if the child has been placed in foster or residential care. The hours of all of the services that comprise child welfare will have to become very flexible, extending into evenings and weekends. Child welfare agencies will have to be very careful that children are not being placed in out-of-home care for reasons of poverty.

Beyond the conflicting goals regarding parenting and employment, welfare reform contains other provisions that will create hardship for families and necessitate changes in child welfare practice. Currently many relative foster homes receive TANF payments to help with the maintenance of the children they have taken in. In this way children are supported who would otherwise require foster care maintenance payments through the child welfare system. As the time limits on TANF payments begin to take effect, depending on state law, such homes may have to be converted to regular foster homes, resulting in less control of decision making for the relative foster parents and greater expense to the state.

Substance abuse is a pervasive issue among families involved in the child welfare system. The TANF provision that anyone who has been convicted of a drug-related felony can never receive income maintenance or food stamps is going to mean that it may be almost impossible for some families to keep or be reunited with their children.

Even if children can remain with their families, welfare reform presents other difficulties. TANF is based on the proposition that parents should be in the workforce, and policy makers have recognized that this will require child care. But whether funding will be sufficient, and whether adequate child care resources exist or can be developed, remains to be seen. Affordable, high-quality child care is a need of families at all income levels. Quality child care has been demonstrated to be critical to the development of the children who spend time in day care while parents work; it can be delivered only by well-trained and adequately reimbursed

personnel. If government subsidies are not adequate, poor children could
bear the added burden of poor child-care experiences.

Outcomes

The standard of care that the community expects for its children changes,
as we have seen, over time. The first chapter reviewed how, as standards
rose, formerly acceptable parental behaviors were identified as problems.
In the last half of the century alone, physical child abuse has been "discovered," followed by child sexual abuse. Substance abuse became so
widespread that it pushed its way to recognition as a threat to children.
Most recently domestic violence, heretofore looked upon as a difficulty
to be worked out within the family, has been identified as within the
scope of the child welfare professional's concern. Each of these changes
has brought increased demand and increased complexity to the practice
of child welfare service.

At the same time, the community has become less able to provide support to families struggling with these difficulties. Changing social mores,
increasing mobility and the consequent lessening of extended families'
ability to help, the increase in single-parent families, the expectation that
women will join the workforce—all of these have strained families caring
for children. Poverty is a pervasive problem, making every other difficulty
harder to resolve. Poverty-stricken communities are often violent and
unsafe. Schools in poor communities often do not offer children the same
opportunities as those in more affluent neighborhoods. Meeting the needs
of children can become an insuperable challenge for parents.

Considering the changing community expectations of child welfare
services, the increased numbers of families and the expanded responsibilities that have fallen into the domain of public child welfare agencies,
and the anticipated impact of new legislation, how should child welfare
service outcomes be conceptualized and measured? What do we want
from child welfare services; what is it reasonable to expect; and how can
those outcomes be measured?

The articulation of expected outcomes has been difficult for the child
welfare profession, as has the development of outcome measures. As part
of ASFA, Congress has mandated the measurement of the outcomes of
child safety, permanency, and well-being. How these terms should be
defined is far from obvious. Does the outcome of permanency mean
just a place where a child can grow up, or do we want children to have

continuity of care in a family home? Is living with or retaining contact with one's own extended family an important outcome? Well-being includes adequate shelter and nutrition. If the goal is to enable children to remain with their own families, this can be accomplished only through coordination with other systems. Children's well-being requires care that meets their developmental needs and enables them to grow to their full potential; these are difficult attributes to measure.

Expanding Expectations

The outcomes we expect from child welfare services change over time—probably more as a matter of emphasis than in absolute terms. Nevertheless, the outcome emphasized is that by which a child welfare agency measures its success.

Safety In the nineteenth century, child safety was the primary goal of child welfare services. Orphanages in which children were sheltered and fed, and in which they received a "moral" education, were the primary means of achieving this goal.

Safety and care in a family home Gradually, in the late nineteenth and early twentieth centuries it came to be expected that families would be provided for children. A growing body of theory concerning infant and child development reinforced this change. Foster homes became the principal means of achieving the goal.

Safety, care in a family home, and permanency In the last quarter of the twentieth century, establishing a permanent home for each child became the major goal of child welfare services, as a growing body of empirical literature demonstrated that children were spending many childhood years in foster care, and moving often. There was renewed interest in parental visiting and the return of children home from foster care. Adoption resources were expanded, particularly for older children.

Safety, care in a family home, and permanency within the extended family Late in the twentieth century, the preferred outcome became a home for the child within the extended family. The passage of the Indian Child Welfare Act, expression of concern by the African American community, and agitation by relatives, particularly grandparents, served to expand the concept of family and emphasize its importance. Family preservation services were the means of achieving this goal.

Rates of reabuse or continued neglect of children who returned to their original families remained high—not surprisingly, given the limited services that many families received. Family homes within the kinship network often experienced distress as they struggled to cope with the problems of children who had been through bad experiences; many of these families needed more support than was available.

Safety, care in a family home, permanency, maintenance of family connections, high-quality care and nurture At the end of the century, with the passage of the Adoption and Safe Families Act, the focus has shifted from whose home the child is in, to the quality of the care the child receives in a permanent home. Adoption became an important means to the goal of high-quality permanent care. The Multiethnic Placement Act removed racial matching from the adoption placement process. Open adoption is being explored as a way for a child to maintain connections with extended family. Parents' rights are not to be protected unless they demonstrate a commitment to creating a caring home for their children.

The Impact of Outcome Measures on Service Provision

Clearly, as expected outcomes change they also become more demanding. The measurement of these outcomes becomes increasingly complex, and emphasis is usually on evaluating the most recent addition. For most of the 1980s and 1990s agencies demonstrated their success, and measured the job performance of their workers, by measuring the achievement of permanency—return home or adoption for children.

Current federal outcome measures are based on the data being collected by the AFCARS and the NCANDS systems. The current content of the data systems has restricted the measurement of safety to reports of reabuse or neglect in open protective service cases, and reports of abuse and neglect in out-of-home care. The first reports of outcome statistics, for 1998, were disappointing in that only twelve states reported usable data on safety, although thirty states reported data related to permanency (U.S. Department of Health and Human Services [hereafter, U.S. HHS], Children's Bureau 2000). The number of states reporting will increase over time.

Though child welfare systems cannot be held responsible for the incidence of reported abuse and neglect, they are indeed responsible for preventing reabuse or continued neglect among those children and families being served. The safety outcome is thus measured through a count of those children with substantiated instances of maltreatment who are reabused or neglected in the twelve months following the substantiation. The data, though incomplete, are encouraging, including reports that 89 percent of the children do not experience any recurrence of abuse or neglect within a twelve-month period.[2] However, the large amount of missing data, including data from some of the largest states, limits the usefulness of the measure.[3] A clear picture of the success of the child welfare system in protecting the children it serves will not become available until subsequent years, when more complete data are available and trends can be noted.

The information about permanency is more complete and is based on a sample of the thirty states that reported the most complete statistics. Permanency with a family was achieved for 80 percent of the children who left foster care: 66 percent were reunified with their original families; 14 percent were adopted by new families or their foster families. Almost half of the children who were adopted had been in foster care for forty-eight or more months prior to adoption, and the longer a child had been in foster care, the higher the probability that the child had had three or more placements (U.S. HHS, Children's Bureau 2000:4-9-4-11).

Return home is not always permanent, however; of the children who entered foster care in 1998, 10 percent were entering within twelve months of a prior episode, and 7 percent a longer time after a prior episode (U.S. HHS, Children's Bureau 2000:4-10). Inadequate services, or inappropriate services, may be a factor in this rate of return to foster care. It is also possible that the use of permanency as an outcome measure puts pressure on workers to return children to their homes when the homes are not ready. Implementation of ASFA could increase this tendency.

Measurement of well-being was not attempted by the Children's Bureau, although it is included in congressionally mandated outcomes, because there were no measures within the NCANDS or AFCARS systems that could be used. Many child welfare practitioners are anxious about the inclusion of measures of child well-being as an outcome. Barth (2000) found child welfare agency managers to be concerned that "measuring affective, cognitive, and physical well-being . . . would create the expectation that child welfare services were intended to promote optimum development (rather than just prevent the increasing trauma of repeated abuse)" (pp. 764–65). The author, however, supports such measurement, arguing that although child welfare agencies need not "provide lifetime case management services to children," the involvement of the agency "indicates significant risk to the child" and represents an investment of public resources; both the risk and the investment warrant follow-up evaluation (p. 765).

If we are to achieve the ultimate outcome of children and youth who grow into productive members of our society, the field must, as Barth contends, turn its attention to child well-being. Unless children are well cared for as they grow, this outcome will not be achieved. A major research and policy issue in the next decade is going to be the development of measures of child and adolescent well-being, which will serve as markers to indicate whether children are progressing along the path of positive development.[4]

Effective Intervention to Achieve Outcomes

Safety Ascertaining whether a child has been maltreated, and assessing the risk of further maltreatment, is perhaps the most agonizing part of the child welfare worker's job. There is no escaping decision making in protective services, and each decision has serious consequences. Lindsey, in an extensive review of risk assessment, finds neither a consistent theoretical base for, nor reliable agreement about, the practice of assessing risk. In fact, as noted in chapter 5, he reports that poverty and uncertain source of income is the strongest predictor of a decision to place a child outside the home (Lindsey 1994).

Workers have a dual role in their initial contacts with families, that of investigating what has happened and estimating the risk of recurrence, and that of helping the family cope with whatever difficulties have led to the report of maltreatment. It takes a skilled worker to competently handle both roles. The difficulty of this dual role has given rise to the suggestion that the police take over the investigatory function in protective services, a proposal that will be discussed in a following section. However, when these two roles are handled well, it is to the great benefit of family and child. Such complex roles, of course, raise the issue of adequate education, training, and supervisory support for protective service workers. It also raises issues concerning agency structure. Reorganization of agency structure so that protective service is recognized as a difficult, specialized area of service, and is differentially compensated so that it will attract the most experienced workers, is a policy option that merits consideration.

Family preservation A wide variety of approaches are used when the state intervenes to prevent further maltreatment of children. All are aimed at improving parenting skills and knowledge. The interventions range from the teaching of child development and behavior management skills to therapeutic interventions that may change basic attitudes. Contextual factors surrounding maltreatment suggest that income maintenance and substance abuse treatment might be the most important services. Unfortunately, it is often not within the power of the child welfare worker to make these services available.

Many community-based family support programs are important in meeting the needs of families. Self-help groups, home-visiting programs, family resource centers, parenting programs—all are thought useful and have as one of their aims the prevention of maltreatment. However, when these programs are evaluated with rigorous designs, with few exceptions it is found that they do not modify parent behavior or affect child development to the extent one would hope. Either we are using the wrong research methodology, which is certainly possible, or, because we do not know the cause of child maltreatment, the programs are unable to focus their efforts effectively.

The evaluation of family preservation programs, reviewed in chapter 4, may be the most extensive test to date of the impact of services based on the idea that parenting behaviors could be modified through cognitive and therapeutic techniques. The most common outcome measure for these studies was placement in foster care, and families receiving family preservation services and those not receiving them had children placed in about the same proportion. However, this is a limited outcome measure, and it may well be that many families benefited greatly from these services. It may even be that children received greater protection, for the intensive involvement of a worker with a family during family preservation services may reveal problems that necessitate placement but would go undiscovered without the services. Reanalysis of the data from these studies using family well-being as an outcome measure could yield different, and more optimistic, conclusions.

Foster care Foster care is a relatively infrequent intervention, but is used when it is thought a child can benefit more from foster care than from remaining in the original home. Protecting the well-being of children, and seeing that they have a permanent home that will provide adequate care, is a complex part of the task of the child welfare worker. Out-of-home care keeps most children safe, but we have noted in earlier chapters that care in poorly trained and supported foster homes, and multiple moves, can do great harm to children.

Foster care is a core service of the child welfare system. It is intended to be a brief service while family crisis is resolved, but the complex problems of families today take a long time to resolve. Substance abuse in particular—a factor in the situations of 70 to 80 percent of families involved in the child welfare system—has a common recovery pattern that involves multiple remissions and may last over years; for about a third of families recovery is never achieved. Children can remain in foster care much too long waiting for their families.

Foster care is one of the points of crisis in the child welfare system; the shortage of foster homes is acute. The more severe the shortage becomes, the more likely a child is to be placed in an available home that may not meet his or her individual needs. Such a placement sets the stage for a move, and each move is damaging. Long stays in foster care, in turn, increase the probability of moves.

Chapter 6 examined ideas for investing in foster care to develop a service for children that could be used as a short-term crisis intervention or a long-term care alternative, as appropriate. Other suggestions focus on reduction in the use of foster care. Supporting children's own families is one alternative. This requires good coordination of services, and also requires that communities build supports around these troubled families and keep cases open for years if necessary. Another way, also using children's own families, is through placement with relatives; thus children remain within their extended family, though formal permanency may not be achieved. A third way of reducing numbers in foster care is the use of institutional care, which can provide permanency and maintain a family connection but does not allow the child to participate in family life in a community. The fourth, being implemented through the provisions of ASFA, is by moving children fairly rapidly into adoptive homes, using open adoptions when appropriate.

Toward More Effective Service: The Ideas of Major Scholars

Critics of the child welfare system stress that individual child welfare workers do the best work possible given the circumstances. Heavy workloads, inadequate training and supervisory support, constant decision making, and the threat of public anger if the decision is wrong—all make child welfare work difficult. Several writers have in recent years suggested structural changes in the system that they think would remove barriers and make better use of the efforts of child welfare workers. These are major scholars, and the following brief reviews of their ideas do not do them justice. The serious student will find it rewarding to read these writers' arguments in their entirety.

Freeing Workers from Investigations

The amount of time that child welfare workers spend on the investigation of reports of abuse and neglect is a vexing problem. We want to have all reports investigated; we also want appropriate services delivered in a timely manner when maltreatment is discovered. Three recent writers have suggested freeing worker time, and returning child welfare agencies to a service orientation, by ending the emphasis on investigation (Pelton 1989; Lindsey 1994; Costin, Karger, et al. 1996). All would turn the investigation of "serious abuse and neglect" over to police and the justice system. Such an approach would free the worker from the "dual role" of helper and investigator. Costin and Karger couple this with the idea that punishment as a criminal would deter abuse, just as such an approach has had an impact on domestic violence.

There are at least three problems. (1) It will be difficult to define "serious" maltreatment—though ASFA has made a first step. And it will be difficult to determine whether maltreatment is serious without investigation. Costin, Karger, et al. (1996) suggest that the initial contact of troubled families should be with a child welfare worker, and that police should take over the ongoing investigation of serious abuse; it is not clear how this change would impact the distribution of caseworkers' efforts. (2) Most investigations do not involve serious maltreatment—most involve family difficulties that do not warrant state intervention. Social workers are best qualified to work with these families, helping resolve problems with brief service and making referrals for voluntary work with community agencies. (3) The initial contact with a family sets the tone for continuing work. If it is adversarial, that tone is likely to persist, thwarting attempts to engage families in services. If it is one of engaging the parents in planning to meet the needs of their children, this too is likely to continue, resulting in the family's productive use of services.

The inordinate amount of time that protective service workers spend in investigating complaints is certainly a serious concern, as are the protection of children and the protection of the civil liberties of their parents. Ideas that address those concerns deserve serious consideration.

Increased Use of Adoption

Bartholet (1999) has a different idea for resolving the systemic problems of the child welfare system. Her concern is that each child have the opportunity to be the cherished child of a family to whom it belongs. Given the intractable problems of many families, she sees time spent in family preservation efforts, and attractive new programs that empower parents, such as community partnerships and group decision meetings, as obstacles in movement toward that goal. Children, she writes, need the protection of a strong, authoritative stance on the part of the child welfare system. And, unless parents make changes rapidly, children who have been maltreated need to move quickly into adoption.

> We need to revamp our child welfare policies so that we remove children and make it possible for them to be adopted much earlier. We need to limit the number of reunification attempts that can be made. We need to use concurrent planning to place children immediately into preadoptive homes, so that they can begin to recover and to bond, and so they won't have to suffer additional disruption and damage if the decision is made to terminate parental rights. We need to reach out to the entire community for adoptive homes. . . . All this would take a huge change in the cultural mindset of those within the child welfare system, most of whom still believe that children belong in some essential way in their families and communities of origin. But cultural mindsets can change.
>
> (BARTHOLET 1999:242–43)

These ideas seem unfamiliar to social workers, educated and experienced in a long tradition of family-based practice. They also deserve serious consideration, however. Empirical work has consistently suggested that adoption is a good solution for children who cannot remain with their own families. The passage of ASFA suggests that our society is beginning to move away from its recent emphasis on the importance of kinship ties. Empirical work has also demonstrated that children need to be in permanent, nurturing homes as early in their lives as possible. This is truly a practice reform idea that puts the welfare of children ahead of all other considerations, although it discounts the benefits to children of remaining within their biological families. Clearly this approach recognizes that the child is the primary client in a child welfare setting.

Community-Based Practice

Along very different lines, a third idea is emerging in the child welfare literature. It envisions a new function of child welfare practice: that of building community strengths so that communities can support the families and children within them. Meezan (1999) outlines it in his writing on community-building. Costin, Karger, et al. (1996) develop the idea in a chapter on a new model of comprehensive services for children and families, which they name the Children's Authority. And Waldfogel (1998) writes of an effective protective services system that uses all the resources of the community.

> To achieve an adequate level of child protection, we must move forward, and quickly, on two parallel tracks of reform. First, we must take steps to improve the effectiveness of CPS in responding to children in need of protection. Second, we must take steps to build the capacity of other partners in the community to join with CPS in providing a more effective response to children in need of protection. These steps will lay the groundwork for the future of child protection: a more fully differentiated child protective services system in which CPS and its community partners provide a customized response to each child in need of protection, intervening more aggressively and authoritatively on the high-risk cases, more helpfully and comprehensively with the lower-risk cases, and earlier and more proactively with the cases in need of prevention.
>
> (WALDFOGEL 1998:233)

These are the community partnerships discussed in chapter 3, and the types of services described in chapters 4 and 5. Individualized intervention packages can be delivered by these partnerships so that families receive appropriate services. Vital to the success of such an integrated system would be funding mechanisms that allowed purchase of these customized services, many of which do not fall into commonly funded categories—such as a furnace so that a family can remain in a home during the winter, a neighbor to come in after school and mentor a mother as she works to improve her parenting, the modifications needed to bring a grandmother's home up to safety standards so that she can take care of her grandchildren.

This approach is more familiar to social workers. It rests on the assumption that people are striving to be the best parents they can. A community network could evolve to the point of providing needed supportive services for anyone in the geographic area who needed help, the caseload becoming thus a mix of voluntary clients with a range of problems, and involuntary clients who are involved in the justice system or have maltreated children. A community partner system would work with the community as well as with individual families, striving to build capacity in both.

The Eradication of Poverty

Poverty is considered by some to be outside the scope of the child welfare system. The association between poverty and child maltreatment is so strong, however, that poverty is bound to be one of the chief concerns of child welfare professionals.

> The problem of poverty among lone-parents and their children has become the core social problem of North America. The problem has been cast as the collapse of the family, a plague of illegitimacy, an epidemic of child abuse, and a crisis for children. At the core all stem from the same problem, child poverty.
>
> (LINDSEY 1994:327)

It is possible to eradicate poverty; it was almost accomplished for the elderly through Social Security and the indexing of its benefits to inflation. Such a universal approach has never been tried in this country for children. Perhaps the elderly are more appealing; they vote, and almost all of us will become elderly one day. During the War on Poverty in the 1960s, great strides were made in reducing child poverty. Now, however, these gains have been lost, and almost 20 percent of our children are poor. Among children of color, the percentage is much higher.

Lindsey (1994) notes that a key time for a young person is the transition from adolescence to adult years; it is at this time that the young person needs the resources to make varied opportunities available. He proposes, in addition to the development of an economic safety net for families, government-funded Child Future Security Accounts. These accounts would be paid into throughout a child's growing years; parents could add to them, and young people could add their own earnings, without changing the amount of government contribution. When the young person was eighteen, money would be there for college, vocational training, or any other "approved" educational venture. Lindsey sees this as a means of beginning to equalize the opportunity structure of our society, and of lifting young people out of the cycle of poverty and limited opportunities.

Child welfare workers are in a key position to see the impact of child poverty and to make that impact known. If community-based patterns of child welfare services become prominent, they will be in an even better position to influence health care, child care, and schools, all of which prepare young people to take advantage of opportunities. As social work reenters the child welfare arena, perhaps poverty and income maintenance will become key concerns of the child welfare system, rather than worrisome issues that belong to another system.

Critical Issue: Recruitment, Education, and Retention of Child Welfare Workers

The recruitment and retention of well-qualified caseworkers presents a huge challenge to child welfare agencies. Public and private agencies work to find and hire men and women who seem to have promise as child welfare workers. Having done so, they invest in further agency-specific training to enhance employees' skills. It is important that they be able to retain those workers. When workers leave, the agency's investment is lost, along with the practice wisdom that a worker has gained during time in the position. Vacant positions mean that the agency infrastructure is strained, as other workers carry larger caseloads and supervisors assume additional duties. They also mean that families and children lose the opportunity to work continuously with a single worker whom they know and whom they believe understands them and their situation. High turnover rates thus constitute a critical issue for child welfare practice.

Turnover Rates

Turnover rates in the child welfare system are unacceptably high. In the fall of 2000 the American Public Human Services Association (APHSA) surveyed both private nonprofit child welfare agencies and public child welfare agencies.[5] Average turnover rates for one year for public agency workers were just under 20 percent, meaning that almost one-fifth of the workers left the agencies between July 1, 1999, and June 30, 2000. Average turnover rates for private nonprofit agencies were much higher; about 40 percent of the workers left during that same time period. Interestingly, turnover rates for supervisors were much lower, about 8 percent for public agencies and 28 percent for private agencies (Drais, Cyphers, et al. 2001:11). Anecdotal reports tell of agencies with much higher turnover rates among caseworkers, and in any gathering of agency managers the disruption caused by turnover and vacancies is a dominant topic. Clearly these turnover rates are high enough to cause significant disruption in the functioning of the agencies and in the services provided to their clients.

Correlates of turnover What are the factors associated with this high turnover rate? In the same survey, 97 percent of the managers and supervisors in the public child welfare agencies identified heavy workloads as a major impediment to retention. Specific workload issues identified were large caseloads and too much time spent on travel and paperwork. Low salaries were named as a factor by 88 percent of the managers and supervisors in private agencies and by 74 percent of those in public agencies. Public agency managers (87 percent) also said that workers not feeling valued was a retention problem; that factor was not noted by private agencies (Drais, Cyphers, et al. 2001:18, 23). This combination of factors creates a situation in which workers do not have enough time or resources to meet the needs of all their clients, and thus do not feel rewarded either professionally or monetarily.

Surveys of workers themselves use intention to leave as a predictor of turnover, because it is of course very difficult to survey workers who have left an agency. Organizational commitment emerges as a critical factor in retaining workers. These surveys find, not surprisingly, that workers with high job satisfaction generally do not intend to leave; job satisfaction is positively correlated with organizational commitment. Organizational commitment can disappear abruptly when a shock (such as a violation of the employee's value system) causes the employee to reevaluate his or her attachment to the organization (Morton 2002a). This commitment to the organization's values and mission was also found important by Ellett (1999), who reports that child welfare workers tend to stay as long as they believe they are making a difference, even in the face of low salaries or high caseloads. This speaks to the need for a clear mission statement that is operationalized in the policies and practices of the agency, so that workers see themselves as carrying out that mission in their everyday work.[6]

Retention Morton (2002a) points out that although much is written about engaging clients, we seldom discuss engaging staff members and securing their commitment to the organization. Retention of workers, he suggests, may be less dependent on external factors, such as funding, than on changes in management.

Training and supervision are necessary supports for any worker in a position as demanding as that of the child welfare caseworker. Many of the people who staff public child welfare agencies begin their employment without any prior training in child development, interviewing skills, the legal framework of public service, or the values and ethics of child welfare. Some agencies require at least a bachelor's degree in social work or another helping or human service profession; however, many others, due to budgetary constraints or to difficulties in recruitment, hire staff members who lack an educational background in human services. Reliance on "trial by fire"—a loose combination of on-the-job and in-service training for new employees while they carry a full caseload—is particularly problematic when the new workers do not have the appropriate educational background.

Nationally there is increased focus on the quality of agency-based child welfare training programs. The Children's Bureau, the Child Welfare League of America, the Council on Social Work Education, and the National Association for Staff Training and Development of the American Public Human Service Association have launched collaborative initiatives, convened conferences, and responded in other ways to increase the quality of training offered by agencies and the quality of educational preparation offered through schools of social work. Increasingly, public agencies are drawing on federal Title IV-E funds to pay for training programs, a strategy that reduces the tendency to cut back on training when there is a state budgetary crisis.

Although training is more often discussed and evaluated, and numerous training curricula exist, supervision is an equally or more critical factor in assuring quality services. Child welfare practice is complex and requires a high degree of sophistication. Development of the necessary values, attitudes, and skills requires supervision and coaching over time. Four interlocking aspects of supervision have been identified: administrative, clinical, educational, and supportive (Kadushin 1976). A child welfare agency will have to provide supervisors who are skilled in all aspects of supervision in order to retain competent workers and provide good collaborative services. In the APHSA survey described earlier in this section, problems with the amount or quality of supervision were mentioned by 82 percent of the managers in public child welfare and by 60 percent of those in private child welfare agencies. A frequently implemented retention strategy was increased or improved supervisor training. Other frequently used retention strategies were increased or improved in-service training, efforts to increase worker safety, physical plant improvements, efforts to reduce caseloads and increase salaries, and, in private agencies, development of flex time (Drais, Cyphers, et al. 2001:27, 35).

Workers need to feel a sense of competence and pride. The demands of the work can be alleviated by structures within the agency that provide support in decision making and facilitate access to the needed resources. A work environment that affirms that the caseworker is valued is also important—not only decent office space, but also safe cars, cellular phones so that workers can stay in touch with the office or summon needed help, and a constant effort to simplify reporting requirements (and provide clerical support) so that time can be spent with families rather than on paperwork. A supportive agency culture, in which staff members are recognized and good work is rewarded, makes a difference in staff retention and enhances the organization's ability to work with other agencies (Glissen and Hemmelgarn 1998).

Social Work Education and Child Welfare

Social work has a long history with child welfare; it is the only discipline that provides curricula in child welfare as a part of the degree program. The components of social work education fit with the demands of child welfare work, and a social work background may enhance a child welfare worker's ability to work effectively and make a difference. As child welfare administrators begin to professionalize child welfare service work, education in social work is becoming a prominent strategy. There is some evidence that the social work profession is beginning to turn away from therapy and private practice and to invest more energy in those who have limited opportunity in our society. Social work may be reentering the child welfare arena.

The usefulness of professional education in child welfare work is beginning to be recognized by child welfare administrators. Ritter and Wodarski (1999) describe the skills needed by the direct service worker at the various stages of casework: During investigation, the worker needs "integrated knowledge of psychopathology, advanced assessment techniques, and intervention strategies . . . to work with resistant families" (p. 222); at the intervention stage, "intensive family services require highly trained social workers knowledgeable in family dynamics, family-based interventions, crisis stabilization, advocacy, and brokering services" (p. 228). The authors add that knowledge of child development is necessary in the assessment stage, and that skills in direct work with children are needed to help children deal with issues of disrupted attachments (pp. 225–27).[7]

As recently as the 1960s, the need for such skills was widely recognized, and a master's degree in social work was a common requirement for child welfare practice. As the volume of child abuse and neglect investigations swelled, and agencies became stressed, a common way of stretching lean budgets was to hire workers with fewer qualifications. As child welfare agencies increasingly worked with involuntary clients, and as the authority of the court was increasingly invoked, social workers deserted the field, finding that the nature of child welfare work no longer fit with their beliefs or with their training (Costin, Karger, et al. 1996: 96–98). Social work education reflected this stance, offering little curriculum with direct application to child welfare work. Consequently, child welfare administrators became less interested in hiring MSW graduates, who were apparently no better trained for the work than those without a graduate degree, who could be employed for less.

In the last decades, social work educators have begun to reexamine and even to reverse this stance, offering a broader, family-focused curriculum applicable to more settings, including the child welfare system. The bachelor of social work degree (BSW) was developed in part to meet a need for workers who would command lower salaries but had some relevant training. These workers have made a strong contribution to child welfare service, and it has been suggested that the generalist practice taught in BSW programs makes this the most appropriate credential for certain aspects of protective service work (Ritter and Wodarski 1999). An increasing number of schools of social work, supported by a combination of state and federal (Title IV-E foster care) funds with matching funds from the universities, offer stipends and curricula for master's degree programs intended to educate professionals specifically for practice and administration in child welfare.

Using this Title IV-E funding, many agencies are investing in the social work education of their staffs. In 1988 only 28 percent of the workers in public child welfare had a social work degree (Lieberman, Hornby, et al. 1988). More recent data are not available, but as partnerships proliferate between agencies and schools of social work—provided child welfare agencies can retain the personnel they educate—the percentage is expected to increase. The National Council on Accreditation, which sets standards toward which agencies aspire, requires that staff members at an accredited agency possess a "masters degree in social work and two years of supervised direct practice; or a bachelor's degree in social work or another human service field and two years related experience and are supervised by a person with a master's degree in social work and experience in the delivery of child protective service" (Council on Accreditation of Services for Families and Children 1997).

Ellett (1999) makes the point that the factors that induce workers to leave may not be the same as the reasons they decide to stay; supportive supervision, manageable workloads, and a feeling of competence in accomplishing work were associated with retention of staff members.[8] Lieberman, Hornby, et al. (1988) judged those with social work training to be best prepared for child welfare work, and found that states that required social work degrees for child welfare work had the lowest turnover rates. Presumably social work education gave these workers a sense of competence in their work.

It is important, however, to recognize that child welfare is an interdisciplinary field. Social work skills provide an excellent core. However, expert knowledge from a variety of disciplines provides depth that, when used in team decision making, informs good decisions and supports the workers who make them. Nor is there any implication here that the professionalizing of child welfare work will solve all of the problems of retention. It will be but one element, an element that should improve services to children and families.

Social Work and Child Welfare: The Nature of the "Fit"

Assumptions

Social workers begin with the assumption that parents are doing their best and that they have strengths on which better lives can be built. This outlook makes it difficult for social workers to adopt approaches that throw families immediately into adversarial systems. Training that teaches the uniqueness and value of each individual makes social workers most comfortable with helping systems that enable them to engage families in cooperative work.

Social workers believe that children grow best in their own families. It is not that social workers believe that children necessarily belong to their families; children are individuals with rights, not possessions. But they recognize that children suffer when separated from their homes, however distressed those homes may be; and they are familiar with a body of child development research that emphasizes the importance of sustained attachment to a single caregiver. Social workers are also realists, and are skilled at assessment. If children are unsafe, if families cannot mobilize to make changes, if family and community supports are lacking, social workers move children to safe homes, using their knowledge of child development to minimize the trauma.

Social workers thrive on engagement and joint problem solving. They dislike, and are not trained for, confrontation. The court system, then, as it presently functions, is uncomfortable for social workers. They are unsure of their role and sometimes angered by confrontational lawyers who do not seem to recognize their professional knowledge. The supervision of the court often seems to the worker to be an expression of the court's distrust of social workers' judgment and actions. An understanding of legal procedure helps, but does not wholly eradicate the feeling. Thus, for the social worker, the child welfare agency's partnership with the courts is more difficult than those with other community service systems.

Values and Ethics

The Social Work Code of Ethics (National Association of Social Workers 1996) lays a sound value base that undergirds child welfare practice and provides guidance in many situations. The code of ethics is, however, akin to policy. It lays down general guidelines but does not resolve specific issues.

> Specific application of the Code must take into account the context in which it is being considered and the possibility of conflicts among the Code's values. . . . Ethical decision making is a process. There are many instances in social work where simple answers are not available to resolve complex ethical issues. Social workers should take into consideration all the values, principles, and standards in this Code that are relevant to any situation in which ethical judgment is warranted. Social workers' decisions and actions should be consistent with the spirit as well as the letter of this Code.
> (NATIONAL ASSOCIATION OF SOCIAL WORKERS 1996)

Pine (1987) suggests a working model for thinking about ethical dilemmas in child welfare, a process in which the professional answers the following questions:

1. What are the conflicting values?
2. From what aspect of the social intervention—policy, target group, implementation, or outcome—do the major issues arise?
3. What are the practitioner's duties or obligations in this case? From what sources do they arise? Are they conflicting?
4. What are the uncertainties or unknowns? How can they be diminished?
5. What are the sources of power? Is the distribution of power equal? What can be done to equalize it?
6. Have the parties voluntarily consented to or participated in the choice of alternatives? Do they have the information and capacity to consent?
7. What are the needs and rights of each party—the right to freedom, privacy, well-being, protection from harm? Are these rights in conflict with one another? Which rights have priority?
8. What is the nature of the limited resources available to support this intervention? On what basis will their distribution be justified?
9. To what extent are there ethical conflicts among the various professions involved in this case? How are they in conflict?

(PINE 1987:319–23)

Social Justice

The Social Work Code of Ethics is very specific about social workers' responsibility for social justice. Education for practice encompasses principles of self-determination, the uniqueness of the individual, and the empowerment of people to make decisions about their own lives. In broader terms, social workers are educated to be concerned about any group of people that do not enjoy equal opportunity in society.

Signs of racism in the child welfare system, reviewed as the critical issue of chapter 3, are thus of particular concern to social workers in the field. Social workers can also influence child welfare practice so that it is shaped to empower the poor and those perceived as "lower-class." Costin, Karger, et al. (1996) and Swift (1995) have written about how class consciousness and a patriarchal society can shape child welfare practice, and Pelton (1989) and Lindsey (1994) focus on the impact of poverty. The interaction of race, class, and poverty with entry rates, service provision, and outcome variables in child welfare practice must be examined on a multisystemic level to weed out biases and inequalities and to develop promising practice and policy solutions, and the educational background of a social worker creates a good basis for this examination and weeding.

Advocacy

Social workers are advocates. Advocacy is among their ethical responsibilities, rooted in their responsibility to promote social and economic justice, and it is a part of their education. Advocacy has been variously defined in recent years. A Child Welfare League definition in 1981 emphasized the educational aspect of advocacy. Other definitions have stressed social action, influencing public policy, and intervention on behalf of clients (Downs, Moore, et al. 2000:466). Advocacy in the context of individual cases is probably most familiar to social workers. When cases seem to fall into a pattern, and clients face a common barrier to social justice, a class of people can become the subject of advocacy. Also familiar in child welfare is the use of class action suits to force reform of child welfare systems that are failing to meet the needs of children and families.

The families that social workers encounter in the child welfare system—poor, often persons of color, sometimes homeless, with serious problems such as substance abuse and mental illness—provide inspiration for advocacy. Presenting data, presenting issues, presenting the needs of "their" families to the agency, to the community, and at the state and national levels, social workers are at their best. And as responsibility for programs tends to move from national to state to community levels, their voice becomes louder and their advocacy has more effect.

Will the hiring of additional social workers mitigate the problem of worker turnover in child welfare? That remains to be seen, and will depend in part on the child welfare agency's ability to retain the social workers currently being educated under Title IV-E programs. If social work is a good educational background for child welfare, social workers should feel competent in their work, and that is one factor associated with job satisfaction and retention. The challenge to the child welfare agency is to create the conditions under which social workers are actually able to use their skills, and thus feel that they are making a difference.

Conclusion

These, then, are the critical issues that those working in child welfare will face in the coming years. Policy directions will have an enormous impact on children and families. Ideas abound, coming from a variety of value systems and sets of assumptions, each with some merits. Choices will have to be made.

What is clear is that many of the families and children served in child welfare systems are poor and relatively powerless. Social justice demands that the eradication of poverty must be a dominant policy agenda; it is a hard agenda to sell in a country that believes poverty is a mark of individual failing. The need of families for supportive communities is evident; the development of such communities is one of the great challenges of the coming years. Certainly it is evident that services that prevent abuse and neglect, and that promote healthy childhood experiences, are preferable to those that attempt to remedy harm; how such services are to be promoted in an age when immediate outcome measures are increasingly demanded is another challenge. Flaws in the structure of the child welfare system itself that discourage workers and disrupt services to families present another challenge. And so the challenges mount.

Social workers have a responsibility to take a leadership role in meeting these challenges. The value system of social work, and its ethical code, provide structure for work in child welfare. The clinical training of social work teaches skills that can be used with some of the most difficult families, and can inform the most difficult decisions, encountered in child welfare practice. Social work values call for supporting all of the policies and practices that enhance families' capacity to make choices about their lives and influence the systems that serve them. Child welfare work demands skills in community partnerships and community development, and offers opportunities for management in very complex organizations. And there is no group that needs the advocacy of social work more than the parents and children in our child welfare system.

Notes

1. The implication in this legislation that families are entitled to a minimum income base is offset by recent welfare reform, which does not provide support for parenting, but focuses on getting parents into the workforce.

2. Maltreatment in foster care will not be reported until later years.

3. States reporting maltreatment data were Colorado, Florida, Illinois, Louisiana, New Jersey, Oklahoma, Pennsylvania, Rhode Island, South Carolina, Utah, Vermont, and Wyoming.

4. The reader interested in greater depth concerning outcome measures would find an excellent starting place in J. Poertner, T. P. McDonald, et al., "Child Welfare Outcomes Revisited" (*Children and Youth Services Review* 22, no. 9–10 [2000]: 789–811).

5. There are some problems with representativeness in this sample, particularly among the private agencies. Those surveyed by the Alliance for Children and Families had only a 30 percent response rate. Of the 551 agencies eligible, the Child Welfare League of America contacted a random sample of 314; only 39 percent returned surveys. It is possible that those agencies that returned surveys tended to be those agencies having serious difficulties with turnover. The estimates are, however, the best available.

6. Staff retention and training is a challenge not only for the public agency; other parts of the system also struggle to recruit and retain trained personnel against similar odds. For example, for attorneys, practice in child welfare as a public defender, a state's attorney, or an attorney representing CASA programs is rarely as remunerative or considered as prestigious as other kinds of legal practice, and the legislature rarely provides sufficient funding for the number of legal professionals needed to meet the demands of these programs. Few lawyers or judges are educated in dependency law or prepared to deal with the intense emotions and life-or-death decisions that can be called for in child welfare casework. To address the education challenge, some law schools (for example, the University of Michigan, Loyola, and the University of Washington) have established child advocacy clinical training programs to prepare law students for this kind of practice. The National Council of Juvenile and Family Court Judges and the American Bar Association Center on Families and the Law have invested heavily in developing training, scholarship, and other professional resources for attorneys and judges practicing in this field.

7. This is an ambitious article. It attempts to analyze the varied tasks of personnel in child welfare and to match those tasks with the skills taught in BSW and MSW programs. Its focus is narrow in that it does not recognize the interdisciplinary nature of child welfare work and the need for contributions from other disciplines.

8. The survey of workers described earlier in the chapter noted that low salary, large caseloads, and too much time spent on travel and paperwork were cited as reasons workers intended to leave (Morton 2002a). These factors might be conceptualized as the impediments to developing a sense of accomplishment.

References

Barth, R. P. 2000. "Outcomes After Child Welfare Services." *Children and Youth Services Review* 22(9/10): 763–87.

Bartholet, E. 1999. *Nobody's Children: Abuse, Neglect, Foster Drift, and the Adoption Alternative*. Boston: Beacon Press.

Costin, L. B., H. J. Karger, et al. 1996. *The Politics of Child Abuse in America*. New York: Oxford University Press.

Council on Accreditation of Services for Families and Children. 1997. *Accreditation Standards*. New York: Council on Accreditation of Services for Families and Children.

Downs, S. W., E. Moore, et al. 2000. *Child Welfare and Family Services: Policies and Practice*. Boston: Allyn and Bacon.

Drais, A., G. Cyphers, et al. 2001. *The Child Welfare Workforce Challenge: Results from a Preliminary Survey*. Washington, D.C.: American Public Human Services Association.

Ellett, A. J. 1999. "I Quit! Can Higher Education Diminish Turnover in Child Welfare?" Louisiana State University School of Social Work, Baton Rouge.

Glissen, C., and A. Hemmelgarn. 1998. "The Effects of Organizational Climate and Inter-organizational Coordination on the Quality and Outcomes of Children's Services Systems." *Child Abuse and Neglect* 22(5): 401–21.

Kadushin, A. 1976. *Supervision in Social Work*. New York: Columbia University Press.

Lieberman, A., H. Hornby, et al. 1988. "Analyzing the Educational Backgrounds and Work Experiences of Child Welfare Personnel: A National Study." *Social Work* 33(6): 485–89.

Lindsey, D. 1994. *The Welfare of Children*. New York: Oxford University Press.

Meezan, W. 1999. *Translating Rhetoric to Reality: The Future of Family and Children's Services*. Ann Arbor: University of Michigan.

Morton, T. 2002a. *Engaging Staff*. Duluth, Ga.: Child Welfare Institute.

———. 2002b. *Failure to Protect?* Duluth, Ga.: Child Welfare Institute.

National Association of Social Workers. 1996. *Code of Ethics*. Silver Spring, Md.: National Association of Social Workers.

Pelton, L. 1989. *For Reasons of Poverty: A Critical Analysis of the Public Child Welfare System in the United States*. New York: Praeger.

Pine, B. 1987. "Strategies for More Ethical Decision Making in Child Welfare." *Child Welfare* (July/August): 315–26.

Ritter, B., and J. Wodarski. 1999. "Differential Uses for BSW and MSW Educated Social Workers in Child Welfare Services." *Children and Youth Services Review* 21(3): 217–38.

Swift, K. J. 1995. *Manufacturing Bad Mothers: A Critical Perspective on Child Neglect*. Toronto: University of Toronto Press.

U.S. Department of Health and Human Services, Children's Bureau. 2000. *Child Welfare Outcomes 1998: Annual Report*. Washington, D.C.: U.S. Government Printing Office.

Waldfogel, J. 1998. "Rethinking the Paradigm for Child Protection." *The Future of Children* 8(1): 104–20.

Internet Resources

All of the listed sites contain links that will take the reader into specific areas of interest.

Annie E. Casey Foundation. An excellent Web site from an organization dedicated to advocacy and to the development of public policy to benefit children. The foundation's annual *Kids Count* data book and other publications can be downloaded. http://www.aecf.org

Casey Family Programs. The Web site of a major child welfare organization with a focus on long-term foster care. Current material covers many aspects of child welfare in addition to foster care, with an emphasis on examination of critical issues and examination of practice and policy. http://www.casey.org

Child Welfare League of America. A major source of information and numeric data about child welfare services. The data system allows display of customized tables to meet individual needs. The site lists conferences and contains an extensive catalog of publications. http://www.cwla.org

Children's Bureau Express. A part of the Administration for Children and Families, the Children's Bureau Express is an electronic publication that covers news, issues, and trends. The latest research findings and promising practices are presented. Articles often include links to full-text documents. One can subscribe to the publication. http://www.calib.com.cbexpress

Children's Defense Fund. The site of a major advocacy organization, promoting children's welfare with particular emphasis on issues affecting African American children. It contains discussion of current issues, policy, and laws. Excellent publications can be ordered, and some are available online. http://www.childrensdefense.org

Evan B. Donaldson Adoption Institute. An easy-to-use and informative Web site covering many aspects of adoption. It contains reports of surveys, conferences, reviews of laws, material on the costs of various types of adoption, and other hard-to-obtain information. http://www.adoptioninstitute.org

National Center for Children in Poverty. An excellent site that contains data and policy discussions. Many discussion papers and publications can be downloaded. http://www.cpmcnet.columbia.edu/dept/nccp

National Clearinghouse on Child Abuse and Neglect Information. The clearinghouse is a national resource on the prevention, identification, and treatment of child abuse and neglect and related child welfare issues. It provides information to meet the specific needs of users. Print and online materials are available. http://www.calib.com/nccanch

National Indian Child Welfare Association. A Web site that contains material of particular interest to those concerned with child welfare issues among the Native American population. Material about conferences, newsletters, discussions of policy issues, and presentations of research are available. The site contains information that is often difficult to find. http://www.nicwa.org

The Clearinghouse on International Developments in Child, Youth, and Family Policies. The Web site is to serve as a single source of information about other countries' child and family policies. The clearinghouse also disseminates an electronic "Issue Brief." To date the site includes information on twenty-three advanced industrialized countries. http://www.childpolicyintl.org

U.S. Department of Health and Human Services, Administration for Children and Families, Administration on Children, Youth, and Families, Children's Bureau. A major source of information that is quite easy to use. The Web site contains links to the AFCARS data reporting system as well as fact sheets reporting recent statistics on all aspects of foster care. Laws and policies are described. Children's Bureau program descriptions and funding announcements are available, and many government publications can be downloaded. http://www.acf.dhhs.gov/programs/cb

Index

abandonment, 33, 227
Abbott, Edith, 17, 65
Abbott, Grace, 17, 65
abortion, 292, 302
abuse, 4, 14; causes of, 35, 110–11,
143, 169–72, 219; and child rescue
movement, 8; and child welfare
services, 28, 91, 384, 410; and
class, 182; and community, 28, 34,
37, 97–98, 395; consequences of,
111, 125n6; and criminal justice
system, 38, 109, 255, 397; data
on, 95, 169, 218; definitions of,
29, 32–40, 72, 164; and
developmental disabilities, 38, 111;
and domestic violence, 29, 38, 42;
and early sexual activity, 360; and
family income, 120; and fatalities,
29–30, 84, 170, 218; in foster care,
124n3, 218–19, 274, 275; in group
home care, 280–81; investigation
of, 105, 168, 394, 397; legislation
on, 71, 72, 95, 116, 167–68;
mandatory reporting of, 71, 72,
90, 93, 97–98, 118, 167, 168, 386,
387; National Center on, 71, 139,
168, 274; nature and extent of,
164–65; and poverty, 111, 160,
169–72, 213, 400; prevention of,
70, 71, 144, 184; public education
on, 37, 97, 386; publicity on, 115,
116, 165; registry of child, 255;

repeated, 181, 190, 391, 392;
reports of, 28, 90, 91, 93, 96, 97,
99, 168–69, 184; in residential
care, 274–75, 280–81; risk
assessment in, 38; and runaways,
353, 354; and single parents, 23,
170–71; studies of, 28, 35, 96,
124n2, 164, 170, 193; and teen
parents, 361; treatment of, 71,
72. *See also* neglect; physical
abuse; psychological abuse; sexual
abuse
Addams, Jane, 17, 19, 47n4, 61, 62,
65, 138, 151
ADHD (Attention Deficit
Hyperactivity Disorder), 177, 180
adolescents: and abuse, 40, 353, 354;
and adoption, 83, 310, 311,
337n8, 338n10, 358; African
American, 24, 358, 359, 361;
Asian, 359, 370; at-risk, 40,
345–82; and child welfare system,
345–46; communication skills of,
362; and criminal justice system,
23, 24, 268, 374–76; and family
treatment, 187; and foster homes,
208, 212, 277, 278, 283n4; and
group homes, 208–9, 261, 269,
278, 279; and guns, 370–71;
Hispanic, 359, 361, 379n6;
homeless, 24, 348–57; homeless *vs.*
runaway, 354; homosexual, 337n8,

adolescents (*continued*)
   357–58; and independence, 364;
   and juvenile justice system, 109,
   365–78; minority, 358; Native
   American, 359; nonconformity of,
   23–24; opportunities for, 379, 400;
   as parents, 350, 352; peer group
   influence on, 376; and
   psychological abuse, 40;
   rehabilitation of, 24; runaway,
   346, 353–57; services for, 364; and
   society, 23–24, 379; with special
   needs, 357–59; statistics on at-risk,
   347; transition to adults of, 400;
   well-being of, 394
adoption, 288–338, 384; in 1970s,
   87n9; of adolescents, 83, 310, 311,
   337n8, 338n10, 358; and adoptive
   homes, 307–8, 313, 317, 329;
   adults and, 308–9, 310; African-
   American, 292, 300, 330; and
   attachment, 338n14, 353; black
   market, 299–300, 304; and child
   development, 311; and children,
   291, 307, 308; of children with
   special needs, 311, 312, 314,
   329–30; and child welfare services,
   296; from China, 321; and
   community, 335; confidential,
   324–25, 326; cost of, 298;
   decision-making in, 307; definition
   of, 288; disrupted, 312, 315, 327;
   and domestic violence, 45; and
   foster care, 123, 234, 297, 300,
   336, 337n3, 396; of foster
   children, 100, 202, 215, 216, 237,
   259, 300, 306–7, 336; foster-
   parent, 313, 327; funding for, 66,
   94, 313, 329–31, 333, 335; by gay
   and lesbian parents, 314, 315–17;
   history of, 289–94; increased use
   of, 397–98; independent, 293, 299,
   303, 308, 317, 321, 323, 337n1,
   338n11; infant, 290, 291–92,
   302–4, 310–11, 327; and
   infertility, 291; international, 289,

293, 298, 308, 314, 320–24;
   legislation on, 294–96 (*See also
   particular laws*); and "life book,"
   337n4; and mediation, 297; and
   mental health, 301, 311, 332, 335;
   mutual consent registries in, 305,
   308; nontraditional, 84–85, 296,
   298, 312–27, 313; numbers of
   children involved in, 300–301; of
   older children, 292, 300, 306, 307,
   311, 313, 324, 327; open, 290,
   293, 296, 298, 303, 304, 324–27,
   328, 331, 338n12; from
   orphanages, 290; outcomes of,
   310–12; and parental rights, 79,
   289, 295, 296, 297, 306; paths to,
   296–300; and permanency, 55–57,
   60, 79, 83, 84, 90, 131, 184, 208,
   308, 312, 391, 392, 393; and
   policy issues, 335–36, 385; and
   poverty, 304, 320, 321; private,
   298; through public agencies,
   296–98; and quality of care, 392;
   and racism, 123, 318; with respite
   care, 296; and search for birth
   parents, 293, 308–9, 310, 328,
   338n15; single-parent, 298,
   313–15, 331; state data on, 95;
   state regulation of, 290–91, 293;
   transcultural, 289; transracial,
   74–75, 123, 289–96, 314, 317–20,
   328, 331, 392. *See also*
   placements; postadoption services
Adoption 2002, 294
Adoption and Foster Care Analysis
   and Reporting System (AFCARS),
   95, 208, 214, 216, 246n6, 268,
   270, 300, 301, 392, 393
Adoption and Safe Families Act
   (ASFA; 1997), 83–85, 349, 350,
   392, 393, 396–98; and children's
   safety, 64, 93; emphasis on
   adoption in, 184, 294, 313, 329;
   and foster care, 123, 297; and new
   forms of adoption, 85; and
   parental rights, 199; and

permanency, 131; provisions of, 125n7; and reasonable efforts at reunion, 69, 191–92; standards for foster homes in, 218, 255, 258, 275; timelines in, 237, 245n6

Adoption Assistance and Child Welfare Act (1980), 69, 82, 106, 107, 108, 295, 329

Adoption Attitudes Survey, National, 301, 310, 317

Adoption Information Clearinghouse, National, 314

adoption rights movement, 308–9

advocacy: and child labor laws, 15; and community, 14; and court-appointed advocates, 107, 108, 115; in criminal justice system, 411n6; and postadoption services, 334–35; and roles of women, 27; and social work, 5, 7, 116, 409, 410

AFCARS. See Adoption and Foster Care Analysis and Reporting System

AFDC. See Aid to Families with Dependent Children

African Americans: and abuse and neglect, 170; adolescent, 24, 358, 359, 361; and adoption, 292, 300, 330; children of, 120–23, 181, 213, 214, 251, 263, 297–98, 317; and extended family, 391; families of, 122, 206; and foster care, 170, 238, 257, 261, 318; in juvenile justice system, 370; and poverty, 20–21, 124, 330; and universal education, 18; and youth violence, 24

AIDS (Acquired Immune Deficiency Syndrome), 353, 361–62

Aid to Dependent Children (ADC; 1935), 75, 78, 151, 167

Aid to Families with Dependent Children (AFDC; 1962), 72, 76, 178

alcohol, 362, 363

Alcoholics Anonymous, 144

alcoholism, 25, 26, 130, 178. See also substance abuse

Allen, J., 332, 335

Allen, M., 139, 140

Allen, R. I., 234, 236

almshouses, 56, 200, 276

American Humane Association, 166

American Public Human Services Association, 96, 208, 403

anger management training, 44–45

animal protection movement, 166

Annie E. Casey Foundation, 97, 346, 371

apathy-futility syndrome, 36, 171

ASFA. See Adoption and Safe Families Act

Asians, 20, 213; adolescent, 359; adoption of, 321; in juvenile justice system, 370

attachment, 59–60, 90, 109, 155, 283n5; and adoption, 338n14, 353; in foster care, 215, 225, 230, 231; problems in, 81

autism, 111, 262

baby brokers, 291

Baran, A., 303

Barnardo's (child welfare agency), 245n4

Barth, R. P., 122, 178, 260, 279, 311, 329, 332, 333, 393, 394

Bartholet, E., 178, 184, 188, 320, 397–98

battered child syndrome, 71, 167

battered women. See domestic violence

Becerra, R., 32

Beer, E. S., 152

Benchmark Survey (1997), 294

Berrick, J. C., 279

Berrick, J. D., 263, 267, 273, 278, 279

Berry, M., 327

Besharov, D. J., 346

biological parents: and adoption, 291, 293, 297, 299, 301–5, 309,

biological parents (*continued*)
  311, 313, 320, 323, 327, 338,
  384; fathers, 304; and foster
  children, 219–21, 225; and foster
  parents, 210, 230, 231–33,
  259–60, 265; mothers, 290, 293,
  302, 303, 304, 324, 325, 326,
  337n2; search for, 293, 308–9,
  310, 328, 338n15; visiting with,
  223–25
Birnie-Lefcovitch, S., 145
birth control. *See* contraception
Birtwell, Charles, 205
Black and Blue (Quindlen), 48n10
Black Social Workers, National
  Association of, 74, 318
Bland, D., 232
The Book of Ruth (Hamilton), 48n9
Botsko, M., 181, 222
Bourguignon, J. P., 332
Bowlby, J., 80, 322
Boyle, P., 349
Brace, Charles Loring, 8, 202–3, 204,
  205, 242, 245n3
Bradshaw, D., 273, 279, 280
Breckinridge, Sophonisba, 17
Broffenbrenner, U., 146
Brooks, D., 311, 332, 335
Brown, P., 139
Bruner, A., 362, 363
Building Blocks for Youth, 370
Burford, G., 176
Burt, M., 346, 347, 359, 364
Bush, M., 282
Buzi, M., 361

Cahn, Katharine, 89–124
Cameron, C., 145
capital punishment, 365
CAPTA. *See* Child Abuse Prevention
  and Treatment Act
Carp, E. W., 337n5
Carroll, Richard, 206
Carstens, C. C., 166–67
CASA. *See* court-appointed special
  advocates

case examples, 10; of adoption, 303;
  of child care costs, 153–54; of
  child fatalities, 31–32; of foster
  care, 147, 220–22, 224, 226,
  228–33, 237; of incarcerated
  parents, 134; of kinship foster care,
  254, 256–59; Mary Ellen, 166; of
  medical neglect, 33; of mental
  health issues, 132; of protective
  services, 173–74, 176, 177–78,
  180, 183; of residential care,
  270–72; of respite care, 136–38; of
  special-needs children, 262,
  264–66
caseloads, 403, 406, 411n8; pressure
  of large, 99, 114, 115, 179–80,
  230, 244; and retention rates, 401,
  402
Casey Family Services, 226, 266, 267,
  334, 335
CASSP. *See* Child and Adolescent
  Services System Program
Cautley, P. W., 229
Census Bureau, U.S., 21
cerebral palsy, 311
Chalmers, M. A., 171
Chamberlain, P., 283n3
Chapin Hall Center for Children
  (University of Chicago), 209
charities, 5, 19; scientific, 8
Charities and Corrections, National
  Conference of, 203, 205, 206
Charity Organization Societies, 19,
  75, 141, 166
Chicago Bar Association, 61, 62
Chicago Home for Unfortunates, 200
Chicago Orphan Asylum, 202
Child Abuse and Neglect, National
  Center on, 71, 139, 168, 274
Child Abuse and Neglect, National
  Incidence Studies of (NIS), 96,
  124n2, 164, 170, 193; Third
  (1996), 28, 35, 120, 121, 169
Child Abuse and Neglect Data
  System, National (NCANDS), 95,
  169, 218, 392, 393

Child Abuse Prevention and
Treatment Act (CAPTA; 1974;
amended 1996), 71, 72, 95,
167–68
Child and Adolescent Services System
Program (CASSP), 112, 136
child care, 2, 150–59; after-school,
257; and child welfare policy, 385;
community, 154, 387; costs of,
153–54; vs. employment, 147–48,
389; federal policy in, 156; and
foster children, 242, 257; market
approach to, 157–58; military
system of, 157; need for, 15, 157;
need for more research in, 158;
and opportunity, 401; parental
preferences in, 153; quality of,
155–56, 158, 159; reexamining,
156–57; resources for, 154–55; and
single-parent family, 23; and teen
parents, 139, 361; wages in, 154,
155, 159; and welfare reform, 389;
workers in, 158, 159; and working
women, 22, 76
Child Care and Development Block
Grant Act (1990), 156, 157
Child Care Development Fund, 157,
158, 159
Child Citizen Act (2000), 323
Child Future Security Accounts, 400
Child Health and Human
Development, National Institute of
(NICHD), 155
child labor, 5, 166; Constitution on,
18; and education, 15–18; laws
against, 8, 14, 15–18; reform of, 1,
65
children: at-risk, 29, 40, 163, 191,
219; dependent, 86n4, 200, 206,
276, 281; needs of, 55–60, 68;
nurture and guidance of, 58–59
Children's Act (1975; England), 309
Children's Aid Society, 203, 204, 205
Children's Authority, 399
Children's Bureau, 7, 37, 52, 66–67,
108, 151, 194, 208; and child

welfare training, 403; and federal
government, 93; inception of
(1912), 92, 167; and measurement
of outcomes, 393
Children's Defense Fund, 96, 259, 371
Children's Justice Act, 67
child rescue movement, 8, 34,
165–66, 183
child support payments, 23, 78
Child Welfare (journal), 67
child welfare agencies, 80, 89;
changing role of, 90–106; differing
perspectives in, 118–19; formal
oversight of, 114–15; and foster
parents, 219; informal oversight of,
115–16; international, 277; and
investment in foster homes, 256;
power of, 193; public, 160,
168–72, 296–98; public vs.
voluntary, 102, 103, 104, 105–6;
state, 140; supervision of, 255;
voluntary (private), 102–4, 298
Child Welfare League of America, 67;
on annual turnover, 102; and child
welfare training, 403; on
confidentiality, 305; data of, 95,
96; definition of kinship care by,
253; and group care, 267, 269;
and new practices, 103, 167; and
private agencies, 104; and
transracial adoptions, 73, 317
child welfare services: availability of,
386–88; bureaucratization of, 167;
change in nature of, 71;
comprehensiveness of, 386–88,
399; criticism of, 28, 30–31, 64;
definition of, 1–2, 383;
expectations of, 391–92; federal
role in, 70, 92, 93, 103, 114; goals
of, 52, 53; innovations in,
396–401; interdisciplinary work
in, 117–18; outcomes of, 390–96;
privatization of, 102, 104;
professionalization of, 167, 404,
406; and racism, 21, 120–25, 170;
reprofessionalization of, 383–84;

child welfare services (*continued*)
  residual, 386, 387, 388; and
  responsibility, 114; standards for,
  70, 103, 114, 390; state role in,
  70, 92, 93, 94; under stress, 2–5,
  98–99; traditional definition of,
  383; and wrap-around services,
  112, 119
child welfare workers, 74, 85–86,
  101–2; education of, 385, 394,
  403, 406; effective use of, 396; and
  foster care, 222–23, 229;
  investigatory function of, 63–64,
  71, 97–98, 165–69, 172–74, 394,
  397; paperwork of, 402, 404,
  411n8; professional skills of, 2, 3,
  5; retention of, 102, 385, 401–4,
  406, 409, 411n8; salaries of, 402,
  403, 411n8; and school system,
  118; and social work education,
  404–6; supervision of, 402, 403,
  406
China, adoption from, 321
civil rights movement, 317
class: and abuse, 182; and culture,
  182; and domestic violence, 41;
  middle, 22, 26; and social work
  values, 408; working, 22, 313
class action suits, 409
Clinton, Hillary, 349–50
Clinton, William Jefferson, 293–94,
  349
community: and abuse, 28, 32, 34,
  37, 90, 97–98, 395; and adoptive
  families, 335; advocacy in, 14; and
  alcohol use, 363; changes in,
  14–27, 91, 390; child care in, 154,
  387; and child fatalities, 30–31;
  and child poverty, 18–19; and child
  welfare, 6–7, 9, 46–47, 85, 89, 93,
  97–98, 192, 283; and child welfare
  services, 164, 384, 387; and
  domestic violence, 44; and families,
  7, 128–60, 177, 200, 387; and
  family preservation, 192, 387, 395;
  funding of programs in, 13, 14,

387; and homosexuality, 362; and
  individual, 8; as intervention
  target, 365; mental health services
  in, 132, 387; and physical abuse,
  34, 37, 390; and psychological
  abuse, 40; as risk antecedent, 346;
  and risk-taking behaviors, 347;
  services based in, 13, 14, 128–60,
  357, 387, 398–400; and sexuality,
  362; social work in, 187; standards
  of, 3, 13–14, 29, 32, 58, 98, 182,
  244, 390; and substance abuse,
  25–26, 373; supports in, 28–29,
  128–29, 138–40, 166, 217–18,
  277; and universal education, 18;
  and youth, 23, 24, 357, 365
Community-Based Family Resource
  Program Grants, 67
community-based model, 377–78
community-centered practice, 187–88
Community Facilities Act (Lanham
  Act), 151, 152
community partnerships, 409, 410;
  and criminal justice system, 399;
  funding of, 384, 399; and
  opportunity, 400–401
Comprehensive Child Development
  Act (1971), 156
confidentiality, 117, 305; of adoption,
  324–25, 326
congregate care, 200–202, 244
connectedness, youth, 346, 347, 352,
  362
Conroy, J., 228
continuity of care, 55, 301, 308
contraception, 292, 302, 362
Convention on the Protection of
  Children and Cooperation in
  Respect of Intercountry Adoption
  (the Hague Convention), 323
Cook, R., 350–51
Cook County Juvenile Court
  (Chicago, Illinois), 366
Coontz, S., 22–23
coordination of systems, 112–14
Costin, L. B., 94, 182, 397, 399, 408

court-appointed special advocates
(CASA), 107, 108, 115
Courtney, M., 6, 122, 267
courts: dependency, 86n4, 108–9,
125n4; family, 56, 61–63, 65, 68,
92, 106–9, 125n4, 221. *See also*
criminal justice system; juvenile
justice system; legal system
Courts, National Center for State, 300
crack cocaine, 26, 83, 172, 208
Crawford, S. L., 178
Crenson, M. W., 206, 245n5
crime, 14; causes of, 365–66, 373,
376; and gender, 371–72; and
guns, 371; juvenile, 365–78; and
mandated sentencing, 374–75;
percent reported, 367–68;
perpetrators of, 368; prevention of
juvenile, 373–78; property, 367,
368, 372; and punishment of
children, 61, 365; and recidivism,
376; and risk-taking behavior, 345;
and runaways, 355; violent, 369,
370, 372; violent *vs.* property,
367, 368; and young children,
370, 372
Crime in the United States (Uniform
Crime Reports; FBI), 367
Crime Victim Surveys, 367
criminal justice system, 4, 109, 165;
and abuse, 38, 397; child advocacy
professionals within, 411n6; and
community partnerships, 399; and
domestic violence, 41, 44, 45;
elements of, 369–70; families in,
129, 211; and incarcerated
parents, 133–34; juveniles in, 368;
social work perspective on, 407;
training of lawyers in, 411n6;
youth in, 24, 268, 374–76. *See also*
juvenile justice system
criminology: classical, 373–76;
classical *vs.* positive, 365–66, 373;
positive, 376–78
crisis intervention, 163–93, 267;
family treatment model of, 186;

home-based model of, 186, 187.
See also Homebuilders
crisis nurseries, 136
Crisis Nurseries Act (1986), 136
Crittenden, P. M., 36
culture: and definitions of abuse, 32;
and domestic violence, 41; of drugs
and violence, 121; and physical
abuse, 34, 37, 182; and social
class, 182
custody, 73; and family court, 109,
125n4, 244; of father, 21; loss of,
274, 304, 333

Dave Thomas Foundation for
Adoption, 294
Davies, L., 232
day care. *See* child care
decision-making: in adoption, 307; in
child welfare, 116, 177, 222, 255;
family, 109, 174, 176, 177, 245,
251; and foster care, 175, 183; and
Native American tribes, 74, 295; of
parents, 192, 221; and safety, 175,
185, 194n6, 228, 295
DeHaan, B., 31
deinstitutionalization movement, 282
delinquency, 14, 23–24, 86n4, 109,
125n4, 243, 268; causes of,
376–77; data on, 367–69; and
discrimination, 378; and drugs,
372–73; environmental factors in,
377; future rates of, 368–69; and
gender, 371–72; "get tough"
approach to, 366–67, 373–76;
and guns, 370–71; preventive
models for, 377–78; and race, 21;
research on, 366–67, 376; and risk
markers, 346; and runaways, 353,
354. *See also* adolescents
depression, 36, 45, 111, 360
disabilities: and abuse, 38, 40, 111;
and child welfare, 6, 268; and
coordination of systems, 112, 113;
developmental, 38, 110–11;
funding for, 67, 72, 113, 136; and

disabilities (*continued*)
  independent living programs, 352;
  and school, 113
disconnectedness, 346–47. *See also*
  isolation, social
discrimination: and delinquency, 378;
  and sexual minority youth, 357
divorce, 22
domestic violence, 14, 40–46, 165,
  259; and abuse, 29, 38; and
  battered women's shelters, 41, 118,
  134, 135; and behavioral problems,
  44; and child welfare services, 6, 89,
  109, 119, 130, 385; and community
  standards, 390; coordination of
  services on, 45–46; and criminal
  justice system, 41, 44, 45; as
  criminal offense, 397; and early
  childhood services, 45–46; and
  family preservation, 42–43, 190;
  and foster care, 211, 212;
  involvement of children in, 42, 134;
  statistics on, 41–42; and substance
  abuse, 46; and success of programs,
  190; *Woman's Day* survey on, 42;
  against women, 41, 134–35
Dore, M. M., 111, 190, 263, 264
Downs, S. W., 62, 86n5, 92, 163
Down syndrome, 311
drug violations, 23, 370, 372–73.
  See also substance abuse

Earned Income Tax Credit, 78, 388
Eastern European orphanages, 36, 40
Eckenrode, J., 354
ecological approach, 377
economy, 369; changing, 152–53,
  157; and women, 21–22. *See also*
  poverty
Edna McConnell Clark Foundation,
  187, 193n3
education, 2, 5, 9; and advocacy, 409;
  and child abuse, 28, 37, 386; and
  child labor, 15–18; of children, 58,
  59, 68, 128, 147; of child welfare
  workers, 385, 394, 403, 404–6;

and community services, 390;
  compulsory, 14, 16–18; and
  democracy, 15, 16; in early child
  welfare, 8; and early sexual
  behavior, 360, 362; and fatalities,
  30; and independent living
  programs, 348, 350, 351; low
  attainment in, 190; and migrant
  workers, 17, 18; and neglect,
  33–34; and opportunity, 18, 401;
  and pregnancy, 360, 362;
  programs for batterers, 44–45;
  public, 30, 37, 157, 159, 166, 386;
  and roles of women, 27; and
  runaways, 356; school-site health,
  362; and school system, 113, 118,
  125n5; and sexual minority youth,
  357; social work, 5, 116, 403,
  404–6, 408, 409; and STDs, 362;
  universal, 15–18, 59, 65, 387
Education, Council on Social Work,
  403
Education, Department of, 151
Edwards, S., 174, 193n2
Eisenberg, M., 155
Elizabethan Poor Laws, 76
Ellett, A. J., 402, 406
Elmer, E., 38
emancipation, legal, 353
Emlen, A., 153
employment, 149; and child abuse,
  28, 38, 170; *vs.* child care, 147–48,
  389, 410n1; and independent
  living programs, 348, 350; lack of,
  38, 170, 369; and runaways, 356;
  and welfare reform, 389; of
  women, 3, 22, 27, 57, 76, 83, 100,
  198, 242, 390
Engler, R., 82, 214
environment, 86n2; and delinquency,
  377; *vs.* heredity, 290
Epstein, W. M., 229, 282
ethical issues, 407–8
Etter, J., 325, 326
Evan B. Donaldson Adoption
  Institute, 294, 301, 321

Fagan, J. A., 376
Fahlberg, V. I., 58–59, 81, 238
failure to thrive, 36
Fair Labor Standards Act (1938), 18
families: abusive, 28, 81, 170; and
    adolescents, 187, 353, 356, 357,
    359, 365, 378; adoptive, 289, 292,
    296, 331, 335, 336; African-
    American, 122, 206, 391;
    autonomy of, 61, 65, 71;
    biological, 223–24, 305 (See also
    biological parents); blended, 22;
    changing structure of, 3, 14,
    21–23, 91, 98, 160; and child
    welfare services, 1, 8, 53, 386; of
    color, 190, 213; and community, 7,
    128–60; in criminal justice system,
    129, 211; decision-making by, 109,
    174, 176, 177, 245, 251; definition
    of, 54, 68–69; establishment of, 2,
    235–36; extended, 23, 54, 56, 57,
    60, 69, 79, 84, 85, 183, 184, 189,
    192, 195, 207, 228, 236, 250–51,
    257, 295, 313, 332, 391, 398;
    female-headed, 21, 22, 76,
    170–71; gender roles in, 20; and
    geographic mobility, 22–23; high-
    risk, 99, 187, 189; Hispanic, 172;
    homosexual, 22, 68–69, 289;
    income support for, 65 (See also
    income maintenance); and
    independent living programs, 352;
    initial contact with, 397;
    intergenerational ties in, 22–23;
    intervention in, 9, 48n12, 53–55,
    60–61, 64, 65, 68, 69, 85, 172–83,
    222, 263; low-risk, 99–100, 188;
    meetings of, 176, 177, 222; needs
    of, 138–40, 146–50;
    nontraditional, 22, 68–69, 184,
    289, 292, 336; nuclear, 54; and
    poverty, 19; psychological, 81;
    reunification of, 8, 199; as risk
    antecedent, 346; and risk-taking
    behaviors, 347; rural, 22, 122; vs.
    safety, 193; separation from, 81,
    240, 289; and sexuality, 362;
    single-parent, 21, 22, 23, 27, 35,
    76, 100, 120, 152, 170–71, 198,
    211, 292, 390; social work
    perspective on, 406; stability of, 3,
    385; strengthening of, 139, 143,
    167, 176, 191, 272; and substance
    abuse, 373; treatment for, 2, 186,
    187, 259, 355, 378; urban vs.
    rural, 122; visiting with biological,
    223–24; young, 21, 25, 28. See
    also domestic violence
Families, Inc. (Iowa), 194n4
Families First, 194n5
Family-Based Services, National
    Resource Center on, 194n4
family homes, 85; vs. institutional
    care, 57, 60, 205, 244. See also
    foster homes; group homes
family preservation, 2, 4, 122, 129,
    163–97, 199, 384; and abuse, 29,
    93, 164–65; vs. adoption, 398;
    appropriate use of services for,
    189–93; and child fatalities, 31;
    and child protective services,
    165–83; and child welfare policy,
    385; community programs for,
    187–88, 192, 387, 395; crisis
    intervention and, 185; and
    domestic violence, 42–43, 190; as
    expectation, 391; and foster care,
    198, 214, 251, 254; and home-
    based treatment, 185; intensive
    service models for, 185–87;
    interventions for, 394–95; and
    kinship foster care, 188–89, 259;
    and social change, 385; social
    work perspective on, 407; and
    states, 140; and welfare reform,
    389
Family Preservation and Support
    Services Act (1993), 139
family resource centers, 140–41
Family Service Plans, 113
Family Support Act, 76
Fanshel, D., 223, 234, 236, 266, 267

fatalities, 29–32; and abuse, 29–30, 84, 170, 218; and bad decisions, 191; and child welfare services, 30–31, 164; from domestic violence, 41; in foster care, 31, 218; and interdisciplinary review teams, 30; and neglect, 30, 84; rates of, 30; risk factors for, 31
fathers: birth, 304; children without, 83; and child support payments, 23, 78; foster, 229, 230; and incarcerated mothers, 133; role of, 21, 23, 174
Faver, C. A., 178
Federal Bureau of Investigation (FBI), Uniform Crime Reports of, 367
Federal Child Abuse Prevention and Treatment Act (1974), 37
Fein, E., 226
feminism, 27, 135; on domestic violence, 41; and neglect, 35; and sexual abuse, 38
Festinger, T., 181, 222, 235
Fiegelman, W., 314
Finch, S. J., 236, 266
Finkelhor, D., 39
Fishman, M., 362, 363
Flaks, D. K., 316
Flower, Lucy L., 61
Foley, R., 131
food stamps, 78
Forty Assets (Search Institute), 347
foster care, 3, 198–246, 384; abuse in, 218–19, 274, 275; and adoption, 123, 216, 234, 297, 300, 336, 337n3, 396; African American recruiters for, 238; and African Americans, 170, 238, 257, 261, 318; age of children in, 212; attachment in, 215, 225, 230, 231; case examples of, 147, 220–22, 224, 226, 228–33, 237; characteristics of, 213–18; and child fatalities, 31, 218; and child welfare policy, 385; and child welfare workers, 222–23, 229;

contemporary, 207–37; cost of, 193n3, 280; and decision-making, 175, 183; difficulties of, 198; and domestic violence, 211, 212; exclusive vs. inclusive, 232, 260; expansion of, 199, 250–83, 292; in families, 54, 56, 57, 250, 256, 391–92; and family preservation, 198, 214, 251, 254, 395; funding for, 66, 104, 124n1, 168, 283n2; and homelessness, 25; vs. institutional care, 205, 206, 284n5; in institutions, 54; and interventions, 395–96; leaving, 216–17; length of stay in, 213–15, 297; long-term, 55, 56, 131; and minority children, 120, 121, 212, 358, 359; number of children in, 83, 93, 94, 199, 207–8; and parental rights, 84, 199; payment for, 241–43, 245, 283nn2,4, 284n6; and permanency, 82–83, 213–14, 216, 393; placements in, 73, 80, 90, 99, 100–101, 114, 121–22, 165, 186, 189, 205, 209, 215–16, 236, 261; and private agencies, 101, 103, 124n3; programs to provide, 70, 79, 80–81, 90; and race, 21, 121–22, 212–13; reasons for entry into, 210–12; reentry into, 217–18; at request of parents, 210; and runaways, 353, 355, 356; shelter, 252; specialized, 105, 261–67; state data on, 95; and substance abuse, 26, 130, 131; and "time clock of the child," 215; transition from, 216, 348–53; types of, 210; and welfare reform, 389; whole-family, 250–51, 259–61. See also kinship foster care
"foster care drift," 82, 212, 214, 330
foster children, 60, 216; as adults, 234–37; as at-risk youth, 348–53; and biological parents, 220–21, 225; characteristics of, 210–13;

experiences of, 219–33; self-
sufficiency of, 234–35; sexual
minority, 357
foster families, 219, 237, 329
foster homes, 83, 90, 165; and
adolescents, 208; and adoptive
homes, 234, 337n3; assessment of,
238–40; and criminal background
checks, 239; establishing, 237–40;
group, 268; kinship, 218, 253–59,
266; licensing of, 239; medical, 26;
minority, 238; vs. orphanages, 205,
206, 284n5; and private agencies,
101, 124n3; respite, 137; retaining,
241–44; shelter, 252; shortage of,
4, 57, 100, 188, 198–99, 214, 216,
218, 244, 251–54, 259, 385, 396;
and stable care, 199
foster parents, 205, 216, 218, 223,
229–33; assessment of, 238–39;
and biological parents, 231–33,
259–60, 265; and children, 233; as
colleagues, 243–44; and emergency
shelter care, 252; and independent
living programs, 352; payments to,
242, 279, 284n6; recruitment of,
237; retention of, 241–44, 245;
and social workers, 241; support
groups for, 241–42; training of,
240–41
Freud, Sigmund, 6
funding: for adoption, 66, 94, 313,
329–31, 333, 335; block-grant, 70,
72, 77, 93, 113, 156, 157, 159,
255, 388; and child poverty, 20;
for child welfare, 47, 119–20; of
child welfare services, 94, 383; of
community partnerships, 384, 399;
of community programs, 13, 14,
384, 387, 399; definition of
capped, 124n1; for disabilities, 67,
72, 113, 136; for family
preservation, 139–40; of family
support services, 139, 140; federal,
66–67, 356, 388; flexible, 119–20;
for foster care, 66, 104, 124n1,

168, 283n2; for independent living
programs, 349, 350; for legal
professionals, 411n6; for practice
reform project, 10; and role of
fathers, 23; for runaways, 356,
357; Title IV-E, 66, 94, 283n2,
333, 349, 356, 403, 405, 409; and
universal education, 18; and
welfare reform, 389; of worker
training programs, 403; of youth
services, 364

Gabor, P., 233
Garbarino, J., 39–40
Gardiner, K. N., 346
gay men, 22, 68–69; as adoptive
parents, 315–17. See also
homosexuality
Gelles, R. J., 36
gender, 20, 371–72
Germany, 277
Gerry, Elbridge T., 166
Gibbs, D. A., 329, 332, 333
Gibson, D., 260
Gingrich, Newt, 277
Giovannoni, J. M., 32
Gordon, M., 151
government, federal: and child labor
laws, 17–18; and Children's
Bureau, 93; and child welfare
services, 70, 92, 93, 103, 114, 156;
and domestic violence, 46;
expanded intervention by, 167;
funding from, 356, 388; and
homelessness, 25; and independent
living programs, 349–50; and
parens patriae, 61, 62, 165, 366;
and parental rights, 366; and
protective services, 165, 167;
responsibility for children of,
60–65; and role of fathers, 23; and
social welfare, 15, 17–18;
standards set by, 388
governments, state: and adoption, 95,
290–91, 293; and block-grant
funding, 388; and child abuse, 37,

governments, state (*continued*)
67; and child welfare, 10, 70,
92–94, 95, 140, 366;
communication among, 388;
expanded intervention by, 167
grandparents: child care by, 133, 136,
153, 158; and crisis intervention,
176, 177; and kinship foster care,
183, 254, 256, 257, 283n1, 391;
organizations of, 116
Great Britain, 277, 337n1
Great Depression, 20, 75
Greene, J., 354
Grotevant, H. D., 325, 326, 338n12
group home care, 250, 251, 261,
267–68, 276–82; abuse in,
280–81; cost of, 279–80; and
runaways, 353, 355; and sexual
minority youth, 357; for young
children, 278–79
group homes, 253, 268–69, 277, 316
Groze, V., 314, 328
guardianship, court-ordered, 79–80
Guatemala, adoption from, 321
Guttmann, E., 39–40

Hamilton, Jane, 47n9
Hart, Dr. Hastings, 203
Hawaii Department of Public Health,
139
Hayes-Bautista, D., 172
Hazel, N., 267
Head Start, 46, 110, 138–39, 145–46,
157, 158, 159
Head Start Performance Standards,
158
health, 9, 155; and homelessness, 25;
maternal, 6, 8, 93; public, 89, 92.
See also mental health
Health and Human Services, U.S.
Department of (HHS), 275
health care, 2, 110, 128; for children,
59, 93; and community standards,
58; lack of, 15, 148; through
Medicaid, 149; and opportunity,
401; and runaways, 353, 356;

school-site, 361–62; and sexual
minority youth, 357; universal,
148, 387; and working women, 22
Healthy Families America (HFA), 141,
142
Healthy Start (Hawaii), 139, 141
Hernandez, D. J., 152
HFA. *See* Healthy Families America
High/Scope Perry Preschool Project
(Ypsilanti, Michigan), 146
Hispanics: and child poverty, 20–21;
children of, 124, 170, 213; families
of, 172; in juvenile justice system,
370; and universal education, 18;
youth of, 359, 361, 379n6
Holt International Adoption Services,
322
Homebuilders, 186, 187, 193n3
homelessness: adolescent, 24, 348–58;
and children, 149, 150, 202; and
domestic violence, 44; and former
foster children, 235; and
independent living programs, 349;
and mental health, 132–33; and
risk-taking behaviors, 347; and
sexual minority youth, 357, 358;
statistics on, 25; and street kids,
354, 355, 358; and whole-family
care, 259
home schooling, 33, 34
home-visiting programs, 139, 141–43,
146
homosexuality: adolescent, 337n8,
357–58; and adoption, 314,
315–17; and child welfare, 358;
community attitudes towards, 362;
and families, 22, 68–69, 289; of
parents, 69, 313, 316; *vs.*
pedophilia, 316
Horn, W. F., 131
Hornby, H., 327, 406
housing: affordable, 149–50; and
child abuse, 28, 170; and
independent living programs, 348,
351; lack of, 179, 188; percent of
income for, 25; public, 149, 150;

and runaways, 355; safe, 149–50; subsidized, 150
Howell, J. C., 374, 376
Hudson, J., 266
Hull House, 24, 47n4, 61
Hurtado, A., 172

ICWA. *See* Indian Child Welfare Act
IEPA. *See* Interethnic Adoption Provisions Amendment
Immigration and Nationality Act, 323
imprisonment, 365; of parents, 133–34, 190; of youth in adult facilities, 375–76
income maintenance, 8, 70, 75–79, 94, 113, 147–48, 184; and adoption, 320, 329; and child poverty, 20; and child welfare services, 89, 93, 128, 386, 401; data on, 95; and Earned Income Tax Credit, 78, 388; for families, 65; and family preservation, 394–95; and placements, 175; in Progressive Era, 14; and social work, 5; universal, 387–88; and welfare reform, 150, 389, 410n1; widows' pensions, 151
Incredible Years Training Series, 143–44
indenture, 56, 165, 201, 202, 244, 245n2, 279
independent living programs, 66, 216–17, 348–53; federal role in, 349–50; and minority youth, 358; need for, 348–49; outcomes of, 351–53; and runaways, 355, 356; Title IV-E, 349, 356
Indian Adoption Project, 73
Indian Affairs, American Association on, 73
Indian Affairs, Bureau of, 73
Indian Child Welfare Act (ICWA; 1978), 72–74, 75, 86n7, 123, 294–95, 296, 317, 391
individual, 7, 8; and adoption, 288; rights of, 408

Individual Education Plans (IEP), 113
Individuals with Disabilities Education Act (IDEA; 1990), 113
industrialization, 16, 17, 18, 22
infant mortality, 207
In re Gault (Supreme Court case), 62, 68
institutional care, 4, 54, 55, 65–69, 135, 165, 320; and abuse, 28, 274; and child welfare policy, 385; correctional, 370; cost of, 242; for dependent children, 47n3, 276–82; *vs.* family homes, 57, 60, 205, 244; *vs.* foster care, 205, 206, 208–9, 284n5; outcomes of, 281–82; and permanency, 396; and poverty, 19; private, 128; and race, 21; and runaways, 355; and safety, 391; for young children, 178–279; and youth, 24. *See also* orphanages
Intercountry Adoption Act (2000), 323
Interethnic Adoption Provisions Amendment (IEPA; 1996), 75, 123, 295–96
interventions: crisis, 163–97; expansion of state, 167; in families, 9, 48n12, 53–55, 60–61, 64, 65, 68, 69, 85, 172–83, 222, 263; and outcomes, 394–96; treatment, 264–66
isolation, social: and abuse, 38, 40; *vs.* connectedness, 347, 352, 362; and minority youth, 359; as risk marker, 346–47

Jivanjee, P., 265
Job Corps, 349
job satisfaction, 406, 409; of child welfare workers, 404; factors in, 411n8; and retention rates, 402
job training programs, 76, 77
Johnson, E., 233
Johnson, Lyndon B., 345
Johnson, P. R., 228
Justice, U.S. Department of, 367
Justice Statistics, Bureau of, 367

juvenile justice system, 1, 8, 348, 365–78; and child welfare policy, 385; and classical criminology, 345; clientele of, 370–73; and community programs, 387; coordination of services in, 373; "get tough" approach in, 366, 373–76; and independent living programs, 352; and mandated sentencing, 374–75; minority youth in, 359, 370; origins of, 24, 366; rehabilitative ideal in, 366, 376; young children in, 370, 372

Kadushin, A., 38, 171, 205, 241, 309, 310, 311–12, 322
Karger, H. J., 94, 182, 397, 399, 408
Karr-Morse, Robin, 86n1
Kelley, Florence, 17, 65
Kent Project (Kent, England), 267, 283n4
Kent v. United States, 68
Kids Count Data Book (Annie E. Casey Foundation), 346, 371
"Kids Count," National, 96
Kingsolver, Barbara, 86n7
kinship foster care, 4, 23, 133, 208, 218, 250, 253–59, 385; advantages of, 131, 244, 266, 282, 396; and African Americans, 121–22, 251, 257, 391; case examples of, 254, 256–59; and family preservation, 183, 188–89, 192, 193, 259, 391–92; payment for, 255, 283n2, 389
Kirk, David, 292, 338n13
Knitzer, J., 45–46
Knudsen, D. D., 274
Kools, S., 359
Koprowitz, C., 363
Korea, adoption from, 321
Korean War, 321, 322
Kreuger, L. W., 6

labor unions, 17, 166
Landsman, M. J., 185

Lanham Act (Community Facilities Act), 151, 152
Lathrop, Julia, 20, 24, 61, 65
laws: on child support payments, 23; enforcement of, 2, 53, 118; against physical abuse, 37. *See also particular laws and acts*
legal system, 22, 52, 53, 70–79, 90, 128, 383; and child protective services, 39, 89; and children's rights, 55–60, 68, 69, 166; child welfare professionals in, 117, 411n6; and child welfare system, 106–10, 175, 244; and due process, 62–63, 68. *See also* courts; criminal justice system; juvenile justice system
lesbians, 22, 68–69; as adoptive parents, 315–17. *See also* homosexuality
Lieberman, A., 406
Lindsey, D., 4, 31, 175, 178, 383, 394, 400, 408
Littner, Ner, 81, 225
Lock, J., 357
Lyon, T. D., 45

Maas, H., 82, 214
McCroskey, J., 190
McCullough, C., 106
McDermott, M. T., 299
McDonald, T. P., 234, 235, 236, 275
McFadden, E. J., 231, 259
McKenzie, R. B., 281, 297
McRoy, R. G., 326, 338n12
maltreatment, 28–40, 163–97. *See also* abuse; neglect
Maluccio, A., 27, 260
managed care, 104–6, 223, 271, 273
marijuana, 362
Martin, J., 38, 171, 199, 214, 246n7, 309, 310
Marx, Karl, 6
Mead, Margaret, 52
mediation, 297, 304, 377

Medicaid: and adoption of children with special needs, 329–30; and drop in infant mortality, 149; health care through, 149; and independent living programs, 349; referrals for, 178; waivers in, 136, 149

Medical Neglect/Disabled Infants State Grants, 67

Medicare, 149

Meezan, W., 7, 190, 327, 399

Meier, E., 235

mental health, 9, 38; and adoption, 301, 311, 332, 335; changes in, 271; and child welfare, 6, 111, 116, 130, 132, 179, 188, 190; and crime by young children, 372; and domestic violence, 42; and foster care, 230, 236; and homelessness, 132–33; and runaways, 353, 355; and whole-family care, 259, 260

mental health services, 89, 110, 119, 268; and child welfare policy, 385–86; community programs for, 132, 387; legislation on, 113; school-site, 362

MEPA. See Multiethnic Placement Act

Merkel-Holguin, L. A., 275

migrant workers, 17, 18

Miller v. Youakim, 283n2

Milne, A. A., 198

minorities: children of, 181, 212, 213, 251, 295, 297, 317, 318; and child welfare services, 213; and juvenile justice system, 370; negative self-identification of, 357, 359; and poverty, 400; and racism, 26, 358, 359; and risk-taking behaviors, 347; sexual, 357–58; youth of, 357, 358, 359. See also particular groups

Moore, E., 62, 86n5, 92, 163

Morton, T., 43, 122, 402

Moses, adoption of, 289–90

mothers: attitudes about role of, 156, 159; birth, 290, 293, 302, 303, 304, 324, 325, 326, 337n2; foster, 229–33, 250, 264, 265; parental rights of, 45, 134; pensions for, 65, 92, 151, 166, 184; protection of children by, 42–44; separation from, 220, 266; single, 22, 76, 147, 170–71, 206, 211, 257, 260, 292, 360; support for incarcerated, 133–34; teenage, 355, 356, 360–61; unwed, 293, 349; working, 150–52, 157

Mothers Against Drunk Driving (MADD), 363

Mulry, Thomas, 205, 206, 282

Multiethnic Placement Act (MEPA; 1994), 74, 75, 123, 125n7, 295–96, 298, 318, 319, 392

national data system, 92, 94–97; and out-of-home care, 95–96

National Rifle Association (NRA), 371

Native Americans: and adoption, 294; and child poverty, 21; children of, 73, 74, 75, 115, 120, 121, 123, 181, 213, 251, 295; and Indian Child Welfare Act, 72–74, 75, 86n7, 123, 294–95, 296, 317, 391; in juvenile justice system, 370; Natchez Indian massacre, 200; tribal decisions of, 74, 295; youth of, 359

NCANDS. See Child Abuse and Neglect Data System, National

neglect, 35–36, 91, 105, 168; and community, 28; definitions of, 29, 32–34, 164, 182; educational, 33–34; effects of, 99, 110, 111; emotional, 34; and fatalities, 30, 84; and foster care, 210–11, 212; investigation of, 397; and malnutrition, 36; medical, 33; and out-of-home placement, 210, 212; physical, 33; and poverty, 35, 36, 211; programs to prevent, 70, 184; and protective services, 210, 211; repeated, 391, 392; in residential

neglect (*continued*)
care, 274–75; and runaways, 354; statistics on, 35; and substance abuse, 26, 35, 36, 171; and teen parents, 361; and urban families, 122. *See also* abuse
Nelson, K. E., 185, 191
Nelson, K. M., 260
"Never Shake a Baby" campaign, 30
New Deal, 15, 70
New York: independent living programs in, 349; juvenile justice system in, 376
New York Society for the Prevention of Cruelty to Children, formation of (1875), 166
NICHD. *See* Child Health and Human Development, National Institute of
NIS. *See* Child Abuse and Neglect, National Incidence Studies of
Nixon, Richard, 156
Noble, D. N., 260
North American Council on Adoptable Children, 331
nutrition, 36, 78–79
Nutter, R., 266

Office of Juvenile Justice and Delinquency Prevention, 283n3
O'Malley, F., 271
Omnibus Budget and Reconciliation Act (1993), Court Improvement Program of, 108
Oregon, 33, 210–11; mandated sentencing in, 374, 375
Oregon Health Plan, 149
Oregon Project, 208, 217
Oregon State Office for Services to Children and Families, 10
orphanages, 56, 81, 92, 102, 103; adoption from, 290; debate about, 277, 279; Eastern European, 36, 40; *vs.* foster care, 205, 206, 284n5; history of, 200–202, 244, 281; and private agencies, 298; in

Romania, 278, 283n5, 304, 322. *See also* institutional care
orphans, 56, 203; shipment West of, 8, 57
outcomes: of adoption, 310–12; of foster care, 234–37; impact of measurement of, 392–94; of independent living programs, 351–53; of institutional care, 281–82; and interventions, 394–96; mandated measurement of, 390–91; of protective services, 180–81; of residential care, 275–76; of specialized foster care, 266
out-of-home care, 1, 2, 129, 178, 193, 228, 246n8; alternative forms of, 199, 250; and block grants, 388; and children of color, 120–22, 197–298, 212–13, 257, 263, 317–20; decisions about, 175; history of, 199–207, 244; and mental illness, 111; number of children in, 208; reasons for, 29, 210–12; temporary, 167. *See also* foster care; institutional care; residential care

Pacific Islanders, 20
parens patriae, 61, 62, 165, 366
parental rights: and adoption, 79, 289, 295, 296, 297, 306; and domestic violence, 45; and foster care, 84, 199; in Germany, 277; limits on, 392; of mother, 45, 134; and preserving families, 189; and state intervention, 199, 366; termination of, 398; violation of, 48n12, 74
parenting: attitudes toward, 145, 188; *vs.* employment, 147–48, 389, 410n1; skills of, 136, 139, 143, 193, 361
parents: adoptive, 291, 292, 293, 302, 304, 305–7, 314, 315–17, 323, 326, 338n15; civil liberties of, 71,

108, 397; as clients, 118; decision-making of, 192, 221; and domestic violence, 109; gay and lesbian, 69, 313, 314, 315–17; incarcerated, 133–34, 190; reunion with, 293; rights of, 63–64, 65, 68, 69, 71, 79, 84, 108, 224; separation from, 225; services for, 384, 389, 394–95; social work perspective on, 406; teen, 139, 259, 350, 352, 361; training programs for, 2, 143–44, 387, 398; and whole-family care, 259; working, 150, 160; working-class, 313. See also biological parents; foster parents; single parents

Parents Anonymous, 144–45

Parnell, J., 176

parole, 365, 369, 373–74; and inmate behavior, 374, 379n7

Parry Center (Portland, Oregon), 200

Partridge, S., 327

Patch Project (Iowa), 187–88

patriarchy, 33, 38, 408

Pecora, P. J., 28, 268, 276

pedophilia, 316

Pelton, L., 408

Perkins, Frances, 151

permanency: and adoption, 55–57, 60, 79, 83, 84, 90, 131, 184, 208, 308, 312, 391, 392, 393; and ASFA, 131; and foster care, 393; and institutional care, 396; and legislation, 295; measurement of, 390–91, 393; outcomes of planning for, 266, 392; planning for, 53, 70, 79–85, 86n8, 93, 100, 119, 224, 245, 259, 292; theoretical base of, 80–81

Personal Responsibility and Work Opportunity Reconciliation Act (PRWORA; 1996), 76, 156

Pfeiffer, S. O., 264, 266

physical abuse, 14, 29, 30, 37–39, 71, 111, 167, 171; of at-risk youth, 354; and community, 34, 37, 390; and culture, 34, 37, 182; and domestic violence, 41; and foster care, 210, 275; laws against, 37; prior to adoption, 312; vs. punishment, 34, 37, 59, 182; and success of programs, 190. See also fatalities

Pine, B., 27, 407–8

placements: adoptive, 73, 74, 87n9, 114, 264, 289, 307–8; crisis, 108; decision about, 175; foster care, 73, 80, 90, 99, 121–22, 165, 186, 189, 205, 209, 236, 261; with gay or lesbian families, 289; immediate, 252; inadequate supervision of, 218; interethnic, 72–75; nineteenth-century, 203–4; number of, 215–16; in out-of-home care, 178, 189, 193, 209; and poor children, 211; preparing for, 227; protective service, 210; rates of, 189–90; with relatives, 84, 188, 199; stable, 122; successive, 271; transracial, 289

Poertner, J., 275

Polansky, N., 36, 171

positive youth development model, 347, 357

postadoption services: and advocacy, 334–35; need for, 327–29; range of, 329–35; and residential care, 333–34; and respite services, 334–35; subsidies for, 329; and support networks, 331–32

post-traumatic stress syndrome, 39

poverty, 9, 14, 165; and adoption, 304, 320, 321, 330; and African Americans, 20–21, 124, 330; among white children, 20–21; causes of, 19–20, 27, 76, 94; child, 18–21, 77; and child labor, 15; and child welfare services, 4, 6, 18–21, 384, 386–87; and community services, 390; and delinquency, 378; and domestic violence, 44; elimination of, 166, 400; extreme,

poverty (*continued*)
190; and female crime, 372;
feminization of, 27; and
homelessness, 25; and hope, 172;
impact of, 188, 244, 257; and
juvenile justice system, 370; and
maltreatment, 38, 40, 111, 160,
169–72, 213, 400; and minimum
wage, 21; and minority youth, 358,
359; and neglect, 35, 36, 211; and
policy, 385, 410; as risk antecedent,
346, 347; and risk-taking behavior,
345; and runaways, 355; and
safety, 394; of single parents, 23,
120, 360; and social work values,
408; and universal education, 18;
War on, 15, 73, 103–4, 400; and
welfare reform, 389; and youth
services, 365
Powers, J., 354
pregnancy, 293, 349; and education,
360, 362; teenage, 355, 356,
360–61
Prevent Child Abuse America
(National Committee to Prevent
Child Abuse), 141, 142
privatization, 102, 104, 105–6, 124n3
probation, 24, 366, 369, 379n2
Progressive Era, 8, 14, 15, 166
Progressive movement, 92
Promoting Safe and Stable Families
program, 66
Protective and Preventive Services,
National Study of, 122, 213
protective services, 1, 54, 124n2, 129,
135, 145, 210; agencies for, 61, 72,
89–90, 221; and block grants, 388;
case examples of, 173–74, 176,
177–78, 180, 183; and civil
liberties of parents, 71, 108, 397;
community role in, 97–98, 164;
competing philosophies about,
166–67; crisis in, 168; cultural
issues in, 181–83; development of,
165–83; and domestic violence,
43–44; education for, 405; extent

and appropriateness of, 178–80,
188; and family preservation,
165–83; federal role in, 92–97,
165, 167; focus on, 3, 8, 91–92;
and foster care, 100;
interdisciplinary, 115, 124;
investigatory function of, 394,
397; and legal system, 39, 89;
measurement of, 393; outcomes of,
180, 234–37; problems of, 384;
and publicity, 115, 116, 165; and
safety, 192, 394; and welfare
reform, 389; workers in, 177
psychological abuse, 34–35, 59, 354;
and at-risk adolescents, 39, 40;
and domestic violence, 41; fiction
about, 47n9; rates of, 39
punishment: of crimes by children, 61,
365; of foster children, 239; *vs.*
physical abuse, 34, 37, 59, 182;
and recidivism, 376

Quindlen, Anna, 48n10

Rabb, J., 274
race, 190, 213; and child poverty,
20–21; and out-of-home care, 120,
122, 212–13, 257, 263, 297–98,
317–20; and STDs, 361. *See also*
minorities
racism, 14; and adoption, 123, 318;
and child welfare services, 26,
120–24, 257, 385; and female
crime, 372; and minority youth,
358, 359; and out-of-home care,
212, 213, 251; and roles of
women, 27; and social work
values, 408; and universal
education, 18
Reddy, L. A., 264, 266
rehabilitative ideal, 366, 373, 376–78
Reindfleisch, N., 274
Reitz, M., 288, 326
religion: in early child welfare, 8; and
neglect, 33; and poverty, 19; and
private agency adoptions, 298

relocation programs, 8, 57, 202–4,
    245n4
residential care, 260, 263, 266, 268,
    269–76; abuse and neglect in,
    274–75, 280–81; and communities,
    276; and continuum of care,
    271–72; management of cost in,
    273–74; outcomes of, 275–76; and
    postadoption services, 333–34
Resnick, G., 346, 347, 359, 364
respite care, 2, 135–38, 258, 296,
    328, 334–35
restorative justice model, 377
right to privacy, 7
Ringwalt, C., 354
risk: antecedents of, 346, 347, 357,
    365, 379; assessment of, 38,
    172–74, 176, 180, 182, 255, 359,
    379, 394; markers of, 346–47
risk-taking behavior, 345–46, 360–65;
    solutions for, 364–65; statistics on,
    347
Ritter, B., 404
Rodenborg, N., 122
Rogers, Carl, 6
Rolock, N., 266
Romania, orphanages in, 278, 283n5,
    304, 322
Roosevelt, Theodore, 66
Rosenthal, J. A., 312, 314, 328
runaways, 24, 209, 216, 346, 353–57,
    366
Russia, adoption from, 321
Ryan, P., 231, 259
Rzepnicki, T. L., 122

SACWIS (State Automated Child
    Welfare Information Systems), 95
safety, 52, 57–58, 90, 113, 116, 118,
    173, 275; and ASFA, 64, 93; vs.
    family preservation, 193;
    intervention for, 394; measurement
    of, 390–91, 392; and placement
    decisions, 175, 185, 194n6, 228,
    295; and protective service system,
    192, 394; vs. risk, 174

Scannapieco, M., 255
Scarr, S., 155
Schmitt, B., 106
Schneiderman, M., 263
Schorr, L. B., 345
Schuerman, J. R., 122
Search Institute, 310–11; Forty Assets
    of, 347
self-esteem: and domestic violence,
    42; enhancing of, 143, 145; and
    family suppport, 276; and foster-
    care status, 316; and knowing
    birth parents, 327; and minority
    youth, 359; nurturing of, 59; and
    transracially adopted children,
    319
self-help groups, 144–45
separation trauma, 1, 81, 240
Service Delivery, National Study of,
    181, 209
settlement houses, 7, 138, 140, 141,
    151, 166, 187
sexual abuse, 14, 29, 34, 38–39, 59,
    109, 354; of boys, 39; and
    community standards, 390; and
    domestic violence, 41; prior to
    adoption, 312; rates of, 34, 210; in
    residential care, 274–75
sexuality: and early sexual activity,
    360; and family, 362; and risk
    markers, 346; and risk-taking
    behavior, 360–62
sexually transmitted diseases (STDs),
    353, 360, 361–62
Shapiro, Michael, 337n2
Shared Fate (Kirk), 292, 338n13
shelters: assessment, 208, 252–53;
    battered women's, 41, 118, 134,
    135; and runaways, 355, 356
Shireman, Charles, 345–82
Shireman, J., 320, 327
siblings: and group shelters, 253, 278;
    separation from, 225–26, 227,
    231, 266
Sickmund, M., 368
Silverman, A., 314

single parents, 150, 151, 190, 220,
    289, 290; and abuse, 23, 170–71;
    adoption by, 298, 313–15, 331;
    and child care, 23; mothers as, 22,
    76, 147, 170–71, 206, 211, 257,
    260, 292, 360; and poverty, 23,
    120, 360
slave poem, 13
Smith, E. P., 280
Snyder, H., 368
Sobel, A., 275
social justice, 379, 408, 409, 410
Social Learning Center (Eugene,
    Oregon), 283n3
social reform, 24, 56; and child labor,
    1, 17, 65; and poverty, 19; and
    social work, 6, 7, 15
Social Security Act (1935), 400;
    amendments to, 104; and child
    welfare agencies, 92–93; and
    disability payments, 72; and foster
    care, 208; as source of income for
    children, 77; Title IV-B Child
    Welfare Services of, 139, 167; Title
    XX of, 72, 93–94, 156, 168. See
    also Aid to Dependent Children
Social Statistics, National Center for,
    300
social survey movement, 7
social work, 1–11, 385; and advocacy,
    5, 7, 116, 409, 410; and child
    welfare, 85–86, 101–2, 406–9,
    410; community, 187; and
    delinquency, 377; education for, 5,
    116, 403, 404–6, 408, 409; history
    of, 5–10, 46–47; and juvenile
    justice system, 366; and parental
    support services, 384; and poverty,
    19, 401; and protective services,
    397; and psychotherapy, 6; skills
    needed in, 115, 404–5, 410,
    411n7; and social reform, 6, 7, 15
Social Work Code of Ethics, 407–8
social workers: African American, 74,
    318; attitude of early, 151; and
    birth mothers, 303; and child

welfare, 406–10; and community
    partnerships, 399; and day nursery
    system, 152; and foster care, 219;
    and legal system, 107, 117; as
    mandated reporters, 97–98
Society for the Prevention of Cruelty
    to Children, 34, 65
Solomon's Sword (Shapiro), 337n2
Sorosky, A., 303
Specht, H., 6, 7
special-needs children: adolescent,
    357–59; adoption of, 311, 312,
    314, 329–30; case examples of,
    262, 264–66; and independent
    living programs, 352; services for,
    15, 55, 261, 262; and specialized
    foster care, 105, 261–67
Spencer, J. W., 274
Staff, I., 226
Staff Training and Development,
    National Association for, 403
State Automated Child Welfare
    Information Systems (SACWIS), 95
State Comprehensive Mental Health
    Services Plan Act (1986), 113
Steiner, H., 357
stress: and abuse, 28, 40; and
    homelessness, 25; and neglect, 35;
    post-traumatic, 39; and single-
    parent family, 23
substance abuse, 14, 89, 94, 109, 119,
    141, 165; absence of, 276; and
    abuse, 38, 171; and child welfare
    services, 99, 122, 129, 179, 384;
    and community, 25–26, 373, 387,
    390; and confidentiality, 117; and
    delinquency, 372–73; and domestic
    violence, 45–46; and early sexual
    behavior, 360; and family
    preservation, 395; and foster care,
    26, 130, 131, 211, 220; impact of,
    188, 190, 244; and independent
    living programs, 352; and neglect,
    26, 35, 36, 171; and policy, 363,
    385; and poverty, 172; prenatal
    exposure to, 111, 311; and

psychological abuse, 40; relapse from, 237; and risk markers, 346; and risk-taking behavior, 345; and runaways, 353, 354, 355, 356; and sexual minority youth, 357; statistics on, 362–63; treatment for, 118, 130–31, 144, 178, 191, 192, 265; and violence, 26, 121; and welfare reform, 389; and whole-family care, 259; by youth, 362–63, 373
substitute care, 29, 199, 206, 267
suicide, 354, 355, 357
Sullivan, A., 315, 316
Supplemental Food Program for Women, Infants and Children (WIC), 78
Supplemental Security Income (SSI), 78, 110, 113
Supreme Court decisions, 6, 67–69, 86n5, 110, 283n2, 304
Survivor's Insurance program, 77
Swift, K. J., 27, 32, 408

Temporary Assistance to Needy Families (TANF), 77, 133, 148, 149, 157, 255, 389
Temporary Care for Children with Disabilities, 136
Testa, M., 266
Title IV-B Child Welfare Services, 139, 167
Title IV-E funding, 403, 405; Adoption Assistance, 66, 94, 333; Foster Care, 66, 283n2; and independent living programs, 349, 356; and social work training, 409
Title XX, 72, 93–94, 156, 168
Toth, J., 228, 282
Towner, Deborah, 283n5
Transitional Living Services for Homeless Youth, 349
Triseliotis, J., 239, 309, 320
truancy, 346, 366
Turnell, A., 174, 193n2
Tvedt, Karen, 128–60

Uniform Crime Reports (UCRs; FBI), 367

VanTheis, Sophie, 234, 236
VCIS. See Voluntary Cooperative Information System
Victims of Child Abuse Legislation (VOCAL), 116
violence: and child fatalities, 31; against children, 28, 134, 190; debates about, 58; and drugs, 26, 121; fiction about, 48n10; impact on young children of, 86n1; and minority youth, 358, 359; reduction of, 190; as risk antecedent, 347; against women, 41, 134–35; youth, 23–24; and youth services, 365
Viorst, Judith, 220
Voluntary Cooperative Information System (VCIS), 96, 100, 214, 215, 216
Volunteers in Service to America (VISTA), 138

Wald, Lillian, 65
Waldfogel, J., 97, 187, 384, 399
War on Poverty, 15, 20, 73, 103–4, 400
Watson, K., 288, 326, 332
weapons, 24; and delinquency, 370–71; and runaways, 354, 355
Webster-Stratton, C., 143
Weinstein, Eugene, 225, 227
welfare programs: and child poverty, 21; and domestic violence, 46; and independent living programs, 349
welfare reform, 21, 46, 76, 78, 110, 148, 157; and child welfare policy, 385; impact of, 171, 388–90; and income maintenance, 150, 389, 410n1; and orphanages, 277; and teen parents, 361
well-being: of adults vs. children, 53–54; child, 90, 113, 117, 118, 227; of former foster children, 236; measurement of, 390–91, 393, 394

Wells, K., 269, 276

West, shipment of children to, 8, 57

White House Conferences, 65, 66; on Care of Dependent Children (1909), 206

Whittaker, J. K., 28, 268, 275, 276

Whittington, D., 269

WIC (Supplemental Food Program for Women, Infants and Children), 78

Wiley, Meredith, 86n1

Wilson, L., 228

Wineman, M., 361

Wodarski, J., 404

women: as caretakers, 14, 22; empowerment of, 44; expectations of, 27, 28, 35; in factories, 16, 22; and neglect, 35–36; in poverty, 19–20; rights of, 21–22, 65; roles of, 14, 27, 151; and sexual abuse, 38; as single parents, 22, 76, 147, 170–71, 206, 211, 257, 260, 292, 360; violence against, 41, 134–35; in workforce, 3, 22, 27, 57, 76, 83, 100, 198, 242, 390; "worthy," 19–20. See also domestic violence; mothers

World War II, child care in, 151–52

"worthy poor," 19, 20

Wyatt, E., 276

Yelton, Susan, 270, 271

Young, L., 36, 37–38, 171

youth, at-risk, 345–82. See also adolescents

Zaslow, M. J., 155

Zimring, F. E., 371